DATE DUE

DE 10 '93			
JA 3 '94			
NO 2 '95			
DE 1 '95			
RENEW			
MY 30 '96			
AR 17			
MY 10 '99			
OC 20 '99			
AP 24 '00			
OC 2 '02			
NO 11 '04			

NARCOTICS INVESTIGATION TECHNIQUES

ABOUT THE AUTHOR

Paul Mahoney has been a member of the Denver Police Department for over twenty years. He has been assigned to the Vice/Drug Control Bureau for the past nine years. Since 1987 he has served as a supervisor on the Denver/Aurora Crack Task Force. In addition to his experience in vice and narcotics investigations, Sgt. Mahoney was in patrol for nine years. He has also served as an instructor at the Denver Police Academy and in the department's internal affairs unit. Sgt. Mahoney received a B.S. degree in Criminology and Law Enforcement from Metropolitan State College in Denver and has a M.A. degree in American Studies from the University of Notre Dame. He has been married for twenty-five years and he and his wife, Carol, have four children.

NARCOTICS INVESTIGATION TECHNIQUES

By

PAUL T. MAHONEY

Sergeant
Denver Police Department

CHARLES C THOMAS • PUBLISHER
Springfield • Illinois • U.S.A.

Published and Distributed Throughout the World by

CHARLES C THOMAS • PUBLISHER
2600 South First Street
Springfield, Illinois 62794-9265

© *1992 by* CHARLES C THOMAS • PUBLISHER

ISBN 0-398-05803-2

Library of Congress Catalog Card Number: 91-40073

With THOMAS BOOKS *careful attention is given to all details of manufacturing
and design. It is the Publisher's desire to present books that are satisfactory as to
their physical qualities and artistic possibilities and appropriate for their particular
use.* THOMAS BOOKS *will be true to those laws of quality that assure a good
name and good will.*

Printed in the United States of America
SC-R-3

Library of Congress Cataloging-in-Publication Data

Mahoney, Paul T.
    Narcotics investigation techniques / by Paul T. Mahoney.
        p.   cm.
    Includes bibliographical references and index.
    ISBN 0-398-05803-2 (cloth)
    1. Drug traffic—Investigation.   2. Drug traffic—United States—
Investigation.   I. Title.
HV8079.N3M34   1992
363.2'5977—dc20   91-40073
                                                                                    CIP

This book is dedicated to all police officers who, never losing their respect for the system, go about their duties daily, trusting that they can make a difference. Through their collective "blocking and tackling," they do make a difference. It is also dedicated to their families and, of course, to my family.

A WORD FROM THE AUTHOR

This book has been written for the local police narcotics investigator and those supervising narcotics investigations and operations. It is written from a practical standpoint, describing investigative and operational techniques which have street-proven effectiveness. It is hoped that the experienced narcotics investigator will find it valuable and further, that the newly assigned investigator will be able to supplement his training through this book.

The book includes some very basic material in the area of case initiation and development and then building on and often emphasizing the basics, discusses six general areas of techniques and operations; Informants, Search Warrants, Raid Planning and Execution, Special Street Operations and Investigative Situations, Undercover Operations, and Enhanced Investigations. The book concludes with a very brief discussion of attitude and professional responsibility.

I have written the book from my perspective having spent over twenty years as a policeman and nine as a narcotics investigator and supervisor. A great many of the finest policemen I have ever worked with or observed have been narcotics investigators.

Among them I have seen dedication and a collective sense of professionalism and craftsmanship to a degree that the general public does not realize exists. Similar to other professions, the specific operations and techniques used by narcotics investigators have developed gradually and unsystematically over a number of years. The craft of a narcotics investigator is passed on informally. It is hoped that through a systematic discussion of these techniques in this book, the skill and professionalism and ultimately the ability of each narcotics investigator to survive, personally and professionally, will be enhanced.

CONTENTS

NARCOTICS INVESTIGATION TECHNIQUES

1

CASE INITIATION

INTRODUCTION

The single most important distinction between narcotics cases and most other types of police investigations is that most narcotics investigations begin before a crime is officially reported. There are, of course, those cases where an officer, generally a patrol officer, has made an arrest, has made an offense report, and has a suspect in jail for possession or distribution. Although these types of cases are important and result in a significant amount of work, they are not the bread and butter of a narcotics officer. The success of a narcotics investigator will generally be directly proportional to his or her initiative. Being a self-starter is important to the success of any investigator, but it is imperative for a narcotics investigator.

To obtain the maximum benefit of individual initiative, it is essential that intelligence information be handled properly when it is received. This chapter discusses many of the factors involved in case initiation, sources of information, prioritizing information, interagency cooperation, and case development within the context of community responsiveness.

Much of what follows, particularly in the early part of this chapter, centers on very basic issues and concepts. Some of these are not normally given much consideration as being within the responsibilities of the individual narcotics investigator or supervisor. However, each investigator and supervisor should have some role in ensuring that they receive

3

information which is so critical to their success and that the information is initially evaluated and distributed effectively.

There is, no doubt, a great deal of worthwhile information which is lost because the people and the systems relied upon to handle the information are inefficient to some degree.

SOURCES OF INFORMATION

Telephone Complaints

Complaints received by telephone from anonymous as well as named complainants represent a vast resource for narcotics investigators. The paranoia of drug dealers is well founded. Sooner or later somebody is going to turn them in; the motives for doing so vary. Telephone complaints can be an annoyance during a hectic day, but just when it seems that there will be nothing more than an endless number of irate citizens reporting neighborhood nuisance complaints, a call will come in from a shunned ex-lover of a dealer, a former business associate, a concerned relative, or a disgruntled customer which has the potential to become an outstanding case.

If complaints are taken by a civilian clerk, the civilian should be trained to ask the right questions to elicit information that is not volunteered. This is particularly true when the complainant is an anonymous caller who may never call again. Information must be solicited through a series of careful questions.

The civilians working in this area of a police department should be carefully screened for the obvious reasons of ensuring the integrity of intelligence and criminal files. Much of the specific training which they will need must be provided by the narcotics investigators and supervisors who rely on the information. Phone complaints, taken by civilians and officers alike, must be reported systematically if the information is to be of consistent value. Standardized report forms should be routinely used as they contribute to the efficient flow of information. Figure 1-1 is a sample checklist which can be used to ensure that several important questions are asked. This is particularly critical in the case of an informant who is willing to participate in the investigation.

This type of checklist should be used in conjunction with a standard intelligence information or complaint sheet (Figure 1-2). It is necessary

```
                  NARCOTICS INVESTIGATION UNIT
                  ADDITIONAL COMPLAINT QUESTIONAIRE

     This form should be used to supplement the Intelligence
     Information Sheet.  After the intelligence sheet is
     complete, this checklist should be used to make certain
     that all information which may help a potential
     investigation has been taken.

     DATE:_____COMPLAINT #_____CALL TAKEN BY_____

     ASCERTAIN THE FOLLOWING FROM THE CALLER:

     1)   Is your knowledge of the drug dealing first hand?  Have
          you seen him/her deal?  Seen him/her in possession?  When?

     2)   Have you personally bought drugs from him/her?  When?

     3)   Would you be willing to assist in this investigation?
          Can you buy from him/her currently?  Do you know anyone
          else who can buy from him/her?

     4)   Would you be willing to testify if a criminal case is
          developed?

     5)   Will you call back if more information becomes available?



                           EVALUATION

     Was the caller intoxicated?_____

     Did the caller indicate what his/her motive for making this
     report is?_____
     _____



     (The information from this form can be incorporated into the
     information on the intelligence sheet.  Too often, the
     person debriefed is not asked pertinent questions such as
     those listed above.  Asking these questions will generally
     elicit other valuable information.)




                           FIGURE 1-1
```

to get more than the standard report details (who, what, when, etc.). The caller should be asked pertinent questions such as, Have you seen him deal? Have you bought from him in the past? When was the last time you were in his apartment? and so on. The appropriate follow-up questions to these should also be asked. The complainant should be asked if he or she will be willing to leave a name and number where an investigator can call back. The caller must be assured that someone is interested in making the most of out of the information which he is providing. Asking the proper questions will make it easier to determine whether the information should be assigned for investigation or whether it should be filed as intelligence without specific assignment.

Some calls will require the immediate attention of an investigator. For example, all calls reporting a drug deal in progress should be referred to an investigator. While many of these will be complaints of street deals which are daily occurrences about which little can be done, some calls will demand some quick, direct response. Some street dealing locations, particularly in cities with crack problems, will generate an inordinate number of complaints. It isn't possible to respond to each and every one of these complaints as a rule, nor is it necessary. But it is important that the information be properly directed so that the investigator can make the appropriate decision. If an investigator is working on a certain location or subject, he should inform the complaint clerk or secretary that any information which is received be directed toward him.

Criteria should be established for assigning information sheets after the calls have been taken by the clerk. If the clerk has asked all the right questions and gotten all the information available, the supervisor can then make the determination whether or not to assign the information for investigation. Not all information should be assigned to an investigator. Information which is not assigned should be made available in the captain's folder, electronic mail, or other similar temporary reservoir of information. That way, investigators have a place to look for new or current information about a subject which they are investigating. The information in the captain's folder or electronic mail should be rotated on a regular basis and transferred to a permanent intelligence file. The following are some commonsense factors used in determining the disposition of incoming intelligence information:

☐ Is the information current?

☐ Does the information pertain to known drug dealers or locations or subjects currently under investigation?

☐ Can the complainant contribute further?

☐ Is the informant or complainant willing to participate in the

```
              NARCOTICS INVESTIGATION UNIT
        INTELLIGENCE INFORMATION AND COMPLAINT FORM

COMPLAINT #:_____DATE OF REPORT:_____TIME:_____

The following intelligence information/complaint was received
by the narcotics investigation unit.  It is not intended for
general distribution and is for the information of commissioned
officers only.

COMPLAINANT:_____ADDRESS:_____
COMPLAINANT'S PHONE NUMBER:  HOME:_____WORK:_____

LOCATION OF COMPLAINT:_____

DRUG TYPE(S):_____

                  SUBJECT OF INFORMATION

NAME:_____ALIAS:_____

DOB:_____POLICE DEPARTMENT #:_____

ADDRESS:_____PHONE NUMBERS:_____

DESCRIPTION: RACE_____HEIGHT____WEIGHT____HAIR____EYES____

VEHICLE INFORMATION:  MAKE_____YEAR_____LIC. NO._____
ADDITIONAL VEHICLE INFO:_____
                      ASSOCIATES
NAME:_____ADDRESS:_____

NAME:_____ADDRESS:_____

                     INFORMATION


                     DISPOSITION


REPORTED BY:_____SERIAL NUMBER:_____
ASSIGNMENT:_____DATE:_____DUE:_____

                    FIGURE 1-2
```

investigation, either as a citizen informant/witness or as a confidential informant?

☐ Is the information sensitive in nature? For example, if a high-profile public official or celebrity is the subject of a complaint, the complaint should be investigated fully to allay any claims of corruption. This is done as much in the interest of clearing any person who might be the target of a malicious, completely false complaint. It is inappropriate and irresponsible to put sensitive information in an intelligence file without determining its validity. If a complaint is received naming a councilman as a drug dealer, for example, that information should not be put into an intelligence file without some investigation. If the complaint is unfounded, the completed investigation should be filed for future reference. The first step in these investigations is to interrogate the complainant thoroughly and get as much specific detail as possible. If the complaint has no basis in fact, that will usually be determined after a thorough interrogation of the complainant. This applies not only to public officials and celebrities but to others who have a position of public trust such as teachers, school bus drivers, nurses, attorneys, etc. To whom this information is assigned for investigation is also an important decision.

☐ Does the alleged activity have an impact on a significant number of people? Drug dealing in parks, near schools, or in other public places are examples.

☐ Finally, does the complaint fall within the purview of the investigative mission? Many times, complaints will be received which do not rightly belong to a narcotics investigation unit. Complaints of people congregating in a park, thought to be involved in drugs, for example, probably should be referred to the patrol division for initial response and investigation. Officers in uniform are better suited to handle such things than are plainclothes investigators. There are places in every large city where people will gather to sell and use marijuana. An example would be a large city park where marijuana dealing and use is an ongoing thing. Occasional users of the park see what's going on there, become incensed, and call for immediate action. The truth is, with the manpower demands on most investigative units, and the low priority given these cases in the court system, it is not cost effective for narcotics investigators to spend much time on these things. However, these situations will provide the opportunity for low-level undercover experience, hence training, and can be used for that purpose when time allows.

There are other factors which will determine whether a complaint is assigned for investigation or not. Availability of manpower will certainly be a factor. The best of all possible situations would be that sufficient manpower were available to investigate each and every intelligence lead. This is not often the case. Also, the danger exists that as investigators spend more and more time checking out complaints, they have less time for using their initiative and putting their own deals together. So it is important that undue emphasis is not put on the investigation of minor complaints having very little substance.

Another factor, always considered, is the size of the deal. Narcotics investigators will always respond to a report of large amounts of drugs. And while it is a valid indicator of the importance of a case, it is not the only factor to be considered. It is common knowledge among informants, people in the drug business, and the public at large that police respond differently to a complaint from which large seizures may result. Because of this, in an effort to get attention, exaggeration of the size and scope of a deal is not uncommon. Streetwise investigators will consider the size of the deal within the context of other factors and are usually quick to recognize misinformation and exaggeration.

Whenever doubt exists as to whether or not to assign a complaint, that doubt should be resolved in favor of assigning the information. A preliminary investigation may make it clear whether further action is possible or feasible. This preliminary investigation often consists of nothing more than discussing the information with other people in the office.

Drug Hotline Complaints

A designated telephone line and number for taking drug complaints can be a very important dimension of the any community's antidrug effort and a great source of information for drug investigators. There are some key elements of any successful drug hotline program.

☐ Number must be well advertised and circulated in the community.

☐ It must be made clear that the number is for reporting drug dealers, it is not an addiction help number.

☐ Community support and response have to be solicited. The community has to develop a sense of responsibility for ridding itself of drug dealers.

☐ Complaints have to be followed by action.

Most departments will not have the necessary manpower to assign someone around the clock to handling a drug hotline. It would be ideal if that were the case. If volunteers are available—senior citizens help programs, Explorer Scout programs, or something of that nature—they could make an important contribution by handling a drug hotline. If the hotline is manned, then guidelines similar to those just outlined for answering telephone complaints should be followed. It might be necessary to make a custom checklist depending on the purpose and objectives of the hotline.

It is most probable that there will not be sufficient manpower and that the hotline must be connected to a telephone recorder or message center. A line handled by a recorder does have some advantages, the most obvious being that some people feel a greater sense of anonymity when leaving a message on an answering machine than when talking to an investigator. For some reason people who may have some guilt feelings related to being a "snitch" will feel better talking to a recorder than a live person. They can rationalize their behavior and overcome their reluctance to get involved.

The message on a drug hotline should be succinct. It should be clear to the caller that there is interest in what they have to report and that something will be done if possible; make it clear to the caller what information they should leave in the message. Also make it clear that anonymity is okay, but if they wish to be contacted by an investigator, they should leave a number where they can be contacted. If the message is carefully worded, further cooperation can be requested, and a name and callback number can be politely solicited. A bilingual message should also be considered. English/Spanish is the most obvious combination, but others might be necessary depending on the makeup of the community. For example, if the hotline serves a public housing unit, maybe the hotline message should be in English, Spanish, and Vietnamese. If the message is multilingual, it should be especially short.

The most serious drawback to a recorded drug hotline system is that for every call received, time must be spent listening to and transcribing the call. If, however, there is a systematic approach to dealing with the recorded calls, the hotline can be a tremendous source of information. Figure 1-3 is a sample of a drug hotline transcript.

The essential details—date and time of call, location, or subject of complaint—and a synopsis of the call are all that is needed. Rather than just a typed list of the calls, it is far preferable to enter the information into a computer data base. A whole range of standard data base products can be purchased inexpensively and readily adapted to specific needs.

```
                    CRACK HOTLINE, 09-07-90


   DATE        TIME      ADDRESS              INFORMATION
   _____    ____      _____           _____

   09-06-90    1444      5300 E. 35th       Corner of Glencoe and
                                            35th, lots of guys in
                                            and out of there,
                                            appear to be gang
                                            members dealing crack.


   09-06-90    1800      715 E. 26th        Black male named Big
                                            John dealing drugs to
                                            people in the 715 Club.


   09-06-90    2130                         Party named Rob dealing
                                            cocaine from pager.
                                            Pager number is 890-1113.


   09-07-90    0005      1000 W. 14th       Heavy trafic late in the
                                            afternoon and early
                                            evening.

   09-07-90    0230      1200 Block Penn    Drug dealing day and
                                            night.  Please do some-
                                            thing about it.  You
                                            can't even walk down the
                                            street without being
                                            bothered.

   09-07-90    0900      1451/59 Detroit    The whole building has
                                            been taken over by crack
                                            dealers.  Janice is
                                            dealing in #201.  James
                                            Wilson lives in #204 and
                                            he deals too.




                         FIGURE 1-3
```

Since drug hotlines are usually part of a coordinated community antidrug effort, there will be a need to study the data at a later date. Total numbers of calls, numbers of calls on a particular location, or subject, and similar date will be requested at some point. Also, officers working on a certain location or subject will need to know the frequency and substance of calls on a particular location. Developing information for a historical type search warrant is the most obvious situation where this information will be valuable. Researching such information is much easier if the drug hotline files are computerized.

The data base should have the potential for query by any of a number of fields, separate files for each call, and custom report capability. Having these capabilities makes it possible to create coherent and comprehensive files. When a call is being transcribed, the location or part thereof should be entered on the mask. If the location has been previously reported, it will then be possible to add the new information to the existing file. If it is a new report, a new file will be created. See Figure 1-4 for a sample drug hotline file.

Since drug hotlines generally involve street-level activity, it is probable that some locations or subjects will be the subject of repeated complaints. Therefore, the files should be designed large enough to accommodate several calls. The files should also have a response field for reporting action taken. This may not be required in all cases, but in nuisance cases where a number of calls are generated, provisions should be made for the investigator assigned to document his or her actions. Doing this makes them part of the permanent file and will be useful for public nuisance actions as well as for meetings with citizens' groups who may feel that nothing is being done about their complaints.

The printouts of daily hotline calls should be put in a central location, such as a hotline book. In addition, copies of the printouts should be disseminated regularly within the department. It has been necessary to shed some time-honored traditions in implementing these programs. Traditional philosophy would prohibit the dissemination of valued intelligence on a broad scale. Information and intelligence has always been carefully guarded, to the point sometimes that investigators would not even share it with each other, let alone anyone else in the department. In many jurisdictions today, however, the volume of drug dealing activity has increased to the point that a team effort is required to deal with it effectively. This team approach has also meant that more and more units within the department are working drug investigations peripherally if not as their specific mission. With this there has been a commensurate need for increased cooperation and coordination. The advantages of information sharing on a systematic basis far outweigh the disadvantages. Other units within the police department should and will be expected to play an important role in any drug enforcement strategy, it only follows

```
                    CRACK HOTLINE COMPLAINT FILE

COMPLAINT NUMBER:_____

1)   DATE:_____TIME:_____LOCATION_____

     INFORMATION:_____

     _____

     COMPLAINANT: ANONYMOUS (Y or N)____NAME_____

     CALL BACK NUMBER_____

     ACTION TAKEN_____


2)   DATE:_____TIME:_____LOCATION_____

     INFORMATION:_____

     _____

     COMPLAINANT: ANONYMOUS (Y or N)____NAME_____

     CALL BACK NUMBER_____

     ACTION TAKEN_____



     Each complaint has a separate file except in the case of
     subsequent complaints on one particular location.  Those
     complaints are entered in the same file as the intial
     call.  Each file has space for five complaints.

     Following the third complaint on a given location, the
     complaint is forwarded to the appropriate sergeant for
     assignment.

     A computerized file such as this can be queried by any of
     the data fields.




                         FIGURE 1-4
```

that they should have access to intelligence information pertaining to street-level dealing. In most cases, effective communication will prevent the separate units from duplicating each other's efforts. If investigators are working on a street level place and there are aggressive patrol officers working in the area, their cooperation should be solicited.

It may not be necessary to assign investigators to handle complaints from the drug hotline. If the officers working the problem area served by the hotline are doing their job aggressively, they will check the hotline printout first thing when they come to work. In fact, a system which allows for officers to assign themselves complaints out of the book will generally take care of all the calls with substance. What may be necessary from time to time is to assign nuisance complaints to officers for follow-up action. This is particularly true in the case of a nuisance problem which has gotten out of hand. Many times, the cause of the nuisance complaints is not only the drug dealing, but all the attendant problems such as rising crime, loitering, heavy foot and vehicular traffic, and the general decline of the neighborhood. These types of complaints will require the help of the patrol officers in the area if any effective solution is to be reached.

Crimestoppers-Type Reports

Most police departments have crimestoppers programs. Due to the public relations nature of these programs, they are quite often attached to the community services or community relations section of the department. Crimestoppers programs have been an excellent source of information during their relatively short existence. They have also been valuable in as much as they have solicited community involvement and generated a greater sense of community responsibility for effective law enforcement. There are a few inherent problems which, however, are not insurmountable.

The objectives of these programs usually involve gaining information about major crimes. Homicides, rapes, assaults on the elderly, robberies, and certain other crimes that gain notoriety are generally the crimes about which information is solicited through the television and radio media. That and the fact that the calls are handled by clerks attached to the community relations or other such office makes it difficult to utilize this research for narcotics investigations.

People calling the crimestoppers are motivated, at least in part, by the offer of a monetary reward. The systems for control and payment are built into the program, and this generally prohibits the narcotics investigators from dealing with the complainant firsthand. Instead, they are given a report which has been filled out by the crimestoppers clerk. The informant is identified by an internal control number only. Getting additional information regarding past reliability of the caller is sometimes difficult because of the guidelines of the program which quite naturally have the confidentiality of the caller as a main priority.

As a rule, the crimestoppers information is very good. The problem is that it may be incomplete in the form in which it is received. The investigators are called on to investigate the complaint and report their findings without the benefit of debriefing the informant. If it is possible to provide a little informal training to the civilians or officers handling these calls initially, the value of this resource can be enhanced. The complaint clerks should be instructed on the right questions to ask and to ascertain if the callers are willing to participate in the investigation by making a controlled buy or doing an introduction. The best solution would be to have crimestoppers refer all drug tips to a certain contact person in the drug investigations bureau. Then, those who wished to work as active informants could be developed, and the other tips could be investigated as they are now. Unfortunately, there are usually guidelines that have been set up to facilitate the crimestoppers program and that do not allow direct referral.

In spite of the shortcomings, crimestoppers programs are an excellent information source. When investigating a case and exhausting all information sources in the process, crimestoppers reports should be checked for possible information on the subject. Crimestoppers reports which come to the attention of the drug investigations unit should be assigned for investigation. Again, part of that investigation should include an effort to make firsthand contact with the caller.

Complaints from Official Channels

Complaints from the mayor's office, the chief's office, and the offices of members of city council, through the chain of command, will require immediate attention. Generally the substance of these complaints will be nuisance-type locations, and in these cases the real source of the complaints will quite often be a neighborhood action group. There have been a number of citizens groups which have taken shape in an effort to assist the antidrug efforts of a community. These groups can be an excellent source of information; members of the community will report to each other more readily than they will contact the police. This is particularly true in communities which have traditionally felt alienated from the police department. The power of these groups should not be underestimated. Nor can a drug investigator afford to assume a negative posture.

It is important that drug enforcement efforts be responsive to the needs of the community. More of that will be discussed later in this chapter. What should be emphasized at this point is the value of the community as a source of information as well as a potential source of support. Through their collective political clout, these groups have been responsible for upscaling drug enforcement efforts: adding personnel, allocating additional funding, and changing city ordinances. To cultivate these groups as a source, it is necessary to meet with them. Generally this responsibility will fall on the drug unit supervisors or commanders.

A well-informed supervisor, familiar with what's taking place on the street, on both sides of the fence, can effectively deal with these groups. What can result is that contacts made will become sources of information and help in the future. Not only will they call directly with information, no longer feeling the necessity to exert political pressure, but you can call them. Another aspect of these positive community contacts is the potential opportunity to develop good future jurors who are sympathetic to the objectives and problems of narcotics law enforcement. While community relations officers should handle most of these meetings and deal with these groups, they are not in a position to talk about particular drug problems from the informed position as are key people from the drug enforcement unit.

Information from Officers on the Street

Most successful narcotics investigators quickly learn the importance of effectively communicating with officers working the street in the patrol division. This communication is not automatic. It must be developed, and it is the responsibility of the investigator to develop it. There is a little natural alienation between patrol officers and officers working plainclothes, particularly narcotics investigators. Patrol officers often view the investigators as prima donnas, and too often these impressions are justified. Most of the time it is not alienation, but a total separation of job duties and a lack of contact which causes communication to break down. Whatever the causes, narcotics officers should work to overcome them and cultivate patrol officers as a source of information and assistance in investigations.

A good street officer can provide valuable information on a case. There are certain tasks for which the patrol officer is ideally suited. If there is a need to know who drives a certain vehicle or who lives at a certain address, a patrol officer can get the information and make the contact appear routine, arousing no suspicion. Drug dealers do not view patrol officers as a threat unless they are holding (currently in possession of drugs). Patrol contacts are not viewed as an extension of a narcotics investigation. Officers can make what is ostensibly a routine traffic stop or even go to a place of residence on the ruse that they have received a call of some sort.

Many times, patrol officers will have been called to a location and investigators planning a search warrant can gain valuable intelligence about the layout, the construction of the doors and locks, and even the disposition of the residents by asking the officer who works the area. Involving patrol officers in an investigation usually pays dividends in the future in the form of additional information. Another benefit is the opportunity to provide informal training. Most officers will respond to constructive criticism given in the right spirit. Many officers shy away from drug enforcement because they are not entirely confident that they know what they are doing. In addition, they may not realize what an important role they can play. Given encouragement and exposure to narcotics investigations, most officers will respond positively.

Whenever manpower needs permit, patrol officers should be encouraged to develop information which they have into a prosecutable case. This may require a short temporary assignment. It will certainly require that an investigator work closely with the patrol officer and teach him the basics of a routine drug case. Street officers will often develop good informants but do not have the means to compensate them or the time to work their information. Nor are they usually experienced at reading informants and determining the relative value of the information. Furthermore, the intricacies of using an informant to make a case in such a way that it can be prosecuted yet keep the informant confidential are not common knowledge among patrol officers. Writing a search warrant is not something that every officer knows how to do, but most officers would like the opportunity to learn.

If an investigator will take the time to work with a patrol officer and teach him or her these various things, the investigator, the officer, and the entire department benefits.

Sharing information with and soliciting the help of uniform officers opens lines of communication. Acknowledging the help of the officers will keep the lines of communication open. It only takes a minute to write the officers an acknowledgment if not a commendatory letter. Figure 1-5 is a sample acknowledgment.

Developing Information from Jail Cases

Jail cases, cases which are assigned to an investigator resulting from an arrest made by a uniform officer, represent an excellent, often untapped, source of information. These cases are generally assigned to specific people or a specific unit for filing. In most departments where this is the case, those assigned to this task will not have time to work cases proactively. Filing jail cases becomes a full-time assignment. The value of the suspects in these cases as potential informants often has to be overlooked because of time constraints.

Evaluating these cases for filing always includes going over the circumstances of the arrest, whether the officer had probable cause for the arrest, whether the search was good, the record of the suspect, etc. Any such evaluation should also include looking at the suspect as a potential source of information. It is worth the time to talk to these people and see if they are willing to cooperate. Many of them have serious records and shouldn't be worked, many of them won't cooperate under any circumstances, and some of them don't have any worthwhile information. However, there will be the small percentage who will talk to an investigator, who are willing to become informants if only to a limited degree to get help on their case. Do not make promises regarding case consideration; the prosecutor must make those decisions regarding recommendations to be made to the judge. Dealing with informants is the subject of the next chapter, where this type of informant will be discussed at length. The point to be made now is that suspects in jail cases can be an excellent source of information.

Another source of information in these cases, which is also often overlooked, is the officer who made the arrest. Those officers with a particularly keen interest in narcotics cases will become obvious because they will consistently be making good arrests. An effort should be made to get to know these officers. Many times they will have information

```
                 NARCOTICS INVESTIGATION UNIT

                ACKNOWLEDGEMENT OF ASSISTANCE


   DATE:_____

   TO:_____SERIAL NUMBER:_____

   ASSIGNMENT:_____

   RE:_____

   COMMENTS:_____

   _____

   _____

   _____

   _____

   _____

   _____

   _____



   CC:_____

      _____



   Thank you for your continued interest and support in drug
   investigations and other matters of mutual concern to the
   patrol and investigations divisions.


                       _____

                          Investigator Assigned


                       _____

                          Commanding Officer
                  FIGURE 1-5
```

which can be turned into a good case, but they don't have the time to work on it. As mentioned before, good, effective communication with patrol officers will stimulate coordination in cases and the entire department and community profits. Again, writing the officers an acknowledgement for their work and notifying them of the disposition of the case is a good idea.

Soliciting Information from Outside Sources

A narcotics investigator in the process of initiating a case has an almost endless supply of sources outside of his unit from which information and help can be solicited. The patrol officer has already been discussed as probably the most valuable source of information. The next most obvious would be investigators working other assignments. The link between narcotics and other crimes is well documented. It is common for investigators from other assignments to check narcotics bureau files for information on possible suspects; this is particularly true of those working crimes against persons. A good example of this is found in communities that have experienced problems with Caribbean drug traffickers. Some cities had to assign homicide and assault detectives to work with the narcotics investigators because of the volume of violent crime attendant to the drug dealing.

The same can be said of street gang drug dealing, where there is a great deal of attendant crime and violence. Investigators from homicide or assault units will contact narcotics investigators and search the files in the process of handling a case. Too infrequently do narcotics investigators check with these other investigators for information. It is possible that their files may have more current information than the narcotics unit concerning current addresses, associates, vehicles, etc.

Theft and burglary detectives can be an equally important source. Many old-time drug users and small-time dealers have traditionally supplemented their incomes by shoplifting (boosting). These detectives could have had several misdemeanor cases on a dealer since a narcotics investigator last had contact with him. Investigators working burglaries and thefts also have a tremendous potential supply of informants; suspects in cases which lend themselves to working some kind of deal, that is, information on drug dealers in exchange for help on their case.

Vice officers also represent a great source of information. In many departments, vice and narcotics investigations are performed by the same unit or even the same person. Consequently, there is usually pretty good communication between the two units. Vice officers will develop a tremendous amount of intelligence with respect to drug dealing due to their daily presence on the street, their constant dealing with prostitutes, and the close relationship between prostitution and narcotics. Prostitutes, as potential informants, are well recognized. But there are other people with whom vice officers will be in close daily contact who are also good sources of information. Vice officers can often develop a limited, but useful, rapport with bar owners, pimps, and small-time gamblers, and information from these people will be forthcoming.

Other criminal justice professionals, most notably parole officers and probation officers, are good sources of information. Because of the way the system operates today, there is very little likelihood that a first-time offender is going to be sentenced to prison, certainly not for any considerable length of time. It is highly likely that the first-time offender will take a plea to a lesser offense and be granted probation. Even second- and third-time offenders may be given a sentencing alternative, such as a treatment program, a halfway house, or home detention. In any of these situations, the people become clients of the probation and parole department.

Probation and parole officers will have current information on their clients and will usually have a good feel for whether their client is continuing his or her criminal behavior. Establishing rapport with probation and parole officers can be mutually beneficial. These officers will generally have broader powers to search their clients and their residences and to question them than police officers will have. It also has to be understood that they will have their responsibility to the client as their first concern, and that fact must be weighed in deciding how much information is shared with them.

There are countless other local government agencies which are potential resources. The excise and licensing authority, the state treasurer's office, the city tax assessor's office, and social services are just a few. The division of motor vehicles is an obvious source of information and photographs.

The local telephone and public utilities companies are excellent sources of information. These are particularly helpful early in an investigation when attempting to identify suspects and residents of suspect locations. Telephone subscriber information, even on nonpublished numbers, used to be easily accessible. For whatever reasons, this is not generally the case any longer. Subscriber information for numbers other than nonpublished numbers can be easily obtained, but more confidential information, including subscriber information for nonpublished numbers, toll records, call forwarding information, etc. will require an administrative subpoena or a search warrant. Search warrants for these types of records are not difficult to obtain, but they do require time, and of course it becomes public record that an inquiry was made.

A great deal of discretion must be used when telephone and utility subscriber information is obtained. In fact, the indiscreet use of this information in the past is partially responsible for the increased difficulty with which this information is obtained today. In any case, this information is critical to most investigations sooner or later.

People in the business community are too often overlooked as a source of information. There is always the risk that the people contacted may not be trustworthy, and for that reason the decision is made to avoid talking to them. Those who can be trusted can be a wealth of information. This is particularly true of motel/hotel owners, bar and restaurant people, money express operators, and others. Keep in mind that these people are in business to make money and don't object offhandedly to a drug dealer renting their rooms, or paying the going rates to wire money, or spending money in their bars and restaurants. It is probably a good policy not to involve these people in an investigation if there is any serious doubt that they can be trusted.

The owners and employees of hotels and motels can be a tremendous source of information and one that's not too difficult to develop. Even if the management is not contacted for fear that they cannot be trusted, motels and hotels should not be overlooked. Good cases are frequently made by alert investigators observing the vehicle of a known dealer, or the dealer himself at a hotel. A subsequent surveillance will often result in the development of probable cause for arrest or a search warrant.

Pharmacists are another excellent contact person within the business community. They will invariably have information on suspicious prescription deals and people that they commonly do not report because they are not sure a criminal act has occurred. Although there may be specialists assigned to compliance investigations, pharmacists can be an excellent contact and source of information for anyone working narcotics. Generally, due to the pressure to work street cases, the investigation of these types of cases, fraud and deceit, compliance, etc., will not be a top priority. The ideal situation is to have a full-time compliance unit which is responsible for making regular contact with pharmacists.

Confidential Informant Information

Without question, informant information provides the basis for most narcotics investigations. Informants are the subject of Chapter Two.

PRIORITIZING INFORMATION

Information coming to the attention of a narcotics investigator or unit usually takes one of three forms. It is information which has the immediate- or long-range potential of being developed into a case, it is intelligence which has some basis in fact but in its present form is too general and untimely to develop, or it is totally without basis in fact. Fortunately most of the information received falls into the category of either intelligence information or case information. Only rarely is information received which is totally untrue, given for some malicious reasons.

In determining whether information has case potential or is intelligence information, the first test is the timeliness of the information. If the information is stale, however detailed, it will probably become intelligence at least until further information becomes available. Again, timeliness is a very subjective concept with respect to drug dealing, and it must be considered in the context of the whole picture. If the information pertains to a complete unknown and nothing can be corroborated either about the person or location or associates, then timeliness of the information alone will probably not be enough to turn the information into a case. The exception of course is when information about a deal is received in advance of it happening or while it is happening, and in that case timing gives the call greater importance. The Supreme Court of the United States has recently held that an anonymous tip corroborated by independent investigation can be sufficient reasonable suspicion to make an investigatory stop.[1]

When a tip is provided anonymously by a first-time informant, it is necessary to corroborate some of the information in order to establish some basis of credibility for the substance of the information and thereby develop reasonable suspicion to make an investigatory stop. In *Alabama v. White,* officers received a call with very specific information that Vanessa White would be getting into a brown Plymouth station wagon with a broken right taillight at a certain location and time and that she

---

1 *Alabama v. White*, 110 S.Ct. 2412 (1990).

would be going to a certain motel and that she would have a brown attache case in the car which would contain about an ounce of cocaine. The officers located the vehicle where it was reported to be, saw a woman get into the vehicle, and followed her to the reported destination. To that extent, they corroborated the information received from the anonymous informant. They had her stopped by a patrol unit just short of her reported destination and got her consent to search the vehicle and the attache case which they found in the car. They found marijuana in the attache case and later found cocaine in the woman's purse.

It was the timeliness of this tip which made it so valuable. Had the call come after the fact, the information would have been possibly good intelligence that the woman was dealing, at best. As it was, it was acted on as a hot tip and developed into a prosecutable case.

So timeliness is a factor, but not the only factor. If information is received about a known drug dealer and the information concerns ongoing activity, it may well be the basis of a case initiation regardless of whether it is fresh or not.

The major distinction between case information and intelligence information will be whether the totality of the information, the subject, the timeliness, and the other factors represent enough facts to initiate an active investigation. Some amount of preliminary investigation and surveillance may be necessary. If serious constraints on an investigator's time do not exist, he or she may have time to work intelligence information and with time can possibly develop it into a case.

Informal discussion between investigators is a great distilling process for intelligence information. Each investigator represents, to some extent, an independent intelligence file. Running the information through this process has a way of naturally refining it to a point where it can be better evaluated.

Prioritizing Information by Task

Logic dictates that the individual investigator as well as those performing a supervisory function will begin the prioritization process by looking at the task involved, the type of investigation necessary. In a small agency, the same investigators may handle all types of cases regardless of whether they are street cases or major cases. In an agency with several investigators, the work is generally separated by tasks. If one is assigned to work crack cases, information on a heroin case, regardless of how good it is, should be turned over to the officers working those cases. Investigators working a street team who receive information regarding a major peddler should turn it over to the people who are working those types of cases. While this is a very simple concept, the failure to follow this logical method of information handling is what causes more trouble among narcotics investigators than anything else. There is a reluctance to turn information over to someone else, particularly where the case involves good, current information on an upper-level dealer.

Each investigator has a responsibility to evaluate information and determine whether it falls within the parameters of his or her assignment. What happens all too often is that this process is done only on information without great potential. In other words, if the information isn't particularly promising, then it is turned over to the people who are supposed to handle it; if it has significant potential, it is often not turned over. Anybody with narcotics investigation experience can attest to the fact that there is a great deal of friction caused by what is perceived as somebody stealing someone else's case. An example of this occurs in the area of crack cocaine. Very few want to work the low-level, nuisance dealers involved in this problem to the exclusion of other more interesting, rewarding cases. But if somebody not assigned to the problem gets information regarding a major dealer with a large quantity of crack and possibly cash, it is probable that they will want to have continued participation in the case. The key in any situation of this type is teamwork: the initiating officer will want to be involved in the case and he or she should be. At the same time, that officer should not work it independently of those whose assignment it is to investigate crack dealers or whatever.

If the investigator fails to prioritize correctly the information on which he or she works, based on task. the supervisor has to intervene and do so. Narcotics enforcement, more than any other type of investigative work, is a team proposition. To achieve maximum efficiency, each investigator, each team, has to take care of its part of the problem and allow the rest of the team to do their part.

That information not immediately prioritized by task will naturally be done so by other factors. Geography is one key factor, particularly in larger cities where investigative responsibilities are broken down by districts of the city. Even where that is not the case, each investigator will prioritize information according to geography based on his or her own background and experience. An investigator who has spent his entire career working a particular side of town with a certain type of dealer dealing a certain type of drug is going to give a low priority to information pertaining to another part of town about which he knows nothing. When this situation arises, the information should be passed on to someone who is working in that area. Both can still participate in the investigation to some extent if it is so desired and if time allows. Time is the key; and generally there is not time to work on all the information which is received.

Information will be further prioritized according to individual preference. If an investigator has made a career out of working street-level heroin dealers, he's probably not going to give much priority to information about a coke dealer in a downtown bar. Ethnic distinctions become very important also. Narcotics investigators are like everybody else in that they develop patterns and begin to feel comfortable working in a certain way and with certain groups of people. As a result, they tend to work the same areas of the city and with ethnic groups who deal primarily in specific drugs. It should be pointed out that this may have little or nothing to do with their own ethnic background. Each group of people has its own idiosyncrasies, and once the investigator has learned them and is comfortable, he or she may not change unless an investigation which is exceptional in nature presents itself.

Each investigator should prioritize his or her cases by informant availability. If an investigator gets information about an area in which she has no informants, she should probably pass the information on to somebody who has or work with them to develop the information. Again, time is a key factor. If she has the time, she may be able to put the case together without informants or develop them as the case progresses. The point is that if information and the investigator already has an informant who can be effective there, that case should be given priority over one in which there is a total lack of informants. Informants are an important resource in most cases; in fact, in many cases there will be no progress without them.

Very important in prioritizing investigative work is some kind of objective determination of the relative importance of the case. What impact on the community is this particular drug problem having? The size and scope of the dealer, the location of his activity, his clientele, and what kind of drugs are being sold will all have a bearing on deciding the importance of each case. A guy selling marijuana near an elementary school may be representative of a problem demanding a more immediate solution than a guy selling grams and half grams of cocaine in a bar. If both these cases fall within the parameters of the same assignment, a decision must be made.

In most jurisdictions, selling cocaine is a more serious felony than selling marijuana. In fact, difficulty is routinely encountered in getting a prosecutor to file a case on a small-time marijuana dealer, and it will almost certainly be pleaded to a lesser charge if it is filed. But the public has no tolerance for drug dealing of any kind near a school. This intolerance is recognized by prosecutors, and marijuana cases near a school or involving children will be regarded as important, whereas a regular marijuana case may not. Impact on the community has to be considered in prioritizing cases.

Likelihood of prosecution is another factor which must be taken into account, and this is, or should be, related in some way to the impact the community is suffering. In most jurisdictions, the systems are so overloaded that drug cases cannot have priority status unless they are the types of cases which are having a serious impact on the community. The person's record is taken into account as well. If a person has two or three prior convictions, the likelihood that he will be prosecuted and receive a jail sentence is greater than a person with no prior record. What happens is that the high-visibility street-type dealers end up being arrested multiple times. They generate a lot of complaints, and after two or three or four convictions, they may get sent to prison. The low-profile dealer, who is either at an upper level or operates in a low-visibility manner, may not get arrested if he is careful and discreet.

When the investigator evaluates two people for potential investigations, he will find a record of one, and the other, who may be a more serious dealer, who may be putting more drugs on the street, may not have a criminal record. The criminal record of the suspect must be researched and considered, but it cannot be automatically assumed that the person who has been caught several times should be a priority target over the person who has not. A good example of this would be white-collar dealers who operate under the guise of respectability. They often have good jobs, dress nicely, have no criminal records, and deal with relative impunity. This class of dealers should be actively worked when the opportunity presents itself.

Consideration of assets for potential seizure has become an important factor in weighing the prospects of a drug investigation. This should not be the most important factor, but it will often be the deciding one. The question, What kind of car does he drive? was formerly asked for identification purposes. Now that question, with respect to a narcotics investigation, is followed up by, Is it paid for? That this trend has developed is only logical. Asset forfeiture is a vital part of narcotics enforcement. And it has made those efforts much more effective. The prospect of losing assets is a more effective deterrent because of the relative swiftness and surety of the punishment, quite unlike the criminal prosecution for the offense itself.

All other things being equal, if one potential target has a brand new truck which is paid for, and which he uses for delivering his product, and the other doesn't own a vehicle, the one with the truck will be the priority target. An unfortunate side effect of this trend toward profit-motivated enforcement is that forfeiture considerations may become more important than a criminal case at some point and decisions will be unduly influenced. Plea bargain arrangements, even though they shouldn't be, might be influenced by forfeiture concessions on the part of the defendant. Nonetheless, assets for potential seizure should be considered when weighing the prospects of a case.

DEVELOPING A CASE

This portion of the chapter deals with techniques generally applicable to all types of cases. In low level street cases, these steps may be taken quickly and informally but they are still part of the developmental process. Conversely, the more difficult, complex, and long term a case is going to be, the more these techniques apply.

Initial Case Planning and Investigation

Case Initiation Reports

Regardless of the type of case, once an investigation is initiated, a case initiation report will have to be made. The format and depth of this report will vary according to the nature of the case. Investigators working street-level cases and initiating 10 to 15 a month will document the initiation of a case quite differently from an investigator working major dealers and initiating only a case or two a year.

Figure 1-6 shows a sample case initiation report. Reports of this type would be more commonly associated with complex or long-term investigations. Anyone who has ever been involved in a case with the

Drug Enforcement Administration (DEA) will recognize the basic content arrangement if not the format. It should be noted that DEA has an excellent reporting system. The format requirements of its reports are conducive to thoroughness, comprehensiveness, and standardization.

```
                 NARCOTICS INVESTIGATION UNIT

                    INVESTIGATIVE REPORT


    REPORTED BY: Sgt. Paul Mahoney          DATE: 08-19-90

    CASE NUMBER: TF 90-08-30

    TYPE OF REPORT: CASE INITIATION REPORT

    INCIDENT: CASE INITIATION - Neal Ross, DPD #444555

    OTHER OFFICERS: Det. Bernie Montoya

    SYNOPSIS: On this date, Information was received that Neal
              Ross, DPD #444555, is dealing crack cocaine from
              3155 24th St.  Informant states that he can make
              an introduction of an undercover officer who can
              then buy directly from Neal Ross.

    PROPOSED PLAN OF ACTION:

    1) Make a controlled buy from Neal Ross utilizing the
       previously reliable confidential informant.  That buy
       will allow the informant to re-establish his contact
       with Neal Ross. It will gain intelligence information
       to corroborate the CI information and setup the under-
       cover introduction.

    2) Following a successful controlled buy, the informant
       and Det. Bernie Montoya will go to the location for
       the purpose of an introduction.  The informant will make
       a small controlled buy and Det. Montoya will make a small
       buy as well.  Ross deals in only $50 and $20 quantities.

    3) Following that introductory buy, Det. Montoya will go
       back and attempt to make at least two more buys from
       Ross without the CI.

    4) After undercover buys have been made, a search warrant
       will be prepared for 3155 24th St. and an arrest warrant
       prepared for Neal Ross.  Through surveillance, it may be
       possible to identify Ross's source.  If this is not the
       case, a final buy will be made and Ross will be arrested
       and the search warrant executed.

    INDEXING:  ROSS, NEAL
                    FIGURE 1-6
```

What is important in case initiation reports is that they clearly present the subject of the investigation and the intentions to proceed. The case initiation report provides documentation for supervisors, command officers, prosecutors, and other participating investigators who will not be as familiar with the case as the primary investigator. Should, for one reason or another, there be a failure to complete the case, the case initiation report will provide valuable information for any future investigations.

The case initiation report also allows the investigator to evaluate his own case more accurately. Until he takes the time to organize his information and put it down in a report, he may be putting off getting started. Figure 1-7 is an optional format for a case initiation report. This has some advantages: Most notably it is brief and can be used for nearly all types of investigations. It serves the same purpose as the more lengthy narrative report. The fill-in-the-blanks format makes it simpler to use while at the same time providing a comprehensive workup on the subject of the investigation. For street-level cases this type of report is probably preferable in that the format makes it easier to review quickly.

Figure 1-8 is yet another sample. This sample represents a report which can be used for keeping track of a case from beginning to end, and is actually more of a case summary sheet than a case initiation report. It was designed for use by a street-level crack unit with a very high enforcement output and a minimum of long-term investigations. It allows for subject identification, a record of expenditure activity, and a seizure summarization, as well as a narrative summary of the investigation. The system requires that an internal file number be taken for each investigation. Each investigator would submit the file sheets for his cases at the end of each month. All sheets would then be entered in the data base for permanent record. Incomplete cases are turned in as such.

This type of report will not take the place of a case initiation report in a case of any substance. It will, however, do so in some routine street cases. It has the advantage of serving multiple purposes. It tracks investigation expenditures, it provides for additional documentation of CI activity and payment, and it summarizes seizures, cases filed, and arrests.

There are any number of variations of the three samples which have been shown here. There should be some official documentation of case initiation; the format isn't really important as long as the content adequately expresses the investigative plan.

```
                    INVESTIGATIVE LEAD SHEET

    Case Initiated By:_____Date:_____

    Suspect's Name: _____DOB:_____
    AKA:_____Nickname:_____

    Race:_____Sex:_____Height:_____Weight:_____Eyes:_____

    Hair Color:_____Other Identifying Traits:_____

    Suspect's Address:_____

    Utility Company Information:

    Public Service:_____

    Telephone Company:_____
```

```
                    INVESTIGATIVE PLAN AND NOTES
    _____
    _____
    _____
    _____
    _____
```

```
                    VEHICLE INFORMATION

    1) _____
        License number    Make       Model        Year     Color

    2) _____
        License number    Make       Model        Year     Color

    Listing #1_____

    Listing #2_____
```

```
    P                              Suspect Identification
    H
    O                              Police Dept. #_____
    T
    O                              Drivers License #_____
    G
    R                              NADDIS Check   [ ]   [ ]
    A
    P                                             yes    no
    H
```

```
                        FIGURE 1-7
```

Goals and Objectives

An experienced narcotics investigator begins formulating the goals of an investigation from the very beginning. Along with that comes ideas for ways of achieving them. These may not be put into writing immediately,

```
                    NARCOTICS INVESTIGATION UNIT

                           FILE SHEET


   FILE NO.:_____   DATE:_____   REPORTED BY:_____

   CASE NUMBER:_____

   SUSPECTS:

   1)  NAME:                        2) NAME:
       ADDRESS:                        ADDRESS:
       DOB:                            DOB:
       PD #:                           PD #:

          (LIST ADDITIONAL SUSPECTS IN NARRATIVE BELOW)

   SEIZURES -     DANGEROUS DRUGS:              TYPE:
                  CURRENCY
                  WEAPONS:
                  DESCRIPTION OF WEAPONS:
                  OTHER SEIZURES:


   EXPENDITURES -
                      EVIDENCE PURCHASED

   1)  DATE:           AMOUNT:          TYPE OF DRUG:
       AMOUNT PAID:                     PROPERTY NUMBER:
   2)  DATE:           AMOUNT:          TYPE OF DRUG:
       AMOUNT PAID:                     PROPERTY NUMBER:
   3)  DATE:           AMOUNT:          TYPE OF DRUG:
       AMOUNT PAID:                     PROPERTY NUMBER:

   INFORMANT PAYMENTS -

   1)  DATE:           VOUCHER NUMBER:          CI NUMBER:
       AMOUNT PAID:       EXPLANATION:

   2)  DATE:           VOUCHER NUMBER:          CI NUMBER:
       AMOUNT PAID:       EXPLANATION:

   3)  DATE:           VOUCHER NUMBER:          CI NUMBER:
       AMOUNT PAID:       EXPLANATION:

   TOTAL ARRESTS:            TOTAL DRUG CASES FILED:
   TOTAL EXPENSES:

   NARRATIVE SUMMARY:

                          FIGURE 1-8
```

or at all for that matter, but formally or informally they are the basis of the investigation. An experienced investigator will instinctively recognize good information and begin thinking of ways to turn it into a case. In more complex cases it is necessary to formulate a written game plan and get approval for it. While an investigator does not want to make the mistake of precluding any of his options, he will usually have a good idea from the beginning whether he will be able to make undercover buys leading to a buy/bust; develop information for a search warrant through surveillance, historical background, controlled buys, or a combination thereof; initiate a financial investigation, etc.

Deciding on an initial course of action doesn't mean that it can't be changed in the future as needed, or as new option become available. Having an idea of how to achieve the goals, what investigative techniques will be used, is an essential part of any case. The game plan is based, of course, on the information at hand. If the informant says that there is no way that this particular suspect will meet anyone, the investigation should not be based initially on the idea of doing the case with undercover buys. Another method should be used to start with, and the plan adapted as necessary.

Target ID

Identification of the subject is essential to any intelligent evaluation of the case. Identifying the subject may require a good deal of resourcefulness on the part of the investigator. Identification will not necessarily include the person's correct full name, date of birth, and social security number. Certain Caribbean nationals involved in drug dealing present an excellent example of this. Identities change so frequently that often even after the case is closed and the subject is imprisoned or deported, the investigator is still not sure of who he has.

Nevertheless, identifying the subject of the investigation is a critical first step in evaluating the case and corroborating information. And the first step in identifying the subject will be a criminal history check. In many cases the investigator is immediately familiar with the subject from his past experience. This will be true in cases involving well-known dealers—most of them have a previous criminal history. Checks for local and state criminal history should be made and then National Crime Information Center, motor vehicle license and vehicle records, field contact cards, traffic violations files, traffic accident reports, offense reports, and other similar sources should be checked as should firearms purchase and registration records. Preliminary identification of the subject doesn't conclude the process; it should continue, aimed at a full suspect profile.

Check with federal law enforcement agencies also. If the subject has a drug trafficking history, and has come to the attention of DEA in past investigations, DEA's computerized information systems are an excellent source of information. The Bureau of Alcohol, Tobacco and Firearms will have comprehensive records of firearms transactions which could help identify the subject as well as provide potentially life-saving intelligence regarding gun possession. It is not suggested that an investigator contact each federal agency in every case, but they should be considered as potential sources of assistance.

A critical part of identifying a subject will be ascertaining whether he or she is currently the subject of somebody else's investigation. What occurs all too frequently is that two or more separate investigations will be active on the same subject at the same time. Which brings up the next point. Other investigators should be contacted in an effort to ascertain if somebody else is working or has information on the same subject. This entails checking intelligence file as well as making personal contact with other investigators. In metropolitan areas with any number of law enforcement agencies and drug task forces in place, many with multijurisdictional authority, there is going to be duplication of effort.

The ideal situation is to have a regional computer network wherein subjects are flagged as they become the subject of a narcotics investigation.

Surveillance may be necessary to identify the subject. It may be that the subject is known only by a nickname or an alias and that there is no record of him, his vehicles, or his associates. Surveillance is frequently overlooked, or minimized, as an investigative tool, probably because it can involve long, tedious, and boring hours. Surveillance may be the only way of identifying a subject, however. It may be necessary to sit on an apartment building where the subject is thought to reside, or a bar where he is known to hang out, or a possible workplace. Sooner or later the investigator will get a break—the subject will get in a vehicle, or the investigator will be able to see the apartment into which the subject goes.

Patrol officers should be utilized as a resource in these situations. The investigator may have to have the subject stopped solely for the purpose of identifying him. The stop should be made to look routine so as not to arouse any suspicion and the officers making the stop should be briefed on what questions to ask and what type of identification will be acceptable. The possibility exists that he may be able to brief the patrol officers on what he is trying to do, alert them regarding what to look for, and have them do sporadic surveillance and, in essence, do the legwork for him. There is also the other possibility that the patrol officers may already know who the person is and a great deal else about him.

Identifying the target of the investigation is essential, and once there is a name, even if it isn't the proper name, a vehicle, an address, and some associates, the investigator is in a position to evaluate further action. The case may move rapidly, and he will have an opportunity to flush on a buy before the subject is completely identified. Traditional policy does not permit spending buy money (flushing) on a subject who is not identified. For obvious reasons this is a good policy, but each situation will be different, and there are probably no hard and fast rules which can be applied in every case. Making an undercover buy before there is any idea who the subject is, his criminal history, or his status as a dealer is inadvisable except in street-level situations where this may be done occasionally. Even in those cases, however, there will be some background knowledge which will guide the decision-making process. For example, if there is a nuisance problem where many dealers congregate regularly, the investigator may wish to make a series of buys, identifying the dealers as he goes along, and then do a roundup all at once. The risk is that he won't get some of the people identified, and he might also buy imitation substance and not end up with a prosecutable case. As a general rule, identify the subject; then consider the options.

Estimated Expenses and Manpower

An essential part of planning an investigation is estimating the manpower and expenses which the investigation will require. This does not have to be done in any great detail and certainly doesn't have to be exact. But the investigator is not operating in a vacuum. Cases are influenced by the availability of time, manpower, and investigative funds. Dividends will be paid here for work done to this point. If he or she has identified the subject, corroborated informant information, done some surveillance, and figured out some goals for the investigation, the investigator is in a better position to estimate the manpower and expenses necessary to get it done. When the whole package is presented to the supervisor, he will be better able to make his decisions and to assist in the case. Likewise, fellow investigators will be reluctant to get involved in an ill-conceived venture, so proper planning of a case is necessary in order to gain their support.

If special hours or shifts are going to be necessary, this should be anticipated and included in the initial case planning. This is another aspect of the case which the investigator is going to have to sell. Other investigators are not going to volunteer to work midnight to 8 A.M.

unless they are sold on the importance of it. Likewise, the supervisor won't disrupt the operations of the team unless he has been shown the necessary justification.

Estimating expenses should include all investigative expenses—informant payments, buy money, money for rental of a surveillance post, money for travel, and other like expenses anticipated. It may be necessary to solicit help on a case based on anticipated expenses. If this happens, the initial case initiation reports and planning take on an enhanced importance. Once again the investigator is selling the relative value of his case.

The need for special equipment also has to be anticipated as part of the case planning.

The case planning process just described will occur to varying degrees depending on the size and scope of the case. An in-depth investigation will require more planning. Street-level buy/busts or search warrant cases may require less planning in some respects, but it will still be a key ingredient of any successful case or operation. Time spent planning pays dividends in the end, most notably in terms of officer safety and successful prosecutions. Planning without proper documentation, however, loses much of its value. The investigator must invest the time to document carefully the investigation from the beginning.

Continuing the Investigation

Surveillance

Once all the necessary work involved in initiating an investigation has been done, surveillance will play a large part in corroborating the initial information and determining the future of the investigation. Regardless of the type of investigation, there is no substitute for surveillance as part of a narcotics case. Surveillance is the number one fact-finding tool of a narcotics investigator. Outside of the informant, there may be no witnesses to interrogate or interview. Very rarely will an investigator interrogate the suspect during the investigation. Interrogation, such a valuable tool to other investigators, is of limited value to a narcotics investigator because of the covert nature of the investigations and the fact that most potential witnesses are also somehow involved in the illegal activity.

In a narcotics investigation, questions are answered by surveillance. The information provided by the informant has to be corroborated and supplemented by surveillance. Seldom, for example, will the informant be able to give the license number of the suspect's vehicle at the beginning of an investigation. He will tell the investigator that the guy drives a red truck with a camper, possibly a Ford, and the investigator must find the license number. Through surveillance, this and other valuable information will be learned.

When information is received on a street dealer, the informant may give an address or a location and a description of the place. Surveillance is necessary to corroborate the informant information, get the exact address, and ascertain if the foot traffic is consistent with street-level drug dealing. Surveillance provides firsthand knowledge of what is taking place. To be effective, surveillance must be documented. Surveillance notes should be converted into a surveillance report as soon as possible. The surveillance report may become the basis of later testimony. Decisions in the case will be made on what is learned in surveillance; if the surveillance isn't properly documented, a good deal of the value of the surveillance will be lost. If several officers are involved in a surveillance, somebody should be designated as the scribe. At the end of the surveillance, the case agent should be given either the notes or a finished surveillance report.

Surveillance, early in an investigation, may shape the rest of the investigation. In order to be effective, the surveillance has to be long enough in duration, and it has to be done during the right hours for the particular case. Sporadic surveillance has its place also. If enough surveillance is done, if it is done well and documented properly, the investigation is given a chance to develop. Photographs always add to the value of a surveillance if it is possible to get them.

Surveillance and further identification of the suspect and knowledge about his habits and patterns go hand in hand. As the case is developing, the investigator will also be developing the profile of the suspect. Does the suspect live alone, does he have a dog, does he work, with whom does he associate, what does he drive, does he have many visitors at home — these and similar questions can be answered through effective surveillance.

It may be necessary to include moving surveillance as part of the initial work on the suspect. Doing a moving surveillance on a streetwise drug dealer will be difficult at best. Several vehicles will be required if the surveillance is to have any chance of success. Remember, to learn anything from a moving surveillance, it will be necessary to follow the suspect to some destination. Watching the suspect drive around won't shed any light on the case. The risk that the suspect will become aware of surveillance has to be weighed against what can be gained. It doesn't pay to be paranoid about getting burned, but on the other hand, there is a substantial risk in any moving surveillance that the suspect will be wary and elusive, in which case he may either become aware of surveillance or lose it, or both. Before undertaking a moving surveillance, particularly early in a case when little is known about the habits of a suspect, the decision to follow him or not will be based on instincts as much as anything else. It might be necessary to start a cautious moving surveillance, prepared in advance to abort it if the suspect shows any signs of awareness.

As the case develops, the suspect becomes known, initial case information has been corroborated, so also do avenues of further investigation become clear. The challenge becomes interesting at this point. The growth and sophistication of the drug dealing business at all levels is apparent when one looks at the growth and sophistication of the drug enforcement profession over the last 30 years. The standard methods of bringing a case to fruition have changed even in the last few years.

Nonetheless, the formula for a successful case remains pretty much the same: good, fresh, and specific information acted on in an appropriate and timely fashion equals good results. The relative value of the information will both determine and be determined by the results. Any inappropriate decision with respect to course of action or timing can negate the value of the information and will either ruin the investigation or put it on hold.

In the development of a case, the investigator must remain open to all possible courses of action. It is helpful to discuss the case with experienced people and solicit their input.

Discussing this development process brings to mind a case in which controlled buys were being made from a guy who delivered off a pager system. It had taken a couple of buys to get the informant past an unwitting to where he was able to call the dealer direct. He had gained the confidence of the dealer, and during one of the deliveries it was possible to follow the suspect a great distance to his residence. Through that surveillance, information was developed about his identity, particularly his criminal record, that indicated that he was a substantial dealer. He had done time in federal prison for weapons charges, he was potentially dangerous, and he was very careful about letting anyone know where he resided. Through the informant buys and surveillance, it was possible to get enough information for a search warrant for the car, the residence, and the person of the suspect. The plan was to make one more controlled buy, stop the suspect immediately following the buy, search his person and his vehicle, and then search his residence. This plan has proven effective repeatedly. The suspect's residence happened to be in a suburb, and the narcotics investigators in that city were notified of the investigation. It was agreed that they would be called after the buy had been made and the suspect stopped.

Several investigators from the other jurisdiction made the decision to put the suspect's residence under surveillance. They went to the suspect's house at about the same time the informant had paged the suspect. The suspect had responded immediately to our call, and in the subsequent call indicated that he had what was ordered and would be there in 10 minutes. In the meantime, the surveillance at the house was recognized — someone from the house called the suspect and told him to respond there immediately, that something wasn't right, and that there were police officers sitting down the block watching his house. Unfortunately, the suspect didn't complete his delivery to us, instead going directly to his house. He subsequently refused to deal with the informant, he changed his pager number, got rid of his car and bought a different one, and then moved from his residence of at least three years. That was the end of the case on him for the time being.

In evaluating this case and what went wrong, it would be easy to say that the other agency should not have been notified until it was time to do the warrant. The fact is, there was a good working relationship between the two agencies, and notifying them of the investigation in their jurisdiction was the right decision. If anything, they should have been notified earlier and participated actively in the case. Likewise, it could be said that the decision to set up on the house was faulty, in light of the type of neighborhood it was in, the time of day, etc. The problem in the case was caused by poor communication. Had they been involved in the investigation all along, they would have realized, based on the nature of the case, that a daytime surveillance was not advisable. The other decisions made in the case were good, the timing was perfect, but an incomplete case was the result nonetheless. In the meantime, the target of the investigation continues to deal crack, he is more wary and circumspect about his dealings, and he will be more difficult to investigate successfully in the future.

This case is an example of the difficulty involved in getting a case from the drawing board to fruition. There are any number of potential errors which can be fatal to the case. One thing is for sure: the information will never become a prosecutable case without the investigator taking some risks in an effort to develop it. There are several techniques which can be employed in developing the case.

Controlled Buys

Among the several investigative techniques commonly practiced today is the controlled buy. The controlled buy is essentially an intelligence gathering technique. A controlled buy can resolve doubt as to the credibility of the informant in a particular case, it can provide information as to the quality and quantity of product on hand at a given time, and it can set the stage for possible undercover buys in the future. In common terminology, the controlled buy is distinguished from the undercover buy in that a controlled buy is made through an informant whereas an undercover buy is made by an officer.

Generally speaking, controlled buys are made with no intention of filing them in court as sale counts. However, these buys must, as the term implies, be controlled. There are several common steps involved in such control. Following is a list of them:

1. Make a money list, either by making a photocopy or by listing bill denominations and serial numbers.

2. Establish enough surveillance on the buy location that the informant can be observed to whatever extent is possible. Viewing the actual transaction is not necessary, for example, if the informant goes into the suspect's residence.

3. Brief the informant on things which he should look for and learn while he is inside.

4. Search the informant prior to sending him into the location. This is necessary due to the fact that the investigator may not witness the actual transaction. It is important that he can say what the informant had on his person before he went in and that when he came out he no longer had the official funds but instead had the drugs purchased with the funds. What is found when the informant is searched might be surprising. If the informant is allowed to go into the place with his own currency, make sure he has the same amount when he comes out.

5. Wire the informant. This isn't essential, but it does provide a way of witnessing the transaction beyond the limitations of visual observa-

tion, thus corroborating the information of the informant. Use a standard body mike as opposed to any new technology. It's a fact of life that the confidential informant (CI) today may be a suspect next week, and there is no reason to assume otherwise and give away any edge that might be needed in the future. Wiring and recording the transaction amounts to the same quality of documentation existent in an undercover buy. If the investigator is later forced to reveal the CI, and have him testify, buys made by him can be filed, Again, control of the buy does not necessarily include wiring the CI.

6. Make good surveillance notes whether the buy is being recorded or not. Electronic surveillance never supplants the need for surveillance notes and reports.

7. Take immediate custody of the evidence purchased. If the buy involves a delivery and subsequent surveillance on the delivery vehicle, the control officer will not immediately be part of that surveillance. His responsibility is to meet the CI, debrief him, and take custody of the evidence. Search the CI after the buy. This is done to keep him from "pinching" the buy (taking some of it), getting product or a kickback as his commission from the dealer, and buying something for himself. A properly controlled buy does not allow for any of these things happening.

When the buy has been completed, the informant should be debriefed thoroughly regarding the transaction. A controlled buy is an attempt to learn all that is possible about the suspect and the location. How many people were inside? Were any weapons seen? Were there children present? Was the door locked? How much was the suspect holding? Did the suspect talk at all about his business? All these things are important in determining what to do next. The CI might return to the investigator and tell him that everything in the house was packed up and the suspect indicated that he was moving. Or the CI might learn that the suspect is expecting a delivery at any time. Intelligence gathered from controlled buys can be extremely important if it becomes necessary to plan a raid at some point in the future.

The controlled buy is a good technique for setting up an undercover buy. Often the CI can make a backhanded introduction of the officer to the suspect. This works well with street-level situations, but the technique will work in other situations too. The technique plays on the relationship between the CI and the suspect. If this is good, any sense of alarm the suspect may feel at the sight of a stranger at his door might be disarmed or at least minimized by the sight of the CI. Of course, if the suspect doesn't trust the CI to start with, this could work in a negative way and he could refuse to deal because of it.

The controlled buy is also used to determine the mood of a place before sending an officer to the door. Often in street-level deals, the suspect will not be identified fully, and many other factors are unknown as well. A CI of proven reliability can test the waters. The CI may come back and say, "They are really nervous and uptight; I don't think it's a good idea to send the undercover officer there now." Or he may say, "The door is wide open, everybody's laid back, no problem." Using a controlled buy for this purpose can significantly reduce the risk the undercover officer is taking and can increase the possibility of making a successful undercover buy.

Paperwork from any controlled buys will not become part of the case filing unless the CI is going to testify and the buys he made are then filed. Otherwise, keep the paperwork pertaining to the controlled buys with other original paperwork as part of the permanent case file. Putting controlled buy documentation at the back of the file, separate in some way is recommended. The facts pertaining to the buys, including lab results, notes, dates, and times, may be subject to discovery at some point. In addition, something unusual may go wrong with the case and the investigator will need careful documentation of the investigation including controlled buys. An example would be a case in which a search warrant is prepared based on CI information and controlled buys. Should a police shooting take place during the service of the warrant, it will probably be necessary to produce everything pertaining to the case, including the CI, in order to assist in the investigation of the shooting. There is also the possibility that the investigation may not be successfully concluded for one reason or another. When the next investigator picks it up, controlled buys, as well as the rest of the previous investigation, will form a good basis for the subsequent case.

Other Techniques

If surveillance and controlled buys are unsuccessful in moving the case along, it may be time to reevaluate the game plan. There are several other things which can be done depending on the circumstances. A pen register could be used depending on the estimated level of the violator and whether or not he uses the telephone to conduct business. These represent a lot of work and some expense and do require a court order. Pen registers will be discussed thoroughly in Chapter Seven.

Trash covers may also be a possibility. Since these involve going through the trash which the suspect has discarded, some imagination is required in doing it unobtrusively. If the suspect lives in an apartment complex with a common dumpster, determining which trash was discarded by the suspect will require surveillance. After the trash from the suspect's apartment has been thrown out, there is the problem of going through it without arousing suspicion. Legally, it is generally accepted that a person has no expectation of privacy with respect to trash that he or she has discarded and that is in essence in plain view for any and all to examine. One exception has been in the state of California, but the U.S. Supreme Court, in a recent ruling on a California case, found that such warrantless searches of trash did not violate the Fourth Amendment.[2]

Specific investigative techniques as they apply to certain types of investigations will be discussed at length in Chapters Five through Seven.

During the early development of a case, surveillance and controlled buys are the most common techniques used. If unable to make progress and build on the initial information by surveillance and or controlled buys, it may well be that at least a temporary impasse in the case has been reached. Chances are, if sporadic surveillance is continued, if information on the subject as well the informants who can provide it, is actively sought, the case will eventually come together. Again, careful documentation is so important to an investigation. Invariably, the same players keep resurfacing, and if a previous investigation has not been documented, if it resides only in some investigator's head, it may not be of much help when it is needed to provide some impetus for a search warrant in a future investigation.

COOPERATION WITH OTHER AGENCIES AND UNITS

Interagency cooperation is essential to effective drug enforcement. In developing a case, it is important that the investigator be mindful of the fact that some other law enforcement officer or agency may well have an interest in this case. In fact they may already have an investigation in progress. In an earlier part of this chapter dealing with identifying the subject of the investigation, it was mentioned that a critical part of that identification process involves determining whether somebody else is

---

2 *California v. Greenwood,* 43 Cr L. 3029 (1988).

already working on him. The animosity that often develops between investigators and between agencies can usually be avoided by communication and cooperation in the early stages of an investigation.

The lesson that is learned eventually is that cooperation between units and agencies is essential to getting the job done. Effective communication is required in achieving an acceptable level of cooperation. When communication breaks down, usually over duplicate investigations, the cooperation falls apart as well. Each investigator has a responsibility to see that communication between agencies and units does not break down. There is no way to avoid duplicate investigations completely, but following some general rules and using some common case etiquette will prevent problems. If an investigator gets information on a case in another jurisdiction, he should check with the investigators in that jurisdiction before proceeding too far. Again, if rapport has been established and good communication exists, cooperation on the case will come easily. It is common for a dealer to be operating in multiple jurisdictions, particularly in metropolitan areas. The dealer may live in a remote suburb but do all his dealing in the center of the big city.

If information is received and the investigator is aware that someone else is already working on it, or is of a type that he knows falls within someone else's area of responsibility, the information should be passed on to them. Anything other than a teamwork approach to drug enforcement will be counterproductive in the long run.

The task force approach to drug enforcement has been very successful in fostering good case cooperation and communication. Drug task forces consisting of federal and local officers are common, as are task forces consisting of various local and state officers. For years, DEA state and local task forces have enhanced the ability of local police officers to complete their mission. Through these task forces, good working relationships have developed which have improved communication and cooperation. DEA has made their resources available to the locals participating in the task force, has provided some excellent training to the officers involved, and through this approach, has enhanced local drug enforcement efforts. Problems will still arise, but as long as the lines of communication remain open, they can be resolved. Organized crime drug enforcement task force programs are another example of the success possible when full advantage is taken of the interagency approach to drug enforcement.

In evaluating how to proceed on a case, taking the case federally can be an option. Certain types of cases have no place in the federal system, and the quantity of drugs involved, while important, is not the sole determining factor. For example, when crack cocaine emerged as a law enforcement crisis in many cities in 1986 and 1987, many small-time crack dealers were successfully prosecuted in the federal system. The impact of taking some of these cases federally was an important aspect of the strategy used to reclaim cities from the crack dealers. The same can be said of the Caribbean drug dealing crisis that developed: working these cases cooperatively, local and federal law enforcement officers were able to get things done that working independently of each other would not have accomplished.

COMMUNITY RESPONSIVENESS

To be effective, narcotics enforcement must be responsive to community needs. In most communities the number one priority will be to clean up the streets, to do something about the highly visible drug problem. People want to walk down their streets without being accosted and harassed by drug dealers, and the community will keep pressure on the police department to eradicate this problem. They won't be placated by the rationale that the narcotics investigators are working on upper-level cases which are really more cost effective. Consequently, if only a limited number of people are available to work narcotics investigations, street-level cases will get the attention over other cases which may involve a better chance of successful prosecution, significantly larger seizures of drugs, and the arrest of suspects who, though not highly visible, may be having more adverse effect on the community welfare than the street-level dealer.

Frustration can result from trying to do more than the limits of one's assignment allows. It is frustrating to work nothing but street level deals, to be constantly handling complaints and seizing small amounts of drugs and paraphernalia. Many small departments do not have enough people assigned to narcotics investigations to allow them to work anything but the street complaints. The best situations allow for enforcement efforts to target all levels with equal effectiveness.

The needs of the community will be reflected in the attitudes of the prosecutors as well. Cases that investigators think should be pushed through the system will often be pleaded out before the preliminary hearing because the system is overloaded and other cases are considered more important.

2

THE INFORMANT

INTRODUCTION

This chapter addresses what is consistently the most important factor in narcotics investigations, the informant. It is the critical role played by the informant that distinguishes narcotics investigations, taken as a whole, from other types of investigations. The ability to develop and manage informants properly will correlate closely to the success of a narcotics investigator.

This chapter discusses how to develop informants in narcotics cases, the various types of informants, and their motives. It also covers the legal considerations involved in the proper use of informants as well as procedural and emotional control of informants.

It is impossible for an officer not assigned to narcotics to realize the role that the informant plays in narcotics cases. It is not generally understood that an informant is a factor, to varying degrees, in most narcotics cases at some point. And even if this is understood, the extent to which personal and professional attitudes have to be compromised to work with informants this extensively cannot be imagined.

The narcotics investigator must be willing and able to establish rapport with all types of unsavory criminal types in order to get the job done. Some animosity arises because of these misunderstandings, and narcotics investigators are left in a position where they are almost apologizing for their widespread use of informants. Part of the misunderstanding is rooted in the traditionally unfavorable light in which our society looks at a "snitch" regardless of the situation. Where patrol officers are concerned, some of this misunderstanding relates to street contacts with these people who may flaunt the fact that they are working with a narcotics detective in order to get out of a minor legal problem. The informants who are repeatedly being contacted by uniform officers will generally be the small-time street crooks who can be extremely effective informants working street-level dealers. They can also be abrasive, indiscreet, and totally without tact when they are contacted by a patrol officer. The resentment that the officers may develop for this person will transfer to some degree to the narcotics investigator who is working with him in some instances.

Likewise, the newly assigned investigator, even if he has worked with informants as a patrol officer, will have no idea how difficult, complicated, frustrating, and potentially disastrous dealing with informants day in and day out can be. This chapter focuses on techniques for making effective use of informants in narcotics cases while minimizing the liabilities.

DEFINITIONS

☐ *Informant:* The informant is literally one who informs or gives information, particularly in the context of law enforcement incriminating information.

☐ *Confidential Informant:* A confidential informant is a person who provides law enforcement officers with information regarding the commission of criminal offenses but who is working on the premise that his identity will not be disclosed. However, this is never guaranteed. Implicit in the definition of a confidential informant is the fact that those controlling the informant have the person completely identified and that identification is documented. Part of the identification is a complete criminal history check, driver's license check, and so on; and in the case of a person who has been employed previously as a confidential informant, an informant background check.

☐ *Previously Reliable Confidential Informant:* A previously reliable confidential informant is one who, working confidentially with a given officer or several officers, has established a basis of reliability.

Through information given previously, it has been established that the confidential informant is reliable, that he has not provided false information in the past, and that his information has resulted in some enforcement action. Information received from a previously reliable confidential informant is given more credibility in the eyes of the court than is that received from a first-time confidential informant or an anonymous informant, but less credibility than a named citizen informant who, by virtue of the fact that he is named, takes on the status of a witness.

☐ *Anonymous Informant:* An anonymous informant is distinguished from a confidential informant inasmuch as nobody, not even the officer receiving the information, knows the identity of the informant. In the case of an anonymous informant, there will be no basis of reliability established as to the veracity of the information. However, there may be times when a person will call the same officer anonymously several times with information which turns out to be true when corroborated independently, and to that extent there is a basis of reliability.

In narcotics enforcement, when the term informant is used, it is commonly used to refer to a confidential informant and most often a previously reliable confidential informant. It is these types of inform- ants with which a narcotics investigator most commonly deals. In today's jargon, an informant is politely referred to as a CI. The substance of this chapter has to do with this type of informant for the most part, and when not otherwise specified, it is this type of informant, a confidential informant, to whom reference is being made. However, since the term informant refers generally to anyone providing incriminating information, the issues discussed will apply generally as well.

INFORMANT POLICY

It is essential that each agency has guidelines in place which classify types of informants, define how informants can be used, specify what types of informants will be eligible for use, stipulate payment of informants, delineate case consideration, etc. This policy should be clearly written and should be among the first things brought to the attention of the newly assigned narcotics investigator. The policy must place restrictions on the use of certain types of informants. It must also clearly assign responsibility and accountability for compliance with the guidelines.

Arguably the most important aspect of any comprehensive informant policy relates to identification and documentation of the informant. It is imperative that confidential informants, particularly those working for pay should be thoroughly identified. The first step in corroborating an informant's information involves thoroughly checking the informant's background. It is important that this be documented, and that should the need arise, the confidential informant can be fully identified by commanders and supervisors with a need to know. If the informant lied about his criminal history, it is a bad sign.

Informants should be classified according to their criminal background. Generally this classification need only provide for three categories: those with serious criminal records, those with only a minor record or no criminal record at all, and those with records for violent crimes or such extensive ongoing criminal history that they are disqualified for use as informants.

Classification of Informants

☐ *Class One:* those with serious criminal records. Serious, though subject to interpretation, would certainly include most felonies and some misdemeanors. Any career criminal behavior regardless of the crimes involved would constitute a serious criminal record. Many informants utilized by narcotics investigators will have serious criminal records. Any use of a person with a serious criminal record as an informant in an investigation should be done only with the approval of a supervisor.

☐ *Class Two:* all persons without what is considered to be a serious criminal record or with no criminal record at all fall within this classification.

☐ *Class Three:* those disqualified for use in an informant capacity based on their criminal record. Those people with a propensity toward violence, with records for aggravated robbery, sexual assault, aggravated assault with a weapon, and assault to a police officer would be peremptorily disqualified for use as informants. Likewise, people currently on probation or parole would probably fall in this category. Only in special circumstances, with the approval of a commanding officer, should these people be considered for use as informants.

Once informants have been classified, categories of participation must be defined. An informant is a participating informant, acting at the direction and under the control of a police officer, or a nonparticipating informant. Informants in the last category act independently of police input, and quite often provide information anonymously. The key distinguishing factor between the two categories of informant participation has to do with control and direction. If an informant's actions are being directed by a police officer, he is a participating informant and the use of that type of informant will require strict monitoring. Nonparticipating informants provide information in the absence of police direction.

Narcotics investigations most commonly involve participating informants, informants who are actively involved in an investigation and are acting at the direction and under the control of a police officer. Obviously, a nonparticipating informant creates no special difficulty for the individual or the department. This category of informant participation would include all the people who call anonymously with tips and who do not wish to get involved any further.

INFORMANT DEVELOPMENT

Aside from classifications established by official informant policy, informants can be generally categorized according to their situation. There are those working off a case or cases in the criminal justice system; there are those who are doing it as a means of making money; and there are those who are doing it only for personal motives, such as cleaning up their neighborhood, helping a relative overcome addiction, or subscribing to the lofty goal of making the world better and drug free.

Identifying Informant Motivation

What all three types have in common is a motive of some kind. It is important to identify the specific motives of informants. Doing so allows the investigator to determine more accurately the veracity of the information as well as the extent of informant participation which will be possible.

There is usually more than one motivational factor involved. An informant working off a case has a reason, hence, a motive, for going to work. What cases the informant will provide information about will be determined by secondary motives. For example, an informant told that he has to provide information resulting in at least three cases in order to get any consideration on his case, will probably choose which three he gives up (informs on) based on several considerations. Human nature dictates that an informant won't take on any unnecessary risk of reprisal. Therefore, he may not volunteer information on a particularly danger- ous dealer. Likewise, an informant who is also a regular user or addict will be reluctant to give up his regular connection. Informants probably aren't going to volunteer information on friends or relatives. Conversely, an informant may choose to give information about people against whom he has a grudge.

Identifying the motives of an informant must be an ongoing process, critical to informant control, particularly in the case of paid informants who are active for a long period of time.

Rules for Informant Handling

Regardless of the situation of the informant, there are several common sense rules which apply to informant handling. The rules have more application where a criminal-type informant is concerned, but they apply in general to all informants. These concepts will be discussed again throughout the chapter as they apply. They are mentioned in short form here to set the tone for further discussion.

1. Control the informant; don't allow him to dictate case decisions. This is much easier said than done. Many informants will attempt to control a case by taking advantage of the fact that they may know more about the suspects and their tendencies than the inves- tigators do. They will, out of necessity, have some input in decid- ing when and how to make a move; it remains the responsibility of the investigator to make the decision and see that what the inform- ant does is in compliance with that decision. Along that same line, informants working for pay have a tendency to push real hard when they need money badly. Often, the compassionate narcotics investigator, attempting to reward a loyal informant, will try to be accommodating and in doing so allows the informant to take control. The informant is not capable of deciding what cases

should be worked and in what manner they should be worked. Stay in control.

2. Keep the identity of the informant confidential assuming that is part of the bargain. Do not, however, promise confidentiality at all costs, because that promise may be impossible to fulfill. There will be times when an investigator is forced to reveal the identity of an informant. It is preferable to use criminaltype, Class One informants, in a confidential manner. Doing so will enable them to be used again and again, whereas if they testify, they will be of diminishing value in the future. There is also the possibility that they will be harmed, possibly killed, if they are not kept confidential.

   And finally there is the likelihood that if they are put in a position of testifying, their veracity, credibility, and motives will be attacked to the point that it will hurt the case more than it will help.

3. Do not allow the informant to be exposed to every other undercover officer in the unit. Doing so gives the informant an advantage should he be the subject of any future investigation.

4. In debriefing an informant, don't give him more information than he gives you. Too often, investigators will, through questioning, tip their hand on an investigation. Don't let the informant work you to see how much you already know.

5. Treat the informant with respect but don't patronize him either. Keep the relationship on a professional basis rather than a personal level. Make it clear that ongoing criminal behavior will not be condoned or tolerated.

6. Do not make promises to an informant that may be impossible to keep with respect to case consideration or payment or relocation or whatever the case may be.

7. As a general rule, two officers should be charged with controlling an informant. One will usually assume primary control. Dealings with informants should not be done one on one as a rule. This happens frequently for various reasons, but as a matter of practice, using two officers makes for a better situation. This is most assuredly the case when the officer and the informant are of different sexes.

8. Informants should be paid for work performed. Putting informants on a retainer for limited periods of time may be necessary, but

it is not preferable. The practice of advancing money on cases will usually come back to haunt an investigator in the form of unreasonable informant expectations. It is better to stick to the practice of paying when the work is done and paying based on what the final product is. It makes for better informant control. Informant payments should be witnessed.

9. A narcotics investigator should never lose sight of the fact that he is dealing with an informant, in most cases, a person who has a criminal record. If the person is a drug dealer, this is a person who may well be investigated in the future. In the course of an investigation or several investigations, a bond may develop between the informant and the investigator who is the control officer. While this is natural, it is potentially disastrous to the investigator and the department. Informants with criminal backgrounds can be as personable as anybody else. They are conwise and streetwise and when they are treated as equals to officers in a case, they have the opportunity to begin influencing the direction of the case.

    In addition, when an officer/informant relationship becomes a friendship, the officer's decisions regarding the informant will become tainted by the personal relationship. Many outstanding careers have been finished by judgment errors made in handling informants. Most of these errors were precipitated when the personal relationship between the officer and the informant supplanted the professional relationship which initially existed. The informant, once a personal relationship has been established, will no longer settle for being treated as an informant. The informant will use the personal relationship. It follows that if a personal relationship between an informant and the control officer is inappropriate, any type of sexual relationship will be far more devastating. As outlandish as this sounds, it happens, and it happens to outstanding police officers as well as the mediocre.

    Inherent in the professional management of an informant is the corroboration of as much of the informant information as possible in an effort to determine its validity. To assume that any information is true before a basis of reliability has been established is inadvisable.

10. Follow established informant procedures. Particularly important are those dealing with identification and documentation of the

informant and the guidelines for what types of people should not
be used as informants.

Most of these rules apply to confidential informants who do not have a
criminal record as well as those who do. In fact they apply in general
terms to every officer/informant relationship. The key to all these guidelines is control. To whatever extent possible, the officer must remain in
control of the informant and the situations in which the informant is
placed while under the control and direction of the officer. When an
informant begins to assert his control, the interests of law enforcement
may be adversely affected. All informants, whether they have a criminal
background or not will not fully understand the objectives of the police
department in any given case. This will not, however, deter them from
attempting to force their will on an investigation for any of a variety of
reasons. To ensure the safety of the officers as well as the informant and
the success of an investigation, the investigator must remain in control if
the informant.

Consider the example of a concerned citizen who, for motives of his
own, wished to help the vice squad rid the town of escort services. He was
a businessman whose heart was in the right place, who was truly interested in assisting the vice officers any way he could. He had a nice
residence, a listed telephone number which could be verified, and at first
suggested that we use it for setting up escort deals. He had a personal
crusade going against escort services, one large organization in particular,
and was demanding that action be taken. It was explained to him that
difficulty was being experienced in getting the suspects to respond to a
hotel or motel because they were wary, and an undercover apartment
with a verifiable telephone listing was not available at the moment. An
attempt was made to assure him that his complaint would be investigated.
He insisted that his residence and his home telephone, even his name, be
used to set up some undercover prostitution deals which would then
enable the arrest of those operating the escort services. The dangers of
this were explained to him, but he could not be deterred. He adamantly
wanted some action taken.

After several deals, some obscene threats of violence were made on the
phone against this well-intentioned citizen informant, some windows
were broken out of his house and his cars, and it dawned on him that
what he was doing was potentially very dangerous. He continued to offer
assistance in other ways, but he could clearly see that compromising his

own personal safety by using his own house for these deals was ill advised and admitted that our initial warnings against doing so had been right. At the beginning of this case, this informant had no idea what all was involved in this type of investigation or how potentially dangerous it could be.

TYPES OF INFORMANTS

Informants Working for Case Consideration

It is this type of informant with which the narcotics investigator most commonly works. Most informants who end up working for pay on a case-by-case basis start by working off a criminal case. That is, they have been arrested and have a case pending, and as a way of securing the most beneficial plea bargain, they work with the police as informants to some degree. The decision regarding how much consideration is given them on their case will ultimately be that of the judge, although the prosecutor must approve and make any recommendations based on input from the police officers involved.

Usually, people who have been arrested for narcotics violations in the past are those who will ask to talk to an investigator for the purpose of working off their current case. They know how the system works because they have been through it before. Whereas probation may be almost automatic on the first case or the first couple of cases, people with prior convictions realize that they may go to jail, and one possible way of avoiding that is to become an informant. First offenders may not realize how the system works, that working off their case is an option, and for that reason, they may not ask to speak to the investigator handling their case. Or, conversely, they may know exactly how it works and realize that they aren't going to do any time regardless of whether they try to work their case off or not, so they don't take the risks attendant to being an informant. Investigators who take the time to talk to people in jail on drug cases will continually develop informants.

The use of informants developed out of pending cases should be subject to the approval of a supervisor. Such a system will protect both the individual and the department from claims of impropriety. The decision to "turn" a person (make him an informant) and allow him to work off his case must be weighed in light of several factors which go beyond the initial approval to work such an informant.

First, compromise is a well-recognized principle of our criminal justice system. Plea bargaining is a case load necessity. This is particularly true with respect to narcotics cases. Nonetheless, the prosecutor must be consulted before any arrangement for disposition of a case is even suggested. The investigator should not make promises about what type of consideration will be given the informant on the case. This is within the domain of the prosecutors, and they must be consulted beforehand. No deals can be made without their input. Even then, there will be limitations on what can be done on a given case depending on its nature. Drunk driving cases, for example, or misdemeanor domestic violence cases are cases where the prosecutor may have very little latitude in offering a deal. By statutory classification these cases do not rank among the most serious, but in terms of public opinion they are very important. The courts will take a really close look at any deals regardless of what the trade-off is.

Another obvious factor involved in the decision to work off a case relates directly to the record of the potential informant versus the possible gain. The record of the informant should be given first consideration. There are many drug dealers, who when they are finally caught on a solid case and are looking at a jail sentence, will want to turn. Consider the needs of the community in making this decision. Some people, regardless of who they are willing to turn, should go to jail. Sooner or later somebody has to go to jail. Not everyone can be allowed to work when it is finally critical to them to do so. If a person has been a career drug dealer, on the street, for example, and is finally caught on a good, solid case, allowing him to work the case off could well be the wrong decision. This person has negatively impacted so many people in the community, and has been a continuing source of drugs on the street and all the attendant problems, that very little consideration for him is warranted. If he wants to work on limited terms, for sentencing considerations, for example, that might be acceptable.

The same philosophy applies to a greater degree to upper-level players. If a person is arrested with an amount which will aggravate his case and dictate a mandatory sentence, what kind of consideration does he deserve? These can be tough decisions to make. If an investigator has a case on a small-time dealer and he is willing to turn his source, which would potentially take a large quantity of drugs off the street, there is some responsibility to do that'as well. Bargains made in this regard should be such that the system gets as much as possible while giving up as little as necessary.

A case comes to mind regarding an alleged street gang drug dealer. According to intelligence reports which had been received, this 18-year-old kid was responsible for large amounts of crack cocaine being brought into the city and was a criminal hardened beyond his years. He was finally arrested on a small-time delivery of an ounce or two of crack. Failing to live up to his reputation, this dealer cried like a baby and immediately began making overtures of working off his case. A very short time later he was arrested again on a weak criminal impersonation case. The investigators handling the case made the decision to allow him to work off the criminal impersonation case while giving no consideration on the drug case. He turned a fairly good deal for several ounces and a good-quality offender. The system profited while giving up very little.

Another factor in deciding what, if any, consideration should be given the informant on his case is, of course, the level at which he is capable of working. It is quite common for informants at a fairly high level to turn people below them. This may not be obvious from the beginning but will generally become apparent rather quickly. The pyramid theory would dictate that any trade of information for consideration move upward to a higher-level of offender, not laterally and certainly not down. There are times when trading laterally is okay, as when, for example, the other suspect is by some objective standard a better quality violator than the one in custody. This situation would be particularly applicable to street-level dealers. While the lower level may all be about the same quality of dealers, some are career criminals and may be dangerous. Some are just difficult to apprehend.

Another very important factor will be whether it will be possible to keep the informant confidential. In fact, it might be possible to keep him off the witness stand, but in reality it will be apparent that he set up the deal. This becomes a factor, particularly in higher-level cases, when the informant is working for sentencing consideration but will probably go to jail. If he participates and it becomes known that he did, a situation may develop where the informant and the dealer he informed on end up in jail together. In this case, the informant may be in real danger. If there is substantial risk that the informant working off a case is going to be hurt or killed, either in prison or on the street, using the informant should probably be reconsidered. If the informant is to be used in spite of these risks, it may be necessary to relocate him and take other precautions as well. Those eventualities should be planned for well in advance so that the necessary approval can be obtained and the appropriate arrangements made.

Along with that is the prospect of the informant becoming a testifying witness at some point. If this is part of the plan from the beginning, the value of the informant as a witness should be assessed. Some informants, by virtue of their criminal history or their demeanor, will be such terrible witnesses that it shouldn't even be considered.

Paid Informants

Many informants who started by providing information in exchange for case consideration will eventually become paid informants. Generally they will have to participate in more than one investigation to get any consideration on their case, and by that time, the investigator and the supervisor will have a feel for what type of person the informant is, what type of cases he is capable of putting together, how dependable he is in terms of keeping in touch, and the reliability of his information. It is a natural progression. By the time the informant has worked off his case, some evaluation of his potential will be possible. Those who are particularly good should be cultivated for use as paid informants.

Paying informants is an issue in the eyes of the general public in part because the perception exists that they, the taxpayers, are paying double for the same services. They are paying sworn law enforcement people to make drug cases who in turn are paying informants, from tax dollars, to help them make the cases. It is, in fact, not a matter of paying double, it is a matter of paying for two different services. Regardless of how good a police department is and how good a narcotics investigator is, informants are absolutely essential to narcotics enforcement, and other aspects of police work as well. Informant work, the information they provide, is like any other commodity: the better the quality, the higher the price that it can demand.

In fact, the use of paid informants probably improves the overall cost effectiveness of a narcotics enforcement unit. An informant introduction can take the place of many hundreds of person-hours involved in getting an undercover officer to a point where he can get an introduction himself and make a buy. Likewise, inside information provided by a reliable informant can establish much better probable cause for a search warrant than numerous hours of surveillance and investigation can do. Timely informant tips can result in maximum seizures of drugs and cash and weapons while action without those tips can be nothing better than guesswork at times.

The value of paid informants to narcotics enforcement efforts is well substantiated. In a street enforcement unit where the primary enforcement tool is a search warrant based on probable cause provided by informant information the amount of money spent on the purchase of evidence and the amount spent on the purchase of information will be very close to the same. When other payments categorized as purchases of services, such as rent for apartments used by informants, bus tickets out of town, etc., are added into the cost of purchasing information, which they really are, more money will be spent purchasing information than purchasing evidence.

Paying informants demands a system of careful accounting and documentation. This aspect of informant control will be discussed in detail later in this chapter.

Drug unit supervisors should know the informants working for their investigators. This principle applies to all informants but is particularly true with respect to those being paid. This does not imply that the supervisor should be involved in the day-to-day control of the informant, but it is important that the supervisor have some feel for the informant as a person. This enables him to give appropriate counsel when it is needed; in addition, it will allow the supervisor to evaluate the informant's work subjectively. While there may be objective guidelines for informant payments, subjective considerations are inevitably a factor when it comes to amount of payment.

Payment amounts are related to any number of factors, the foremost being the availability of funds. A unit with adequate funds available for reasonable informant payments will fare better than will those without. That notwithstanding, there must be a payment schedule, albeit an informal one, for making informant payments. A department's informant policy should also have provisions requiring command approval for payments exceeding a given amount, $300.00, for example.

Among the objective considerations for amount of informant payments would be the danger factor. If the informant is subjected to considerable danger, he should be compensated more for that case than for a routine case. An informant making buys under conditions of implicit violence or in which guns are flourished should be compensated for the added potential danger. Anticipated danger to the informant from possible future retribution will also be a factor given consideration at times.

Usually the most persuasive factors in determining amount of payment are the weight of the seizure and the level of the violators. These two factors taken together largely define the quality of a case. Also considered in the process will be the track record of the informant. A reliable informant who has been working consistently for a year or two will generally be paid more for a case than will a first-time informant for the same level of case.

All things considered, informants, like other people doing piecework, should be paid for the overall quality of their work. Some informants will do a lot of their own investigation in an effort to get the case to go. The informant who pays particularly close attention to details, such as exact addresses, license numbers, last names, description of suspects and weapons, and the like, are worth more to the investigator. They are obviously tuned in to what is needed to make a case successful. They have been paying attention during debriefings and improving their performance accordingly. This extra effort should be rewarded, and the informant should be told that he is being paid a little extra for an unusually good piece of work.

Informants should, as a rule, be paid when the work is done. This is almost essential in search warrant cases. Paying the informant before the results are in, before the warrant is served, is not recommended. If the informant is a regular, paying small amounts for controlled buys leading up to the warrant is acceptable. These payments should be small, and total payment made for the success of the case, if any, should be adjusted to account for these buy payments. Many informants would rather not take small payments for buys made, waiting instead for the payoff on the case success. Some informants exist on the street-level deal, and if they are setting up one warrant after another, the policy of paying $20.00 or $25.00 for each controlled buy will keep them working. The danger in paying informants as a search warrant case progresses is that the incentive that the case be successful is reduced. In fact, if it is a small-time deal, the street-level informant who is part con man, and most of them are, will figure it out that he makes out better taking a small payment for a controlled buy if the chances that the warrant will be profitable and yield a case are slim. Informants may also be tempted to double-cross and collect a payment for a buy and then tip off the dealer that the heat may be on for which he may be paid in cash or drugs.

There are many jurisdictions which require that the identity of an informant be revealed when the informant's information forms the basis of probable cause for a search warrant or an arrest. In some of these jurisdictions, the informant may be revealed at the preliminary hearing stage. For various reasons, the courts in these jurisdictions require that the prosecutor be prepared to reveal the identity of the informant without any motions, hearings, or rulings on the issue. This applies to possession cases which result from search warrant recoveries, where the warrant was based on CI information, and other cases where the confidentiality of the informant is generally protected. If this is the case, the informant should be advised up front that he will, in all likelihood, not be kept confidential.

Many times, the informant will agree to testify if it is necessary and the controlled buys will be made as if they were undercover buys. A statement will be taken from the informant, the buy will be recorded, and the paperwork will be prepared as if it were going to be part of the case. In these cases, an informant willing to testify might be paid more for each controlled buy than those who are not. The same problems mentioned earlier with respect to an informant's testimony exist. The other inherent difficulty with this type of arrangement is that the informant is actually being paid more, in advance, for his promise to testify and for possible retribution which he may suffer. He is being paid more based on the probability that the case will go to trial and that his identity may be revealed and that he may testify. Since most cases are plea bargained, the informant will usually not testify. If this happens, there is no trial, no testimony, and no revelation of the informant's identity, and, hence, no retribution. Also, when it comes down to actually testifying, it never seems like such a good idea when it becomes imminent. What looked alright to the informant when he was getting $50.00 for a controlled buy doesn't look nearly so appealing when it is almost certain that he will have to confront the defendant in open court from the witness stand.

The informant may back out at the last minute, and the entire case, if hinged on his testimony, might be dismissed. The informant may not feel any sense of obligation to keep his part of the bargain. Any sense of obligation that is felt may be overcome by the inherent aversion to being a witness in court.

There are professional informants who move from one place to the next working as paid informants. Paying these people for deals they set up is one thing; paying them, banking on the fact that they will be around to testify, isn't advisable.

Informants Motivated by Other Factors

In addition to those working off a case and those working for pay, there is an additional small category of informants who are working for a variety of personal motives. Often they don't work for any considerable duration; in fact, most of these will work on one deal and then disappear. Motives for this type of informant cover a wide range. It is also a distinct possibility that some of these motives will also influence those informants being paid and those working off a case.

Among the most common personal motives causing a person to inform on another is retribution. This often occurs with lovers who have been cast off for another or abused in some way. An informant with this motive can be extremely valuable. The time factor is critical. If they turn the person immediately, their information is fresh, and as ex-lovers they are in a position to know a great deal more about the suspect's habits, his financial affairs, the way he deals, etc. than is someone who is merely a friend or a customer would know. The key to handling this type of informant is to take action quickly before the burning desire to seek retribution has dissipated or before reconciliation takes place. This is a distinct possibility, which is also an important consideration inasmuch as the informant may have to testify.

It is important to isolate this particular motive and identify it for what it is. Retribution as a motive can be so powerful that the informant may go to any length to fulfill it. Such motivation can easily stimulate a false report or at least cause the informant to embellish the story in an effort to assure that some action is taken. Assuming the informant is serious about turning an ex-lover, he or she should be in a better position to do it than anybody else, although not able to participate, make a buy for example, if the relationship has been permanently severed.

Retribution is also commonly a motive where other types of relationships exist or have existed between the informant and the suspect. An ex-partner or associate in the business of drug dealing may be motivated to become an informant. These informants can be particularly helpful in providing historical information on the suspect but probably have lost the trust and confidence of the suspect, and therefore, using them in a participating role may be precluded much as in the case of the ex-lover. Again, the fact that revenge or retribution is the motivating factor has to be weighed in order to assess accurately the value of the information. Valuable information can be learned from this type of informant with respect to dealing habits, financial affairs, and associates.

Like retribution, personal gain of one type or another motivates people to become informants. Relatives of drug users will often become informants in an effort to help the relative. People working on this motive will be quick to admit it, and they are sincere. They are not often in a position to help in a participating role: while they may know the identity of the dealer, they probably don't buy from him. They may have access to phone numbers and know last names and such, and they may know the dealer well enough to establish sufficient rapport for a controlled buy if that's the direction decided upon.

Informants will also come forward in an effort to clean up their building or neighborhood. Again, personal gain, ridding one's own neighborhood of drug dealers, is the motive. These informants will usually be of the nonparticipating classification and as a rule can only provide general intelligence information. Some apartment managers will become informants on a limited basis to help cure a particular problem. They are in a position to provide background information as well as floor plans and keys, surveillance apartments, etc.

Then there are those informants with lofty motives, such as saving the country from the drug plague. Many paid informants are motivated by the desire to improve the world while at the same time making amends for past misconduct. Some of these informants tend to overestimate their contribution and minimize the role of the police departments at the same time. They begin to consider themselves secret agents who are making the police look good. Control of these informants can be difficult because of the self-delusions and the fact that many are frustrated people who wanted to get into law enforcement but never made it, usually because of their criminal history, or lack of education, or both.

It is important to identify the motives of an informant. There are usually secondary motives operating, and those have to be recognized for what they are. The motives of the informant have a direct bearing on what kind of work he is capable of performing.

LEGAL AND ETHICAL CONSIDERATIONS

Confidentiality

Confidentiality is necessary to the free flow of information from private citizens to the government. This principle is well recognized. That confidential informants are necessary to effective law enforcement, particularly narcotics enforcement, is also recognized and widely accepted. There are, however, no fixed rules by which all courts in all jurisdictions are forced to abide regarding the disclosure of the identity of the informant.

In *McRay v. Illinois,*[1] the Supreme Court ruled that the trial court in Illinois, in permitting the officers to withhold the informant's identity, did not violate the defendant's right to confrontation and cross examination under the Sixth Amendment. Mr. Justice Stewart, writing the majority opinion quoted from *Cooper v. California,*[2] "Petitioner also represents the contention here that he was unconstitutionally deprived of the right to confront a witness against him, because the State did not produce the informant to testify against him. This contention we consider absolutely devoid of merit."[3]

In getting to that conclusion, the majority opinion in *McRay* touched on a number of key factors regarding what is referred to as the "informer's privilege":[4]

> In sum, the Court in the exercise of its power to formulate evidentiary rules for federal criminal cases has *consistently declined to hold that an informer's identity need always be disclosed in a federal criminal trial, let alone in a preliminary hearing to determine probable cause for an arrest or search.* Yet we are now asked to hold that the Constitution somehow compels Illinois to abolish the informer's privilege from its law of evidence, and to require disclosure of the informer's identity in every such preliminary hearing where it appears that the officers made the arrest or search in reliance upon facts supplied by an informer they had reason to trust. The argument is based upon the Due Process Clause of the Fourteenth Amendment, and upon the Sixth Amendment right of confrontation, applicable to the States through the Fourteenth Amendment . . . We find no support for the petitioner's position in either of those constitutional provisions. (emphasis added)

---

1 *McRay v. Illinois,* 386 U.S. 300 (1967).

2 *Cooper v. California,* 386 U.S. 58 (1967).

3 386 U.S. 300, 313 (1967), quoting from 386 U.S. 58, 62 (1967).

4 386 U.S. 300, 312 (1967).

The Court went on to say in the majority opinion that the officers had testified in this case as to what basis of reliability the informant had, that they had been carefully cross-examined, and that the judge had been satisfied that the officers were being truthful and did not force disclosure: "Nothing in the Due Process Clause of the Fourteenth Amendment requires a state court judge in every such hearing to assume the arresting officers are committing perjury."[5]

It must be understood that no jurisdiction is mandated to keep an informant's identity confidential either. "The informer's privilege does *not* dictate that a magistrate *must* keep every informant's identity confidential; rather, it provides that it is not unconstitutional for a jurisdiction to give a magistrate the discretion to allow the prosecution to keep an informer's identity confidential where the affiant's testimony relating to the content and circumstances of the informant's information is otherwise found to be intrinsically believable."[6]

Each jurisdiction will treat the confidentiality issue differently, and the investigator must be familiar with the policy in his or her jurisdiction. Some cities may be located in two or more counties, and officers may encounter different policies in the separate jurisdictions. While one may allow search warrant affidavits based, in part at least, on hearsay information from a confidential informant without disclosing the informant, the other may not and may force the disclosure of the identity of the informant if the evidence from the search warrant is to be used.

Informant Participation

The level of informant participation in a given case may determine whether or not disclosure of the informant is eventually required. Challenges to the informer's privilege frequently hinge on the informant's level of participation. If the informant is an eye and ear witness to the offense for which the suspect is charged, and as such if he is a material witness, critical to determining guilt or innocence, disclosure may be ordered.

With respect to informant participation, *Roviaro v. United States* remains

---

5 Ibid., at 313.

6 John M. Burkhoff, *Search Warrant Law Deskbook* (New York: Clark Boardman Company Ltd., 1990), p. 4–7.

the most definitive case.[7] A 1957 decision, it was cited in the majority opinion in the *McRay* decision and others since. The *Roviaro* decision is a very good one to examine in that the circumstances of the case are so similar to cases being set up today in spite of the passage of 33 years. The dilemma remains, however, as to how to keep the informant from participating to the extent that he has to testify.

The informant met with Roviaro, who was a suspected heroin dealer with whom the confidential informant had dealt in the past. At a certain location in Chicago, they met, Roviaro got into the informant's vehicle, and they drove to another location where Roviaro, the passenger in the vehicle, got out of the vehicle and went to a spot near a tree and came back a short time later with a package of heroin. There was a Chicago police officer hidden in the back or trunk of the informant's vehicle, and he later testified regarding the conversation between Roviaro and the informant.

Roviaro and the informant were arrested and taken to a police station, where the informant, playing out his role, which was to look like another suspect rather than an informant, denied knowing Roviaro in front of him. Roviaro was charged, and in his defense, disclosure of the informant was requested. The informant's identity was not disclosed. The Supreme Court ruled that in not disclosing the informant the trial court had acted wrongly in this case. The reasons given centered on the informant's level of participation in that the informant "had taken a material part in bringing about the possession of certain drugs by the accused, had been present with the accused at the occurrence of the alleged crime, and might be a material witness as to whether the accused knowingly transported drugs as charged."[8]

The Court ruled further that while "no fixed rule with respect to disclosure is justifiable," the "identity of informer must be disclosed whenever the informer's testimony may be relevant and helpful to the accused's defense."[9] The decision also discussed other factors to be considered in determining when disclosure will be required: the availability of other witnesses, the likelihood that the testimony of the informant would differ from other witnesses (in this case, the police officer who testified about the conversation Roviaro and the informant had), and the

---

7 *Roviaro v. United States,* 353 U.S. 53 (1957).

8 Ibid., at 55.

9 Ibid., at 61, 62.

availability of the informant. In *Roviaro,* there was some basis for belief that the informant may have been dead by the time of trial. Also to be considered is the identity of the informant known to the defendant. In this case, the defendant, Roviaro, figured out who the informant was from the way the deal was set up, but the identity of the informant was not disclosed by the government. If it is likely that the identity of the informant is known to the defendant, the privilege against disclosure may no longer apply.

The level of an informant's participation, as in this case, can lead to an entrapment defense, although Mr. Justice Clark noted in his dissenting opinion that entrapment had not been claimed by Roviaro. The majority opinion noted that the testimony of the informant might have established entrapment.

State courts followed *Roviaro.* If the informant is involved to the extent that he is actually "setting up the crime and is present at its commission or when the informant actually takes part in the crime," disclosure will no doubt be ordered.[10,11]

Disclosure of the informant may take the form of an *in-camera* hearing where the prosecution is ordered to present the informant before the judge in chambers. This has been ordered in cases where there is some question about the informant, possibly even the existence of the informant, in an effort to balance the need for confidentiality with the rights of the individual.[12]

Cellmate Informants

Narcotics investigators will occasionally receive information from informants who are incarcerated regarding drug dealing activity of cellmates. These are usually not the type of situations where constitutional issues preclude the use of the informant's information. Restrictions on the use of cellmate informants do not generally apply to information about ongoing criminal activity, such as drug dealing, or information about criminal activity which is going to happen in the future.

---

10 *State v. Lanigan,* 528 A.2d 310 (R.I. 1987).

11 Burkhoff, *Search Warrant Law Deskbook,* p. 4–7.

12 *People v. Flores,* 766 P.2d 114, 123 (Colo. 1988). Also, see Burkhoff, Search Warrant Law Deskbook, p. 4–8.

If an informant is in the cell with a dealer, they will sometimes be able to set up deals from jail. The necessary contacts and introductions will be made from jail, and these types of communications would not be privileged. In addition, cellmate communications regarding past criminal activity unrelated to the charges for which the suspect is currently being held, where the informant solicits the information at the direction of the police, are excluded from the Fifth Amendment *Miranda* protections. There is no need to advise a suspect prior to using a cellmate informant or an undercover officer even though the suspect is in custody *if the information pertains to a crime or crimes other than that for which the suspect is being held.*[13]

If, however, a cellmate informant or undercover officer is used to obtain information about a case currently pending and for which the suspect has been formally charged, Sixth Amendment protections regarding right to counsel become a factor. Information gained from an informant in this situation can be used only if it pertains to unrelated crimes or to the crime charged if the informant assumes a passive posture, listening and reporting but not soliciting any information. Merely placing an informant in the cell with one who has been charged for the purpose of *listening* does not compromise a violation of the defendant's Sixth Amendment right to counsel if the informant makes no deliberate effort to elicit information about the crime charged.[14]

Investigative Application of Legal Considerations

It is necessary for a narcotics investigator to understand when the confidentiality of the informant is likely to be respected in the legal system and when disclosure is probable. In order to make sensible case decisions with respect to the role of the informant, this is essential. Too often, the narcotics investigator operates on what he has learned informally with respect to use of confidential informants rather than what case law, the rules of evidence, and the courts in his jurisdiction have mandated.

It is important to realize that while the principle of the confidential informant is well founded, it is not, by any means, absolute or guaranteed. As mentioned earlier, the informant should be told beforehand that

13 *Illinois v. Perkins,* 110 S.Ct. 2394 (1990).

14 *United States v. Henry,* 447 U.S. 264 (1980).

while every effort will be made to keep his identity confidential, the situation may arise where his identity will be disclosed in court.

The value of an informant's information will usually be directly related to the amount of risk, disclosure of identity or personal safety, or both that the informant undertakes. The closer that an informant is to a deal, the more likely that he will be disclosed as the informant, that he will testify, and that he may suffer some form of retaliation.

Those narcotics cases involving the highest degree of informant participation are undercover buys and introductions. In some cases it will be prearranged that the informant will testify. In those cases the informant will make controlled buys which will be prepared as undercover buys for presentation in court. The informant will be wired, good surveillance will be in place, and the informant will be debriefed after the buy. If it has been arranged that the informant will testify, and usually this is because it is impossible to introduce an undercover officer, these cases present no particular problem.

What is a constant source of difficulty is the case in which the informant does not wish to testify, yet the deal requires a high level of informant participation. An example would be a case where an informant tells an officer of a person dealing in ounce quantities who does not wish to meet anyone. The suspect will deliver to the informant. He will not let the informant come to where he lives under any circumstances. The informant knows this party is a foreign national living in this country illegally, knows him only by a nickname, does not know where he lives, and does not know what type of car he drives. The informant has provided information in the past which has resulted in good seizures and good arrests. In this case, he has seen this suspect deal cocaine in ounce quantities and above. The informant is experiencing serious cash flow problems and needs to generate some income and is pushing the case.

Assume that it is decided to have the informant contact the suspect and try to make a buy for some quantity smaller than an ounce. The strategy is to flush on an informant buy in an effort to establish the suspect's identity through surveillance and identify the suspect's vehicle. If the surveillance is particularly good, it might even be determined where the suspect is staying.

The investigator may not wish to flush on an ounce controlled buy to gain this intelligence, but a quarter ounce or a half ounce may be acceptable. The informant contacts the suspect and asks about making a buy. The suspect tells the informant that he is in possession (in pocket, holding, etc.); in fact he has just been resupplied (re-upped), but his brother got arrested last week dealing an ounce to an undercover police officer, and because of that the suspect has developed a new policy of dealing nothing less than quarter pounds. The informant tells the suspect that he might have a buyer in mind, but a quarter pound may be more than he can handle at once. The suspect tells the informant to call him and he will bring the cocaine once he has seen the money and is certain that everything is okay.

The informant reports back with the new information. The information would encourage the belief that the suspect is probably worth some time and effort. The informant still does not know who the suspect is nor does he know where the suspect lives. As the scenario now exists, there are several options available, and most of them involve future informant participation to the point that he will have to be disclosed. Not having the suspect identified, the investigator is probably not in any position to flush on a buy of the size which the suspect demands. That's out. Assume that the informant is able to give some clue where the suspect hangs out, for example, where he meets him, since he is not allowed to go to the suspect's home. It may be possible to stake out that location and through extensive surveillance, identify the suspect. Once he is identified, it might be possible to find out where he lives and the options have then been expanded. Through identification it might be determined that the suspect is a high-level dealer, and it might be possible to gain support, financial and otherwise, to do a full-length complex investigation.

Assuming that none of that is true, however, the factors discussed in *Roviaro* would seem to dictate that the informant's participation will be of such an extent that he will have to be disclosed. If the informant arranges for the delivery of 4 ounces, with the purpose of arresting the suspect immediately after the informant has seen the cocaine and left the suspect to call the investigator, the defense may later assert that the informant is a material witness even though he is not there when the arrest and seizure takes place. If he is there when the arrest is made, he could be arrested, as was the informant in *Roviaro*, to take the heat off him and then released when he is found to be clean. In both scenarios, the investigator would articulate the probable cause for arrest as information from a previously reliable confidential informant, that the suspect was in possession of cocaine at such and such a location now, and that exigent circumstances prevented the obtaining of a warrant. This would be true, but there is a significant chance that the disclosure of the informant's identity will be ordered at a motions hearing or some other proceeding prior to trial because of his extensive involvement and the fact that he may be a material witness to the defense of the suspect. In addition, the defense may already know or have a good idea who the informant is and, therefore, not disclosing his identity serves no purpose in terms of protecting his personal safety.

Another complication with this plan, aside from the involvement of the informant already detailed, is that the suspect may demand that the informant give him the money first, before any further dealing takes place. This creates the untenable situation of having to front the money (give the suspect the money on his word that he will deliver the drugs), and it places the informant in a position of even greater participation.

Informants will often report that there is no way a suspect will meet anyone when that is really not true. Under the right circumstances, the suspect could be induced to meet someone. Greed may become a factor and may prevail over the suspect's sense of street survival. Even if able to get an undercover officer introduced, the investigator still may have the problem of having to bust the suspect immediately rather than flush a large amount of money, and that will leave the informant in the position of a material witness, right in the middle of the deal. The best course of action would seem to be to persuade the informant to testify or hold off an any immediate action and work on the deal and try to develop it to the point that the involvement of the informant is significantly diminished.

The most common means of getting the informant out of undercover negotiations involves making an introductory buy in the presence of the informant, setting up future buys directly from the suspect without any informant involvement. The initial buy is not filed as a criminal case charging the sale to the informant. The subsequent buys can be filed as the informant is not a participant. In reality, it may be obvious in time that he set the suspect up, but he is not a witness to the offenses charged.

Informant information and controlled buys, used as the probable cause foundation of a search warrant, are usually the cleanest types of cases in terms of informant involvement. The case may be that a previously reliable confidential informant calls and reports that the suspect is at a particular location, now, and that the suspect is in possession. If there is no exigency, a search warrant can be obtained. If the suspect is standing on a street corner, sitting in a car, or whatever, and exigent circumstances do exist—the suspect will be leaving any minute, the car is running, etc.—investigators can respond and arrest the suspect based on probable cause that he is in possession of drugs in violation of the law. The suspect can be searched subsequent to arrest and charged. There is a good chance that the identity of the informant will not be disclosed in a suppression hearing.[15] Likewise, if a search warrant is based on information from an informant where the informant is providing a tip rather than participating, depending on the jurisdiction of the case, as there are no hard and fast rules, the identity of the informant should be protected.

If controlled buys are made and they then become the basis of probable cause for a search warrant, the informant, although he is a participant to the extent that he made a buy, is not a material witness since no particular sale is charged, only possession. At that, the defense will push for disclosure of the informant for the simple reason that they know the prosecutor does not wish to reveal it and may dismiss the case rather than do so. Depending on the circumstances of the case, the jurisdiction, and the way the warrant is written, disclosure may be ordered. This will be discussed in more detail in the next chapter pertaining to search warrants.

Cellmate informants are not uncommon in narcotics cases. Cases come to mind where an informant called from jail and stated that he was in with a person from whom the informant had made a purchase of drugs in the very recent past before either of them went to jail. In this case the informant had been to the suspect's apartment on the morning that both were arrested. At that time he had seen over an ounce of cocaine in the apartment. Investigation revealed that the suspect had been jailed at about 10 o'clock in the morning after he was stopped for a traffic violation and subsequently arrested for a concealed weapons charge. The suspect had keys and identification which supported or corroborated the informant information with respect to where the suspect lived and in what apartment he lived. By coincidence, the informant had also been arrested at about the same time as the suspect in an incident which was totally unrelated. Based on the freshness of the informant's information, the fact that it could be corroborated, and the fact that the suspect had a

---

15 *McRay v. Illinois,* 366 U.S. 300 (1967).

past history as a drug dealer, known to carry weapons, a search warrant was obtained for the suspect's residence. Over an ounce of cocaine was recovered from the apartment along with documentation that the suspect lived there, and he was charged with possession of a controlled substance.

The information obtained by the cellmate informant did not pertain to the case for which the suspect was currently charged; it related to a separate criminal offense. In fact the information was not obtained during the time that the suspect and informant were cellmates, but the fact that they were cellmates prompted the investigation, and while in the cell with the suspect, the informant was able to ask the suspect if the police had taken his drugs. The suspect told the informant that they had not, that the cocaine was still in the apartment. This information was valuable in deciding to act on the probable cause which existed; it was not added to the probable cause factors in the warrant because to do so was unnecessary and may have tended to identify the informant.

There have been many other cases where an informant is a cellmate with a drug dealer and by virtue of that fact is able to provide information which leads to additional drug charges on the suspect or charges on associated dealers to whom the informant is given a referral. The suspect in one case told the informant that he was in jail on a drug case, that he needed to generate some money badly and that in order to do so he needed a good source for a large amount of cocaine. That way, his people could deal it for him while he was in jail, and he could continue his business of making money. The cellmate informant told the suspect that he knew of a good source whose prices were right and offered to put the two in contact. The undercover officer was then able to deal directly with the suspect by telephone, and a reverse deal in which the suspect in jail was to be the buyer of 3 kilos was set up. The suspect was charged as a conspirator in that attempt to purchase a controlled substance, as were the people who physically did the deal for the suspect in jail. A large amount of cash was seized.

The informant was not a material witness to the deal. He arranged the contact between the officer and the original suspect, but was not a party to the negotiations, the exchange of money and drugs, or the arrests. As a matter of fact, the suspect knew that the informant put the deal together, but the use of the informant did not violate the suspect's Fifth and/or Sixth Amendment rights as detailed earlier, nor did the informant participate to the extent that he was a material witness.

MANAGING THE INFORMANT

Procedural Control

Proper informant control begins with a comprehensive policy governing the use, documentation, and payment of informants. Such a policy should include the following elements:

1. Classification of informant types, including those precluded from use by their criminal history or other reasons;

2. Categorization of informant participation, which delineates what types of informants can be used in what capacity;

3. Format and requirements for complete informant identification as well as informant documentation;

4. Requirements for documentation of informant contacts, payments, and other considerations;

5. Provisions for informant integrity. The identity of informants should be available only on a need-to-know basis. The system for informant management must at once protect the integrity of the department and the identity of the informants.

Classification of informant types and categorization of informant participation levels was sufficiently discussed earlier in the chapter. These provisions, be they very restrictive or open ended, must be clearly written so that there is no misunderstanding what types of people are qualified for use as informants and what approval is necessary.

A comprehensive informant policy must ensure that each informant is properly identified and documented. Standard informant records should be developed for the purpose of permanent identification of the informant and for documenting informant activity. Figures 2-1 and 2-2 illustrate sample documentation records. Figure 2-1 is a permanent informant identification record. It provides for the recording of all information necessary to complete informant identification. This informant record serves much the same purpose as a application for employment. In addition to the standard identification information, this form should also include drivers license numbers, police department numbers, FBI numbers, social security numbers, etc. This documentation report should also include background data on the informant in short narrative form.

The identification and documentation should be complete and submit-

```
PERMANENT INFORMANT IDENTIFICATION FILE

CODE NUMBER:_____CONTROL OFFICERS:_____SER.#_____

CODE NAME:_____          _____SER.#_____

DATE ACTIVATED:_____DATE DEACTIVATED:_____

LAST NAME:_____FIRST NAME:_____MI_____

ALIASES: 1)_____2)_____

                      INFORMANT HISTORY

ADDRESS:_____BUSINESS ADDRESS:_____

SS#:_____-_____-_____,FBI#:_____PD#:_____

DRIVERS LICENSE NUMBER:_____DATE OF BIRTH___/___/___

PREVIOUS ARREST HISTORY:_____

CURRENT CASE INFORMATION:_____

ASSOCIATES:_____


PRIOR HISTORY AS AN INFORMANT:   YES [ ]   NO [ ]

PREVIOUS CONTROL OFFICER:_____SER.#_____

WAS INFORMANT DECLARED            YES [ ]   NO [ ]
    UNDESIRABLE

P                          R F
H                          I I
O                          G N
T                          H G
O                          T E
G                            R
R                          I P
A                          N R
P                          D I
H                          E N
                           X T

NOTES:————————————————————————————————————
```

FIGURE 2-1

ted to a supervisor before the informant is worked. Normally, a prospective informant will be debriefed, that is, investigated, to determine identification and background, and documented before approved for use.

If the informant has ever worked for any other law enforcement agency in the capacity of an informant, this should be noted as well as the results of the background check related to that employment. This is done for two obvious reasons: The first stems from the fact that, if the inform-ant has ever worked for another agency or another officer within the same agency, checking on his past work gives some idea what type of informant he was at that time. The other officer who worked him will be able to illuminate the officer currently working him, or contemplating working him, with respect to reliability, dependability, and criminal behavior.

Dependability and reliability are not the same thing. Being reliable pertains to the information provided and whether it is true and accurate. Being dependable has to do with calling when he says he will call, showing up on time, not showing up drunk, and all those types of things. Many extremely reliable informants are some of the most undependable people.

If another officer in the same agency has worked the informant, and if a good system for informant identification and documentation is in place, that fact should be apparent before a control number is issued. That being the case, it will be easy to look at past work.

The second reason for checking out an informant's past track record has to do with professional etiquette. If the informant states that he has worked for another agency or another officer in the past, he may still be working for them. The other officer in that case will have a vested interest in what the informant is doing, going to another agency for work. Maybe the informant is shopping for the best deal for his information, and in that case he may be supplying information which has already been given to the other officer. Whatever the case may be, much bad blood between officers and agencies is generated by what is perceived as informant stealing. Certainly this is true where narcotics officers are concerned. If an informant indicates that he has worked for somebody else in the past, that should be researched and documented.

In discussing this, a case comes to mind regarding an informant who contacted the narcotics unit wanting to work. He had information on a couple of small deals but they didn't look too bad. The officers doing the background check on the informant had the informant in the car when a reference the informant had given was checked out. The informant stated that he had worked for a large police department in the Midwest. One of the investigators involved immediately called the agency from his cellular telephone. He was able to reach the officer for whom the informant said he had worked in the past. That officer asked him, "Do you have him with you now, is he there in the car with you?" to which the detective responded in the affirmative. The officer in the Midwest then stated, "Do me a favor, lean over and shoot that son of a bitch in the head."

It was learned that the informant had in fact worked with the officer whom he listed as a reference. But the informant's version of his work record and the officer's differed in detail. In fact, it was learned that the informant had worked extensively with the officer in a long-term undercover investigation. The case had been set up so that grand jury indictments would be issued all at one time. The suspects would all be arrested at once in a roundup, and due to his level of participation, the informant would testify. The informant got nervous after the roundup and disappeared. An extensive effort had been made to locate him and get him to return for the pretrial proceedings.

The informant contacted the officer and stated that he was out of town and needed money for transportation back. The officer sent him the money, by way of Western Union, believing him to be across the country. The informant picked up the money, not across the country, but in the same city that the investigation had taken place. He had never left town, merely gone underground, and after taking the transportation money he did leave town and was never heard from again. The final straw, the reason the officer suggested that the informant be shot in the head (frustrated though he was, the officer made this suggestion in jest), the informant had worked the officer for about $3,000.00 in advance payments including the transportation money. The money had been given to the informant in good faith, but not in strict compliance with informant policy, and the officer ended up taking the $3,000.00 out of his own pocket rather than violate the department informant policy.

If the informant is working for case consideration, some notes pertaining to his case should be included in the documentation.

What is sometimes not included in this documentation package is the photograph. A photograph could be very important in what is the unforeseen future of the informant. Should the informant not have a criminal record or a driver's license, arrangements should be made with the department's identification bureau and a policy established that enables informant photos to be made easily. Not to require that a photograph is part of the informant documentation file is to assume that the informant is not going to do anything for which he may become a suspect, that he is always going to be on "our side." This is the wrong assumption to make. If any assumption is to be made, it is that the informant is going to go bad and will be a suspect in one crime or another in the future.

Every informant should be given a control number and a code name. The control number and the code name should be included on the permanent informant identification record. The control number system should apply to all informants in the department, not just those being worked by narcotics investigators. Ideally, the numbers should include an identifier which indicates the year that the informant is activated.

The date of activation is an important part of an informant documentation record. In addition, the record should provide for the date of deactivation and the reasons that the informant was deactivated.

The names and serial numbers of control officers should be a part of the permanent record. The record should be set up so that the serial number is a separate information field. In this manner, the files can be searched, assuming a computerized system is in place, by control officers' numbers as well as names.

Once the informant identification record is complete and the use of the informant has been approved, the permanent record should be personally hand delivered to the designated custodian of these records. At that time they should be entered in a secure computer system and the hard copy locked in a limited access safe. Whatever system is in place, it must protect the confidentiality of the informant. The integrity of the department is guaranteed in direct proportion to the quality of the informant policy in place, the enforcement of the policy, and the accuracy of the informant identification record.

Figure 2-2 is an example of an informant activity record. This record should provide documentation of all informant activity, whether payment was made or not, which resulted in enforcement action. If, for example, an informant is working for case consideration, this card should still be used in conjunction with the informant record, even though payment is not made. Some advocate the official documentation of every informant contact. It is preferable that this activity record be used only to record information that resulted directly in enforcement action and when the informant is paid. If the substance of the information was true but a case did not result, there should be an entry on the card for that as well. In fact, depending on how much work the informant did, he may be paid a small amount under such circumstances even though a case did not result.

Investigators should have further documentation of contacts with

---

INFORMANT ACTIVITY RECORD

CODE NUMBER:_____CONTROL OFFICERS:_____SER#_____

_____SER#_____

DATE OF DOCUMENTATION AND ACTIVATION:_____

DEACTIVATED:_____

CODE NAME:_____PAGE ___OF___PAGES

DATE	CASE NUMBER	ACTIVITY SUMMARY	AMT PAID	VOUCHER

FIGURE 2-2

informants in their case journals and notebooks. In fact it is a good idea to document as many of the informant contacts as possible in the investigator's journal. To expect that all will be documented is unrealistic, but brief notes on informant contacts can provide valuable details for future reference.

The official activity record should also be used to document informant tips which did not for one reason or another prove to be true. If all informant activity is accurately recorded, a true picture of the informant is available should it be necessary for documenting reliability or assessing the relative worth of the informant or whatever. Very seldom will a steady, previously reliable informant give information which is totally false. By the time action is taken, circumstances may have changed, and the evidence may not be recovered, but the information was right to varying degrees, when it was reported.

An informant who gives information which is totally false should be evaluated. The concept of reliability implies that the informant is truthful in every case and precludes any tolerance of lying on the part of the informant. Most informants will exaggerate, which is tolerable, but lying is unacceptable and destroys an informant's credibility to the point that he is of no value as a participating informant.

Lying is just one way that an informant can destroy his credibility and thus make him undesirable for future work as an informant. In general, the characteristics which may make a person an undesirable employee in a normal job might also seriously diminish his value as an informant. If a person is so totally undependable that he can't be counted on at all, he probably isn't much good. If the informant jeopardizes the safety of police officers working him, he is of no value.

If, for whatever reason, an informant has been determined to be undesirable, he should be placed on the undesirable list. All too often this undesirable informant list exists only informally, and only after a bad experience does an investigator learn that somebody has already been through the same thing. A good informant management system will provide for a separate file for undesirable informants which is cross-referenced in the other files.

A good informant management system comprises three files: the Permanent Informant Identification File, the Informant Activity Record File, and the Undesirable Informant File (see Figure 2-3).

If a prospective informant is being checked and is determined to be undesirable, the informant should be given a code number, the

```
                    COMPONENTS OF INFORMANT FILE SYSTEM

    ┌─────────────────────────────────────────────────┐
    │ PERMANENT INFORMANT IDENTIFICATION FILE           │
    │                                                   
        Query limited to need-to-know basis.

        Input is limited to informant applications.

        Comprehensive informant identification is provided.

        Periodic updates from informant activity record are made.

        Undesirable informants are flagged in this file.

        Outside access to the other two files must go through
        this file.

    ┌──────────────────────────┐
    │ INFORMANT ACTIVITY RECORD │
    └──────────────────────────┘
        Maintenance is at working level.

        Periodic updates forwarded to permanent ID file.

        Access is limited to control officers and supervisors
        and the command officers directly responsible for the
        administration of the system.  Command officers and
        supervisors not involved in the administration of the
        informant system would not have access.

        Undesirable informants are flagged, and information is
        forwarded to Permanent Informant ID file and Undesirable
        Informant File.
    ┌──────────────────────────┐
    │ UNDESIRABLE INFORMANT FILE│
    └──────────────────────────┘
        There is no direct access to this file.

        This file is cross-referenced from other two files.
```

FIGURE 2-3

informant identification documentation should be completed, and the information immediately forwarded to the Undesirable Informant File. Documenting one who is unfit for use as an informant is important no matter at what stage in the process that determination is made.

Practical Control of the Informant

The day-to-day use and management of informants requires emotional control as well as compliance with procedures and policies designed as external controls. The controlling officer must be in control of his own emotions in order to control the emotional climate under which the informant works. What is referred to as emotional control encompasses all of the feelings and personality influences involved in a successful officer/informant relationship. Managing informants, while not totally unlike managing or supervising any other type of worker, does require certain skills, some of which are very tangible and learnable and which contribute to emotional control and success. Some of the skills required are intangible and relate to factors such as the chemistry between two people and intuition and feel.

Successfully dealing with an informant requires, first, that the relationship between the officer and the informant be established and maintained at a strictly professional level. Almost all difficulties encountered with informants can be traced back to the failure to do this. Either the relationship never was on a professional level or what was at one time a sound relationship was allowed to deteriorate.

The first step in establishing a professional relationship has to do with the mind-set of the controlling officer. The officer should look at the informant in much the same way that he would look at any other contract laborer. A plumber, for example, being contracted to do work, is not evaluated on personality; he is evaluated on whether he can successfully complete the job at some terms acceptable to both parties involved. A plumber will probably not respond well if he is treated in a condescending manner as if he were somehow less important than the people hiring him. A perception that this attitude exists may adversely affect the way the job is done.

The officer must get past the fact that he is dealing with an informant in order to establish rapport while at the same time never forgetting he is dealing with an informant. The purpose of the contact with the informant is self-serving from both points of view. The informant is working for some reason and the law enforcement agency is contracting with the informant in order to get a job done. To accomplish this, the informant should be treated with the respect due any person. Terms such as snitch, or rat, or other such pejorative expressions that would degrade the informant should not be carelessly used. Informants don't seem to mind the term informant or confidential informant or CI.

Initial Interview

When a first-time informant is being debriefed, establish the professional nature of the relationship immediately. Doing so involves learning certain things about the informant and asking a number of questions. If the informant is interested in working off a case, he should be encouraged to describe his case and articulate what he hopes to accomplish by turning somebody else. If the informant wishes to work for pay or to satisfy some other motive, he should also be encouraged to talk about that as explicitly as possible. In doing so it is possible to determine what the expectations of the informant are and whether or not they are realistic. At this point, the informant should also give some background information about himself. Much of this to this point will be no different from most other employment interviews.

Once the employee has detailed his motives and expectations, he should be interrogated to ascertain what he knows. The informant should not be allowed to give general information or teasers of information and hold the rest of the information ransom, pending the fulfillment of the investigator's part of the bargain. This situation typically sounds something like this:

> I know this guy who sells pot, and if you help me with my case, I'll get him for you. I mean this is a big-time dealer and you guys can't catch him, but I know him. I'm not telling you his name until I find out what you're all about. How do I know I can trust you to keep your end of the bargain. I might do all this work for you and then you'll forget about helping me.

When this takes place it is time to set some of the ground rules. Normally it is not necessary to go over these rules this early in the initial contact, but in this case the informant has forced the issue. The informant should be firmly advised that he is not in charge. The determination as to whether any working relationship will be established has not been made yet. He should be told what details are necessary. It may be that he really does not know anything specific. Most of the time, however, the informant is feeling out the situation.

It is necessary to learn three things at this stage of the initial informant contact:

1. Expectations of the informant

2. Motives of the informant

3. Preliminary evaluation of what the informant knows

Once this has been accomplished, it will be possible to make some evaluations regarding a course of action. If the informant does not know anything worthwhile, the interview should be terminated and the informant given some idea of what type of information may be of further interest and instructed to call again if anything should develop. If it is apparent that the person doesn't know anything worthwhile or isn't in a position to participate actively, he should be told so politely and directly.

There are so many people who get the idea that they are going to be informants or superspies, or good citizens, or whatever and come in off the street wishing to make an impression. If the person is of this type and has no information of any relative value, wasted time and frustration should be minimized. Some people, particularly irate citizens who feel they have a legitimate complaint, may not take this dismissal well.

At this preliminary stage of the initial interview, it may well be determined that the informant has unreasonable expectations. For example, in the case of a person who came in and who wanted to be an informant, in the initial contact it became clear that he was probably in a position to provide some valuable information. He was talking about people with whom the investigators were familiar and were working on, and his information was very accurate. He was vague about his expectations, apparently withholding information until the investigators would make some type of commitment to him. He admitted that he needed a little help with a minor civil problem that he had and then, when pushed, went on to say that once that was provided, he was willing to work on the condition he was given a $500.00 retainer and a rental car. He was told that his proposal was ridiculous, was informed of our counteroffer, which was unacceptable to him, and that was the end of that. Regarding the people he would be able to do, he was told what the terms would be and told to call if that became appealing in the future.

The expectations of the informant must be reasonable in light of what is fair and realistic. The informant may want more help on a case than is justified or need more than the prosecutor will be willing to give him. An ongoing professional relationship with an informant requires honesty. If the informant wants more than he can rightfully expect, the investigator should be honest. A course that proceeds on false pretenses and promises that cannot be fulfilled is inadvisable. However, as much intelligence information as possible should be obtained before advising the potential informant that his expectations are unreasonable.

The motives of the informant also have to be evaluated at this early stage. The motives of the informant will be good indicators of potential. All three factors, expectations, motives, and knowledge or ability should be considered individually and collectively. The interview should either terminate or proceed based upon consideration of these factors.

If the decision is made to proceed, it is best to take a break in the interview before going on. At this point the officers interviewing the potential informant should privately discuss the progress of the interview and the potential of the informant. Some preliminary background investigation should be done at this point also such as checking the informant's record to see if it matches his version. What is discovered may preclude any use of the informant, and that will be the end of it. The pending case, if there is one, should be reviewed. It may be apparent that the quality of the case pending is so good that very little in the way of a trade is warranted. Some of the names he is giving should be checked if they are unfamiliar.

Informant Agreement

When the interview is reconvened, the officers conducting the interview should have a good idea of what they intend to do. If the decision has been made to document the informant and begin using him, the terms of the working relationship with the informant should be set at this stage of the initial interview. If the informant is working off a case, he should be told what types of deals will be required and how many. If the informant is to be paid, there should be some discussion about payment arrangements, although specific details regarding any informant payment schedule, if one exists, should not be discussed. The investigator should not get locked in to any details. He should make sure that the informant understands the professional nature of the relationship which is being established. If the relationship starts off on a professional level, it can be maintained at the level. If the relationship is initiated on an overly friendly or personal level, it is tough to get it back on a professional basis.

Establishing the professional nature of the relationship can be facilitated by a written agreement or informant contract. There are several advantages to putting the agreement in writing. The prosecutor should be involved in arranging the specific details and spelling them out in writing. If a case is being worked off, whether the agreement is in writing or verbal, certain issues should be addressed. For example, what exactly will constitute fulfillment on the informant's part. Will he get help on his case for effort alone or must he put some cases on the table? Should the informant's case be filed and the informant charged pending his performance or should the filing be delayed?

Generally, the informant should not be allowed consideration on his case for effort alone; however, there will be circumstances where that is justified. Also, generally speaking, the case should be filed, the informant charged with any pending case and then if he completes his part of the agreement, steps can be taken to get the case dropped or the charges reduced.

Day-to-Day Informant Contact

Surveillance

Adequate surveillance is an essential part of effective informant control. While in most cases two officers are sufficient to handle this, more than two will sometimes be required. What is essential is that enough surveillance is in place to document visually the activities of the informant while at the same time providing enough backup should trouble develop. One officer taking an informant to a controlled buy is not enough. There are types of cases in which this is done as common practice, usually because of the case load and the need for maximum efficiency in setting up ensuing enforcement action, search warrants primarily. If adequate surveillance, at least two officers, is not provided, the informant may read this as a tactical weakness and exploit it to his advantage later. On the other hand, adequate surveillance, professionally and systematically done, will serve to enhance the informant's perception of the professional nature of the working arrangement.

Electronic surveillance helps achieve informant control. It will be difficult for the informant to mislead the control officer if the conversations are monitored and/or taped. This type of surveillance can be excellent documentation. Likewise, when a case requires that an informant make several phone calls to set up a deal, these phone calls should be monitored and recorded for future reference. Listening to these conversations can be extremely helpful to the officer in assessing the potential of the case and the informant. It may become apparent through listening to these conversations that an informant has been misleading about his relationship with the target of the investigation, maybe the informant isn't trusted at all. Conversely, maybe the relationship is stronger than described by the informant, and the potential of the case is significantly better than indicated by initial evaluations.

Searching the Informant

The ideal situation would provide that an informant, regardless of length of service, would be searched before each and every contact with the controlling officer. If such is the case, the informant knows it and will expect it. If searches are done only on first-time informants or in special circumstances, the potential for trouble and misunderstanding exists. It is generally necessary in an affidavit detailing a controlled buy to explain that the informant was searched prior to the buy being made. This search is usually done but only in a cursory manner. The informant should be searched thoroughly, before every contact, certainly every controlled buy.

If the investigator makes a practice of doing this, the possibility that the informant may conceal a weapon, or take drugs with him, or take his own currency with him, is greatly reduced. A thorough search of the informant should be part of the professional relationship. Going through the indignity of being searched every time is something to which the informant will adjust as long as he understands that it is routine policy which must be followed. Not to search the informant is to put an undue amount of trust in him.

Searching the informant is a necessary step in ensuring that the case is done thoroughly and professionally and that the informant does not turn on the officers and set them up in some way. If there is one constant trait among criminal-type informants, it is that sooner or later they will go bad, sooner or later they will take advantage of their situation. The control officer has to guard himself against compromise by the informant, and searching the informant before controlled buys and other informant undercover operations is very important.

Informant Meetings

In the absence of a policy or strict personal discipline which makes searching a fundamental of informant handling, officers become lax in dealing with informants and lose sight of the fact that the informant is, after all, an informant, not a police officer. In the same vein, control of the situation in which the informant is met; the informant should not be allowed to dictate where meetings are going to take place simply because that's his preference. His input is important, but he should not be allowed to take control. If meetings are held at a police facility, the informant should be kept out of restricted areas. The informant should not be allowed to leave the interview room or the undercover phone room and walk freely throughout the office. This is a bad habit and other officers find it offensive. It is potentially dangerous as well. Of course, if offices are set up in an off-sight location, the informant should not be told where that location is or taken there under any conditions.

When an informant is part of an undercover operation about which a briefing is held, the informant has no part in the briefing. It is not a good idea for an informant to see all the undercover officers in the unit and learn more about tactics and technology than he has a right to know. A photograph of the informant should be shown to the officers at the briefing, and they should be provided with a good description so that they will know who the informant is. The informant should not be included in the briefing.

Payments

The informant should be paid consistent with the arrangements that have been made and the existing payment schedule. Most investigators will give in to informant pleas for an advance or a little extra once in a while. It is not a good idea to give the informant more than was arranged or to pay him between deals to keep him going. It is done, and it does generate loyalty and goodwill, but it also spoils the informant if it is done regularly. Payments of such a kind encourage the informant's misconception that he will be paid regardless of what he puts together if he has a good enough sob story.

Payments to informants should be witnessed whenever possible. Figure 2-4 is a sample of an expense voucher used to document informant payments. It provides for code number, signature of informant in code name acknowledging receipt of payment, and signatures of paying and witnessing officers. Ideally, these vouchers should be part of a computerized system. This being the case, a record of payments to each informant, by code number, can be easily accessed and provides for additional informant documentation. The more checks and balances in place, the less likely that an officer will be falsely accused of impropriety in paying informants.

Being Available for Contact

One of the most difficult adjustments that a narcotics investigator has to make pertains to being on call for informants. Regardless of how much control over an informant that an officer exercises, the fact remains that the informant will call when he thinks the circumstances and timing are right. The whole concept of working informants centers on the hope that the informant will call with information that is valuable and timely.

Before the widespread availability of pager systems, it was sometimes difficult for the informant to contact the control officer. Now the pager system has made it possible for an informant readily to contact the officer when it is important. One of the intangibles in informant handling involves the ability of the control officer to distinguish between information that is hot and must be acted upon immediately and information that the informant says is hot and embellishes for selfish motives.

Invariably, informants who haven't called for weeks will start calling before a long holiday weekend because they need to make some money. When they call under these circumstances, the need to make money will cause them to overstate the size and importance of a deal and the urgency as well. The same thing happens often on Friday nights. The informant will want to make some quick money for the weekend and call with a "can't wait" deal.

The circumstances should be evaluated as objectively as possible in deciding if in fact the deal can't wait. A big part of the job involves being called out at times inconvenient to the investigators. When a good deal presents itself, action must be taken. The old adage, "If he's dealing today, he'll be dealing tomorrow" isn't necessarily true. It is usually voiced when the officers aren't in the mood to work late again. There are times when immediate action is essential. Dedicated narcotics investigators adjust to long and uncertain hours, and while nobody minds staying late for a good deal, resentment will develop if people are required to stay late regularly at the whim of a suddenly hungry informant. Informants cannot be allowed to dictate their own hours; generally when they try and force something to happen it won't work out.

```
                    NARCOTICS INVESTIGATION UNIT
                       EXPENDITURE RECORD
                                      DATE:_____

                                      VOUCHER #_____

                                      CHECK #_____

    ITEMIZATION                AMOUNT RECEIVED  $_____

    EVIDENCE      $_____  RENT/UTILITIES   $_____

    INFORMANT     $_____  OFFICE FURNITURE $_____
                               EQUIPMENT

    ELECTRONIC    $_____  TRAVEL           $_____
    EQUIPMENT

    VEHICLE       $_____  VEHICLE REPAIR   $_____
    LEASING                    AND MAINTENANCE

    COMMUNICATIONS $_____  MISCELLANEOUS    $_____

                               TOTAL EXPENSES   $_____

    RETURN RECEIPT NUMBER_____AMT. RETURNED $_____
                            EVIDENCE
    1) DATE:_____ AMOUNT PURCHASED_____ AMOUNT PAID_____
       PROPERTY NUMBER_____LOCATION/SUSPECT_____
       FILE NUMBER _____COVERING OFFICERS_____

    2) DATE:_____ AMOUNT PURCHASED_____ AMOUNT PAID_____
       PROPERTY NUMBER_____LOCATION/SUSPECT_____
       FILE NUMBER_____COVERING OFFICERS_____
                        OTHER EXPENSES

       _____
       _____
       _____
       _____
       _____
       _____


                  INFORMANT PAYMENT RECEIPT

    CODE #_____, DID RECEIVE$_____,ON___/___/___

    FOR INFORMATION OR SERVICES, (_____)

    RE:  FILE NUMBER_____.

    SIGNATURE OF CI (CODE NAME)_____

    PAYING OFFICER_____#_____DATE_____

    WITNESS_____#_____DATE_____

    SUBMITTING OFFICER_____#_____DATE_____

    SUPERVISOR_____#_____DATE_____

    COMMANDING OFFICER_____#_____DATE_____

                     FIGURE 2-4
```

SPECIAL CONSIDERATIONS—SMALL JURISDICTIONS

In a small-town atmosphere, informants may quickly lose effectiveness. Word about a suspected informant will travel fast and does not have to travel very far before the informant is no longer useful. Regardless of how carefully informants are worked, word gets out.

Because of this, it is a good idea for small towns to pool informant resources. Doing so enables informants to move around a regional area. Doing so also requires communication and coordination in managing the informant. Informants will be subject to different control officers as they operate around the region. Records of informant activity being kept at the local level must also become part of the regional informant management system if control of the informant and necessary documentation of his activities are to exist.

The fact remains, an informant operating at a participating level in a small town is not going to remain confidential very long. Informants used on a nonparticipating basis who are providing intelligence but not participating will obviously remain useful longer.

INFORMANT CASE STUDIES

The following case studies and the analysis of each are provided for the purpose of illustrating some of the concepts discussed in this chapter. They are based on actual cases, which while not particularly unique, do offer some interesting problems characteristic to the use of informants in narcotics cases.

CASE NUMBER ONE

Facts

This case, which happened in 1985, involved a narcotics detective who at the time was a four- or five-year veteran. He was by reputation and in fact an excellent police officer and a hard-working narcotics detective. He was 1 of 12 narcotic officers working a street assignment with pretty much free reign in deciding what types of cases were worked. All the officers were also working under serious resource limitations: very limited funds for buys and informant payments, poor undercover vehicles which they did not take home, and only a city telephone paging system which was awkward and uncomfortable for informants to use.

This officer had developed an interest over the years in what was an organized group of speed (methamphetamine) dealers. The group had one certain leader who was well known. The leader of the group had demonstrated an unusual propensity for violence and had reportedly killed several people and then disposed of their bodies in a mine shaft in the mountains. While there was some evidence that these rumors were true, the identities of the victims were unknown, and nobody would come forth with specific information about when the homicides took place and who the victims were.

This group had become a project and a potential informant developed whose mother had long been associated with biker gangs and this particular speeder organization. The informant, a female, knew a great deal about the organization. The detective was able to develop the informant, and the informant made some introductions of an undercover officer to some of the fringe people in the organization, including two of her sisters from whom undercover buys were made. Rapport between the informant and the detective was established in spite of the limited financial resources available. The informant's continued work was related to the rapport between her and the detective as much as anything else. She had been convinced that she was doing the right thing.

As the detective worked more with the informant, it was learned that she had specific information about some of the homicides which had taken place. In fact, she had been present for at least one of them and had been forced to participate as a means of assuring that her conscience didn't at some time in the future prevail upon her to report the incident to the police. According to her, all three people present when the murder took place were forced to put a bullet in the body before it was dumped into the mine shaft.

The detective spent a great deal of time determining the location of the mine shaft and attempting to identify the victims. After many trips to the mountains, the location was tentatively established. The plan was to have the mine shafts excavated. This represented some serious logistical problems as well as a great deal of expense, and the fine points had not been worked out fully when the informant went bad.

The informant who lived the life of a typical speeder had a husband who was also a part-time informant, and they both had a mutual male friend, who through the course of eight months that the informant had been working with the detective, knew about the informant's actions and did some work with the detective himself. One Saturday night, or afternoon, it was determined that there wasn't room for the three of them anymore and the informant and her friend decided to kill the husband. To do so, they arranged for him to take an overdose of insulin, operating on the theory that the cause of death would be difficult to establish and even if it was established, it could not be proven that they had any involvement in his death.

The plan began to go bad when the informant's husband didn't die, in fact he did feel badly and began to suspect what had happened not long after taking his insulin shot. The informant and her boyfriend then decided to finish the job they started in brutal fashion. They slashed the husband's wrists and slit his throat as well. What had been designed as a clean, quiet murder deteriorated into a bloody, brutal mess. The husband finally died. All three had been drinking and drugging before the mayhem took place.

The informant and her boyfriend put the body in the trunk of a car with the intention of taking it to the mine shaft familiar to the informant from the previous homicides she had witnessed. On the way to the mountain site of the mine shaft, the informant's car broke down. Rather than take the body back home, they dumped it along the side of a road and made some effort to conceal it.

Later in the evening the two bragged about what they had accomplished, and somebody called the district attorney's office. While there was no body yet, it was determined through initial response that a homicide might have taken place and the informant and her boyfriend were taken to police headquarters for questioning. At that point, the informant stated that she had nothing to say except that she wanted to get in touch with a particular narcotics detective. The detective was called by the homicide detectives and responded from home. After being briefed by the homicide detectives, he did some preliminary questioning of the informant.

The detective advised the informant pursuant to Miranda and made it clear that this was unlike other communications between them in the past. Subsequent to advisement, the informant proceeded to tell the narcotics detective the whole story. A full confession was obtained, and the informant and her boyfriend were subsequently charged and pleaded guilty to homicide.

The initial investigation into the speed dealing organization was forced to take a different direction. It was learned that the mine shafts had been determined to be unsafe and, through explosives, had been permanently sealed by the state department of mines. Without the informant as a witness to the homicides, there was little, if any, chance of successfully prosecuting the suspects. The main suspect and numerous other principles became the subject of a joint state/federal investigation and were subsequently imprisoned on drug-related charges.

Analysis

There were several things which happened in this case which prevented the situation from being worse than it was. First, the detective took great pains to manage the informant properly in what was a strictly professional manner. Had there been any impropriety, it certainly would have surfaced after the informant was arrested for homicide. As it turned out, the detective had documented his activities with the informant and had any impropriety been falsely alleged, the detective was in a good position to defend his actions as they were properly documented. The informant had been paid cash for work done, and all the paperwork pertaining to those payments was a matter of record.

Second, the rapport established between the informant and the detective was ultimately responsible for the obtaining of a full confession and immediate recovery of the body. The informant had developed some respect for the detective as a police officer and a person. Consequently, when she wanted to confess, he was the person whom she wanted to hear the confession.

Ultimately, the informant pleaded guilty, but in the early stages of the investigation, when she was contemplating a defense, the possibility had been discussed between her and her attorney of using informant-related stress as a mitigating factor. In other words, she contemplated a temporary insanity plea based in part on the pressure involved in helping the police catch a brutal murderer. The dangerous nature of the people about whom she was informing lent credence to her story. Although she was working as an informant of her own volition, she was put in a position of tremendous stress, and the police were at least partially responsible for her predicament. As it turned out, she pleaded guilty and how far the defense would have taken her is unknown.

The most important lesson to be learned from this example involves the transitory nature of informant/officer relationships. What had been an informant with great potential at noon on a Saturday was a homicide suspect by Sunday morning. To lose sight of how quickly informants can turn can be personally and professionally devastating to the control officer in the end. Imagine if this detective had a romantic or sexual relationship with this informant, the facts of which came out after she was arrested for homicide. She could have claimed that the officer had ruined the relationship between her and her husband, put her on a guilt trip which led to an argument, when to relieve her guilt she told her husband about it, and so forth, and so on. It has happened.

CASE NUMBER TWO

Facts

This second case study involves an informant/officer situation which took place in the early part of 1987. The informant had been arrested on a simple *possession case and not a solid case by any means. There were problems with the search and other minor problems also. The officer who was assigned the case was an experienced police officer with about 10 years of service including 2 or 3 years working narcotics. Recognizing the weakness of the case, the officer contacted the suspect and suggested that maybe he could work off the case. The record of the suspect consisted of only minor offenses. He had arrests for possession but no convictions.*

When the officer suggested that the suspect work the case off, the suspect was receptive to the idea. It was arranged that the suspect would do three deals in exchange for consideration on his case. A deputy district attorney was contacted and had agreed not to file the case, and inasmuch as the search was bad to begin with, they really were not trading much.

The informant knew of some Caribbean nationals who were part of an emerging drug dealing organization. He was particularly interested in working on them as they had created a great deal of animosity among locals due to their violence and threatened violence. The detective had used the informant to make two or three controlled buys, which then formed the probable cause basis for successful search warrants. The informant had almost fulfilled his agreement and desired to continue working for pay. He was fairly intelligent, and his descriptions of people and things were accurate.

The informant knew of two people who were dealing from an apartment building in east Denver. There were other narcotics detectives with information on these people, and it was planned that the informant would introduce an undercover officer to these people. The detective who was the controlling officer dropped the informant off at his car one day and gave him $10.00 when it was discovered that he had a flat tire. There was never any further contact with the informant.

About five days later, the controlling detective was contacted by members of the homicide unit wanting information on the informant. The informant had been shot in the head and killed at the drug house of the two Caribbean dealers he was about to turn. I mention the fact that the dealers were Caribbean dealers because it is important to the story. At that time, these Caribbean drug dealers had all but taken over street-level cocaine trafficking in east Denver. In so doing, they had alienated themselves from the local dealers and users, in particular those who were black. They operated on a face-to-face basis and relied on threats and intimidation. Weapons were brandished during these street-level deals, and the Caribbeans openly regarded the locals, black and white, with disdain. Naturally, the locals resented this treatment, but they continued to patronize the Caribbean dealers because of the quality of the product they sold. In other words, the good cocaine made it worth some risk and humiliation.

The informant had gone to the apartment of the two dealers and had purchased some cocaine, some time, not long after the controlling officer last saw him. He was dissatisfied with the product and went back the next day to get more and have them make it right. The informant, underestimating the violent potential of these particular dealers, took a starter pistol with him. When it became apparent that he was not going to be compensated for the bad product of the prior day, the informant pulled the starter pistol and began demanding his money back or some good coke. One of the Caribbeans pulled a .45-caliber semiautomatic pistol and shot the informant in the head. The dealers then picked up a few of their belongings and walked out of the building.

The informant had taken a girlfriend with him that day. She heard the shots and got scared. After waiting a short time, and seeing the two dealers leave, she got behind the wheel of the car and left. Several days later, the body of the informant was discovered by the landlord or apartment manager who called the police.

Analysis

Again, this case serves as an example, not of what the officer did wrong, but what could have happened. The officer was conscientious in dealing with the informant and searched the informant prior to taking him to make the controlled buys. He searched him subsequent to the buys as well. It is entirely possible that this scenario could have happened while the informant was making a controlled buy rather than when making a buy on his own. The control officer was not aware that the informant was carrying a starter pistol for protection. The informant had been searched prior to each controlled buy, and the informant had nothing on him on those occasions. The knowledge that he was going to be searched may have prevented this from occurring during a controlled buy situation. As it was, the control officer had established the procedure of searching the informant prior to all contacts with him.

It is entirely possible, given the violent nature of the dealers involved in this case, and the antagonism that had developed between them and the locals, that this informant, or any other informant, would encounter violence during a controlled buy. Aside from the fact that the informant was carrying a starter pistol, this case is an excellent example of the need for adequate cover in controlled buy situations. Had, in fact, this homicide taken place during a controlled buy, one covering officer would not have been nearly adequate.

Controlled buys are made so often and so routinely without incident that the investigators become complacent.

When this informant was first contacted, he mentioned several people who were street-level dealers from whom he could buy cocaine. He was willing to do so in order to work off his case. The police department, through the control officer, and with the consent of the prosecutor, made an informal, unwritten agreement to this effect. If the informant developed enough information, initially through controlled buys, which more readily established some basis of reliability, for three search warrants, the case against the informant would not be filed. The control officer gave the informant specific direction regarding what type of information would be necessary and what type of informant participation would be required.

The informant was murdered while working as an informant. Had he been given a traffic ticket or been stopped for some minor violation, he might have asked the detective who was the control officer to intercede on his behalf. Informants who are small-time crooks and street-level people frequently put the officer working them in a bad spot because of what they do when not under the officer's direction. In this case, the informant, when not under the ongoing control of the officer, reverted to his normal life-style. The fact that he was working as an informant did not stop him from doing what he did naturally: buy dope and use dope and take other people to buy dope. In dealing with inform-ants who are criminal types, it should not be assumed that they have changed their ways. It must be made clear to them that if they break the law, buy dope, whatever, they are on their own; that behavior is not condoned by virtue of the fact that they are working as an informant.

There is some built-in hypocrisy in the previous concept. The relative value of an informant pertains directly to his knowledge of some criminal element and his ability to deal with them. To tell an informant that he is not allowed to break the law, that it will be neither condoned nor tolerated is one thing. This must be done. But, if in fact the informant "turned over a new leaf" and left all his past associates behind him, severed all ties with the drug dealers he is expected to turn, how will he be able to participate effectively as an informant? He won't.

The fact that this informant was killed in a dope house by two dealers who were the subject of an investigation in which the informant had participated does not reflect negatively on the department or the control officer. The informant was not under the direction of the officer when he was killed. He was committing a felony, buying drugs. While an argument could be made that he was trying to enhance his value as an informant by getting closer to the dealers, the key factor is that he was acting on his own. The informant was a drug user, a small-time middleman who made money by going to the dealer for people who couldn't go there themselves. Technically, then, he was involved in the dealing. He got killed doing what he did best. Chances are that if he had not had anything to do with the dealers, until directed to do so by the detective in control, he would not have been killed. Again, informants are informants; they require strict control and direction, and when left to their own devices they will revert to their own ways and may get themselves killed or kill somebody else. They are not sworn officers, and to trust that they will not put you in a position of compromise is to be naive.

CASE NUMBER THREE

Facts

   This case involves an informant who worked for three and a half or four years. He worked consistently at the street level and would occasionally put something together at a level slightly higher. He began as an informant for a patrol officer who turned him over to the narcotics unit because he had more work than the patrol officer could handle. The patrol officer had been a narcotics unit supervisor with another police department for several years prior to joining our department. He knew how to read informants and realized that this informant had some potential.

   A sergeant of a street-level crack unit became the primary control officer of this informant. This unlikely situation evolved because a natural rapport existed between him and the informant, and the work load of the unit was such that sergeants actually did some cases in addition to supervising and assisting with the other cases being worked. The informant had at one time been a law enforcement intern through a community college program. He had worked in a jail with sworn officers. He was a very intelligent person, who were it not for serious educational shortcomings, probably would have been able to do about anything he wanted to do. As it was, he was a street person who worked at odd jobs and bought cocaine from street-level dealers. He had only a minor criminal record, one or two arrests for traffic violations and failure-to-appear warrants.

   This informant was particularly good when sent in a particular direction to cold hit (make a buy from a dealer whom he did not know and from whom he had never bought in the past). If no informant was in a place about which we had received information, this informant was useful if the dealers were at a level compatible with his experience and general characteristics. The informant would occasionally develop information on his own and that was usually good, but he fell into a pattern of responding to our needs and going where we sent him. He *would call, sometimes every night, and ask what we had going. He would usually accompany that question with a statement of financial need. This informant was not looking for big money, just small amounts on a regular basis. He and his family were on food stamps and welfare, and anything he got supplemented that income and what he could make doing odd jobs. The informant liked to drink and would occasionally call when he was intoxicated and be demanding and belligerent.*

The sergeant who was the primary control officer made the informant available to other officers in need of an informant to work on a specific case. This usually produced satisfactory results, although as the informant gained tenure, so to speak, he also became more brazen and assertive. He began demanding payment, using the fact that he worked for the sergeant as a bargaining point. If he wasn't paid to his satisfaction, he would call the sergeant and complain. Likewise, when the investigators using him had a complaint, they would tell the sergeant rather than risk a confrontation with the informant.

The informant worked effectively at the street level, but like all informants he began to think he was in charge — without him, the narcotics investigators were nothing.

After about three years of work, the informant developed information about some people who were using a pager system and supplying a tremendous amount of cocaine to street-level people who would then convert it to crack for sale in their crack house. The sergeant and the informant worked the case over the course of several months. Several arguments took place, brought on by the informant's various stages of intoxication and his insistence on doing the case his way rather than letting the sergeant provide the direction. In the end, the case was put together in the manner that the sergeant wanted. A kilo of cocaine, several guns, two cars, and $46,000 in cash were seized. The informant did not participate to the extent that disclosure of his identity was ordered, although the defendants were able to figure it out. After several hours of suppression hearings and a lengthy trial, the two principal defendants were convicted.

At about the same time this case was concluded, the sergeant who was the control officer changed assignments and became involved in more enhanced investigations, doing very few street-level deals. As a consequence, the value of the informant diminished. Efforts were made by other investigators to work the informant on the street-level deals, but each ended unsatisfactorily. None could put up with the informant's demanding ways, his drunken tirades, or his threats to call the sergeant. Likewise, the informant did not feel any rapport with the other officers. The informant was eventually put on the undesir-

able informant list after several heated verbal exchanges between the informant and the narcs he had worked with, including the sergeant. Finally, the informant made several complaints of impropriety regarding the conduct of the officers who had worked him. The complaints ranged from racism to threats to laziness, incompetence, and so forth. None of the complaints was found to have any substance.

Analysis

This is a classic case of letting an informant relationship develop into something other than a professional one. There was a natural rapport between the sergeant and the informant. There was a mutual like and trust. The sergeant allowed this to affect the manner in which the informant was treated, particularly with respect to payment. Feeling compassion for the informant's personal situation, the sergeant often paid the informant in advance when he needed the money. Also, when the informant was badly in need of money, the sergeant would try to put something together so he could make some money. The informant was in essence dictating when he worked. Other investigators working with and for the sergeant began to sense the special treatment and often joked about it. Unfortunately, rather than joking, they should have been saying, "Hey, this guy is getting special treatment because he works for you and you like him and he really isn't deserving of it." Not until the situation completely deteriorated was this brought out in the open.

It is at the same time a classic case of informant burnout. The informant was effective at a level natural to him for some time. He developed some very good cases over the years, and eventually did one outstanding case. It might have been apparent to an outsider that the informant had peaked at that time, that both he and the sergeant had about worked the relationship as far as it could be worked. Like any other job, there reaches a point when the employee and the employer are no longer able to communicate, they no longer have the same goals, and consequently the relationship has to be severed.

Informants are not going to be effective indefinitely. It is important that someone is taking an objective look at what informant are doing and can recognize signs of trouble or burnout or unreliability before it develops into a crisis. In looking at the performance of this informant over the last 12 months, there was a noticeable drop in effectiveness with the exception of the one outstanding case. The sergeant was too closely involved in handling the informant to see what was happening, and nobody else familiar with the day-to-day operations would bring it up, except informally.

CASE NUMBER FOUR

Facts

This case involves an experienced streetwise informant and a streetwise cop who was inexperienced as a narc. The informant had worked for various investigators over a several-year period with varying degrees of success. He was known to be capable of putting a real good deal together and while not having ever been completely untruthful, his veracity had been subject to question.

The informant had worked around this particular detective before, although he had never worked directly with him. He came to the unit with information, and when the officer who normally worked with him was unable to do this deal, it was suggested that the other detective do it. The informant related that he knew where 2 kilos of cocaine could be found. He told the officer that he knew the people well and that he had to do some checking and he would get back to him when he had more information. The informant later contacted the officer and told him that he was close to finding out if the deal was right, but was experiencing one minor problem. There was someone, the informant related, who was following him and bothering him and keeping him from doing what he had to do. The informant didn't go into explicit detail, but stated that if it was arranged so that the informant was apparently arrested in front of the other party, the informant would be left alone to get the deal together.

It was arranged that the informant would be at a certain location at a certain time and that he would be stopped as he left the predetermined building. The informant did leave the building at the exact time which had been agreed upon and the investigator stopped him. The informant, adding realism, ran from the officer and when finally caught had to be physically subdued by him. The informant then told the officer that the other person had been watching him and that it had worked out perfectly. The other person, thinking he had been arrested, would now leave him alone.

The informant then left the officer with a promise to call him back in a couple of hours. The informant had already done a lot of preliminary work on the case and had given the detective the suspects' names, address, etc., and the officer was a long way toward putting enough probable cause together to get a search warrant. Much of what the informant had told the officer was corroborated by the records of the suspects and the detective's independent investigation. Both the suspects had records for drug dealing, and other intelligence information regarding them was also discovered. That intelligence information supported the informant's claims that these people were drug dealers.

The informant did call back later in the evening. At that time the informant stated that he had been to the place and had seen cocaine there, described the people inside, and so forth. The detective put the finishing touches on his affidavit for a search warrant and got the warrant signed. When the informant called back, he stated that there was cocaine there, but did not come right out and say that he saw the 2 kilos that he had earlier promised would be there. The detective pushed him, and he assured the detective that it was right and that he should take immediate action. He went on to say that these guys were good crooks, and if we waited too long, the cocaine would be gone. They would either move it or sell it.

The warrant was executed at about 11:00 P.M. The people that the informant described were there, everything was exactly as the informant had described it with the exception of the fact that 2 kilos were not recovered. Trace amounts of cocaine were found, as was paraphernalia and the packaging from at least 1 kilo. The principal suspect was there and he was isolated from the rest of the people in the house and interrogated by the affiant detective. This took place after a thorough search of the house had been done, wall panels removed, ceiling panels checked, etc.

The principal suspect, after being advised, denied any knowledge of drugs in the house. He was contacted the next day regarding some damage done to the house during the immediate entry and was calmed down considerably. He admitted to the detective that he had been a drug dealer. He further admitted to the detective that the trace amount which had been recovered was all that was in the house. He went on to say that he had attempted to buy 2 kilos of cocaine on the day that the warrant was executed. He had gone with the person who was acting as the middleman in the deal to a location where the deal was to have taken place. He had given the money to the middleman to buy the cocaine, the middleman went inside the place and when he came out he was arrested by some police officers who had chased him down the street. Following the arrest of this party, the buyer left the area. The buyer would not tell the detective who the middleman was, what his name was, but did say that he had done business with him before. The buyer went on to tell the detective that after this deal, he was probably going to get out of the business. That he had been lucky, that he had never been arrested, and that he would have been arrested if the police would have waited just a short time before jumping the middleman that day. As it was, all he was out was a great deal of cash.

Analysis

What apparently happened in this case is that the informant set up a scenario in which he and perhaps a collaborator would rip off the potential 2-kilo buyer *for his money. To facilitate this rip-off, the informant was brazen enough to use the narcotics detectives as interference to set a screen for him.*

The original plan of the informant may have been to set up the deal by acting as the middleman and then have the buyers arrested for possession when he was sure that they had it safely in their house. In this way he would collect his fee for arranging the deal, probably taking the form of a small amount of cocaine from the buyer and a fair amount of cash from the seller. In addition, he would be paid a handsome amount of cash by the police department for setting up the seizure of 2 kilos. Recognizing a chance to increase his profit, the informant switched the plan, probably including the potential seller or some third party inside what was represented as the place of the dealer, but not necessarily.

There are several valuable lessons which can be learned from this example. The first involves informant control. It is difficult to maintain control of an informant, any informant, but particularly a crafty, streetwise informant such as the one in this case who was by nature a crook not worthy of trust. The officer who normally controlled the informant was quite experienced in handling informants in general and had dealt with this particular informant extensively. It is entirely possible that the change in the informant's plans took place when he realized that he was not going to do this deal with the officer with whom he usually worked. The inexperienced detective was caught totally unsuspecting; however, he was not capable of the same level of informant control as the officer who regularly handled this informant. This would have been true even had he been experienced. To expect that informants can be worked and controlled with equal effectiveness by different officers is unrealistic. All informants require specific control and that control cannot be transferred automatically from one officer to the next.

The scam that the informant put together, while bold, is not necessarily innovative. Regardless of what type of crime is involved, there is always the potential for the informant to set up someone who is participating at the same level as the informant in the crime. It follows then that it is also possible that the informant will set up an underling or a total innocent to take the fall for him. In this case, if the buy of 2 kilos had gone as planned, and the informant and the buyer would have been arrested immediately thereafter in possession of the cocaine, they would have been equal participants and treated as such by the investigators. If joint possession could be shown, both would be charged.

The point being made is that the informant, even if this deal had gone right, was participating in a crime to a much greater extent than the controlling detective realized. If 2 kilos had been recovered in the search, it would have been because the informant arranged for the buyer to get the 2 kilos, he took the money and bought them, he was paid to middle the deal, and then he turned the buyer. He, in fact, set him up to be arrested in possession of 2 kilos. The informant set this thing up anyway you look at it, and it is this type of informant participation against which any court can be expected to guard carefully.

This situation is similar to an informant calling and saying that he knows about some people who are going to pull a robbery, where it is going to happen, and when. The informant arranges for the police to intervene and arrest the perpetrators. What the police later find out is that the reason the informant was aware of this happening was because he set it up. He picked the target, he recruited the two other suspects to help, he got the weapons, and then he cut himself out by putting the others up front and setting them up to be arrested while he is allowed to get away.

When the informant suggested that he needed help shaking somebody who was bothering him and sticking with him, he was vague about the reasons this was happening, and although the investigator pushed for an explanation, he probably didn't push him hard enough. He wasn't completely familiar with the informant, and while his instincts told him something was wrong, they didn't tell him how completely things were wrong. He was suspicious enough to search the informant after he had to chase him down and handcuff him. When the informant was found to be clean and the informant stuck to his story that this guy was just pestering him, that it was no big deal, the officer's instincts were somewhat assuaged and he backed off. The informant reassured him that now everything was alright—with "this guy" out of the way he would be free to go about his business and check the thing out, and he would notify the officer when it was right. The officer was going to get 2 kilos, and it was going to be a good case. The past seizures for which the informant was responsible and the experience of the investigator, coupled with the desire to do well, to get a significant drug seizure, overwhelmed and dulled the otherwise sharp instincts of an outstanding street cop.

Informants such as this will eventually cost an officer his career if they are not put on the undesirable list. Even though they may be honest 75 percent of the time, even though they have a knack for putting some large deals together, they should not be used. They will eventually compromise the integrity of the controlling investigators. Moreover, they damage the cause of all narcotics investigators, as happened in this case, who are trying to get the job done right, working within the system.

This informant is certainly not above setting an officer up to be indicted or maybe even killed. Treat informants like informants, don't trust them beyond what can be verified, and don't allow them to control a case. While you cannot regulate their participation in criminal activity on their own, you can and must control their participation in your cases.

There is arguably no other aspect of narcotics investigation potentially more disastrous than working with informants.

3

SEARCH WARRANTS

INTRODUCTION

N arcotics cases progress, quite naturally, from the receipt of intelligence information (most often from a confidential informant), to investigation and more information of a corroborating nature, to case culmination and the seizure of drugs and assets. The trend in narcotics investigations during the last 25 years has been toward concluding narcotics investigations with a buy/bust scenario in which the suspect is arrested in immediate possession of the drugs. Doing cases in this manner will many times preclude the necessity of serving search warrants; certainly the search warrant in these cases is not relied upon as the primary investigative technique.

In a buy/bust situation, where the suspect brings the evidence to the undercover officer, the case is often made without any need for a search warrant. Obviously, the search warrant will be used in a supporting role, to obtain supplemental evidence, additional drugs, stashes of money and weapons, financial records, and so on.

Partially responsible for the development and the emergence of undercover investigation techniques are the difficulty and amount of work involved in obtaining search warrants. Drug enforcement prior to the exclusionary rule was a simple two-step progression. Information was received, and the officers responded and seized the drugs and subsequently filed the case. *Mapp v. Ohio*[1] sought to provide a remedy for police searches outside the scope of the Fourth Amendment. Evidence obtained in such cases is inadmissible. *Mapp*, and subsequent decisions which have amplified it and clarified it, put a great deal of extra responsibility on the narcotics investigator. The exclusionary rule demands that precision and detail are put into narcotics investigations. Instead of going from information to seizure, the progression must be information $\rightarrow$ investigation to establish probable cause $\rightarrow$ search warrant $\rightarrow$ seizure. The quality of investigation done to establish probable cause for a search warrant and the correctness of warrant ultimately define the quality of a search warrant case more than seizures, quality of the violators, or any other factors.

The freedom from unreasonable searches and seizures is fundamental to our system of government and rightly so. Understanding that the Fourth Amendment will be carefully guarded, defense attorneys may use this fact to change the focus of a proceeding from guilt or innocence and the facts of a case to the issue of illegal search.[2] Of course, in narcotics cases, suppression hearings are commonplace and in such hearings the entire focus will be the legality of the search which produced the evidence. If the search was bad—if probable cause was lacking or if a warrant was not in existence and the case does not fall into one of the categories excepted from the warrant requirement— the exclusionary rule will be applied and the evidence suppressed.

The search warrant is one of the most important investigative techniques which a narcotics investigator must master. In spite of the undercover tactics which have supplanted the need for search warrants in many cases, the search warrant remains a basic tool. It is essential that the investigator understand and value the priorities of the system and learn to operate effectively within it. Large seizures are meaningless if the case does not result in conviction and sentencing. The Fourth Amendment puts serious demands on the skill, training, and professionalism of the narcotics investigator.

This chapter discusses the legal, technical, and logistical aspects of using the search warrant as an effective investigative tool.

---

1 *Mapp v. Ohio*, 367 U.S. 643 (1961).

2 John M. Burkhoff, Search Warrant Law Deskbook (New York, Clark Boardman Company, Ltd., 1990), Section 2.1, p. 2-2.

LEGAL ASPECTS

Exceptions to Warrant Requirement

It is an unassailable premise that obtaining a search warrant is in every case preferable to acting without one. Courts have made it clear repeatedly that the Fourth Amendment will be strictly interpreted.[3]

> We do not believe that strict enforcement of the fourth amendment will cripple the police or preclude effective law enforcement. Candor compels us to acknowledge, however, that some crimes escape detection, and some criminals escape punishment, as a result of our vigilant commitment to constitutional norms. Enforcement of these norms is not, on such occasions, a pleasant duty; but it is a duty from which judges may not shrink.

Cases in which a search is made without first obtaining a search warrant will be scrutinized due to what is referred to as the "warrant preference."[4]

The warrant requirement of the Fourth Amendment is designed to protect all citizens. It guarantees "the right of the people to be secure in their persons, houses, papers and effects against unreasonable searches and seizures" and further provides "that no Warrants shall issue, but upon probable cause, supported by Oath or affirmation, and particularly describing the place to be searched and the persons or things to be seized."

While the Fourth Amendment makes it clear that people and their places and things will not be subject to search and seizure without a warrant, and further that the warrant must be based on probable cause, there are situational exceptions to the warrant requirement.

Narcotics investigators commonly encounter situations which fall into one or more of the various categories of exceptions to the search warrant requirement. Some of these exceptions will now be discussed in the specific context of narcotics investigations.

Exception to Search Warrant Requirement: EXIGENCY

Exigent circumstances exist where there is probable cause to believe that a crime is being committed or has just been committed and when

---

3 *United States v. Most,* 876 F.2d 191, 200 (D.C. Cir. 1989).

4 Burkhoff, Search Warrant Law Deskbook, p. 3-2.

there are specific factors present which indicate that it is urgent that some action be taken immediately.

1. The amount of time necessary to get a search warrant is not available;

2. The contraband will be moved if immediate action is not taken;

3. The officers on surveillance at the site of the contraband might possibly be subject to some danger during the time that a search warrant is being prepared and signed;

4. The suspects may be aware that the police are watching them currently and may possibly escape;

5. Contraband can be destroyed easily, and disposing of the evidence is behavior characteristic of those involved in drug trafficking.[5]

Narcotics investigators will frequently encounter exigent circumstances. They also commonly encounter what they consider to be exigent circumstances, but which are later determined not to be. The determination of whether or not exigent circumstances exist is usually a decision that is made quickly and followed immediately with some irrevocable action. To avoid making the wrong determination, a narcotics investigator should have a clear idea of what factors need to be considered. Even at that, the courts may rule against the action taken depending on the individual facts of the case. There are several investigative techniques and resulting situations which produce exigent circumstances.

Controlled Buys/Undercover Buys

Narcotics investigators will frequently make a controlled buy or an undercover buy with the intention of going immediately and obtaining a search warrant for the premises. In these instances, surveillance will be maintained on the location until the search warrant affidavit can be written and the warrant signed. Perhaps an informant made a controlled buy, and following that buy he told the investigator that a certain suspect was inside and that he had a large amount of cocaine, as much as the informant has ever seen him have. The determination is made to get a search warrant and hit it immediately thereafter, and surveillance is established to make sure that the dealer does not leave.

Specific information regarding the identity of the dealer and how many other people are inside will be critical. The simplest scenario is

---

5 *People v. Guerin,* 769 P.2d 1068, 1071 (Colo. 1989).

the one in which there is only one person inside, and the informant has told the investigator that the dealer has the cocaine on his person. Then it is clear that if he leaves, he will be stopped and arrested and the house secured until the warrant is ready. The whole purpose of the surveillance is to ensure that the cocaine which was just observed inside the house is not allowed to be taken out of the house. If the dealer leaves, he will be arrested on the basis of probable cause that he is committing a crime, possession of a controlled substance, and/or that he has just committed a crime, the sale of a controlled substance. Whether the sale was to an undercover officer or an informant does not matter at this point except inasmuch as the word of an undercover police officer is objectively more reliable than is that of an informant.

Two of the factors mentioned above in conjunction with the determination of exigency in court are present. First, there is not time to obtain a search warrant, an attempt is being made to get one, but it is not ready and the suspect is leaving. Second, in observing the suspect leave, it is believed, based on information available, that he is taking the cocaine with him. This has created a situation where either immediate action is taken, the suspect arrested and the premises secured, or the evidence will be gone. Background data, developed through the investigation, can enlighten the situation. If, for example, it is known that the suspect leaves at 3:45 P.M. each and every weekday to pick up his child at school and then immediately returns, then to see him leave the house at 3:45 P.M. on a Thursday while a warrant is being prepared, may not create the type of exigency required. Similarly, if there is information that the suspect always hides the cocaine in the house when he leaves, that he never has it with him on his person, then there probably are not exigent circumstances, although probable cause to arrest him does exist depending on what other knowledge is possessed at the time. The point is, no action should be taken, that is, securing the location prior to the warrant being signed unless it is absolutely necessary, unless it is urgent to do so.

U.S. v. Elkins dealt with exigent circumstances presented after a controlled buy had been made and while a warrant was being obtained.[6] The situation took place in 1982 in Tennessee. In that case, agents from the Drug Enforcement Administration and local officers had made a controlled buy from Elkins, and the determination was made to maintain

---

6 *United States v. Elkins,* 732 F.2d 1280 (6th Cir. 1984)

surveillance on the house and a vehicle from which Elkins had been observed taking cocaine until search warrants were prepared.

Not long after the officer left to prepare the search warrant, a male party was observed leaving in Elkin's car. The vehicle which had been determined to be Elkins was stopped at some point in a long driveway leading away from the house and Elkins's son was driving it. Elkins's son and the other male party he left with were both detained and taken back toward the house.

The agents and officers at that time felt that their intentions had been compromised by their actions. In other words, it was probably clear to Elkins and other people inside the house that investigators were watching the house and had just arrested the two people leaving. Making the determination that that was the case, the decision was made to enter and secure the house. That decision was made based on essentially two factors. First, Elkins had been arrested in the past in possession of a submachine gun-type weapon with a silencer and was considered dangerous. Two, the officers felt that Elkins was aware of their presence and being so aware, he would destroy whatever evidence was in the house. The controlled buy had been part of a multiounce arrangement to be completed later, and good information existed that Elkins had a substantial amount of cocaine in the house and possibly in the car as well. The judgment that Elkins would destroy the cocaine was no doubt based on their knowledge of the circumstances in this case as well as their previous experience in dealing with drug dealers; i.e., they will destroy the evidence if they feel that they are about to be arrested.

One of the DEA agents went to the door and knocked while announcing his presence. Elkins and Carol Dichtel, later a co-defendant, emerged from the rear of the house to see who was at the door. They quickly retreated when they became aware of who was knocking. The agent was greeted by a young man who opened the door for him and allowed him into the house. There were two mean dogs preventing the agent from moving into the house any farther than he did and securing Elkins and Dichtel. The young man who opened the door took control of the dogs which eventually allowed the agent to move through the house. While the DEA agent was attempting to get into the house, one of the local officers involved moved around the house to a point outside a bathroom window. He was able to see Elkins and Carol Dichtel in the bathroom dumping cocaine in the toilet. The officer smashed out the bathroom window and ordered them to stop destroying the evidence, but they continued flushing.

The case went to the Supreme Court on the contention of Elkins and Dichtel that the initial entry "to secure the premises was violative of their Fourth Amendment rights."[7] The Supreme Court ruled that "the law is settled that a warrantless entry will be sustained when the circumstances then extant were such as to lead a person of reasonable caution to conclude that evidence of a federal crime would probably be found on the premises and also that such evidence would probably be destroyed in the time necessary to obtain a search warrant."[8]

Furthermore, it was determined in this case that "the warrantless entry was justified by the circumstances. Once having entered the premises, the agents were then required to secure all persons therein and to make a protective sweep for the weapons Elkins was known to favor, for the safety of all concerned. This was done with minimal intrusion, . . . "[9]

The judgments made by the officers and agents of the present circumstances and the urgency created by those circumstances in this case were correct. There were articulable reasons of the kind necessary to support the conclusion that exigent circumstances did exist, and action had to be taken in the absence of a search warrant. While a warrant is preferable in every case, there are many cases of this nature which will require immediate and decisive action.

Extended Surveillance

There are times when an investigator will be doing surveillance on a location for the purpose of building probable cause and end up in a situation where he is taking immediate action in the absence of a search warrant. It is important to remember that, as mentioned, when action is taken based on exigent circumstances, the same standard of probable cause exists. Lacking probable cause, exigent circumstances alone won't justify the action taken.

People v. Guerin, the 1989 Colorado case to which reference was made previously, provides an excellent example of this type of situation.[10] In that case, a narcotics detective had received information from an anony-

---

7 Ibid., at 1284.

8 Ibid.

9 Ibid., at 1285.

10 *People v. Guerin,* 769 P.2d 1068 (Colo. 1989)

mous caller regarding the sale of marijuana at a local tire shop. The detective had been informed by the caller that small quantities were being distributed and that a great deal of traffic was being generated. The detective, unable to corroborate the information from the anonymous caller, decided to do some surveillance. While on surveillance, the detective observed several people go into the tire shop, stay a very brief period of time, and then leave. Obviously, this type of customer contact would be inconsistent with the tire business, and to that extent, it corroborated the information received from the anonymous informant.

Deciding that a crime was being committed, the detective made the decision to enter the business, arrest the owner, and secure the premises until a warrant could be obtained. The detective and three other police officers approached the tire shop and knocked at the locked door with their guns drawn. The door was opened and the officers entered to the smell of burning marijuana. The officer proceeded to frisk the people inside for weapons and asked who was the owner of the business. The owner identified himself, and cocaine was subsequently recovered from his jacket pocket. A plastic baggie was partially exposed sticking out of a closed cash box on the desk. One of the officers recognized it as marijuana packaging, and the baggie was pulled out of the box. It did contain marijuana. The detective left the tire store to obtain a warrant and returned at about 10:00 P.M. with a signed search warrant. Additional evidence was obtained. The initial entry had been made into the store at about 6:30 P.M.

The defense filed a motion to suppress the evidence seized and the statement made by the owner that he was the owner. The trial court ruled that while there was probable cause for arrest, "neither exigent circumstances nor consent were present which would have vitiated the necessity of obtaining a warrant prior to the search of Tire King."[11]

The prosecution appealed the case. The Colorado Supreme Court ruled that "a warrantless search is presumptively violative of the fourth amendment, U.S. Const. amend IV, unless it falls within one of the recognized exceptions to the search warrant requirement."[12] The court went on to detail the factors to be considered, those five mentioned at the beginning of this section. In this case it was ruled that exigency did not

11 Ibid., at 1070.

12 Ibid.

exist. Several aspects of the case were brought up in support of this finding.

First, it was mentioned that the initial call from the unidentified source to the detective detailed the time of drug sales as being from 6:00 P.M. to 9:00 P.M. The detective decided to secure the business at 6:30 P.M. The court ruled that inferring from the initial information the detective could be reasonably certain that the dealing would continue until at least 9:00 P.M. The information received had been that this was activity of an ongoing nature. Therefore, if action was not taken on this night, there was nothing to preclude the possibility of preparing a search warrant and taking action on another night. The court ruled that there was little danger that the evidence would be moved from the tire store and no evidence that the officers on surveillance would be in any danger if action was not taken immediately. Furthermore, there was no evidence that anybody inside the business was aware of the police surveillance. Had they been, marijuana customers would have been turned away, and the police would have probably been denied admittance.

"Finally, while cocaine can be easily disposed of by flushing it down a drain, marijuana is not as easily destroyed. Marijuana in the quantities that would allow the defendant to sell it to a substantial number of persons is much more difficult to destroy."[13]

In coming to its decision, the court went through the five factors which it listed in the ruling as being considered in determining exigency. In this case it was determined that there was no urgency involved; it was 6:00 P.M. and the dealing would probably continue until 9:00 P.M. Furthermore, there was no reasonable belief that the marijuana was about to be removed. Initial information received by the detective indicated that the marijuana was kept in with the tire supply and the cocaine was kept in the pop machine. Considering the third factor, there was no evidence that the police on the surveillance would be in any particular danger. Fourth, as to awareness on behalf of the dealers of police presence; there was no indication that this was the case here. And, finally, the ready destructibility was not a factor according to the court in this case.

Many narcotics cases happen just as this one did, The decision to arrest and secure based on exigent circumstances must take into account all the factors previously mentioned. They need not all be present, but

---

13 Ibid., at 1071.

there must be a combination of factors which add up to exigency. A search warrant should be obtained if at all possible.

Crack houses present similar circumstances on a regular basis. Crack dealing is such a transitory business that seldom can a warrant be obtained before there is a significant change in circumstances inside the crack house. The dealer has sold out, he has moved it to another location, he has gone to re-up (replenish his supply of drugs), or he still has enough left to make the warrant worth doing. Investigative techniques have, out of necessity, been adapted to accommodate the changing nature of the business. Often warrants have to be prepared with the knowledge that they may not be good by the time they are ready, but on the reliance that they will become right again soon. Patience, additional surveillance, and preraid buys can help ensure success.

Buy/Bust Scenarios

Quite often a buy/bust operation will take place and with it will come exigent circumstances requiring action before a warrant is obtained. Obviously the best case scenario would be to have the warrants ready to go, either written as anticipatory search warrants and approval obtained or written based on projected activity and ready for immediate signature after the fact. In a recent case, in which all suspects ultimately pleaded guilty, the situation involved two undercover officers negotiating for the purchase of 1 pound of marijuana. It was anticipated that the middleman would contact his source who would bring the pound, and after the officers observed it, they would be arrested. As it happened, the primary source could not be reached, and the middleman contacted a secondary source. The officers, the middleman, and an associate of his went to a site near the source location. The middleman wanted the officers to front the money for a pound, but they refused to do that. That is, they would not trust him with their money on the promise that he would return with the marijuana. He agreed to get the marijuana and then quickly take the money back to the source after the deal.

The middleman was observed by surveillance officers going into a triplex residential building. He was observed to the point that he descended some stairs which led down to two separate apartments. It could not be determined which of the two doors he entered. He came back to the corner, and when the officers saw the marijuana, both suspects were arrested. The arrests took place approximately 200 feet from the source location.

Investigators went back to the triplex, in an undercover capacity, and knocked on the two downstairs doors. There was no answer at the one, it was dark and quiet inside also. The other door, number 310, was answered by a woman who, when asked if someone had just come to her door responded in the negative. Nobody had been there. Officers left the triplex and went back to the arrest scene down the street. A short time later, two teenagers came down the street and inquired about the situation. They had come from number 310 at the triplex. They were inquisitive about why the people were being arrested. After some discussion, the investigators went back to number 310 and recontacted the woman, this time identifying themselves as police officers. The woman was asked whether she would consent to a search of her apartment, and she refused. She was then advised that the apartment was being secured while a search warrant could be obtained and that one officer was presently on his way to write the warrant.

She had two large pit bulls, and she was told to secure them in the bathroom. She wanted to secure them in a front bedroom adjacent to the living room but she was told to put them in the bathroom, which she did. She was then informed that the officers were going to take a look around the house just to determine if there were any other people inside the house and that once that was done, all would sit in the living room and wait for the arrival of the search warrant. The look for other people inside the house revealed marijuana on top of a dresser, in plain view, in the front bedroom where she had wanted to put the dogs. The woman was immediately advised that she was under arrest and advised of her rights. Following advisement, she volunteered to show the investigators where the marijuana was hidden, so that her house would not be put in shambles by a thorough search. She unlocked a freezer in the kitchen which contained 115 pounds of marijuana in 1-pound bags. The search warrant was subsequently signed and the marijuana seized.

The case could no doubt have been challenged, first on the grounds that there was not probable cause to believe that number 310 was the source apartment and that there was marijuana inside and, then, that exigent circumstances, necessitating entry without a warrant, did not exist. The supervisor at the scene made the decision to secure the apartment after talking to the other investigators involved. One surveillance officer had seen the middleman at the top of the stairs and then disappear, apparently down the stairs, and then reappear a short time later and take the marijuana directly to the undercover officers. Nobody was home in the back apartment, which eliminated it from consideration, so the conclusion was reached that number 310 was the source apartment, and if they gave the middleman 1 pound of marijuana, more marijuana was inside. The middleman had told the undercover officers that this source, although a secondary source to the one the middleman originally planned to buy from, "always had it, and it was good stuff." To the supervisor making the decision, all this added up to probable cause that a crime had been committed in number 310 and that there was marijuana and other evidence in the apartment.

The first plainclothes officer who went to the door of number 310 did not identify himself as a police officer. He acted as if the person who had come to the door was a friend of his and that he was looking for him. Not until the second time that the officers went to the door did they identify themselves as narcotics investigators and explain their purpose. However, the woman was aware of the presence of the police inasmuch as her daughter and another teenager went down the block to investigate and find out who was being arrested. It is important to remember that the woman had fronted the middleman the pound and had reason to be concerned about getting her money for the deal. It was determined that by the time a warrant was prepared, the evidence would be moved or destroyed. The officers had no idea that there were 115 pounds of marijuana inside the apartment and that to move it or destroy it would take some time.

Four of the five factors mentioned in the *Guerin* case existed.[14] There was urgency, and therefore not time to get a search warrant, there were indications that the people at the source location were aware that the middleman to whom they had just sold a pound had been arrested and a risk therefore that those suspects would escape, there was the collective experience which indicated to the officers that those who traffic in drugs will dispose of them if they know they are about to be detected, and because of that it was feared that evidence would be destroyed. Finally, there was a significant chance that other contraband would be moved. Only the factor regarding potential danger to surveillance officers was lacking.

What is difficult for investigators to get used to is that the outcome, the fact that the officers were right, the source location was just as it was thought to be and there was quite a bit of marijuana there, will not

---

14 Ibid.

necessarily qualify the decisions made as the right decisions. It could well have been determined that probable cause did not exist or that there were not enough articulable factors present to create exigency sufficient to justify entry without a search warrant.

These are tough calls to make, and knowledge, skill, and experience are critical to making the right choices. All the experience and skill and knowledge in the world will not guarantee that the choice that is being made will be supported by the courts, although in most cases, decisions made in good faith from an educated, informed perspective will prove to be correct.

Exception to Search Warrant Requirement: CONSENT

Narcotics investigators frequently encounter situations in which they are acting with the consent of a person rather than the authorization of a search warrant. If a person who has authority gives consent, a search warrant is not required. In order to be valid, the consent must be given by one who has "common authority over or other sufficient relationship to the premises or effects sought to be inspected."[15]

Investigators searching based on consent must ascertain that the person giving the consent is lucid, that he has authority to give consent, and that the consent is being given free of any coercion.

Consent searches are commonly used by narcotics investigators when there is not probable cause to obtain a search warrant. Consent is often sought as a last resort.

There are times when seeking a consent to search is an expedient solution to a problem with no other apparent options. Some investigators frequently use the consent search technique in response to citizen complaints about drug dealing at a given location. If all other investigative efforts have failed to corroborate the fact that the people are dealing and complaints persist, knocking on the door and talking to the people is a direct approach to determining if illegal activity is taking place. People will occasionally consent to a police search knowing that in doing so they are incriminating themselves.

Consent searches are also routinely used in airport interdiction cases for the sake of expediency.

The problem with consent search situations involves using the evidence obtained later against the consenting person. The person consenting

---

15 *United States v. Matlock,* 415 U.S. 164, 171 (1974, and Burkhoff, *Search Warrant Law Deskbook,* p. 3–12.

might, when the case goes to court, deny that he or she consented freely and seek to have the evidence suppressed, or if the consenting person is not the person charged, the authority of the consenting person will be challenged. The burden of proof will be on the prosecution to establish that the consent was given freely. Having the consent in writing will allay some of the later difficulty, but it may not do so entirely.

If a consent search is used as an avenue of the last resort, fine. If, however, probable cause to obtain a search warrant exists, *a search warrant should be obtained rather than relying on a consent search.*

Exception to Search Warrant Requirement:
SEARCH INCIDENT TO LAWFUL ARREST

The most commonly encountered exception to the search warrant requirement is the situation where a person is lawfully arrested and searched incident to that arrest. When a person is lawfully arrested, he may be searched, and evidence obtained in such a search is admissible. Likewise, when a person is arrested, the area within his immediate control may also be searched. The area searched in these situations must be limited to that "area from within which" the suspect "might have obtained either a weapon or something that could have been used as evidence against him."[16]

Narcotics investigators will often receive a hot tip which justifies the arrest of a person based on probable cause, without an arrest warrant. The suspect will then be searched incident to the arrest and the evidence recovered will be admissible. As an example, if a previously reliable confidential informant calls and states that Willie C. is at a certain street corner and is currently in the possession of and selling cocaine, there are several considerations in determining if probable cause to arrest him exists. First, has the informant been reliable in the past? If he has, there is not the requisite degree of corroboration necessary as if the informant were a first-time informant or an anonymous caller. Next, the investigator must determine the informant's basis of knowledge. The informant must have firsthand knowledge—he must have seen the cocaine in Willie C's possession. The information should be corroborated to whatever extent is possible. In this case, Willie C. is a documented drug dealer with previous arrests for possession and sale, and numerous intelligence

---

16 *Chimel v. California*, 89 SCt. 2034, 2042 (1969)

entries exist regarding his activity. Finally, what facts exist which indicate that if immediate action is not taken Willie C. will be gone or he will have sold or moved the drugs?

The past experience of a narcotics investigator will have taught him that those dealing on street corners usually hold only small quantities and sell them quickly. Assuming that in this case, there is specific information that Willie C. is going to be leaving soon to go to the dog track. There is not time to obtain an arrest warrant based on probable cause; neither is there time to obtain a search warrant for his person. The decision is then made to go arrest him on probable cause without an arrest warrant for possession and sale of a controlled substance. He is then searched and a case is filed based on the recovery.

This situation is one common to narcotics investigators, particularly those working the street. There are any number of complications which can alter the facts just given and thereby change the course of action. Many dealers will, for example, stash the drugs nearby and, on request, produce only enough for the one transaction. Therefore, when they are arrested by the police officers, they have nothing on them and they are released.

Searches incident to all types of lawful arrests commonly reveal drugs. These cases will then be referred to the narcotics investigators. It is necessary that the search and arrest be done in the proper order. For example, a uniformed officer stops a known drug dealer, and in doing a patdown for weapons, he reaches into his pocket and recovers cocaine. The officer then arrests him and then clears him only to find that he is wanted for failure to appear. The search is not incident to arrest and goes beyond the scope of a patdown frisk or cursory search. The search was before arrest and therefore unlawful. If, on the other hand, the uniformed officer observed the party on the street and did a test clearance on the off chance that he may have an arrest warrant for him, he could then contact the person, arrest him for the warrant, and seize the drugs legally. In fact, this type of situation or a variant thereof occurs frequently.

There are a surprising number of good arrests which never result in case filings due to the failure of the arresting officer to write an accurate statement. Many times the officer will have established probable cause to arrest a person for dealing drugs through surveillance or a combination of surveillance, past experience, and informant information. However, when the report is written, the background information that established probable cause for the narcotics arrest is left out, and it appears as if the officer contacted the suspected drug dealer, searched him, and then arrested him. In fact, what may have happened was that he watched him for several minutes and observed what, based on his experience, were street-level drug sales. In addition, the officer may have learned from an informant earlier in the evening that the suspect had been seen in possession of and selling drugs. Probable cause for arrest was thus developed, and the suspect was then contacted by the officer and arrested for possession and sale of drugs. The search incident to arrest revealed drugs, currency, paraphernalia, etc.

What is suggested here is that, whenever possible, surveillance should be maintained until such point that reasonable suspicion to stop a person pursuant to *Terry* develops into probable cause to arrest. Following arrest, a search is legal. In a stop and frisk situation, there can be no search.[17] In addition, while narcotics investigators will quickly learn from their mistakes by having cases refused, uniform officers may not realize the intricacies involved in these situations and may benefit from some informal training. Narcotics investigators should take the time to give feedback to patrol officers attentive to the narcotics problem in their areas.

Exception to Search Warrant Requirement: AUTOMOBILE SEARCHES

Vehicles are an integral part of the drug trafficking business as they are of any business in which goods are exchanged, picked up, and delivered. The automobile exception to the search warrant requirement is based on the fact that motor vehicles can be readily moved and evidence thereby lost. "One of the circumstances in which the Constitution does not require a search warrant is when the police stop an automobile on the street or highway because they have probable cause to believe it contains contraband or evidence of a crime."[18]

To search a vehicle without a warrant, using exigent circumstances as justification, probable cause must exist. The same probable cause necessary to obtain a search warrant. The courts have created a special class of exception to the warrant requirement for motor vehicles, but the exception "applies only to searches of vehicles that are supported by probable cause. In this class of cases, a search is not unreasonable if based on facts

---

17 *Terry v. Ohio,* 392 U.S. 1 (1968)

18 *Arkansas v. Sanders,* 442 U.S. 753, 760 (1979)

that would justify the issuance of a warrant, even though a warrant has not actually been obtained."[19]

In cases of a more long-term nature, where an investigation is ongoing, probable cause to search a motor vehicle will be developed and a search warrant obtained along with warrants for houses, businesses, etc. In cases where probable cause develops spontaneously and unexpectedly and immediate action must be taken, time to get a search warrant will not be available. In these cases, if probable cause exists, the vehicle should be seized and secured and a warrant obtained. While there is case law that states that it is not necessary to get a warrant to search the vehicle while it is "at the station house,"[20] it is preferable to do so.[21]

Inventory searches of vehicles do not fall under the "automobile exception" class. Inventory searches of vehicles are not based on probable cause; rather, they are conducted as a way of protecting privately owned property and protecting against liability claims. For these types of searches to be valid, the custody of the vehicle must be lawful. A vehicle cannot be seized and then inventoried for no reason. At that, the inventory will be subject to some regulation. The Supreme Court recently held that the search of closed containers for inventory purposes was illegal absent a department procedure which specifically called for the inventory of contents in closed containers.[22]

Other Search Warrant Exceptions

There are several other exceptions to the search warrant requirement, namely, administrative searches, probation searches, searches at border checkpoints, and others, including stop and frisk situations, although as mentioned, a stop and frisk situation does not justify a search per se, only a patdown for weapons. The four categories of exceptions discussed — exigency, search incident to arrest, consent, and automobile searches — are those most germane to narcotics investigations. While the treatment of these situations here was superficial, the purpose was to discuss these exceptions within the specific context of narcotics investigations and to

---

19 *United States v. Ross,* 456 U.S. 798, 809 (1982)

20 *Texas V. White,* 423 U.S. 67, 68 (1975)

21 See, also, *United States v. Ross,* 456 U.S. 798, 807, n.9 (1982); and *United States v. Johns,* 469 U.S. 478, 486 (1985)

22 *Florida v. Wells,* 110 S.Ct. 1632 (1990)

emphasize that while a search warrant is preferable, it is not always possible nor is it necessary in every case.

PREPARING THE SEARCH WARRANT

Defining Probable Cause

The goal in a narcotics investigation is to develop probable cause: probable cause to arrest, such as in a buy/bust situation where the suspect brings the evidence to the officers and thereby provides probable cause for his own arrest, or probable cause to obtain a search warrant for a person, vehicle, or place. This discussion deals with probable cause necessary to obtain a search warrant. "Probable cause" as used in the Fourth Amendment applies to both search and arrest:[23]

> An arrest warrant is issued by a magistrate upon a showing that probable cause exists to believe that the subject of the warrant has committed an offense and thus the warrant primarily serves to protect an individual from an unreasonable seizure. A search warrant, in contrast, is issued upon a showing of probable cause to believe that the legitimate object of a search is located in a particular place, and therefore safeguards an individual's interest in the privacy of his home and possessions against the unjustified intrusion of the police.

In narcotics cases, drugs being contraband, there is not a need to show the reviewing judge or magistrate the drug items being sought are the evidence of a criminal activity, whereas in a burglary case, for example, it is necessary to show that the television set or firearms which are the subject of the search are evidence of a crime. It may be necessary to show the connection to drug dealing actiity of nonnarcotic evidence which is being sought in addition to the drug evidence.

What is necessary in narcotics search warrants is the showing of probable cause that the items sought are presently located in the place named in the search warrant. "In dealing with probable cause, however, as the very name implies, we deal with probabilities. These are not technical; they are the factual and practical considerations of everyday life on which reasonable and prudent men, not legal technicians, act."[24] In an effort to define probable cause, in addition to quoting from *Brinegar,* the Supreme Court in *Gates* went on to say that "probable cause

---

23 *Steagald v. United States,* 451 U.S. 204, 212–13 (1981).

24 *Brinegar v. United States,* 338 U.S. 160, 175 (1949).

is a fluid concept—turning on the assessment or probabilities in particu-lar factual contexts—not readily, or even usefully, reduced to a neat set of legal rules."[25]

Once it has been determined by the investigator that probable cause has been developed and that the time has come to prepare and serve a search warrant, the task becomes one of writing an affidavit in which probable cause is established for the reviewing judicial authority so that the warrant is approved and the search authorized.

Establishing Probable Cause in the Affidavit

Affiant Introduction

The search warrant affidavit should begin with an introduction of the affiant to the reviewing judge. This introduction is not just a formality. It serves essentially two purposes. First, it does introduce the affiant officer to the judge. Beyond that, the qualifications of the affiant which are stated as part of the introduction serve as a basis of training and experi-ence from which inferences will be drawn in the affidavit. The introduc-tion of the affiant should to some extent be tailored to the circumstances of each affidavit.

Special circumstances of a case may require that special training and experience, if any, be listed in the introduction. If a search warrant is being written for a crack house and the affiant has written 200 crack search warrants, that should be noted as part of the introduction. It may be necessary to establish probable cause to search any persons in the crack house, and past experience will be relied upon to justify that request. Likewise, the experience of fellow officers can be incorporated into an introduction.

The following is a sample introduction:

> Your affiant, Sergeant Paul Mahoney, has been a police officer in the city and county of Denver for the past 20 years and is currently assigned to the Vice/Drug Control Bureau as a supervisor in the Crack Task Force. Your affiant has been a supervisor in the Crack Task Force for the past three years. As such, your affiant has been involved in the investigation, planning, and execution of approximately 500 crack cocaine and cocaine search warrants. Your affiant has participated in numerous training classes in the subject of drug investigation

---

25 *Illinois v. Gates,* 462 U.S. 213, 232 (1983)

and has served as an instructor in classes related to drug trafficking and drug investigations.

When establishing probable cause in the affidavit will require drawing inferences based upon experience with crack cocaine and cocaine traffickers, and drug traffickers in general, the foundation of past experience has been set.

Investigative Facts

The search warrant affidavit is best written chronologically, beginning with the details of the information which initiated the investigation. What generally distinguishes narcotics search warrants from search warrants based on other criminal investigations is the role of the confidential informant as a primary source of information. In a criminal investigation, there are several investigative sources of information from which facts are learned and the investigation develops. Among those are fellow officers, citizen informants who are named in the affidavit, documents, and physical evidence which are described and confidential informants. A different standard of credibility exists for confidential informant sources than the other investigative sources. Fellow officers named as sources of information are presumed credible. Likewise, documents and other inanimate objects from which facts are learned are presumably credible and can be evaluated on face value. Citizens who are named in an affidavit are witnesses and the information which they provide to an investigation while presumed credible can be evaluated relative to other facts of the investigation. For instance:

> Mr. John Smith, who resides next door to the victim, at 3333 Cherry, stated that he heard commotion and when he looked out of his bedroom window, he observed a blue Pontiac leaving north on Cherry. Mr. Smith then went next door and found that the front door of 3331 Cherry had been knocked off its hinges. Mr. Smith further stated that he has seen the Pontiac parked in front of the victims house on several prior occasions and that he believes it to be the vehicle of the victim's ex-husband . . .

The facts of the investigation, learned from Mr. Smith who is named in the search warrant, can be taken at face value. The reviewing judge knows who Mr. Smith is, what his relationship to the investigation is, and what he contributed to the investigation. Compare that with the following:

> A previously reliable confidential informant contacted your affiant and stated that crack cocaine was being sold from the location of 5555 Ash St. The informant related to your affiant that within the past 72 hours the informant

was present at that location and observed a white male, known to the informant as "Hippie" in possession of and selling small quantities of cocaine in exchange for currency.

Where the informant is confidential, credibility must be established; it is not presumed.

Confidential Informant Credibility and Reliability

When a confidential informant is used in a narcotics warrant to establish probable cause, the reliability of the informant must be established. The longstanding measure of informant reliability was the *Aguilar-Spinelli* test. This test, developed by case law in the 1960s, requires that (1), the basis of the informant's knowledge must be established and (2), the veracity of the informant's information must be detailed for the evaluation of the reviewing judge.[26]

Under the *Aguilar-Spinelli* standard, an affidavit for a search warrant based on informant information must satisfy the "two-pronged" test. In satisfying the "basis of knowledge" requirement, the affiant must show the reviewing judge how the informant acquired the information. Was the informant present at the house of a drug dealer? If so, when? In what way is the informant familiar with the packaging and appearance of drugs, cocaine, for example? Is he familiar by virtue of previous association as a user? All information which establishes the informant's basis of knowledge must be clearly presented.

Meeting the "veracity prong" of the *Aguilar-Spinelli* test requires establishing the credibility of an informant. By what facts can the judge reviewing the affidavit determine that the information is reliable, that he is being truthful?

In 1983, the Supreme Court rejected the *Aguilar-Spinelli* test in favor of a more general standard. "For all these reasons, we conclude that it is wiser to abandon the "two-pronged test" established in our decisions in Aguilar and Spinelli. In its place we reaffirm the totality-of-the-circumstances analysis that traditionally has informed probable-cause determinations."[27]

While *Gates* provides for a more general approach to determining informant reliability, it does not require that the individual states aban-

---

26 *Aguilar v. Texas*, 378 U.S. 108 (1964), and *Spinelli v. United States*, 393 U.S. 410 (1969)

27 *Illinois v. Gates*, 462 U.S. 212, 238 (1983), footnote omitted.

don the *Aguilar-Spinelli* test. Under *Gates*, the requirements of each "prong," basis of knowledge and reliability, do not necessarily have to be fulfilled separately and distinctly. Instead, the "totality-of-the-circumstances" approach is adopted and confidential informant information is thus evaluated.[28] Such evaluation considers all facts surrounding the situation, including investigative corroboration of informant facts. In *Gates*, the informant was anonymous, and the initial informant tip took the form of a detailed letter. The anonymous informant's basis of knowledge could not be established nor could his reliability, and the Illinois Supreme Court concluded that there was no showing of probable cause. The *Gates* court ruled:[29]

> We agree with the Illinois Supreme Court that an informant's "veracity," "reliability," and "basis of knowledge" are all highly relevant in determining the value of his report. We do not agree, however, that these elements should be understood as entirely separate and independent requirements to be rigidly exacted in every case, which the opinion of the Supreme Court of Illinois would imply. Rather, as detailed below, they should be understood simply as closely intertwined issues that may usefully illuminate the common sense, practical question whether there is "probable cause" to believe that contraband or evidence is located at a particular place.[30]

Gates may have relaxed the "rigid" standard for evaluating informant information, but it did not change the substance of the requirements for establishing probable cause based on information provided by a confidential informant. It is still necessary to establish the informant's basis of knowledge and his veracity, although the two factors, according to *Gates*, may be taken as a whole and evaluated rather than being looked at strictly independent of each other.

Previously Reliable Informants

When the informant providing the information is a previously reliable confidential informant, it is necessary to detail his previous reliability to the reviewing judge. If an informant has been reliable 40 times in the past year, it isn't necessary to detail every occasion of reliability. It is not necessary to give specific details which would tend to identify the informant. It is only necessary to establish reliability:

---

28 Ibid.

29 Ibid.

30 Ibid., at 230.

1. Informant has provided information in the past;

2. Information has been provided on a given number of occasions within a given time period;

3. The information resulted in seizures, arrests, and convictions, or the results of the cases are pending;

4. The informant has not provided information known to the affiant to be untrue.

It is acceptable to establish the reliability of an informant through what he has done for other officers. The same detail is required. It is not necessary to give exact numbers of occasions of reliability. Delimiting parameters can be established; at least three occasions within the past three months, for example. What must be included is enough information regarding occasions of past reliability within a given time period and the action resulting from that information to enable the judge to make a determination of reliability.

Regarding previous reliability, enough specific information should be provided in the affidavit so that reliability is established. What is included in the affidavit is all that will be considered. If there is any question about how much information to include, resolve it in favor of too much information rather than too little.

First-Time Confidential Informants

In the case of first-time confidential informants, there is no established basis of credibility and reliability. It is necessary therefore to establish credibility based on information provided in this, the first instance, through corroboration. The affiant should corroborate as much detail of the information as possible to do. If the informant reports that a certain party is dealing drugs from a certain location, an attempt to corroborate that information is necessary. Does the subject have a record for drug dealing? If he does, is that corroborative of the informant's information regarding the address given by the informant? Hotline files and intelligence files should be checked to determine if this address has been reported as a drug dealing location. If it has, that too is corroborative.

The informant should provide a detailed description of the subject and the location and as much specific detail about the subject's habits as possible. The informant should be taken to the location to point it out.

Showing the informant a photo lineup and having him identify the suspect from that is a good technique.

One of the surest ways of corroborating a first-time informant's tip about a drug dealer is through a controlled buy. Of course, controlled buys are also made to corroborate the information of previously reliable informants as well. The details of a controlled buy in an affidavit show the reviewing judge something of the informant's credibility. If the informant first reported that the suspected dealer was dealing cocaine in grams and half grams and that he wrapped them in newspaper, it is important to include in your affidavit that a controlled buy was made, the quantity purchased was a half gram, and the cocaine was wrapped in newspaper.

It is quite common that the information of a first-time informant can be corroborated through information of a previously reliable informant. For example, a first-time informant may report a subject dealing at a certain location about which a previously reliable informant has already given information. Likewise, information received from fellow officers can corroborate the information given by a first-time informant. Surveillance is also a key to corroborating informant information.

Corroboration is a big part of any search warrant investigation. With respect to first-time confidential informants, (CIs), enough corroboration must be accomplished through investigation so that some relatively high degree of informant credibility is obvious to the reviewing judge.

CI Basis of Knowledge

In writing a search warrant affidavit based on information from any confidential informant, it is necessary to establish that the informant has some basis of knowledge. How does the informant know that the suspect is a drug dealer? The information has to be specific enough to establish that it is not innocent, general information which could be considered almost common knowledge and which of itself does not show any criminal activity. General information will not establish probable cause that drugs are in a certain location at a given time. The informant knows that there are drugs in a certain house because the informant has been there within the past 72 hours and has observed the suspect in possession of the drugs. The informant is familiar with the packaging and appearance of cocaine inasmuch as the informant has used drugs in the past. In addition, the informant was present twice last week, the week of October 31, 1990, when the suspect was in possession of and selling cocaine.

Any specific information which establishes the basis of knowledge should be included with as much detail as possible consistent with the aim of keeping the informant confidential.

Specific Information Versus Confidentiality

Difficulty is encountered in narcotics search warrants balancing the need for specific information which establishes the informant's credibility, reliability, and basis of knowledge with the need to protect the informant's identity.

Specific details included in an affidavit may identify the informant without actually naming him or her. This defeats the purpose of using a confidential informant. If the suspect learns the identity of the inform-ant from facts written in the affidavit, the informant's safety and future value as an informant may be jeopardized. Affidavits based on informa-tion received from a confidential informant must be constructed with a dual purpose: (1) establish probable cause and (2) protect the confidentiality of the informant.

Recognizing this need to ensure confidentiality, courts have permitted some efforts to accomplish it. For example, if an informant was present at the suspect's house on Tuesday and five other people came and went during the time that the informant was there, specific details which the informant learned during that visit may not tend to reveal his identity. However, it is still permissible to list the time of the informant's basis of knowledge within a "window." The 72-hour period spanning the dates of October 1, 1990 through October 3, 1990, rather than Tuesday, October 2, 1990, would be a manner of constructing a time window for informant activity in the interest of keeping the identity of the informant confidential. If the subject is a street-level dealer, dealing to 20 people a day, chances are that specific information regarding the date that observations were made by an informant would not tend to reveal his identity.

In the case of an informant whose information is extremely valuable due to his closeness to the suspect, more difficulty will be encountered in writing specific details in the affidavit and at the same time keeping the informant's identity confidential. An informant who has the trust and confidence of a dealer may learn that the suspect has a large stash in a certain location. If the informant is the only person other than the suspect who has this information, putting this information in the affida-vit and keeping the informant confidential may be difficult if not impossible. The informant may have other, more general information which would not be so uncommon, but which builds probable cause. The informant may know that when the suspect is home and the porch light is on, the suspect is dealing. The informant may know that when the suspect is dealing, he always has an ounce ready to sell. Other people, in addition to the informant probably have this information too. Probable cause can be established without using the other information, which may be the strongest indicator of probable cause. If to use it is to identify the informant, and if you have probable cause without it, it does not have to be included in the affidavit.

The same considerations exist with respect to controlled buys made to establish probable cause. The controlled buy will go a long way toward corroborating initial informant information and establishing probable cause. The details of the buy should be included for that purpose. It is not necessary to include such explicit details about the buy that the informant is virtually identified without being named. If the purpose of a controlled buy was to establish probable cause, enough details to accomplish that purpose should be included. Again, the time of the buy can be reported, framed within a time window. It is not necessary to put the exact time and date. Also included should be the fact that the buy was made in exchange for U.S. currency as well as the results of the presumptive screening which established that the substance purchased was a controlled substance.

If a $50.00 package was purchased, in the interest of conserving funds, but the suspect normally does not sell anything less than a $100.00 package, only doing so because of his relationship with the informant, to include that detail might identify the informant. It is permissible to put that department currency not exceeding $100.00 was exchanged by the informant for the cocaine.

In protecting the identity of the informant, it is essential that the integrity of the affiant not be compromised. There can be no misrepresentation of the facts in the affidavit. The intent is not to mislead or distort the facts of an investigation but to minimize those reported if necessary to protect the informant's identity. The object is to establish probable cause for a search warrant and keep the informant confidential at the same time.

Further investigation—Corroboration

At this point in an affidavit, the officer has been identified, the initial facts of the investigation presented, the informant information has been written into the affidavit and the informant's reliability, credibility, and basis of knowledge have been established. What remains is to detail further investigative facts which corroborate the informant information.

Freshness

Steps which were taken to establish that the information provided by the CI is fresh should be described. The investigation done to this end could take the form of controlled buys, surveillance, discussions with other officers, review of intelligence files, etc. The reviewing judge will need to know the relative freshness of information pertaining to drug dealing due to the transitory nature of the business. Establishing that the drug dealing of the suspect is an ongoing activity will shed light on the freshness issue. A person who was seen selling a bag of marijuana on Thursday may not have any left by Sunday. Theoretically, this may be an isolated case. The suspect may have been in dire need of money and had the opportunity to sell some marijuana and make a fast dollar. He may never do it again. Conversely, if it can be shown that the subject has a history of drug dealing, he has been arrested three times, his house has been on the hotline four times in the last month, and the CI states that he deals "7-24" (7 days a week, 24 hours a day) all the time, and that he renews his supply every night, controlled buy information 72 hours old is relatively fresh.

Confidential informant information and other investigative facts are usually considered fresh if not more than 72 hours elapses between the time the information is learned and the time the warrant is presented for signature. This period of time can be much longer if there is evidence of ongoing drug activity and that information is part of the affidavit. The freshness or staleness of controlled buys and other information will be determined, largely proportionate to any showing of the ongoing nature of the activity.[31]

Other Corroboration

All standard investigative measures to corroborate information and the results of those efforts should be included in the affidavit. Any undercover work should be included. Undercover buys obviously make

---

31 *People v. David,* 326 N.W.2d 485, 487–88 (Mich. Ct. App. 1982): Controlled buy information 3 days old considered stale absent a showing of ongoing activity. *State v. Wise,* 434 So.2d. 1308, 1311–12 (La. Ct. App. 1983): Controlled buy information over 90 days old not stale due to large quantities of drugs involved and evidence of ongoing drug activity. See Burkhoff, *Search Warrant Law Deskbook,* pp. 5–7, 5–8.)

great probable cause. Unlike a controlled buy, an undercover buy provides a witness to criminal activity, and as much detail as possible should be included about the undercover buys in the affidavit. The exception to this might be the case of an ongoing investigation, of which a warrant is just a small part, and where the undercover portion of the investigation is to continue. In that case, to detail the undercover buy would jeopardize the rest of the investigation.

Corroborative information received from fellow officers, including patrol reports, should be supplied. Field contact or interview reports can provide excellent corroboration. Offense reports, arrest reports, driver's license checks, National Crime Information Center checks, Drug Enforcement Administration intelligence checks, utility listings, should also be included as should surveillance results.

If any of these sources provides negative information, that too should be included in the affidavit. If, for example, the public service lists to J. Pearson and your target is E. Pearson, or E. Smith for that matter, this should be included as a fact developed through the investigation. If surveillance was done, the results should be reported, even if the results were inconclusive. At this stage of the investigation, applying for a search warrant, there is a belief that probable cause exists.

Facts in the affidavit should be explained in light of experience where such inferences can be made. For example, in my experience, it is quite common for drug traffickers to have the public utilities at their residence listed in someone else's name. It is also quite common for the apartment to be rented in someone else's name. The fact that no record exists of the suspect living at the reported address is one thing. It does not diminish the fact that in a surveillance I have seen him come and go and seen him standing at the front door talking to people in the street or the fact that the informant made a controlled buy from him at the reported address to which you can find no record connecting him.

Likewise, the fact that a person does not have a record for drug dealing does not diminish the informant information and the other corroborative facts.

Probable cause either exists or it does not, and negative facts which have also been part of the investigation will only serve to keep the investigation in its true perspective.

Immediate Entry

When all the facts have been detailed which pertain to probable cause, the affidavit is complete except to ask for the warrant. Before requesting that the warrant be issued, consider the justification for immediate entry, no-knock entry, if such a provision exists. Many states do not have a specific provision for "no-knock" execution of search warrants. Others have provisions authorizing police officers to use force as is reasonably necessary to gain entry and execute the search warrant. Most states have a "knock and announce" requirement by which officers are required to give notice of their presence and announce their intentions prior to entering the premises to be searched. The federal rule, 18 U.S.C. 3109, provides that:

> The officer may break open any outer or inner door or window of a house, or any part of a house, or anything therein, to execute a search warrant, if after notice of his authority and purpose, he is refused admittance or when necessary to liberate himself or a person aiding him in the execution of the warrant.

The Supreme Court has taken a clear position on the subject, in support of 18 U.S.C. 3109:[32]

> The requirement of prior notice of authority and purpose before entry into a home is deeply rooted in our heritage and should not be given grudging application. Congress, codifying a tradition embedded in Anglo-American law, has declared in 3109 the reverence of the law for the individual's right of privacy in the house.

In spite of this, there are states, Colorado among them, that have specific provisions for immediate entry search warrants. The Colorado law provides for immediate entry authorization, on the face of the warrant, requiring judicial approval separate from and in addition to search warrant approval.

It is necessary, in a search warrant affidavit, to detail facts which officers believe are present and which justify immediate entry. The collective experience of police officers working narcotics cases supports the belief that those trafficking in narcotics will dispose of the narcotics given time and warning of the presence of police officers whose purpose is to execute a search warrant. Likewise, some drug dealers are known to arm themselves against users, other dealers, and law enforcement

---

32 *Miller v. United States,* 357 U.S. 301, 313 (1958)

personnel. Experience of drug investigators has shown this to be the case.

If such particular information is available, if there is a belief that evidence will be destroyed, and if the presence of the police is made known, that should be put in this portion of the search warrant. Likewise, if the record of the suspect and other investigative facts support the belief that the suspect is armed and possibly dangerous, that too should be included in the affidavit. In the absence of specific information about this particular drug dealer, general information and inferences drawn from the experience of the affiant and other drug investigators should be included.

In most jurisdictions, officers are authorized to ignore the knock and announce requirements where there exists a potential danger to the officers or a reasonable likelihood that evidence will be destroyed. Additionally, after the knock and announce requirements have been fulfilled, officers may ignore the reasonable delay requirement if they believe that their safety is jeopardized by waiting or that evidence will be destroyed. In other words, they may immediately make forcible entry after knocking and announcing.

During 1986 and 1987, the city of Denver experienced particular difficulty with Caribbean drug traffickers, over 50 search warrants targeting those dealers were executed. Collective experience indicated that these dealers and their methods of operation were especially violent and that they represented a special danger to law enforcement officers. Partly in response to the violent nature of these dealers, and partly due to the lack of personnel assigned to investigate them, teamwork was developed with the SWAT group, and they routinely did the tactical entries on the search warrants.

Weapons were encountered frequently, and there were many close calls, the only difference between someone getting killed and a clean entry was the dynamic, professional nature of the SWAT tactics. In many of these warrants, it was necessary to deploy tactical diversions, such as stun grenades, when the officers were compromised in one way or another.

In preparing these search warrants, authorization for immediate entry was routinely requested and granted. The method of entry was justified in the affidavit, specifically when specific information was not available and in general based on collective experience in dealing with this trafficking group when specific information was not available. The approach was tremendously successful; no officers were injured, suspects suffered only minor injuries, and drugs and cash and weapons were recovered. In addition, these cases were prosecuted with almost 100 percent success.

This is mentioned here to illustrate one point to be made with respect to immediate entry search warrants, and that is, significant distinctions exist between the state and federal systems. Some of these investigations focusing on Caribbean drug dealers were conducted jointly with federal agencies which were participating in the task force. In one such joint investigation, information was developed and an undercover operation was undertaken. Buys were made through an unwitting (a person unwittingly participating in or facilitating a police investigation) from a Caribbean dealer. State probable cause arrest warrants were drawn up for the unwitting, who was an American, and state search warrants for two apartments were written as well.

However, it was decided that a federal warrant would be written for the main target's residence, considered to be a stash house (location where drugs are stored). That was a reasonable decision in light of the task force approach to the investigation, which had worked well for the most part. A final operation was planned to include one more undercover buy and then the search warrants would be executed simultaneously. The federal search warrant was completed and signed by the magistrate after the last buy was made. The operation had been planned so that the Denver Police SWAT Unit would execute the search warrants, three of them simultaneously, including the federal search warrant at the home of the source. The warrants were executed in a manner consistent with the pattern which had been proven to be effective. At the home of the source, a flash-bang was deployed as a diversion, and then entry was made. The knock and announce requirement of 18 U.C.S. 3109 was ignored.

A substantial amount of evidence was recovered, and the suspect was indicted in the federal system. Defense motions to suppress the evidence based on the contention that the method of entry was unreasonable were denied by the trial court.

The Tenth Circuit Court of Appeals overruled the trial court and ruled that the method of entry was not in compliance with 18 U.S.C. 3109 inasmuch as "the circumstances surrounding the execution of the this warrant were not sufficiently exigent to justify the type of forcible entry employed by the Denver SWAT team."[33] The decision went on to say that,

---

33 *U.S. v. Stewart,* 867 F.2d 581, 584 (10th Cir. 1989).

"In this case, the method of entry used was not formulated in response to an emergency but instead was carefully planned without specific information well in advance of the time the warrant was obtained."[34] Furthermore, not only was an emergency lacking, but only general information supported the method of entry, not specific facts about the suspect or that address.

There was specific information about this subject, which would have sufficiently supported immediate entry on a state search warrant. The case could then have been filed in federal court, and the evidence may not, under those circumstances, have been suppressed.

Information, both specific and general, should be included in a search warrant affidavit to support the belief that evidence will be destroyed and officer safety may be compromised if the presence of the police and their purpose is known.

SPECIAL PROBLEMS AND CONSIDERATIONS

Anticipatory Search Warrants

"An anticipatory search warrant, by definition, is a warrant that has been issued before the necessary events have occurred which will allow a constitutional search of the premises; if those events do not transpire, the warrant is void."[35]

While the Supreme Court has never ruled on the constitutionality of anticipatory search warrants, it has indirectly approved the concept in wiretap cases.[36] Anticipatory search warrants have been given qualified approval by other courts, however. In general, the affidavit for such a search warrant should be written in such a way that factors on which probable cause is contingent are clear and that it is also clear that, without certain events happening to create the necessary factors, probable cause will not exist and the warrant will not be executed. Therefore, the judge is giving his approval, contingent upon the existence of future probable cause. If probable cause is not formed as anticipated, the warrant will not be executed.

Drug investigations present the ideal circumstances for this type of

---

34 Ibid., at 585.

35 *United States v. Garcia,* 882 F.2d 699 (2d Cir. 1989).

36 *Berger v. New York,* 388 U.S. 41 (1967).

warrant situation. In *Garcia*, the court put the question of anticipatory search warrants in this perspective.[37]

> The question thus posed by this case—and by any challenge to a warrant that is issued in anticipation of delivery of an item upon which the government relies to establish probable cause to search—is whether the objective of the fourth amendment is better served by allowing an agent to obtain a warrant in advance of the delivery, or whether it is better served by forcing him to go to the scene without a warrant...we believe that the purposes of the fourth amendment are best served by permitting government agents to obtain warrants in advance if they can show probable cause to believe that the contraband will be located on the premises at the time that search takes place. We therefore explicitly hold today what we assumed in *Segovia:* Anticipatory warrants are not unconstitutional per se, ...

The affiant must have reason to believe that the contraband or evidence sought in the warrant *will* be at the specified location at some time in the future, contingent on certain things happening.[38] There must be probable cause to believe that the items sought will be there, not just speculation based on investigative contingencies.[39]

> To guard against successful challenges to the validity of anticipatory warrants based on alleged loss of judicial control in their execution, officers should place reasonable limiting language in their warrant affidavits specifying that execution will not occur in the absence of a particular contingency, such as: (1) A scheduled time for delivery; (2) a given event; (3) police surveillance confirming that the package has been delivered; or (4) a particular method that allows executing officers to know that the items are in the place to be searched.

Search Prior to Warrant Arrival

In order to expedite matters, particularly where some exigency exists and it is feared that passing time is resulting in the loss of evidence, a warrant will occasionally be executed on the verbal authority of the affiant that it has been signed by the judge or magistrate. It will be executed prior to the warrant actually being present at the premises to be searched. "While it may be foolhardy to proceed in the absence of the physical presence of the warrant, it is not unconstitutional."[40] This decision elaborated that "law enforcement officials are not constitution-

---

37 *United States v. Garcia,* 882 F.2d 699, 703 (2d Cir. 1989).

38 Burkhoff, *Search Warrant Law Deskbook,* p. 4–12.

39 A. Louis Dipietro, "Anticipatory Search Warrants," *FBI Law Enforcement Bulletin,* July 1990, p. 31.

40 *United States v. Hepperle,* 810 F.2d 836, 839 (8th Cir. 1987).

ally required to present a copy of the search warrant prior to commencing a search, so long as the previously issued warrant is presented before the officers vacate the premises," and further, that "the conduct of searches, with a warrant 'to arrive later' should be discouraged."[41]

Generally this is done in cases where the officers may have been on surveillance for a lengthy period of time and feel the need to execute the warrant and commence the search without any further delay. If there is a valid reason for proceeding before the warrant arrives, then it must be done. In cases where the additional time is of no consequence, the arrival of the search warrant should be awaited before it is executed and the search undertaken.

Search Warrant for Persons

When search warrants have been obtained for premises and vehicles, it is quite common for persons, named and unnamed, to be included in the search warrant request. There are particular situations where it is quite important that the search warrant include all persons who are to be in the premises. In crack house search warrants, it is a common request that the search warrant include not only the premises but all persons who are inside and possibly around the perimeter as well. The common presence of lookouts who are associated with the dealing and who may be armed or who may be in possession of drugs necessitates this. A Colorado court of appeals recently upheld the validity of this practice. The case took place in Colorado Springs and involved a classic crack house situation. The traffic to and from the crack house had generated numerous complaints. People on the street were being approached by people soliciting crack business.

Informant information was detailed with respect to the roles of the various people in the business both inside and outside the house. Undercover officers had purchased drugs from some of the people who hung around the outside and served as lookouts. Informant information indicated that weapons were kept inside the house and that the house was also equipped with a police scanner. The house was well fortified. The police obtained a search warrant, and the warrant included "all persons found within or in the immediate vicinity of the residence." When the warrant was executed, there were no fewer than 15 people inside. The

---

41 Ibid.

contention of the defendant in this case was that "the search of his person was invalid because it was unsupported by probable cause."[42]

The trial court ruled that the warrant, and its extension to all people within and in the vicinity, was valid. The court of appeals recognized that " 'all persons' or 'any persons' warrants have been challenged with some frequency as being violative of this fourth amendment requirement" (particularly of place to be searched and things to be seized).[43]

The court went on to point out that a nexus must be shown between the persons for whom a search warrant is requested and the criminal activity. In the case of a crack house such as this, it would be necessary to show that there are no people there who are not involved. There is no legitimate purpose for being at this house. The only reasons people are there are to buy, sell, and use crack.[44]

> Here we agree with the trial court that the nexus necessary for a search of all persons within the house has been amply demonstrated. The residence here was a private place with tightly controlled access through only one heavily guarded door. The extensive drug sale activity occurring there consisted of a sophisticated and tightly organized network of authorized personnel working in concert. To say that anyone who had gained entrance to that fortress-like structure could have been merely a casual visitor would strain credulity beyond the breaking point.

Information regarding persons named in search warrants should be as detailed and specific as facts allow. In the case of crack houses and other similar situations, where there is often no legitimate activity being conducted on the premises, it is advisable to include all persons on or within the premises as subjects for which a warrant is requested. If the identity of the persons is known, the warrants should be specifically requested for those people as well as all other unknown persons. The justification for such warrants is the possible connection between anybody on the premises and the criminal activity. Generally, through controlled buys and other intelligence, descriptions of the parties involved are available. At the very least, those people should be described in the affidavit and search warrants sought for their persons.

Some judges are reluctant to sign a search warrant for persons whether they are named in the search warrant or just described. It is the feeling of

---

42 *People v. Johnson,* XIV Brief Times Reporter 1263, 1265 (Colo. App. 1990).

43 Ibid.

44 Ibid., at 1266.

these judges that probable cause arrest warrants should be obtained rather than search warrants, the basis of the probable cause for the arrest warrants being essentially the same as for the search warrants. Then when the search warrant for the premises is executed, the people for whom the arrest warrants have been obtained will be arrested and searched incident to arrest.

If people are encountered in a drug search warrant for whom neither arrest nor search warrants have been issued, they should be frisked for weapons and secured during the preliminary securing of the premises. If probable cause to arrest them develops based on what the search warrant reveals, they should then be arrested and searched incident to arrest.

It is best to have all the main subjects identified and have the search warrants include their persons or have probable cause arrest warrants prepared for those people.

Delays in Search Warrant Execution

It is common, particularly in street-level drug investigations, that after a search warrant has been obtained, circumstances are not right for it to be executed. Conditions upon which probable cause for search warrants has been based are subject to rapid change. Such changes can cause delays in the execution of warrants until such time as optimum conditions exist. As a general rule, elapsed time and evidence of ongoing drug dealing activity combine to define what would be an unreasonable delay in executing a narcotics search warrant. Preraid buys are commonly used to "freshen up" probable cause when there has been a significant delay in executing the warrant. If the delay in executing the search warrant is caused by efforts to time the execution of the warrant to coincide with the height of ongoing drug dealing activity, and if the warrant is not executed unless it has been determined that there is ongoing activity, the amount of delay will probably not be fatal to the search warrant. That is, of course, providing that the maximum time for warrant validity has not been exceeded.

SAMPLE SEARCH WARRANT AFFIDAVIT

This section of the chapter will be devoted to analyzing a sample search warrant affidavit. The affidavit critique (Figure 3-1) provides an affidavit in the left column, and the right column has comments about certain portions of the affidavit and the investigation as well as some of the arguments brought up in the suppression motions. This is an actual search warrant affidavit written and developed as the investigation progressed. Or as the Supreme Court stated, "drafted by nonlawyers in the midst and haste of a criminal investigation."[45]

The investigation spanned several months, although it was inactive during most of the time period between the initial informant information and the culmination of the investigation. The informant in the case was a long-time, reliable street-level informant. He had initiated several other pager cases at about this same period of time, but in none of those cases was it possible to get to the source location. Rather, those cases were concluded with the arrest of the dealer, the search of his vehicle and cases filed. To build probable cause in these types of cases, pager delivery cases, it is usually necessary to make several controlled buys and attempt to follow a delivery person to the source, unless of course a buy/bust situation is preferable.

There are some comments about the investigation which can be made in the interest of making the affidavit an example from which several lessons can be learned. Like most investigations, some mistakes were made. There were some errors in fact in the affidavit. The errors and mistakes were "good-faith errors," made in the course of trying to do the investigation correctly.

Investigators were very familiar with Charles and Donna Williams from previous investigations and intelligence information. During the surveillances, including those before and after controlled buys, detailed notes were made, and from those, surveillance reports were later written. Those surveillance reports were critical when it came time to writing the affidavit. In all those surveillances, where in the affidavit it appears as if there was no question as to the identity of Donna Williams, it was in fact the belief of investigators that Donna Williams was being followed. The surveillances done were for the most part at night, and visibility was therefore reduced. Also, the suspect was wary and her driving reflected that she was continually checking for the presence of surveillance.

On the night that the affidavit was completed and the warrants signed, the person thought to be Donna Williams had been followed for several

---

45 *Illinois v. Gates,* 462 U.S. 213, 235 (1983), quoting from *United States v. Ventresca,* 380 U.S. 102, 108 (1965).

FIGURE 3-1. SAMPLE AFFIDAVIT AND COMMENTS

Your affiant, Sgt. Paul Mahoney has been a police officer for the past eighteen years and is currently assigned to the Vice/Drug Control Bureau as a supervisor in the Denver/ Aurora Crack Task Force. Your affiant has been conducting and supervising narcotics investigations for the past six years. Your affiant has personally been involved in the planning, investigation and development of approximately five hundred narcotics investigations. A large number of these have resulted in the execution of search warrants. Through this experience, your affiant has developed a certain expertise with respect to the manner in which drug transactions, particularly those involving cocaine base (crack) and cocaine, are conducted.

Affiant Introduction. The experience of the affiant is relied upon throughout the affidavit. Interpretations of facts are made based on that experience.

During the month of April 1989, your affiant and Det. James Nash were contacted by a previously reliable confidential informant. This informant has been reliable to Det. Nash and your affiant on at least three occasions in the last six months, resulting in the execution of search warrants, the recovery of cocaine, crack (cocaine base), and guns. At least one of these cases is still pending in the court system. This informant has never provided information which was later proven to be untrue. This informant is familiar with the packaging and appearance of cocaine and crack cocaine from previous association as a user.

The previous reliability of the informant is established within a given time frame, three times in the last six months. Occasions of reliability actually far exceeded three in that period. The informant knows what cocaine and crack look like and how they are sold: he has bought them in the past. Credibility is established and the basis of knowledge is about to be set.

FIGURE 3-1. (Continued)

In the interest of clarity, this informant will be known as informant #1 in
this affidavit. In April 1989, this informant related to Det. Nash and
your affiant that he/she knew of a 40
year-old white female known to the
informant as "Jackie" and a 30 to
40 year-old black male known to the
informant as "C" or Charles who
were engaged in the sale of cocaine
through the use of a pager.

The facts of the investigation are
introduced as they were presented
to the affiant by the informant. This
begins the chronological presentation of the investigative facts and
details the informant's basis of knowledge as well.

This informant stated that he/she had
been present on several occasions
when "Jackie" and "C" delivered cocaine in response to a pager call.
The informant further stated that
these two had another younger black
male, known as "Rob", working for
them as a runner (delivery man).
The informant related that customers
would call the pager, leave their number and when called back, would
place their order.

The informant further related that
if the customer was unknown to the
dealers, they would not do business
with him or her. The informant went
on to say that these people were
known to drive a tan or brown Cadillac, a red and white Cadillac, a gray
Lincoln, and an older pick-up truck.

His information is presented in light
of that basis of knowledge. He has
seen these people deal cocaine, he has
firsthand knowledge of their pager
number, the cars they drive and what
they look like.

Nothing further was done with this
investigation until September 6, 1989
at which time the informant again
contacted your affiant. At that time,
the informant stated that "Jackie" and
"C" were continuing to deal cocaine

FIGURE 3-1. (Continued)

from a pager and that the pager number was 855-6736. The informant also provided a license number which the informant stated belonged to "Jackie" and "C". That number, AWJ-205, listed to Donna Williams, 2101 E. Colfax, Denver, Colorado on a 1982 Cadillac through Colorado Division of Motor Vehicles. The informant stated that the license number was obtained by the informant while the vehicle was parked at Pierre's Supper Club at 22nd and Downing. Your affiant checked Vice/Drug Control files and found intelligence information that Donna Williams was arrested on 2-18-86 at 2434 Franklin St. after undercover officers ordered $650.00 worth of cocaine and Donna Williams delivered it. Your affiant was present during that incident and personally involved in the arrest of Donna Williams. She was charged with Possession of a Controlled Substance. There is also an intelligence entry dated 2-19-86 that Donna Williams and her husband Charles were engaged in the sale of cocaine by pager 869-3597. A similar entry is on the card of Charles Williams. Your affiant pulled the DPD records of both of these people, Donna Williams, DPD #369924, and Charles Williams, DPD #279463. Photographs of these people were shown to the informant who positively identified Donna Williams as "Jackie" and Charles Williams as "C" or "Charles", about whom,

The information provided by the informant is corroborated through traditional investigative means.

Defense alleged at suppression hearing that affiant had lied in previous arrest and the case thrown out because of that. And that this case resulted from a grudge held by the affiant. That the affiant had lied or been accused of lying was disproved and defense counsel retracted the allegation, on the record, at the direction of the judge.

The informant positively identified both of these photographs. Jackie, whom the informant had dealt with the most, was most familiar to the

FIGURE 3-1. (Continued)

the informant had provided information previously to your affiant.

Your affiant checked the address of 2101 E. Colfax, the address where the 1982 Cadillac lists, and found that it is a cash express/Western Union outlet. In checking drivers license status on Donna Williams and Charles Williams, your affiant found that 2101 E. Colfax #45 is listed as the home address of both people.

informant and his identification of the photograph of Donna Williams was certain. However, following the execution of the warrants the informant identified a photograph of Drew Barker as Jackie and recanted his previous identification. This particular informant had a history of being excellent when it came to physical descriptions and identifications.

It is your affiant's experience that drug traffickers commonly conceal their place of residence in an effort to avoid detection by law enforcement. In checking contact cards, your affiant determined that Charles Williams has been contacted in AWW-769, which lists to him at 2101 E. Colfax on a 1984 Cadillac Fleetwood and in AZK-231 which lists to Drew Barker at 1021 E. 9th Ave. on a 1984 Lincoln Town Car, silver or gray in color. On 1-17-89, Williams was stopped in AZK-231 in front of 1425 Xenia, a known crack nuisance apartment complex. This vehicle information corroborated informant information as to the cars that "C" and "Jackie" were known to drive, two Cadillacs and a Lincoln.

Affiant's experience is relied upon here.

This was an error in the affidavit. Charles Williams had been stopped in the 3100 block of Pontiac on this date in this vehicle. He had been stopped in front of 1425 Xenia on another occasion in another vehicle.

Within the seventy-two hour time period spanning the dates of 9-12-89 to 9-15-89, your affiant conducted a controlled buy utilizing a first time confidential informant. This informant will be referred to as informant #2

The controlled buy made here by a first-time informant is described within a time window. Where it took place, exactly when it took place and how much was purchased would tend to identify the informant and in the interest of confidentiality that information is omitted.

FIGURE 3-1. (Continued)

and is familiar with the packaging and appearance of cocaine from past association as a user.

After determining that this informant had no currency or contraband, the informant was given Crack Task Force funds not to exceed $350.00 The informant then called 855-6736. A short time later, the party known to the informant as "Jackie" arrived in AZK-231 and delivered the amount of cocaine which had been ordered. This cocaine was placed in the Property Bureau with a request for analysis, number 390010. The analysis revealed the substance to be positive for cocaine HCl. This informant identified the female delivering as Donna Williams, from DPD photograph #369924.

This informant identified the photograph of Donna Williams as being Jackie, thus corroborating the first informant's positive identification.

Surveillance had been established at the delivery location within the City and County of Denver and after the transaction with informant #2, AZK-231 was followed for a lengthy period of time and it eventually parked at 3010 S. California Blvd. This plate, AZK-231, is the vehicle in which Charles Williams was contacted on 1-17-89.

Surveillance is used to corroborate some facts learned through other investigative means and through informant information.

Your affiant and Sgt. Castricone did periodic surveillance on 3010 S. California Blvd. during the dates of 9-12-89 and 9-13-89. During this surveillance, your affiant observed Donna Williams in the front room of 3010 S. California Blvd. Your affiant also observed AWJ-205, the Cadillac which

This identification of Donna Williams was positive as was that identification made by Det. Nash on 9-13-89.

FIGURE 3-1. (Continued)

lists to Donna Williams, parked in the driveway at 3010 S. California Blvd.

It was daylight when these identifications were made whereas the other surveillances were done at night.

On 9-13-89, Det. Nash did surveillance on the location of 3010 S. California Blvd. and observed Donna Williams on the front porch with what appeared to be a watering can for flowers. Det. Nash is familiar with Donna Williams from previous contacts and other investigations.

Between the dates 9-11-89 and 9-13-89, your affiant made a controlled buy from Donna Williams utilizing informant #1. Informant #1 was given Crack Task Force funds not to exceed $350.00 after it was determined that the informant had no currency or contraband on his/her person. The informant called 855-6736 and ordered a specific amount of cocaine when the call was returned. Surveillance was established and Donna Williams was observed delivering the cocaine to the informant. Donna Williams was driving AZK-231, the previously described 1984 Lincoln Town Car which lists to Drew Barker, 1021 E. 9th #165.

This controlled buy was made and the informant again positively identified Jackie as Donna Williams. At this point in the investigation Drew Barker had not been identified, there was no photo available. In fact, it was not yet determined that Drew Barker was a real person and not an alias for Donna Williams.

The disposition of the substance purchased and results of the analysis should have been included in the affidavit.

On 9-13-89, surveillance was established at 3010 S. California Blvd. At the time surveillance was established, AWJ-205 was parked in the driveway at 3010 S. California Blvd. That vehicle left that location at 8:45 PM and was observed at 9:45 PM parked in front of 560 S. Holly which is a small

This entire surveillance involving Donna Williams was challenged in the hearing on the motions to suppress. The defense maintained that while the surveillance provided arguably good probable cause, the actions were not those of Donna Williams but of Drew Barker. As such,

FIGURE 3-1. (Continued)

shopping center containing five or six stores. At that time, Donna Williams was observed parking the Lincoln Town Car AZK-231 next to the Cadillac, AWJ-205, and entering one of the shops in the shopping center. Surveillance was maintained.

they should be discounted as probable cause for Donna Williams, her car, or her residence.

At approximately 9:55 PM, Donna Williams was observed driving AZK-231 to the location of Mississippi and Monaco where she met with a male party who exited AUG-143, (Colorado passenger plate), the meeting was short, approximately two minutes. Donna Williams then drove southbound on Monaco and the male party whom she met, got into AUG-143 as a passenger and the vehicle drove northbound on Monaco.

This was, without any doubt, a drug transaction and that point is made later in the affidavit.

During this surveillance, Donna Williams appeared to be checking for surveillance, stopping suddenly, making U-turns, parking for brief interludes, turning her lights out for brief periods of time, etc. She was then followed south on Monaco to Cherry Creek Drive and west on Cherry Creek Drive to Holly where she drove north and parked in the 700 Block S. Holly with her lights on. She had the dome light on and appeared to be scrutinizing something in her hands. At approximately 10:15 PM, Donna Williams drove back to the shopping center at 560 S. Holly and parked next to AWJ-205, the vehicle which lists to her. They were the only two vehicles parked in the lot in front

The surveillance officers were positive that the person being followed was Donna Williams. The fact that the car did not list to her was relatively meaningless as drug dealers often have their own cars registered under another name.

FIGURE 3-1. (Continued)

of the shopping center. At approximately 10:40 PM, Donna Williams got back into AZK-231, left the shopping center and returned at approximately 10:50 PM. Again she parked next to the Cadillac, AWJ-205, which lists to her, and entered one of the shops.

At approximately 11:15 PM, Donna Williams got back into AZK-231 and was followed to the Vickers station at Tennessee and Monaco where Det. Dale Wallis observed her look at a pager in her hands as she walked to a pay phone against the wall on the south side of the Vickers station.

Donna Williams was then followed to the intersection of Tennessee and Oneida where she met a male in 6071-AK (Colorado truck plate) for approximately a minute. Donna Williams then drove south on Monaco to Yale and west on Yale and eventually parked in front of 3010 S. California Blvd. and went inside at approximately 11:55 PM. The Cadillac, AWJ-205, was parked in front of 3010 S. California Blvd. when Donna Williams arrived. It had been parked at the shopping center at 11:15 PM when Donna Williams left and was followed eventually to 3010 S. California Blvd.

A very short time later Donna Williams left 3010 S. California Blvd. and was followed to the area of Colfax and Cook where she met with a male

Defense counsel, moving to suppress the evidence, claimed "a reckless disregard for the truth by the officer affiant," in attributing the actions of Drew Barker or an unknown person to Donna Williams. Drew Barker was dead by the time these hearings and the trial were held and the defense attempted to show that Drew Barker was the drug dealer, that Donna Williams had never been observed by the surveillance officers and that the cocaine and cash recovered from Charles and Donna Williams's bedroom belonged to Drew Barker. Further, they asserted that neither Charles or Donna Williams knew that the cocaine and cash were present in their bedroom.

This would seem like an implausible defense were it not for the fact that Drew Barker, not Donna Williams had been arrested in the gray Lincoln on the night that the warrants were executed. Also, Drew Barker was now dead so they raised the question, did the affiant or the officers *ever* observe Donna Williams in any of the actions attributed to her?

The ultimate question to the jury was, had the affiant been mistaken or perhaps lied? Were Donna and Charles Williams guilty of anything?

FIGURE 3-1. (Continued)

party in the middle of the block after driving around the block once or twice. Donna Williams drove from that location, east on 17th Ave. to Colorado Blvd. and then northbound. Surveillance was discontinued at approximately 29th and Colorado Blvd. at 12:25 AM on 9-14-89.

Based on your affiant's experience, the activity of Donna Williams while under surveillance on 9-13-89/9-14-89 is consistent with that of a person doing drug transactions by way of a pager. Several brief meetings in a short period of time, erratic and unusual driving behavior, and checking for surveillance are all consistent with drug dealing, specifically drug dealing from pager calls.

Your affiant has been in the Vice/ Drug Control Bureau for the past six years. Dealing by pager has become more prevalent in the past three years. Particularly since the crackdown on crack houses.

Drug dealers, confidential sources and concerned citizens and law enforcement officers have all informed your affiant that dealers use pagers in order to make more difficult targets for search warrants and generally make detection of their criminal activity more difficult. These dealers commonly deal only with customers with whom they are well acquainted.

Another reason for the trend toward pager use in drug dealing is that if

What the defense could not overcome were the large amounts of cocaine and cash recovered from the Williams's bedroom.

Throughout the investigation, the residence at 3010 S. California Blvd. was tied in, supporting the claim of the affiant, based on his experience, that it was the stash house. The experience of the affiant is relied upon to interpret the actions of Donna Williams: those of a cautious drug dealer.

This information is specifically included in the affidavit to extend probable cause to the residence. Keep in mind, nobody had been in that residence, nobody had seen drugs in that location. The probable cause for 3010 S. California Blvd. was constructed through surveillance, the actions of Donna Williams and the interpretations of those actions based upon the affiant's experience.

FIGURE 3-1. (Continued)

apprehended, the dealer will not be caught in the "stash house" for all drugs and currency, carrying only what is a minimum for deliveries and "re-upping" or resupplying frequently. Potential losses in product and currency are thus minimized.

On 9-14-89, your affiant took informant #1 past 3010 S. California Blvd. where the Cadillac was parked in the driveway. The informant identified this vehicle, relating to your affiant that he/she had observed "C" as a passenger in this vehicle.

Based on the facts detailed previously, your affiant requests that a search warrant be issued for: (1) 3010 S. California Blvd.; (2) AZK-231, a 1984 Gray/Silver Lincoln used for deliveries of cocaine; (3) AWJ-205, a 1982 Cadillac four-door owned by Donna Williams; and (4) the person of Donna Williams, DPD #369924.

Your affiant further requests that the warrant for the residence at 3010 S. California Blvd. be immediate entry nature in order to ensure the safety of the officers executing the warrant and to prevent the destruction of evidence. Your affiant checked gun registration information on the Denver Police Department computer and found that Charles Williams purchased a .25 caliber, Titan, semiautomatic pistol on July 10, 1988. Further, aside from this specific information, your affiant has learned,

The warrant for Drew Barker's vehicle, AZK-231, was executed at 1:40 AM following a lengthy surveillance. Drew Barker, not Donna Williams, was driving it. Drew Barker was a female, approximately 10 years older than Donna Williams, not nearly as heavy and with a different hairstyle. Cocaine and cash were recovered from her car and she was arrested.

The warrant for 3010 S. California Blvd. was then executed at 2:30 AM. The defense counsel later argued that the affiant had sworn to the facts in the affidavit when it was obvious that he had lied. He had never seen Donna Williams, he had seen Drew Barker. He then, the defense claimed, knowing of the falseness of the affidavit, particularly that portion pertaining to the residence of Donna Williams, went ahead and executed the warrant anyway. This, the defense argued, amounted to a blatant disregard for the system, as the affiant knew there was no probable cause for the residence of Donna and Charles Williams because it had not been Donna Williams performing the ac-

---

FIGURE 3-1. (Continued)

through experience, that it is common for drug dealers to keep guns in their residences and on their persons for protection against other drug dealers, drug users and law enforcement officers.

tions attributed to her in the affidavit.

It was ruled that probable cause had been established for 3010 S. California Blvd. whether or not Drew Barker was the person known as Jackie, rather than Donna Williams.

---

hours continuously. Several apparent drug transactions took place, and the determination was made that the time was right to finish the warrants and get them signed.

Immediately after the warrants were signed, Drew Barker was stopped in the Lincoln Town Car, AZK-231, in the parking lot of what turned out to be her apartment complex. At the time she was stopped, it was believed that Donna Williams was driving the vehicle, Investigators were surprised that it was not, and the possibility of not executing the search warrant at 3010 S. California Blvd., the home of Charles and Donna Williams, was discussed. It was decided, after Drew Barker was arrested and cocaine was recovered, that the facts related to probable cause for the warrant at 3010 S. California Blvd. had not been diminished by the fact that Drew Barker, not Donna Williams, was driving the Lincoln, when it had been certain throughout the investigation that Donna Williams had been the subject of the lengthy surveillances through which probable cause was developed. At the time that Drew Barker was arrested, it was still believed that this was an isolated case, that Donna Williams had been driving on the other occasions.

That being the case, the search warrants at 3010 S. California Blvd., were executed within an hour after Drew Barker had been arrested. Entry was achieved without force in a low-profile manner, due to the time of day (approximately 2:30 A.M.). Charles and Donna Williams were both present in the house as were their daughter and Donna Williams's mother.

Approximately 2 pounds of cocaine, $46,000.00, and three guns, two of which had been reported stolen, were recovered. The defendants secured the services of a competent attorney to represent them. A very short time after the arrests took place, Drew Barker died of an apparent heart attack. It was never determined with certainty, but it was believed that she was a relative of Donna Williams, possibly a sister. Defense counsel prepared a motion to suppress, based primarily on the contention that Donna Williams had not been observed in any of the surveillances, and that it had been Drew Barker whom had been followed by narcotics investigators who then attributed her actions to Donna Williams in an effort to build probable cause for the Williamses' residence.

The fact that both informants in the case had initially identified Donna Williams as "Jackie" and that following the arrest of Drew Barker, informant #1 identified Drew Barker as "Jackie" and recanted his previous identification of Donna Williams was a key issue. Defense argued in the motion to suppress that probable cause, on which the search warrant for 3010 S. California Blvd. had been based, was vitiated by the arrest of Drew Barker. Furthermore, the decision to execute the search warrant at that location amounted to reckless disregard for the truth by the affiant.

In the suppression hearing, the defense attorney brought up the 1986 arrest of Donna Williams and asserted that the affiant in this case had lied in that case and consequently that case had been dismissed. This was totally false. The judge recessed the proceedings while this claim was checked for accuracy. There had never been any accusation that the affiant in this case had lied in that or any other case. There had been, as it turned out, a suggestion made that one of the other officers in that previous case had not been completely truthful, but it was never substantiated; it was not the officer who was the affiant in this case; and that case had not been dismissed on that account. The defense attorney apologized to the affiant before the proceeding continued. The defense argument continued that the affiant had recklessly disregarded the truth in this affidavit and falsely developed probable cause which implicated Donna Williams because the previous case had produced negative results.

The suppression hearing lasted several hours. In the end, the judge ruled that the errors in the affidavit were good-faith errors, and did not suppress the evidence. By the time the trial was held, the defense had been constructed that all the cocaine, cash, and guns found in the Williamses' home belonged to Drew Barker, who was deceased. The jury, after hours of deliberation, convicted both Charles and Donna Williams, and they were sentenced to six years in prison.

This case is an excellent example of the complexity of street-level drug investigations and the search warrant affidavits which commonly result from these investigations. This affidavit was constructed on good faith that Donna Williams was responsible for a large-scale, street-level drug dealing operation. When it was written in the affidavit that Donna Williams was seen driving a certain vehicle and that Donna Williams was seen at 3010 S. California Blvd., officers believed that it was her doing everything attributed to her. The fact that it may not have been Donna Williams being followed on those occasions was not even considered when the affidavit was being written. That possibility did not present itself until Drew Barker was arrested.

Informant #1 had always been reliable and had proven himself to be particularly adept at descriptions of subjects and photo identifications. When he and the second informant identified Donna Williams as Jackie, that left little room for doubt in the investigators' minds that she was the suspect. Also, the Lincoln, AZK-231, had been followed to Charles and Donna Williamses' house before and after deliveries had been made. A public utilities listing had been obtained, which indicated that Charles Williams had the public utilities in his name at 3010 S. California Blvd. It was through an oversight that this information was omitted from the affidavit.

The ruling that the errors were "good-faith" errors, and as such exceptions to the exclusionary rule, was the right decision. No information known to be false was included in the affidavit. Finally, the results of the search warrant bear out the accuracy of the investigation: Donna and Charles Williams were responsible for a significant amount of street-level cocaine dealing.

LOGISTICAL CONSIDERATIONS:

Use of the Search Warrant on a Large Scale

There are a number of factors involved in determining what the role of the search warrant will be in the enforcement strategy of a drug unit. Drug investigations will necessarily involve a large amount of search warrants. However, the search warrant can also be used as a primary enforcement technique for certain drug problems. The search warrant can be the primary weapon, in a manner of speaking. This portion of the chapter will deal with that concept; using the search warrant on a large scale as the primary enforcement technique for street-level drug problems.

Timeliness

The idea of using the search warrant as a primary investigative technique in drug investigations may appear at first glance to be totally impractical. Given the amount of work involved in preparing a search warrant and the time factor involved, the search warrant is often discounted as an unwieldy tool against what is an extremely transitory enterprise. It is also assumed that a lesser quality of case results through the use of a search warrant than through undercover investigations, in which the search warrant is utilized only in a secondary role if at all.

The drug problem of each given community has to be defined within the context of the needs of the community and the ability of the police department to address the problem. Denver, for example, in 1987 was faced with an emerging crack problem which threatened to take over whole neighborhoods in a certain part of the city. A task force approach was adopted, and the decision was made to assign four full-time investigators to the problem as well as two investigators from the other city cooperating in the task force.

The undercover approach was explored as possibly the most effective manner in which the problem could be impacted. The problem had manifested itself in the form of crack houses multiplying in numbers at an alarming rate. The dealers were careful about dealing only to people they knew for the most part. Each undercover operation required at least one introduction and then subsequent buys to make a prosecutable case in which the informant had no participation. This true to form with most street-level investigations. However, the time involved in putting these investigations together was extensive. Each buy was manpower intensive, and although good cases were being made, some of the effect was lost if arrests weren't soon made because the dealers would move on, often before they had been completely identified. Meanwhile the problem was growing out of control.

A great deal of information was forthcoming, and it was impossible, due to the limited manpower, to try and make undercover buys in each location. In addition, undercover officers were at a premium. In order to keep the buy program going, it was necessary to have to have people assigned on a temporary basis, and this created problems as well. By default, actually, a game plan was developed which involved using search warrants based on informant information and controlled buys as the primary technique. Controlled buys do not, of course, require the manpower that undercover buys do. It was possible then to have each team of detectives setting up search warrants simultaneously and then executing them in the natural order that they became ready.

Obviously, to use the search warrant effectively against a street level problem such as this, it was necessary to have help with the tactical part of the operations. The SWAT unit was available 16 hours a day, and its members were, by virtue of a great deal of experience in the previous year or two, highly skilled. The investigators, who were also highly skilled and experienced, were preparing warrants quickly and would proceed with two or three investigations simultaneously. When it was determined that the time was right, the warrants were executed in a manner consistent with tactical considerations. As soon as entry was made, the investigative team would do the search, process prisoners, and move onto the next one. The tactical manner in which the warrants were executed had several desirable side effects, the foremost of which were officer safety and maximum personnel efficiency.

This special approach was applied intensively to this aspect of the drug problem in isolation from the rest of the problem. Search warrants were executed in unprecedented numbers, operating on the theory that if probable cause was there, the crack unit would be there too. In the time period between October 1987 and January 1991, 851 search warrants were executed. Narcotic evidence was obtained in 78 percent of those, non-narcotic evidence was recovered in 17 percent, and in only 5 percent were no recoveries made. To be effective, the investigations, the search warrants, and the resulting criminal cases had to be produced in assembly-line quantities.

This amount of work, performed by a small number of officers, demanded that those preparing the warrants be capable of writing affidavits which were technically correct and able to withstand close courtroom scrutiny. The problem has been significantly diminished in size and scope, and the number of complaints reduced. Certain neighborhoods, which had once fallen into the hands of crack dealers, have been reclaimed, largely through a concentrated enforcement effort relying on the search warrant as the principal enforcement technique.

In the case of street corner dealing, open market style, the search warrant will obviously not be effective as the primary technique but will be used frequently in support of other enforcement efforts.

Case Quality

It is possible to achieve a high quality of cases using the search warrant extensively to control low-level drug dealing problems. Prosecutors have a preference for cases involving undercover buys and investigations due to the fact that in those cases there is an officer/witness who can give direct testimony to the fact that the defendant is a drug dealer. Search warrant cases can result in quality prosecutions for possession and possession for sale, but these cases can be more difficult to prosecute and have a higher built-in potential that evidence will be suppressed. The quality of these cases is defined by the correctness of the warrant. The affidavit discussed at length earlier is a very real example of how intricate details of an investigation can create fatal or near-fatal flaws in a search warrant affidavit. With no undercover buys or investigation, the entire case hinges on the evidence gained from the search warrant.

Cost-Effectiveness

Search warrants can be a cost-effective enforcement technique. Compared to long-term undercover investigations, involving several buys of significant quantities, a search warrant case can be assembled inexpensively. Excluding personnel, most times the only expenses involved are the informant payment and controlled buys.

Regardless, search warrants are a very important facet of drug investigations, whether used as a primary tool for street-level enforcement or used as the need arises in conjunction with an investigation.

DRUG INVESTIGATION

PROBABLE CAUSE DEVELOPMENT AND ARTICULATION

I N T R O	Introductory paragraph should adequately express affiant's training and experience to establish the basis for any inferences to be drawn from that experience. Introduction should be concise.	CRITICAL ELEMENTS THROUGHOUT: Concise presentation. Freshness of information. Corroboration. Suspect identification. Informant credibility and basis of knowledge.

I N V F A C T S	The facts of the case should be presented in such a way that case initiation is clear. The affidavit should then continue, in chronological order or some other logical order applicable to the particular investigation. The presentation should be such that the development of probable cause is clear. INFORMATION SOURCES PRESUMED CREDIBLE: fellow officers, named citizens, documents.

CONFIDENTIAL INFORMANTS

PREVIOUSLY RELIABLE: 1) Establish credibility in the affidavit by detailing occasions of previous reliability; 2) Establish informant's basis of knowledge.

FIRST-TIME INFORMANT: 1) Establish credibility of informant information through detailed corroboration; 2) Establish informant's basis of knowledge.

CORROBORATION OF CI INFORMATION

CONTROLLED BUYS: Commonly used as a means of verifying, or corroborating CI information. This is particularly true in the case of first-time informants.

SURVEILLANCE: Essential to a proper investigation in most cases. Will enhance the investigation and will provide tactical intelligence as well.

INVESTIGATION/UNDERCOVER BUYS: Informant information is corroborated through traditional investigative tactics, such as motor vehicle listings, police department record checks, etc. Undercover buys serve a similar purpose to the controlled buy with more value due to the weight of credibility attributed to police officers.

CITIZEN COMPLAINTS AND OTHER SOURCES.

PROBABLE CAUSE: Probability that evidence sought is at the suspected location (person, place, vehicle) PRESENTLY.

FIGURE 3-2

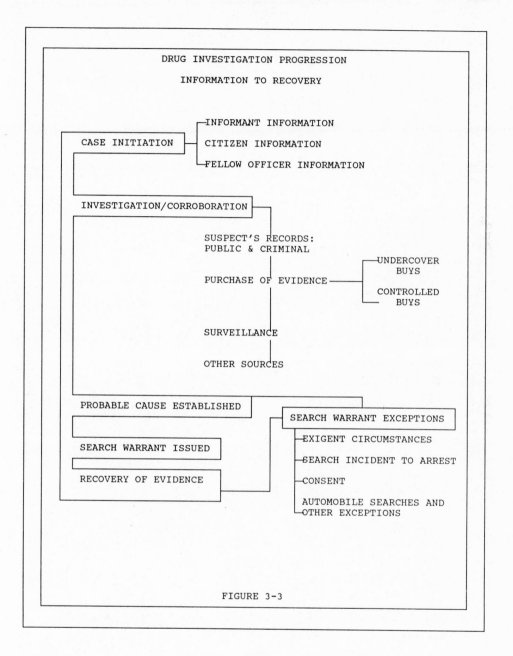

DRUG INVESTIGATION PROGRESSION

INFORMATION TO RECOVERY

CASE INITIATION
— INFORMANT INFORMATION
— CITIZEN INFORMATION
— FELLOW OFFICER INFORMATION

INVESTIGATION/CORROBORATION

SUSPECT'S RECORDS:
PUBLIC & CRIMINAL

PURCHASE OF EVIDENCE — UNDERCOVER BUYS
— CONTROLLED BUYS

SURVEILLANCE

OTHER SOURCES

PROBABLE CAUSE ESTABLISHED

SEARCH WARRANT EXCEPTIONS
— EXIGENT CIRCUMSTANCES
— SEARCH INCIDENT TO ARREST
— CONSENT
— AUTOMOBILE SEARCHES AND OTHER EXCEPTIONS

SEARCH WARRANT ISSUED

RECOVERY OF EVIDENCE

FIGURE 3-3

4

RAID PLANNING
AND EXECUTION

INTRODUCTION

Successful search warrant operations require a significant amount of tactical and investigative planning. Search warrant raids range from the simple or the routine operation to complex operations in which the search warrant is timed and coordinated with other phases of the investigation. While there are other aspects of narcotics investigation as potentially dangerous, there is no operation of such a traumatic nature as the search warrant raid.

Raiding someone's private domain for the purpose of executing a search warrant is implicitly risky. It is an act of calculated, controlled violence, philosophically extreme in the context of a free society. Because of this, it holds considerable potential for disaster; potential danger, potential civil liability, and potential investigative failure. It is essential that search warrant operations be investigatively sound. The investigative success and the tactical success are mutually interdependent. A poor investigation can jeopardize the tactical success of the raid. Likewise, a poorly conducted raid in which evidence is lost can result in wasted investigative effort.

Any search warrant operation, regardless of how simple, requires a good investigation, starting with an affidavit that is legally and technically correct and continuing with investigation and planning aimed at ensuring the tactical success of the raid.

This chapter will deal with search warrant operations: planning, and execution. It will discuss such operations from the earliest investigative planning, through the actual raid, the search, and gathering of evidence, to the after-action reporting.

INITIAL PLANNING

The initial planning for a search warrant raid begins at the earliest stages of an investigation. In narcotics investigations, intelligence gained from informants and other sources is gained with a dual purpose. The investigation is put together and probable cause is developed while raid planning intelligence is gathered and organized. Where search warrants are such a standard part of an investigation, this has to be the case. Raid planning is an ongoing process, beginning at the onset of an investigation and continuing through the execution of the warrant.

Intelligence information pertaining to search warrant operations should be separated into three general categories: that pertaining to the suspect, that pertaining to the target location, and that pertaining to external influences.

PRERAID INTELLIGENCE GATHERING

The goal of preraid intelligence gathering is to accumulate as much information as possible about the suspect, the target location, and any external influences which may exist. Accomplished to the optimum extent, a complete picture of the suspect, the target location, and factors influencing both suspect and target is possible. In doing so, the relative safety of the officers, citizens, and suspects can be maximized, and the success of the investigation and search warrant operations enhanced.

It should be understood that the discussion to follow is based on best case scenario possibilities. It is not possible to accomplish all the raid planning goals in every case, nor is it necessary. The degree of planning necessary is somewhat related to the complexity of the investigation. However, in simple cases, just as in complex cases, success and safety are directly proportional to the amount of planning involved. No search warrant operation is simple in the true sense of that word, and to take an operation lightly is to invite disaster. At the same time, too much planning, to the extent that timing is distorted and chances of success are thus compromised, can be self-defeating. It is always possible to do more planning; it is always possible to find reasons to postpone an operation based on tactical considerations. Successful search warrant operational planning balances the tactical and planning needs with the investigative needs: execution of the warrant in a timely fashion so that evidence is recovered and the suspects prosecuted.

Suspect

Intelligence about the suspect should be assembled to form a composite picture with as much detail as possible. The first step in accomplishing this involves identifying the suspect. There are many occasions where a search warrant is executed and suspect is not identified beforehand. It is understood that it will not always be possible to identify the suspect with any degree of completeness. This is particularly true in street-level investigations.

When a person becomes a suspect in a search warrant investigation, there should be an attempt to identify him through every possible means. Criminal history information will be particularly important in making tactical decisions concerning a search v ar ant operation. In a criminal history workup, particular attention must be given to indicat. 's of violence—weapons violations, arrests for assault, robbery, sexual assault, homicide, domestic violence, and resistance to arrest.

In developing the picture of the suspect's propensity toward violence, specific inquiries of the informant about the presence of weapons should be made. Too often, weapons information is generic. If the informant states that the suspect has a gun, an effort should be made to get the numbers and types of guns and other weapons specifically identified. It is a good idea to have a weapons identification chart available to show informants and other witnesses, police officers included. There are any number of weapons which are commonly referred to as machine guns. Many are not, however, machine guns in terms of firepower or functional capability. An example of this generic characterization of weapons involves street gang drug dealers. Informants will commonly report to the officers that suspects have an "Uzi," when in fact the suspects are in possession of a weapon far different from the Uzi in terms of capability, function, and reliability. Specific information about types of weapons is a very important tactical consideration. For the plan to be appropriately responsive, the intelligence information upon which plans are based must be accurate. Many times, generic weapon information can be developed into specific information through appropriate questioning of the informant and other witnesses and a thorough background investigation of the suspect.

Gun registration information, including weapons recently purchased over the counter, is quite commonly available. Other information about the suspect can also reflect on the possibility that the suspect has weapons. For instance, does the suspect/dealer trade his product for stolen goods. If that is the case, it is a good possibility that some of the stolen goods taken in exchange for drugs are weapons.

Associates of the suspect should be identified, whenever possible, in an effort to obtain a more comprehensive picture of the suspect. If the suspect is a known associate of stickups and burglars, this is some indication that the suspect too might be prone to hard-core criminal activity, that he might be prone to violence, and that he might be in possession of weapons.

Detailed information regarding the suspect's dealing habits should be developed. The suspect that deals on the street level to hundreds of people per month represents a different tactical situation from that of a larger-scale dealer who deals only in larger quantities to select people. The street-level dealer is not necessarily more dangerous, but the amount of traffic alone will contribute to different tactical considerations.

A determination of who lives with the suspect is important. Is he married? Does he have children? Do other people live with him? and so on. Any other personal characteristics which contribute to a suspect's composite should be noted.

Any information regarding the military background of the suspect can also be very important. There are some militant factions involved in drug dealing, the leaders of which have had the benefit of extensive training in military tactics and special weapons. In addition, there are some individuals, not necessarily allied with any militant group, who by virtue of their previous military training may pose a real or potential threat, beyond that which one without their military training or experience may represent.

Any special language characteristics about the suspect also represent valuable tactical intelligence. The suspect who does not speak English must be planned for differently to some extent from those who do.

This detailed composite will not be compiled passively. The investigator must take steps to learn all that is possible about a suspect. This is, of course, true in all investigations, but particularly true in search warrant investigations. While this information is important in an affidavit and the development of probable cause, it is likewise very important background data for tactical planning.

While the suspect profile will never be complete, there will always be more to learn, the investigator must strive for a degree of completeness which allows a picture of what the suspect is, even if he has not been identified. Corroboration of information is important from a tactical sense as it is in building probable cause. A suspect's reputation often exceeds his actual potential; potential as a dealer, potential as a crook, and potential as a man of violence. Informant information must not be taken at face value if it can be verified Informant information with respect to suspect identification and characteristics needs to be corroborated.

Target Location

Target identification begins with the most basic information and develops from there. There are some occasions when the informant knows the location and is capable of buying there, but does not know the address or apartment number. Drug dealers are known to take the address off a building or change the address in an effort to confuse and distract law enforcement people. Make certain of the target location early in the investigation through informant identification and surveillance. Again, given enough time, a thorough target identification is not a tricky proposition, but when putting a warrant together hastily, so that evidence will be recovered before the situation changes, time is a precious commodity.

It may be necessary to do some low-scale undercover work to identify the target. For example, posing as a utility company employee or a salesman may be necessary in order to learn about the address and particular details about its location and construction. If this is possible, valuable intelligence can be learned about possible fortification, etc.

Once the location has been determined, an effort should be made to learn subscriber information for public utilities and the telephone at that location. Many times the dealer will not be the resident of record; rather he will have a rental agreement, with public utilities and the phone in somebody else's name. The involvement of the suspect is thus disguised. Nonetheless, when there is time, these sources should be checked as part of an established routine for identifying both suspect and target location.

When the informant is describing the location, questions germane to tactical intelligence are important. If the informant has ever been inside the location, he can provide a description of the interior, and that can be refined as the investigation continues. If the informant makes several controlled buys at the location, clarification of the description of the target location should occur through each buy. The informant should be given specific information, things to find out about the location before buys are made and debriefed following the buys. The informant should vicariously scout the interior of the location on behalf of the affiant. He should be informed of things which the investigator wishes to learn and be debriefed following the buys.

The investigator should learn all that is possible about doors and windows. If all the traffic to and from a location uses one certain door, that may be a strong indication that the other door is barricaded. Two cases come to mind where this information was critical to formulating tactical plans. In one case, the accuracy of the informant information contributed to a successful raid plan; in the other instance, faulty inform-ant information was very costly.

In the first case, the location in question was a crack house, common and street level. The informant was emphatic that all the traffic came and went from the front door. The informant had seen the suspect come and go from the front door exclusively, never using the back door. In addition, the informant said there was evidence of fortification on the front door which was removed to allow potential buyers to enter the crack house. The informant was queried about possible fortification on the back doors and windows of the house. The informant could not comment on that; outsiders, he said, were not allowed in the back part of the house. The conclusion reached by the affiant/case agent was that the back of the house was fortified and that if a tactical entry were planned, the front door should be targeted.

When entry was made, the front door was the point of attack. Entry was quick and relatively easy, as fortification of that door was minimal.

The back door, on the other hand, was another story. It was braced with three cross-members, one wood 2-by-4 and two steel pipes. The iron supports for those braces were held to the wall by 3/8-inch lag bolts which went entirely through the brick wall. It was sealed by aluminum foil taped against the door. In addition, a refrigerator was firmly in place against the back door. The window adjacent to the back door was sealed with plastic behind the glass and six wooden cross-members were nailed to the window frame. Entry through the back part of the house would have been virtually impossible.

The other case that comes to mind involved a large rooming house building which had originally been a private Victorian-style home. The building had been taken over by crack dealers, and complaints about the dealing and the attendant crimes were numerous. The investigator who was assigned to the problem was under some pressure to come up with a solution. The investigator had an informant who had been reliable on two or three occasions in the past and who had never been unreliable. The informant was shifty and undependable but not unreliable when it came to intelligence information. One of the cases which the informant had put together was particularly successful, resulting in three arrests, a large drug seizure, a large cash seizure, and the recovery of two weapons. In that instance, the informant information was entirely accurate.

In this case, there were two crack dealing locations within the three story rooming house, one on the third floor and one on the first floor. The detective putting the case together had made controlled buys from both locations, and there was sufficient probable cause. There were some problems with the investigation, but in light of the rampant dealing, the numerous complaints, and the attendant violence, the determination was made to execute the warrants after a preraid buy from both locations.

There was a tactical problem in getting to both apartments without the lookouts tipping the dealers that there was a raid in progress. The lower apartment was in the front part of the building, but it had no direct view of the outside front of the building. There were often lookouts from the upper apartment, who had a view of the front of the building, but in cold weather the lookouts stayed inside on the staircase. It was determined that the lookout from the upstairs apartment would be inside and would not be a factor if he could not see the entry team enter the door to the lower apartment. The ideal situation would be to have one entry team approach close to the side of the building and enter the lower apartment from the front while a separate team entered the back of the house and took the upstairs apartment.

There was a three-story fire escape stairway leading up the back of the building. It was unknown where this staircase led, but the informant was questioned about it and stated that it led to a hallway, which in turn led directly to the door of the upstairs apartment for which a warrant had been obtained. The informant stated that he had used that approach in the past. The informant stated that the door was not always open but offered to go and check. A final controlled buy was made from the upstairs apartment, and the informant told the investigator that he had left the back door open and that there wasn't anybody around the back of the lot. The investigator could not get close enough to the building to see the informant enter or leave from the back of the building, and the failure to do this or to provide enough additional surveillance so that this could be accomplished proved to be a serious error.

Following a preraid controlled buy, the affiant and his supervisor met with a supervisor from the tactical unit which was doing the entry as well as the member of that unit who had done a scout of the building. Based on the most recent informant information, it was decided to have one team hit the front and go to the lower apartment and have a second team hit the upstairs apartment by going up the back staircase. It should be noted that the officer who had done the scout stated that he had not seen the back door which led to the fire escape. He stated that he saw two doors opposite the target location, and they were both closed. He had not opened them looking for a back door; he thought they were apartment doors.

The team that went to the front and hit the lower apartment had no problem. Everything went according to plan, and their movement along the side and to the front of the building went undetected by people inside. The team that went to the back found that all the informant information about having used this approach at any time in the past was false. The door at the top of the stairs did not lead to a hallway but led rather to a screened-in porch. After the initial door was rammed to get into the porch, a second door was rammed. This door led to someone's apartment; a small, one-room apartment. The entry team then had to open the door to get out of that apartment and cross the hall to the suspect's apartment. In order to execute the warrant, a total of four doors were penetrated, three of them for an apartment for which there was no search warrant. Fortunately, there was not anyone home in the apartment which had been mistakenly entered.

The informant information was not verified; it was taken at face value, and the result was an embarrassing, potentially tragic situation. It is necessary to rely on informant information in narcotics work, but the lesson clear in this case is that such reliance should not be done nonchalantly. Everything an informant reports should be questioned, and as a supervisor it is often a good idea to question the informant personally in cases such as this, where the information is vital to officer safety. Furthermore, in this case, the informant information contradicted that of the scout officer, although the scout officer was not sure that there wasn't a back door, just that he had not seen one. An assumption was made that the informant was being truthful when for some reason he was fabricating a story about a back door and having used it in the past.

Informant information regarding the target location should be corroborated to whatever extent possible. If there is any doubt about the information, it should be resolved in favor of facts which are known and have been verified. It should be added that for this one case of misintelligence, hundreds could be cited, like the one previously mentioned, where an informant provided extremely accurate details which paved the way for a smooth entry and successful case.

In the case of an apartment complex, tract housing, or public housing, it may be possible to obtain floor plans of the location. If the target location is an apartment building, it may also be possible to get a key for the building security door if not the private entrance. All possible information about the location and its surroundings should be obtained.

Certain locations will call for a significant amount of surveillance in order to learn what is necessary to achieve tactical success. The construction of the building; the doors, locks, and windows; and the presence of security doors and security alarms—all are important factors. Traffic patterns, lighting, and obstacles on the grounds and the premises are likewise very important. A final, preraid scout should be done to finalize the target assessment.

External Influences

The other category of critical preraid intelligence pertains to external influences. There are any number of factors in addition to the suspect and the target location which will adversely affect the investigation and the tactical execution of the warrant. In should be determined how many people in addition to the suspect live at the target location. The presence of children and other persons who are not involved with the drug dealing activity present both tactical and investigative problems. The presence of people who are not involved in the dealing, but are merely living in the place, creates a different tactical situation from one in which the only people in the target location are those involved in the criminal activity.

It is particularly important to determine if there are children in the target location. The presence of children, more than the presence of other presumably innocent people, will not only alter initial tactical planning, it will also affect contingency plans to some extent. For example, in a particularly serious situation, where the entry officers are compromised and their safety is in jeopardy, a diversion such as a stun grenade may be deployed as a contingency which was part of the overall tactical plan. If, however, it is known that children may be or are present, such diversions may be a part of a last-resort, emergency plan only.

The presence of animals is important tactical intelligence as well. Vicious dogs may present problems when encountered in the entry, but any dog is liable to bark and give advance warning that the entry team is approaching. If vicious dogs are known to be present, special weapons might become part of the tactical plan in order to deal with that threat. Occasionally other pets are in the target location which will be a factor. Snakes, for example, will sometimes be kept as pets, and in some cases the drugs will be kept in the area in which the snakes are confined.

One of the most important external factors affecting tactical operations is timing. It is important to learn everything possible about the habits of the suspect so that the search warrant operation can be timed for maximum tactical and investigative success. Too often, narcotics investigators fall into predictable patterns. Executing search warrants during certain hours, just out of habit, can be a dangerous pattern to develop. Each search warrant operation should be timed, based on characteristics of the particular suspect rather than the convenience of the officers involved. There are some situations which dictate that the warrant is executed at peak activity periods, when there are many people coming and going from the location and in the neighborhood. Conversely, there are times when it is best to hit the place when it is quiet. The facts of the investigation will dictate the answers to these and other questions, and the tactical plans have to be adjusted to fit the investigative needs of the case if possible.

The emotional climate of the neighborhood in which the location is situated is also a consideration. If the neighborhood is hostile to the presence of police officers, additional tactical adjustments will have to be made to deal with the potential of interference. It might be necessary to assign a rear guard to protect vehicles and equipment left behind.

Perhaps the most important external factor to be considered will be the presence of confederates of the suspect. The investigator needs to ascertain from the informant and other sources as much information as possible about the role which these people play. Are they lookouts, or muscle men, or just associates who hang around? If they are involved in the dealing, a suspect profile should be developed on them to whatever extent is possible. In that case, they are co-conspirators and subjects of the investigation.

The capability of the suspect to compromise the security of the operation should also be assessed. This entails everything from having a police scanner to having a close friend who works in the police department, the courts, or other sensitive areas. The informant is part of this consideration as well. It is not unheard of for informants to tip off the same individual about whom they have provided information. No informant should be trusted with raid planning details. If the informant is part of a preraid operation, he should not be included in any briefings; he should be kept secure following the conclusion of his involvement until the operation has reached the point where it is beyond compromise.

DOCUMENTARY ELEMENTS OF PLANNING

Diagrams

A diagram is part of every tactical operation. The diagrams will range in detail from a rough sketch on a blackboard of the exterior of a location to a detailed scale drawing of both the exterior and interior of the target location. The more detail the better. Again, intelligence about the inside of a location may often be difficult to obtain. In debriefing an informant, the interior should be sketched as he describes it, or he should sketch. The affiant can clarify the rough diagram through questions. It is necessary to tell the informant the details of which he is expected to make note while at the target location.

Invariably, risk in a tactical search warrant operation is inversely proportional to the quality of the intelligence. If a complete floor plan of the inside of the target location can be provided, risk is reduced. If very little is known about the inside of the target location, the greater the unknown factors and the greater the risk involved.

More often than not, a detailed diagram of the inside of a location will not be available. Figures 4-1, 4-2, 4-3 and 4-4 are sample raid diagrams that do provide quite a bit of detail. Figure 4-1 represents a cocaine dealing location in a particular block, once saturated with drug houses and bootleggers. Several houses in this block have at one time been the subject of drug dealing or bootlegging investigations or both. This house was used by a bootlegger years ago and then became a stash pad for a notorious street-level dealer. This dealer also had a fortified place across the street from which the dealing went on continually for several years. That location was equipped with intense fortification, and a video surveillance system, and nobody was allowed inside. All dealing was done through windows, slots in the doors, etc.

This diagram, Figure 4-1, is a basic floor plan which was sketched following a search warrant at that location in which several ounces of cocaine were recovered from a floor safe. A policy of diagramming the location of each search warrant in the event that a future raid was necessary had been established. This diagram has been used for planning raids on houses of similar construction on the block, of which there are several and of which at least two have been the subject of search warrants since the time that the sketch was made. Such sketches, made at the time a warrant is executed and kept on file, can provide excellent intelligence. In street-level dealing situations, it is common for the same places to be hit more than once. In any case, such diagrams do not require a great time commitment relative to their potential value. In addition, in cases such as this, the drawing is an important investigative document, and becomes part of the case filing. The detail and notes pertaining to fortification and the location of the safe made this diagram excellent for courtroom presentation.

Figure 4-2 is a similar diagram, drawn following a raid for future reference.

Figure 4-3 is an excellent drawing based on informant information and extensive surveillance. The informant in this case had stayed at 3547 Franklin St. and had once been part of the drug dealing operation. The two locations were across the alley from each other and were part of one crack dealing operation. The informant was debriefed at great length to put this diagram together. In addition, the detective who was in charge of this case is not only an excellent investigator but a talented draftsman as well. There were several people involved in this operation between the two locations. In addition, there was a great deal of foot traffic during most of the day and night. As such, this operation represented a difficult

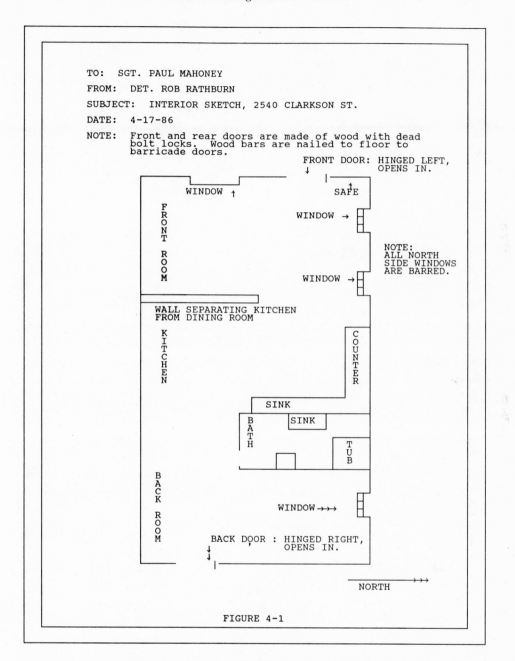

TO: SGT. PAUL MAHONEY

FROM: DET. ROB RATHBURN

SUBJECT: INTERIOR SKETCH, 2540 CLARKSON ST.

DATE: 4-17-86

NOTE: Front and rear doors are made of wood with dead bolt locks. Wood bars are nailed to floor to barricade doors.

FRONT DOOR: HINGED LEFT, OPENS IN.

WINDOW

SAFE

WINDOW →

FRONT ROOM

NOTE: ALL NORTH SIDE WINDOWS ARE BARRED.

WINDOW →

WALL SEPARATING KITCHEN FROM DINING ROOM

KITCHEN

COUNTER

SINK

SINK

BATH

TUB

BACK ROOM

WINDOW →→→

BACK DOOR : HINGED RIGHT, OPENS IN.

NORTH →→→

FIGURE 4-1

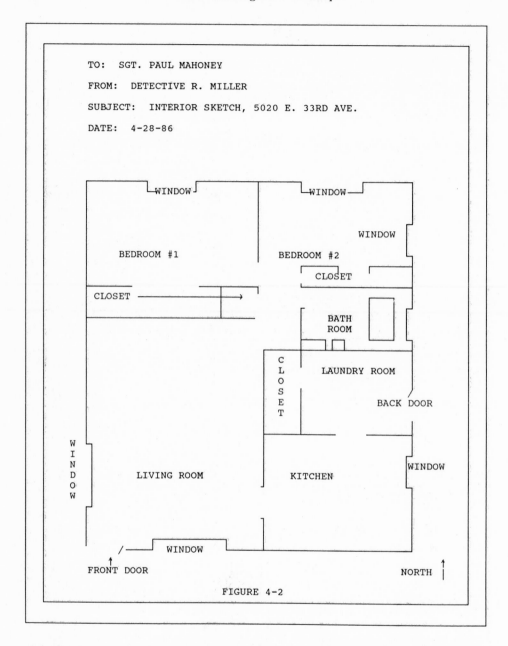

TO: SGT. PAUL MAHONEY

FROM: DETECTIVE R. MILLER

SUBJECT: INTERIOR SKETCH, 5020 E. 33RD AVE.

DATE: 4-28-86

FIGURE 4-2

tactical situation. The diagram provided invaluable preraid intelligence which contributed to a successful operation. Understandably, not every investigator will be capable of this kind of drawing, nor will the intelligence required for this type of drawing be available in most cases.

Figure 4-4 represents yet another preraid diagram. It was drawn by an

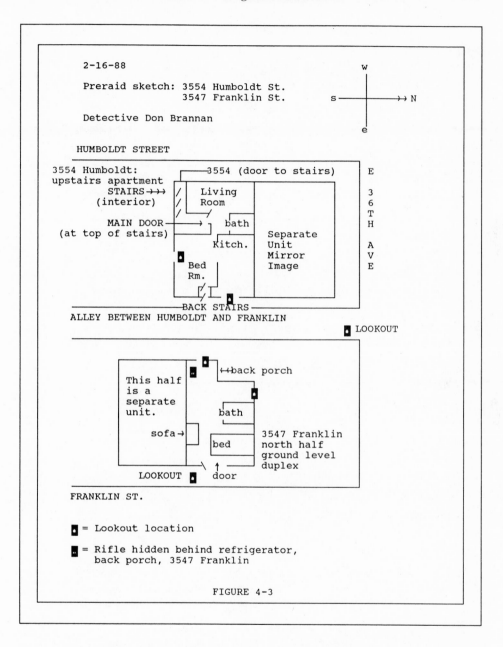

2-16-88

Preraid sketch: 3554 Humboldt St.
                3547 Franklin St.

Detective Don Brannan

```
                                                      w
                                                      |
                                       s——————|——————→ N
                                                      |
                                                      e
```

HUMBOLDT STREET

```
3554 Humboldt:          ┌——3554 (door to stairs)    E
upstairs apartment      │
        STAIRS →→→  /│   Living                       3
        (interior) /│   Room                          6
                   /│                                  T
   MAIN DOOR ———→ ┐  bath                              H
(at top of stairs)    Kitch.   Separate
                               Unit                   A
                    ▮          Mirror                 V
                    Bed        Image                  E
                    Rm.
                      ▯/┐   ▮
————————————————————BACK STAIRS————————————————————
ALLEY BETWEEN HUMBOLDT AND FRANKLIN
                                           ▮ LOOKOUT
```

```
                        ▮ ↩back porch
                     ▪
    This half                    ▮
    is a
    separate        bath
    unit.
        sofa→┌─┐   ┌───    3547 Franklin
            │  │  │bed     north half
            └─┘  │          ground level
     LOOKOUT ▮  ↑ door      duplex
```

FRANKLIN ST.

▮ = Lookout location

▪ = Rifle hidden behind refrigerator,
    back porch, 3547 Franklin

FIGURE 4-3

investigator who had been in both locations in an undercover capacity. It is a basic drawing providing almost no detail about the inside of the target locations. The undercover officer had purchased small amounts of cocaine in each of these apartments on two occasions. In each instance he had a gun held to his head and was given very little opportunity to look around, nor was he inclined to do so. In fact, it was discovered by the suspects during one of the buys that the officer was armed. This resulted in near tragedy; only quick thinking and fast talking saved the officer. He was able to talk his way out of danger, but obtaining raid intelligence was, understandably, a very low priority.

Because of the poor intelligence value of this diagram, additional investigation was done to improve the preraid tactical intelligence. The target locations were part of a public housing unit, and floor plans were obtained. Also, aerial photographs were obtained which, while not improving the intelligence pertaining to the inside of the target, did pinpoint the target locations in relationship to their surroundings and improved the overall quality of the tactical intelligence. These rough diagrams, supported by other intelligence, did suffice.

Raid diagrams should include details regarding the direction which doors open, the locations of plumbing fixtures, walls, closets, and stairways, and the like. Of course, the location that drugs are hidden, if known, or the area within the target in which the dealing takes place is also vital intelligence. Drawings to scale are not necessary, nor are they likely to be part of preraid intelligence. A drawing that is proportionately sketched so that distances can be estimated is sufficient.

Photographs

To be most beneficial, photographs of a target location should either serve to show the relationship of the target to its surroundings and/or show specific details about the location. Photographs are an excellent means of gaining a tactical advantage and ensuring that the location is pinpointed beyond any doubt.

Photographs taken from a distant perspective, preferably aerial photographs, can be important in determining potential sources of tactical difficulty either unrelated or peripherally related to the target. In planning the tactical approach, preraid surveillance, deployment of covering officers, etc., such photographs can be very important.

Photographs can provide a tactical advantage and should be part of prepaid planning when time allows. this is particularly true in large operations where there may be many people involved in the raid who have no prior knowledge about the location, and may have never seen it.

Any photographs of the suspect also provide valuable intelligence. It

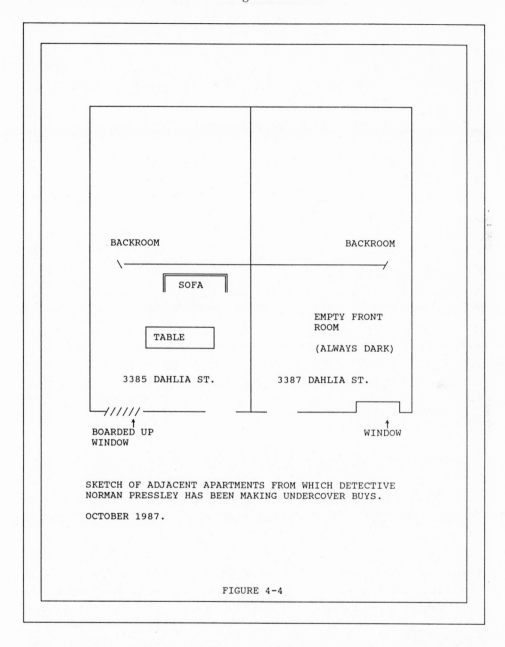

BACKROOM

BACKROOM

SOFA

EMPTY FRONT
ROOM

(ALWAYS DARK)

TABLE

3385 DAHLIA ST.

3387 DAHLIA ST.

//////

BOARDED UP
WINDOW

WINDOW

SKETCH OF ADJACENT APARTMENTS FROM WHICH DETECTIVE
NORMAN PRESSLEY HAS BEEN MAKING UNDERCOVER BUYS.

OCTOBER 1987.

FIGURE 4-4

is preferable to have a police department mug shot or a driver's license photograph. Surveillance photos depicting the suspect will make an adequate substitute if either of those is lacking. Again, there are many cases in which the suspect is not identified. But a thorough identification, which includes a photograph, is preferable in every respect.

Videotapes

Many tactical units utilize videotape for preraid scouting purposes. They have an advantage in that the tape can be narrated by the person operating the camera. The narrator can then comment on the target as it appears. Having a videotape also allows the target to be evaluated, on film, from a number of different angles. The disadvantage can be the difficulty in making the videotape scout inconspicuously. To be of any value, taping must be done in daylight from a relatively close distance, and it is difficult to accomplish this without the suspect's becoming aware of the process. A good undercover vehicle for such a purpose can make the task easier, but there is still a need for caution. The officers doing the scout, particularly in the case where videotape is used, must understand that tactical information gained at the expense of investigative security is probably a waste of effort anyway. Getting burned on a preraid scout mission can cause the dealer to freeze up temporarily, clean up the place, and move or hide the drugs, move altogether, or engage in any number of other things. One of these other things involves the dealer preparing for the raid either by arming himself or by setting an ambush. Granted, the usual response would be to quit dealing temporarily, but some are devious enough to prepare violent countermeasures if they know they are to be raided.

Suspect Profile

Compilation of suspect information, whatever has been obtained through the investigation, is an important element of the preraid planning. Every bit of information which has been accumulated should be organized into a concise suspect profile. The suspect profile should consist of a fact sheet, copies of the criminal history, and photographs.

Any information concerning weapons and previous history of violence should be included on the basic fact sheet. There must be careful differentiation between known facts and unsubstantiated intelligence information. An accurate suspect profile is the goal; rumors and speculation should be represented as just that. For example, it is often rumored that a given suspect will probably shoot it out with the police when the raid occurs. This happens far less frequently than rumors would have it. This is important information, albeit rumor and speculation, and should be imparted at some point to those involved in the raid, but it must be presented as rumor and speculation based on rumor. On the other hand, if there are solid indications that the suspect is dangerous, based on previous history and behavior, distinguish this type of information from the previous type. An attempt should be made to assess clearly the relative threat of the suspect in the profile.

The suspect profile should also include dealing patterns and habits. This information will be as important in planning the tactical portion of the operation as it has been in preparing the investigation to that point.

Probable Cause Package

Some documentation of probable cause will be an essential element of the raid planning. Such documentation need only be a synopsis of the facts leading to probable cause. To plan the tactical operation accurately, those involved in the planning will need to have some basic idea of the investigation to that point. On a small team, working together on most cases, information of this nature is usually exchanged informally as the investigation proceeds. Others who are not part of the investigative team but who are involved in the tactical operation may have no idea of how a case has progressed. A synopsis of the basic facts of the case will ensure that this information is shared at the appropriate time. When those involved in the tactical part of the operation are not narcotics investigators, this information is particularly important.

By this stage of the planning of a tactical operation, regardless of how quickly or how slowly the planning progresses, the search warrant should be about complete, and the documentary elements of the raid planning should be in order. Diagrams, photographs, videotapes, the suspect profile, and a synopsis of the investigation should all be elements of such planning when possible. The process to this point could take a couple of hours or several hours, or it could take weeks or months depending on the size and scope of the case. Regardless of the size of the operation, certain planning steps are essential to the formulation of raid plans.

FORMULATING OPERATIONAL PLANS

The goal of operational planning is to formulate a comprehensive plan that will directly accomplish the objective, execution of the raid, and seizure of suspects and evidence, with a minimum of risk. The plan must fit the situation. It is possible to make tactical plans too complicated. In so doing, safety and success of the operation may both be at risk. A plan can be detailed and comprehensive without being complicated. Nothing should be included in the plan that does not have a purpose. The investigation to this point, all the information and documentation, will contribute to the operational planning.

Statement of Objective

All search warrant plans begin with a clearly recognized objective: execute a search warrant at a given time and location, apprehend the suspects, and seize the evidence. For any plan to be effective, it must encompass all the phases of the objective. Accomplishing the objective may be contingent upon the success of other operations. For example, a search warrant may be planned immediately following a buy/bust. In order for the search warrant to be successful, the buy/bust operation must be successful.

Plan of Action

A primary plan of action, a method of achieving the operational objective, must be developed. In the case of a simple search warrant operation, the first consideration is the target location. All intelligence, diagrams, and photographs of the target location should be reviewed and a primary plan of operation assembled. Every search warrant operational plan will include plans for three distinct phases: the entry, the arrest, and the search.

Entry

The plan for entry will be specifically tailored to the needs of each case. The entry phase of the search warrant operations is a tactical operation to varying degrees. The following discussion is related to search warrant entry plans where the entry will be immediate and/or forced. Alternate methods of entry such as subterfuge will be discussed later in the chapter when we cover contingency planning. In many jurisdictions, tactical units are available to assist with the entry phase of search warrant operations when it has been determined that it is necessary. In formulating the entry plan, the provisions of the search warrant pertaining to immediate entry have to be considered. The target location and the suspect are evaluated in an effort to determine some objective threat level. The tactical skills and training of those responsible for executing the warrant have to be evaluated in light of the other factors.

There are four criteria used in determining the need for the assistance of a tactical unit in making the search warrant entry. If the target location is barricaded or fortified against entry, that is one of the things that does create the need for special tactical expertise. If the suspect has a history of violent behavior or if it is suspected that he is armed and may use the weapon against an officer, those are also indications that a trained tactical unit may be necessary to accomplish the mission. Finally, if a contingency allowing for the arrest of the suspect away from the location and subsequent service of the warrant is not possible, and any of the other factors are present, the situation may call for a level of tactical expertise which exceeds that of the narcotics investigators.[1]

The use of tactical teams to execute immediate entry narcotics search warrants had increased over the past five years or so. Tactical teams have developed special crisis entry methods which combine traditional tactics with the needs of a search warrant investigation. The use of tactical entry teams has been necessitated by changes in the drug dealing business. Ten years ago, narcotics investigators routinely made their own entries. The entry tactics were based on solid police instincts and narcotics training and experience. Essentially, the goal was to get to the target unnoticed, enter as swiftly as possible, and secure the suspects before they could flush the drugs down the toilet, eat them, or throw them out the window.

Trends in the drug dealing business toward fortification and the possession of firearms have stimulated the upgrading of tactics and the need for sophisticated tactical training.

If the tactical demands of a given operation exceed the ability of the investigators, assistance with the entry should be sought. A narcotics unit without such a resource should be trained in entry tactics. Such training should be thorough and, to be effective, should be ongoing. The dilemma revolves around the amount of training required versus the commitment to the primary mission of drug investigations. Tactical training should be done to the extent that the officers are proficient in entry tactics, without compromising the commitment to the primary mission—investigation and apprehension of drug dealers and violators—to any significant degree.

There are distinct advantages in using a specially trained tactical team

---

1 National Tactical Officers Association, "High Risk Warrant Service," unpublished outline.

to do search warrant entries. First, responsibility for that phase of the operation is turned over to a specialized team. If using such a unit is commonplace, teamwork will develop. The tactical unit will understand the needs of the investigators and will give those needs a high priority. Likewise, the investigators will develop the type of intelligence necessary and document it to the satisfaction of the tactical unit. The affiant on a search warrant case usually has many responsibilities just prior to the execution of the warrant. Often the finishing details have to be put on the warrant, which has to be signed, and preraid buys are commonly necessary. Turning the tactical operation over to a highly skilled unit allows the investigator to focus on the other aspects of the investigation.

Also, more investigative work is possible when the entry phase of a search warrant operation is turned over to specialists. It is possible to get more cases done, thus relieved of that big responsibility. It is possible to do multiple warrants in rapid succession where responsibilities are shared. Investigators can be split up for the searches and processing of prisoners and two or three warrants can be done in the time it would take to do one if the investigators also have the entry responsibilities. In addition, the more warrants that a tactical unit does, proficiency increases and coordination is improved.

There are disadvantages to this approach also. Some tactical units are not responsive to the needs of the investigators. For this approach to work, teamwork must be developed so that investigative needs and tactical needs are met. Many tactical units are so deliberate in their planning that it is not practical to get them mobilized for a search warrant operation which may demand split-second timing and swiftness. If too much time passes before executing the search warrant, circumstances may change and if they change before the entry is made, the whole operation may be an exercise in futility. Logistically, it is difficult to coordinate a tactical unit and the narcotics unit. It is something that can be accomplished, but it takes a mutual commitment.

Regardless of whether a tactical unit is used or the investigative unit is making the entry, providing for an entry team is basic to the raid planning process. If a tactical unit is used, details of the entry plan will be formulated by the supervisor in that unit according to his assessment.

Entry Plan Goals

There are certain key goals that figure into the success of every entry plan. Superiority of personnel and firepower, swiftness of execution, the element of surprise, and security of the inner and outer perimeters are critical. To achieve these four goals, it is necessary to have done the proper investigation prior to the planning stage. That is, the quality of preraid intelligence will ultimately determine whether or not these goals are achievable. Tactical skill, training, and a certain amount of luck will be critical in effectively converting the plan into action.

When a search warrant entry is planned, the probability that the suspects are armed should be carefully weighed. Again, good preraid intelligence should determine not only if the suspects are armed but how they are armed. The aim is to guarantee an edge so that firepower superiority is achieved. The entry team should not knowingly enter a situation allowing the suspects to have the upper hand. Likewise, the plan should include enough people to deal appropriately with the number of people to be encountered.

Swiftness and surprise are closely related goals. Surprise requires precision timing and swift movement once the timing is deemed to be right. The element of surprise, if it is maintained, will greatly affect the outcome of the entry. Losing the element of surprise can result in tactical and investigative failure. If the suspects are alerted prematurely to the presence of the entry team, the safety of the team can be compromised, giving a distinct advantage to those inside the location. They can arm themselves and wait in ambush and/or destroy the evidence.

Security of the inner and outer perimeters is directly related to the previous three goals. It will be necessary to have adequate personnel, appropriately armed and deployed in a timely manner to surprise the suspects and gain a tactical advantage. Attempting to do a search warrant entry without adequate personnel can result in breaks in the perimeter security. A great many drug dealers will flee if given half a chance, and the result can be as dangerous as if they stand their ground and fight. Once the perimeter security has been broken, any number of things can happen, and all of them involve a deviation from the established plan. It is far preferable to involve too many people in the perimeter security plan than too few.

Many street level drug raids present serious perimeter problems due to the traffic coming and going from the location and the large number of people that may be encountered inside. Very serious consequences have resulted from an entry team encountering unexpected lookouts or other people on the approach to the target. Every plan should include provisions for dealing with such people. Many times, the lookouts or other people encountered outside, are armed and resist, or they alert the suspects inside of impending trouble. To put these people down and secure them without hesitation and without drawing from the manpower necessary to proceed with the entry should be the plan.

Likewise, security on the outer perimeter may include assigning a rear guard to protect vehicles and equipment left behind. Underestimating the importance of outer perimeter security can be very costly.

Inner perimeter security will also require a varying number of people depending on the individual circumstances of the raid. Again, if the raid involves a street-level drug dealing operation, such as a crack house, any number of people may be inside the target location. A raid in which 15 people are encountered inside the location presents a vastly different problem from one in which only 1 or 2 people have to be secured. This is true not only in terms of officer safety but also in an investigative sense. Proving possession may become a problem if drugs are recovered. Suspects may attempt to dispose of drugs and other evidence and may be able to do so undetected if the number of suspects in the location greatly exceeds the number of police officers.

If these four goals are achieved, the entry plan is calculated to succeed. There are several other important considerations which must be made in determining if the goals can be achieved.

Entry Equipment Needs

Certain equipment is fundamental to the success of a search warrant entry plan. Intelligence pertaining to the target location and the suspect will to a large extent determine what equipment is included in the entry plan. Is the target fortified? Is the suspect armed? If the doors are relatively insecure, or are open most of the time, equipment needs will be minimized. If the target is fortified, the nature and extent of fortification will call for special equipment. The degree to which the suspect is armed will dictate special equipment needs in the way of weapons and diversionary devices.

Basic equipment for a search warrant entry should include the following: battering ram, pry bar or break and rake, protective vests, flashlights, raid jackets, raid caps, and flex-cuffs in addition to the service weapon, spare ammunition, handcuffs, and other equipment routinely carried. This equipment will provide for immediate entry in most cases, ready identification of the officers executing the warrant, and quick security of the suspects inside the target location. Effective use of basic equipment such as a battering ram requires some skill, which can be acquired only through practice. Likewise, using a break and rake to pry open a locked screen door requires some practice. To formulate an entry plan without accounting for the level of training and expertise of those involved is a mistake. The fact that a person is an outstanding narcotics investigator does not mean that he will be skilled in the use of a battering ram and a pry bar. To whatever extent possible, people should be deployed in a raid plan in accordance with their skills.

Beyond that basic equipment, there are a variety of other items which may be necessary and without which the goals of the entry plan cannot be achieved. For example, if the target location has steel security doors, swiftness and surprise will not be achieved short of defeating one of the doors quickly and effectively.

The use of special equipment also carries with it some requisite amount of specialized training. Hooking up a tow chain and pulling a door requires training if it is to be done correctly and safely. Likewise, special equipment called for may include some special weapons, submachine guns, or shotguns, for example. To be effective, the officers called on to use them must have had the necessary training.

The entry plan should include an accurate assessment of any equipment required to get the job done, an explanation of how the equipment facilitates the plan, and who will be responsible for using the equipment.

Entry Team Assignments

The personnel needs of the entry phase of the operation have to be assessed. Included in this assessment should be not only the entry team itself, but all others essential to completing the entry successfully. A search warrant entry plan should provide for enough people to enter the location safely, secure the people inside, and prevent the destruction of evidence, if possible. At the same time, the plan must provide for adequate manpower to perform functions in support of the entry team, such as preraid surveillance and perimeter containment. Basically, preraid surveillance should be in place to assist the entry team by providing up-to-the-minute intelligence, and whatever cover and containment people are required should be in place so that the entry can be accomplished safely and successfully.

The most basic of operations will require containment at the inner perimeter, preferably at least two people. Then a minimum of six people should be involved in the entry and securing of the people inside the target location. To do an entry with fewer than six people is inherently risky. In some cases, where the target location is unusually large or there are many people inside, the configuration should be expanded. There are any number of variations to this team configuration. For example, the ram can be a one-man operation and the ram man and the break and rake man can then team up to make a third entry team, or they can be the trailers, whose responsibility it will be to control and secure those people inside. The people encountered inside the location may not ultimately be arrested and charged, but they most certainly must be secured before the rest of the operation is undertaken.

The entry team should be adequate in size, sufficiently trained, and properly equipped so that the entry can be safely accomplished. The entry team must be able to enter the target location swiftly, gain control of the suspects and other people in the location, and prevent the destruction of evidence. All weapons found in the residence should be secured. Once these things are accomplished and order is restored to the target location, the location is secure, and the team leader can call for the search team.

The ideal plan utilizes the most highly skilled and best trained tactical people on the entry team. Special weapons should be a part of the entry plan only if people with the necessary training in the use of the weapons are available. People who work well together should be assigned together. Members of several agencies or units should not work together on an entry team. Entry responsibilities must, therefore, be assigned to a group of people who have worked and trained together.

Certain search warrant operations will require extensive support for the entry team. The neighborhood may be such that outside perimeter security must be established. Likewise, many narcotics search warrants will require preraid surveillance in order to ensure success. In these cases, the surveillance officers will monitor conditions at the target location and may make the call for the entry team to move into action. The surveillance team can provide covert security for the entry team as they are moving forward.

What is necessary in all cases is some type of close perimeter containment. It is best if all windows and doors from which an exit could be made are covered. Assignments for this task should be based on the individual characteristics of the location and manpower available.

Commonly, in situations where a separate tactical unit is making the entry, narcotics investigators will assume responsibility for the other tasks which must be completed. The decision to have the covering officers in plainclothes or in raid gear will be dictated by external factors. They should be equipped with raid vests in any case, even if worn under their civilian jackets. In some cases, it is advantageous to move containment and perimeter officers into place just ahead of the entry team's approach. To do so without compromising the entry team, the approach has to be made covertly in plainclothes. Again, these assignments should be very specific, and plans should include method and direction of approach.

In cases of drug labs and other situations of potentially extreme danger, an ambulance should be held on standby near the target location. Securing drug labs and entry in other special situations will be covered later in this chapter.

After the plan for entry has been made, equipment needs assessed, and manpower assignments made, contingency plans should be made. Formulating contingency plans, "what if" plans, is essential to conducting search warrant operations successfully and safely. To be fully prepared, it is necessary to consider eventualities which will alter the plan. These range from the simple, such as checking to see if a door is unlocked, if that is a distinct possibility, before ramming it, to more complex problems, such as the suspect barricading himself.

Most contingencies in narcotics search warrant operations involve suspects encountered in the immediate area as approach is being made, suspects leaving the location, and the inability to defeat the door quickly enough, all of which compromise the safety of the entry team. Preraid surveillance on the location and last-minute preraid controlled buys can provide up-to-date intelligence which greatly facilitates the entry operation. More specific discussion on contingency planning, including entry by means other than force, follows in the section of this chapter pertaining to the briefing.

When manpower from other units is being utilized for a search warrant operation, coordination with the appropriate people from that unit is critical if the necessary help is to be arranged. This coordination should be done enough in advance of the operation so that the required arrangements can be made.

Communications

Communication will be critical in the dynamic phase of a search warrant operation. It is best if search warrant operations can be done on a secure radio channel. All members of the operation must have the capability to communicate with each other. Many drug dealers monitor police scanners in an effort to get advance warning that they are about to be raided. This advance warning can be very dangerous as the element of surprise is turned in favor of the suspects. Any advance warning will also surely result in evidence being moved or hidden. Another factor to be considered is that media people commonly monitor vice and narcotics channels in addition to regular channels. Having the media arrive unexpectedly at the scene of an operation can create unnecessary complications.

When the plan for the entry phase of the operation is completed, the remainder of the operation can be planned.

Arrest and Search

Once the target location is declared secure by the leader of the entry team, the arrest and search team will take over. Even though all the occupants of the location have been secured, they are under investigation and may or may not be arrested and charged when the operation is complete. Securing the occupants is part of the entry phase; handling the arrestees and other occupants appropriately belongs at the beginning of the search phase. Generally speaking, if a tactical team is used for a search warrant entry, their responsibilities will end when the target is secure and the investigators must take it from there.

A search warrant operation plan must include the handling of prisoners, processing of paperwork, and prisoner transportation. Having a female officer on the arrest and search team will facilitate the search of any female prisoners. If a person is named or described as a subject for which a search warrant has been issued or if a person has been arrested, that person should be immediately searched. Planning for the search and arrest of prisoners will expedite the operation.

Intelligence gathered in the investigation will be used to determine the number of people necessary for the search and arrest phase of the operation. Plan so that enough people are available to search the target location thoroughly and systematically. It may not be necessary to make specific assignments beforehand. In fact it is often better to make those assignments after the location has been secured and it is possible to assess the needs accurately. In every search warrant operation, at least one person must be assigned to be the scribe, who makes an inventory of the items taken. In some cases, more than one person is necessary.

Search an Arrest Equipment

The plan should include the necessary equipment and stationery supplies to perform this phase of the operation properly. For arrest processing, plenty of handcuffs need be available. The flex-cuffs work well for immediately securing people in the target location, but these should not be kept in place for any extended period of time. Special cutters are necessary for removing the flex-cuffs. If people are arrested, regular handcuffs should be applied after the person is thoroughly searched. Again, having the necessary forms available for initial processing of those arrested so that they can be quickly removed from the scene is expeditious. This is particularly important in cases where numerous people are arrested inside a target location.

Among the items necessary for the search kit, include a camera, evidence containers, markers and inventory forms, some basic hand tools, portable lights, and rubber gloves.

Special Planning Considerations

If the entry and the arrest and search plans are adequately made, very little additional planning is necessary. Individual circumstances will dictate that some special needs be addressed. For example, standard postraid reporting will routinely be done and will suffice in most cases. It is usually not necessary to plan for such, but in the case of major operations, there should be a plan for special notifications. If the operation will generate some media attention, that should be anticipated and advance notification given to the appropriate members of the department responsible for those details that something extraordinary may take place.

BRIEFING PACKAGE

Once the planning has been completed, the briefing package can be assembled. The briefing package, the information to be given to each officer at the briefing, should include the important facts but should not be cluttered with unnecessary details. Standardized forms facilitate assembling the briefing package, but each individual operation will have different requirements. Figure 4-5 is an example of a standard briefing sheet.

The briefing package should begin with a brief statement of the operational plan. Do not go into too much detail in this or any other part of the briefing package. The briefing itself will be a thorough explanation of the operation, and written material should be in outline rather than narrative form. The following is an example of an operational plan written for a briefing sheet:

> On 10-21-87, members of the narcotics bureau and federal agents will be conducting search warrant operations at 12695 E. Albrook #5611 and 5553 Wheeling St. The raids will be conducted simultaneously and are contingent on the successful completion of an undercover buy operation which will take place at 12695 E. Albrook #5611 at approximately 7:00 P.M. The undercover operative will be Det. Dale Krantz who will be buying from Wiley McClain. McClain is expected to go to 5553 Wheeling St. to pick up the ounce and deliver it to Det. Krantz. Krantz will leave the area after the buy, and surveillance will be maintained on 12695 E. Albrook #5611 and 5553 Wheeling St. until the search warrant is completed. The entry phase of the simultaneous search warrants will be the responsibility of the Denver Police Metro SWAT Unit.

A standard briefing sheet can provide an outline for the basic information such as the name and description of the undercover officer, undercover vehicle, etc. If a confidential informant is making a controlled buy, the description of the informant should be included on the briefing sheet. In the case of informant participation, it can be helpful to clarify the extent of the participation with a brief statement in the space provided for informant involvement. For example, in a search warrant operation not contingent on any undercover operation, but in which an informant is making a preraid buy, a simple statement to that effect should be included. Again, see Figure 4-5 for a sample briefing sheet.

The target location is listed by address and the general vicinity described in cases where the address is one that may not be immediately recognized. The suspects should be named and described as well as possible.

Following this basic information, the briefing sheet should list officers involved in the operation by name and radio call number. Their assignments should be listed next to their names. It is not necessary to explain the assignments fully, as they will be explained completely in the briefing.

```
                    SEARCH WARRANT OPERATIONS
                          BRIEFING SHEET

DATE OF OPERATION:_____TIME OF OPERATION:_____

OPERATIONAL PLAN:_____

_____

_____

_____

_____

UNDERCOVER OFFICER:_____

DESCRIPTION OF OFFICER:_____

UNDERCOVER VEHICLE:_____

INFORMANT DESCRIPTION/INVOLVEMENT:_____

_____
```

TARGET LOCATIONS	NAME	NO.	ASSIGNMENTS
LOCATION #1_____			
LOCATION #2_____			
LOCATION #3_____			
SUSPECT INFORMATION			
NAME:_____			
DESCRIPTION:_____			
PHOTO ATTACHED: ☐ YES ☐ NO			
NAME:_____			
DESCRIPTION:_____			
PHOTO ATTACHED: ☐ YES ☐ NO			

FIGURE 4-5

In some cases, it is helpful to have the cellular phone numbers and/or pager numbers on the sheet in the event that communication by means other than radio is required.

In the case of a more complex operation, the plan and briefing package must contain more detail. Not presented here, but included in the actual package, are photos of each of the suspects and copies of their criminal records. The operation described in the plan involved an undercover buy and two subsequent search warrants. Officers involved in the operation had surveillance responsibilities before the operation, during the undercover operation, and after the operation prior to the execution of the warrants. In addition, the officers each had fixed responsibilities for handling arrests and searching.

These officers did not have responsibility for making the entries at the two locations. That part of the operation was turned over to a tactical unit which made all assignments and entry plans. The entries were done simultaneously. A briefing had been held two days prior to this operation between the supervisor in the investigative unit and the supervisors from the tactical unit. The locations were scouted, and the overall plan was worked out in detail. One of the supervisors from the tactical unit attended the general briefing. Likewise, the supervisor from the narcotics investigations unit attended the tactical briefing. Effective communication ensured that everyone was on the same page and that the investigative plans and the entry operations plans dovetailed. Briefing sheets were exchanged, and each of the two teams had a good idea of the general plan. Communication was done on one radio channel common to both the tactical teams and the investigators.

This operation took place in a remote part of the city in which the streets are laid out in a confusing manner. Many of the people involved in the operational plan were federal agents who were not familiar with that part of the city. For that matter, many of the local officers were unfamiliar with that part of the city also. A map of the area was made (Figure 4-6). On that map, certain coordinates were given alpha designations which coincided with some of the surveillance responsibilities. This was done to reduce the possibility that either suspect would be able to drive completely out of the area. The outer perimeter was contained in this manner. Due to the fact that a surveillance plane was being used, it was not necessary to do tight ground surveillance and risk being burned. The map shows location numbers one and two, which were described on the briefing sheet.

Detailed diagrams of the apartment complex were given to the tactical unit for making the entry plan. These diagrams had been obtained from the property management company and included floor plans. In addition, the undercover officer provided a diagram of where the apartment was situated in the building, and this was used in the entry plan as well.

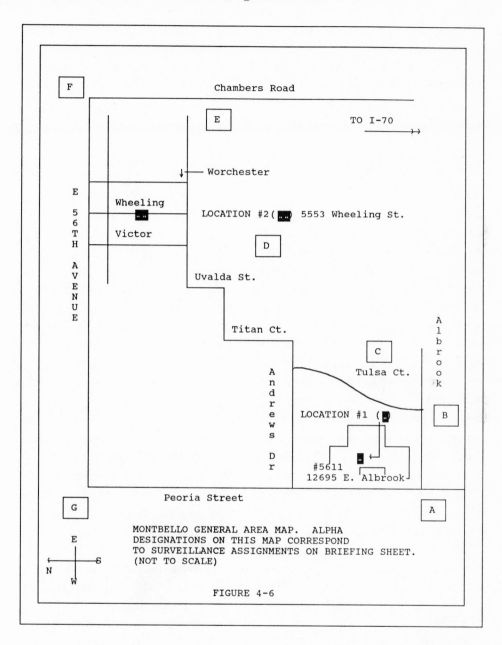

F

Chambers Road

E

TO I-70
→→

— Worchester

E
5
6
T
H

A
V
E
N
U
E

Wheeling

Victor

LOCATION #2( ) 5553 Wheeling St.

D

Uvalda St.

Titan Ct.

A
l
b
r
o
o
k

C

Tulsa Ct.

A
n
d
r
e
w
s

D
r

LOCATION #1 ( )

B

#5611
12695 E. Albrook

Peoria Street

G

A

MONTBELLO GENERAL AREA MAP.   ALPHA
DESIGNATIONS ON THIS MAP CORRESPOND
TO SURVEILLANCE ASSIGNMENTS ON BRIEFING SHEET.
(NOT TO SCALE)

E

N ←——→ S

W

FIGURE 4-6

One of the primary problems of any complex operation is assuring that the target location or locations are pinpointed beyond any question. Any doubt or questions about the target location must be removed during the preraid briefing. Hitting the wrong location is not unheard of in the business of executing search warrants. There is a certain risk of that happening, but that can be minimized by accurate preraid intelligence, a good operational plan, and a thorough briefing.

Involving representatives from so many different agencies in a search warrant operation requires good communication and teamwork in addition to comprehensive planning.

Conduct of the Briefing

General Briefing

The preraid briefing should be conducted by the investigator in charge of the case and the supervisor. If the supervisor is completely familiar with the details of the investigation, which in most major operations he will be, he is in a better position to conduct the briefing than the investigator. The supervisor has more rank, which should not make any real difference, but it might. Also, the supervisor may be enough removed from the investigation to look at the operation more objectively. It is best if the supervisor and the investigator plan the operation together and are both present to conduct the briefing.

The briefing should follow the briefing documentation package filling in the details which are outlined in the briefing sheet. Every person connected with the operation should attend the briefing. This will not always be possible. Frequently, the officers doing preraid surveillance won't be able to attend the briefing. In that case, any officer not at the briefing should be briefed beforehand of the general plan and their role in the plan. The officer in charge of the briefing must apprise the officers not at the briefing of any change in the operational plans that may develop during the briefing.

The briefing should be conducted so that the plan is discussed from beginning to end. Questions and discussion of the plan should take place after the operational plan has been stated. It is common to adjust the plan during the briefing. The officer conducting the briefing should not hesitate to draw on the experience of other officers involved in the operation.

It is important to keep the tone of the briefing as professional and businesslike as possible. Some joking and light comments are natural and help keep everyone relaxed. Too much of this type of behavior is intolerable, however, as it causes the briefing to be drawn off track.

The specifics of the search warrant should be discussed during the briefing. The subject or subjects of the warrant should be clearly identified. The provisions which have been authorized regarding immediate entry should be noted. If the search warrant includes specific persons and vehicles in addition to a physical location, that too should be clarified.

Tactical Briefing

In the event that a tactical unit, separate from the investigative unit is given responsibility for the entry, the briefing for that part of the operation might be conducted aside from the general briefing if the tactical people feel that it is necessary. Also, in large operations, the tactical teams should break into groups for specific tactical planning. This is done when a large number of people is involved and conducting only one briefing is too confusing.

The briefing for the tactical portion of the operation is most critical since it is in that phase that the most danger exists. The diagrams and photographs of the target location should be distributed. Usually, a diagram of the target location is put on a blackboard and assignments written on the blackboard next to the diagram.

Whether a separate tactical briefing is held or whether that portion of the operation is planned in a general briefing, it is at this juncture when contingency planning is discussed.

Contingency Planning

While contingency planning is an ongoing process throughout the investigation and the search warrant planning process, specific contingency plans will most often be made at the briefing. The contingency plans will be stimulated by discussion of the basic plan and by intelligence information which is forthcoming immediately prior to the briefing or during the briefing.

With respect to contingency plans, it is necessary to clarify what circumstances will trigger changes in the basic plan and what the responsive action will be. Discipline is a key ingredient in the success of any tactical operation. It is important that officers involved in the entry plan have the discipline to stick to the primary plan until forced into a contingency and then make the transition to exactly the contingency which has been planned for the given situation. If planning has not allowed for contingency plans, changes in circumstances will force each officer to react on his own and continuity and teamwork are lost.

It is not possible to plan for every contingency. Regardless of how specific planning is, things can happen for which a plan does not exist.

In narcotics raids, the following general situations most commonly trigger changes in raid plans during the execution of the raid.

1. *Suspect movement outside the location:* The suspect leaves the residence as the entry team is moving toward the target location. If the suspect leaves in a vehicle and is away from the location before the entry team is compromised, the suspect can be stopped by perimeter officers, possibly requiring the assistance of a uniform car. The target can be hit as planned, or if the suspect who left was known to be the only person in the target location, an alternate to forced entry will be possible when the suspect is secured. If the suspect leaves on foot as the entry team is approaching on foot, a potentially much more serious situation arises. The suspect, alerted to the existence and purpose of the entry team, may run, go for a weapon, or attempt to destroy evidence. Entry plans should consider this possibility in every case. Some plan should be in place to secure the suspect immediately without drawing from the strength of the entry team, which may by that time be compromised and exposed to danger at the target location.

2. *Suspect movement inside the target location:* Suspect movement inside the target location should be anticipated. At the very least, when the suspect becomes aware of the presence of a raid team, an attempt will be made to get to and destroy the evidence in most cases. This will not necessarily create changes in the basic plan, but it will if the team is slowed down or stopped at the door. In these cases, the suspect may be able to barricade himself in a portion of the house and an entirely different situation is thus created in which the suspect has to be contained until he can be forcefully overcome or talked out of his position.

3. *Fortification:* Fortification is common in the drug dealing business and many tactical entries are planned based on defeating the fortification. It is usually impossible to know exactly to what extent a target is fortified. If the fortification can not be defeated quickly, the officers on the entry team could be in a position of very grave danger. In these situations the deployment of tactical diversions such as stun grenades may be in order. Such diversions can effectively buy time for the entry team.

4. *Lookouts:* If lookouts are an obvious part of a drug dealing operation, that should be fairly apparent, and plans to deal with the lookouts can be made as part of the entry plan. Lookouts can make an entry very difficult if they have enough time to issue a warning and thereby compromise the entry plan.

It is unseen and inconspicuous lookouts which can be most dangerous, and if they remain undetected they almost always give warning, which results in lost evidence if not an armed attack. Some sophisticated drug dealing operations pick a strategic location, one that can be approached only by passing a checkpoint or series of checkpoints. Such lookouts, when they are a known factor, must be dealt with separately and before the entry team moves into place. Sometimes a diversion will work; other times it is necessary to secure the lookout quickly and quietly immediately prior to the entry team making its final approach or almost simultaneous with that approach. A diversion which will draw the lookouts and other people in the area away from the target location is good if it works, but usually the direct approach, securing the lookout, is more effective.

5. *Unexpected number of people:* A large number of people inside a target location can cause changes in the entry tactics. A preraid buy and preraid surveillance can be helpful in determining the number of people inside the target location immediately prior to entry.

6. *Unexpected floorplan:* An inaccurate floor plan on which the entry plan is based will cause immediate changes in entry tactics. Additional floors, additional rooms, and other such unexpected details generally are the result of too little preraid intelligence or inaccurate intelligence. It is almost better to have no idea of what the interior floor plan is like than to make a plan based on faulty intelligence.

Most of the foregoing situations can be prepared for as part of contingency planning. While it is important to be organized and have contingency plans ready, it is also important to keep the planning simple enough so that it has some chance of being consummated. Overly complicated plans will often be unworkable. A big part of successfully reacting to changes in an entry plan, as the plan is in progress, is related to training and experience.

A unit that has trained and worked together on several live operations will react infinitely better than will an inadequately trained unit.

Subterfuge and Other Entry Alternatives

When a search warrant operation is being planned, the most common contingency plans or alternate plans involve the prospects of making entry by some way other than force. In general, these considerations are made based upon both tactical and investigative practicalities. In the end, the two are related. If a place is set up in such a way that entry will be difficult and dangerous, it also follows that the chances of recovering evidence before it can be destroyed are also reduced.

When it appears that there is little chance of success, alternatives to forced tactical entry should be considered. There are several which are commonly used, and they all involve getting the door open without force. Establishing surveillance on the target location and waiting for the suspect to leave is one way. If he can be stopped away from the house, it might be possible to use his key and gain entry. This, of course, will depend on how many other people are inside the location and if having the main suspect in custody removes the threat or greatly reduces it. This is effective but may require doing a significant amount of surveillance.

Another commonly employed alternative is subterfuge—having someone approach the door and getting the suspect to open it without knowledge that a drug raid is imminent. Many times this can be accomplished using a pair of uniform officers acting as if they have been called to the location for some innocuous reason. This will very often facilitate entry on locations of only a moderate or low threat level. Suspects in such cases can be caught off guard. On a fully fortified drug dealing location, this approach may not be sound. The officers sent to the door are exposed to a significant amount of danger.

There are any number of other scams whereby entry can be made using subterfuge. The chances of success and potential danger of alternate methods should be weighted against the tactical entry method and a determination made accordingly.

Another alternative to forced entry involves approaching the target location covertly and entering when the door is opened to allow someone else to enter or exit. This will often work, but the entry team must be prepared, as in the case of all alternatives, to make forced entry if their true purpose is detected.

IMPLEMENTING THE PLAN

Once the briefing is complete and the preraid surveillance has determined that conditions are right to go ahead with the raid, it is best to move forward as quickly as safety permits. Unnecessary delays at this point are distracting and counterproductive.

Staging

It is often necessary to stage following the briefing, en route to the target location. This is done when it is necessary to facilitate transportation and final preparations for the raid. Many times the briefing will be held in close enough proximity to the target location that final preparations can be made immediately following the briefing and no final staging area is necessary. If a staging is required, choose a staging area carefully. To stage too close to the target is inadvisable. The staging area should be out of heavy traffic patterns so as not to invite alarm or warning.

Again, final staging should be done quickly, with as little disruption to the focus of the operation as possible. If notifications are necessary, they should be done following the final staging. The necessary notifications should be made either by telephone or on a secure radio channel, telephone being preferable. The security of an operation can be assured only by limiting knowledge of it to those very few officers who must know. Notifying the communications bureau is important and they do have a need to know. Search warrant operations will generate calls for service from citizens who often mistake the perceptible activity for possible criminal activity. The dispatcher should also be notified when the location is secure.

Approach

The approach to the target location from the staging area should be done as inconspicuously as possible. Usually it is best to limit the number of vehicles transporting the officers to the location. An unmarked van specifically adapted for this purpose is best, as it allows for equipment to be hauled easily and also makes it possible for all officers to arrive simultaneously.

The final approach on foot should be done quickly and as a team.

Compliance with the terms of the warrant with respect to knocking and announcing is very important. In any case, once the entry is in progress, officers should be verbally identifying the operation by yelling "police." There have been tragic occurrences related to the suspects allegedly mistaking a police raid for a break-in by some criminal element. This is a common claim, but proper raid attire and clear verbal identification should make such claims invalid.

However, there was a 1989 case in Florida in which the suspect shot and killed a police officer who was part of a raid team. The suspect was subsequently acquitted of homicide and manslaughter by a jury based on the claim that he did not know that the people who entered his home in masks and dark clothing were police officers.

The Search

Suspects and Other Occupants

Once the entry team has secured all the occupants of the target location, the operation moves into the next phase. One of the leaders of the investigative team should make an immediate effort to identify the occupants and document their precise position in the target location when entry was made. The first few moments after a location has been secured can be chaotic. Adrenalin is running high. In the excitement and the confusion, particularly if numerous occupants are present, evidence may be thrown or secreted by suspects who are being or have been secured. The position of occupants relative to evidence found can be critical to a search warrant investigation.

Officers who made the entry should be questioned as to the whereabouts of each occupant when first encountered. Many times, some or all of the suspects will have been moved by the time the investigators get into the location and events have to be recreated. Figure 4-7 is a report developed for documenting the position of people when a search warrant is executed. It also facilitates the after-action reporting as well as the drug investigation. Figure 4-8 is a generic diagram form designed for use in conjunction with the search warrant report for additional documentation of the location of suspects and other people. This diagram can be adapted to most all situations and captures the names of officers who will be able to testify to the relative locations of suspects and evidence when that becomes critical.

```
                 NARCOTICS  INVESTIGATION  UNIT

                    SEARCH  WARRANT  REPORT


        DATE_____TIME_____TEAM  LEADER_____

        LOCATION  OF  SEARCH  WARRANT_____

        POINT  OF  ENTRY_____

        FORCIBLE  ENTRY   YES  [      ]    NO  [      ]


        AMOUNT  OF  DAMAGE_____

            ARRESTS                              NOTES

     1)   Name_____
          DOB_____
          Address_____
          Position  in  house_____
          Evidence_____

     2)   Name_____
          DOB_____
          Address_____
          Position  in  house_____
          Evidence_____

     3)   Name_____
          DOB_____
          Address_____
          Position  in  house_____
          Evidence_____

     4)   Name_____
          DOB_____
          Address_____
          Position  in  house_____
          Evidence_____

     5)   Name_____
          DOB_____
          Address_____
          Position  in  house_____
          Evidence_____
```

FIGURE 4-7

These forms can be filled out immediately, and while they may not supplant the need for complete statements from officers later, they work very well for initial documentation as a starting point for the investigation at the scene.

Generally, the supervisor of the investigative team is in the best

```
              NARCOTICS INVESTIGATION UNIT

                SEARCH WARRANT DIAGRAM

    DATE:_____TIME_____

    LOCATION OF WARRANT_____

    NAME OF OFFICER SUBMITTING THIS DIAGRAM WHO CAN
    TESTIFY TO THE DESCRIBED LOCATIONS AND POSITIONS
    OF SUSPECTS AND EVIDENCE
                                _____

    SIGNATURE_____SER#_____

    (NOTES IN DIAGRAM DO NOT APPEAR ON THE ACTUAL FORM)
```

	(EACH ROOM SHOULD BE LABELLED ACCORDING TO NEEDS. DEPICT AS MANY ROOMS AS NECESSARY.)
(XXX THROUGH UNNECESSARY ROOM DIVISION LINES).	(INDICATE NORTH)

```
    LEGEND:  /  / = DOORWAY;  (#) = SUSPECT LOCATION

          —xxxx—— = OPEN AREA, NO WALL.

    SUSPECT #1: NAME _____DOB_____
    SUSPECT #2: NAME _____DOB_____
    SUSPECT #3: NAME _____DOB_____
```

FIGURE 4-8

position to do this type of documentation. The supervisor should be familiar with what people, if any, are specifically named in the search warrant. Once the principal residents and/or suspects are identified, the purpose of the police raid should be explained by either the supervisor or the affiant. The appropriate people should be shown a copy of the search warrant. Those people named in the search warrant can be taken into a secure area, one that has already been searched, and they can be thoroughly searched. If people are present who are obviously not involved in the dealing, they can be cleared and then released. They should not be released unless it is apparent that they are not suspects. However, if they are not suspects, and they are clear of any warrants, they should be released as soon as possible to reduce the confusion and number of people in the location.

Searching people who are not named in the warrant and who may or may not be involved in the drug dealing is a decision to be carefully weighed. If evidence has been recovered and probable cause exists to arrest them, they can then be thoroughly searched incident to arrest and the evidence thus obtained will be admissible. To search all occupants merely because they are present, while perhaps the logical thing to do, may result in suppressed evidence later.

In the initial stages of an investigation at a search warrant scene, to search all people routinely simply for expediency is inadvisable. Let the investigation, the search of the location, and evidence recovered be a guide to searching occupants. As mentioned in the previous chapter, many drug warrants are approved with a provision to search all occupants. In these situations, it is necessary to have shown some nexus between the person and the drug dealing activity in the affidavit. If the person to be searched is not named in the warrant, and has no connection to the investigation, a thorough search of the person may later be determined to be unlawful. In *Ybarra v. Illinois,* the Supreme Court reached the conclusion that a "warrant to search a place cannot normally be construed to authorize a search of each individual in that place."[2] If there is probable cause to arrest the person, then a lawful search can be conducted incident to arrest. This probable cause might be independent of the drug investigation, or it might be related to previous sales and/or evidence recovered in the warrant and some clear nexus between the specific occupant and the target location.

Searching

While the supervisor is overseeing the documentation and processing of suspects and other occupants, the case investigator is free to take preliminary steps toward initiating the search. The first of these is to

---

2 *Ybarra v. Illinois,* 444 U.S. 90, 92 n.4 (1979)

survey the entire scene and determine the best approach for accomplishing the search. Next, a work station should be established and cleared to the extent that some work surface is available. Having a supply of paper towels or clean rags in the raid kit is useful for cleaning a table or counter and making a spot to work. The raid kit and other essentials should be brought to the central work station.

After the work station has been established, search assignments should be based either on circumstances at hand, a prearranged plan, or both. To be effective, any search operation must be thorough and systematic. The search must be consistent with the limitations of the search warrant. Generally, drug searches permit the opening of packages, checking in light fixtures, looking in ceiling panels, and undertaking other activities related to searching areas in which drugs might be concealed. It is reasonable that some minor damage might be done during a search operation and that the residence is left in mild disarray.[3]

However, to cause too much disorder in the search operation is counterproductive and inconsistent with being systematic and thorough. Search responsibilities should be assigned so that each room is the subject of two separate searches at least. Searching for drugs is a skill requiring practice and patience. Drug dealers are notorious for their collective ability to hide money and drugs, and a cursory or incomplete search will probably fail to recover all evidence.

The following is a list of potential evidence normally specified as some, if not all, of the items sought in a drug warrant. Many drug units in conjunction with the prosecutors have developed specific wording which is used in all drug search warrants with respect to the things named as items to be recovered. The wording should be in compliance with statutory definitions regarding controlled substances and illegal drugs. In addition to the contraband, items such as those listed here should also be included in the list of things, possibly related to drug dealing which are sought in the search warrant.

Items of Potential Evidentiary Value

1. *Drugs, in any quantity, even trace amounts.*

2. *Cash.* All cash should be checked against money lists for buy money from undercover and controlled buys. Currency generated by drug trafficking will be subject to civil seizure. It may be

---

3 See *Williams v. Alford,* 647 F.Supp. 1386, 1392 (M.D. Ala. 1986)

necessary to have a drug-sniffing dog go over the money in an effort to show that the money is tainted. Cash seized in conjunction with drug evidence should be taken as evidence.

3. *Drug packaging and processing materials.* Items such as paper bindles, plastic baggies, balloons, small pieces of foil, etc., may have evidentiary value, especially packaging material which the particular dealer is known to use. For example, if buys were made in which the drugs were wrapped in magazine paper, an attempt should be made to find the remnants of the magazine in the house and have a documents expert make comparisons. Baking soda, milk sugar, and other substances used in cutting or manufacturing drugs should be seized.

4. *Drug paraphernalia.* Needles, roach clips, crack pipes, hash pipes, etc. may be important evidence. In addition, such common items as razor blades, mirrors, and spoons may have evidentiary value as drug paraphernalia depending on the context in which they were recovered.

5. *Weapons.* Any weapons which may be a part of the drug dealing business should be taken as evidence. There will be some cases where the weapons recovered obviously have no connection to drug dealing; examples are weapons such as antique hunting rifles and the like. However, if there is a possibility that the weapons are related to the drug dealing, they should be taken. They can always be released to the owner later. There is so much violence related to drug dealing that to leave a suspected drug dealer in possession of a firearm which he may be inclined to use as part of the business is not in the best interest of effective drug enforcement, officer safety, or public safety.

6. *Paperwork and drug dealing records.* Paperwork which identifies the residents of the target location will be important evidence. Any telephone and address books which may identify dealing associates should also be examined and taken if they have any information of value in them. Sometimes, undercover phone numbers will be recorded in these books. Personal correspondence which identifies the residents of the location is also important evidence. Records of drug transactions are occasionally detailed and self-evident. Most of the time, however, they are recorded in the form of notes

on scrap pieces of paper, and it is difficult to establish that they are records of drug transactions. Any papers thought to be drug records should be seized and analyzed further when time permits.

7. *Financial records.* Bank records and other financial records such as income tax returns may be important in establishing a case for asset forfeiture. In addition, bank records may lead to further search warrants for safety deposit boxes and bank records.

8. *Keys.* Keys found may be important. If found on a suspect, a key to the target location can be evidence of his direct connection to it.

9. *Police scanners and surveillance equipment.*

10. *Other items with specific relevance to the particular investigation.*

Common Places of Concealment: Fixed Locations

1. *Structural.* Hiding drugs and other items of evidence within various parts of the structure is common. Potential hiding places in the ceiling and walls and floors should be checked as should the attics and crawl spaces. Furnace ducts and areas where insulation is loose, plumbing access panels, and electrical fixtures are used for concealing drugs as well.

2. *Furnishings.* The carpeting should be checked for loose edges and corners. All furniture in the target location should be thoroughly checked. Bedding should be removed from mattresses, and the box springs and mattresses should be searched. It is not uncommon for drug dealers to hide drugs in the rooms of children. Rooms should not be overlooked or searched in a cursory manner merely because they are children's rooms.

Drawers should be removed and the sides of the cabinet and the bottoms of the drawers checked for evidence secured to them.

Drugs and cash are frequently hidden in kitchen appliances. The insulation panels on oven doors and microwaves should be checked if there is any indication that the panels have been removed. Items in the refrigerator should be checked: drugs are often hidden in food containers either separately or mixed in with the food in the package.

3. *Personal property.* The most time-consuming portion of a search operation involves going through the clothing and personal prop-

erty in the location. To be effective, all clothing and personal property must be thoroughly checked for evidence. Money and drugs are commonly concealed in the pockets and linings of clothing in closets and drawers.

Cameras, videocassette recorders, audiocassette recorders, and other such items are all potential hiding places. Too often cameras are not opened and checked, and drugs can easily be hidden in the film compartment. Again, items of property in a child's room should be searched also. Drug dealers have been known to conceal drugs inside their children's stuffed toys and dolls and other playthings.

Food items too should be checked. Cereal boxes and loaves of sliced bread are good hiding places frequently overlooked in a search. Cans of coffee and packages of baking supplies should be searched too.

False-bottom containers, possibly marked as a certain product, deodorant, beer, motor oil, and the like, which are used for hiding money, drugs, and other valuable evidence are likely to be found.

4. *Curtilage and outbuildings.* The search warrant should include curtilage, the area adjacent to and part of the target property, as well as garages, sheds, and other outbuildings which are under the control of the suspect and which may be used as hiding places. It has become popular to bury drugs in the yard. In cases such as this, a good drug sniffing dog may be essential. This is another case where good surveillance can pay off. If there is any indication that the suspect is hiding drugs in such a manner, through surveillance, the suspect may be observed and his hiding places detected. Without some good inside information, drugs and evidence buried in the yard will probably not be found.

    Garages and outbuildings should be searched as thoroughly as the main location. Suspects may use these places to hide their drugs, thereby keeping other people, such as spouse or children inside the target location unaware of their activity.

Documenting the Search

Properly documenting and recording the evidence recovered is as important as any other phase of the operation. A search warrant scene should be processed with the care given other crime scenes. It is a good idea to photograph evidence as it is recovered before it is moved. This is not essential, but it is certainly preferable. Juries are impressed with photographs: they make excellent visual aids in the courtroom presentation. Also, if photographs were not taken, defense attorneys may try to make an issue of that in front of the jury. They may attempt to make the investigation look shoddy or second rate if common investigative techniques such as photographing evidence are not utilized.

The same is true of fingerprinting the packaging material which contained the drugs. Even though it is rare that fingerprints will be obtained, defense attorneys will make a big issue of the failure to request fingerprints. Again, juries do not realize the technical difficulties and other problems involved with getting fingerprints off paper decks or plastic baggies. To a certain extent, the jurors have unrealistic expectations as a result of watching police work dramatized on television and at the movies. Jurors expect that fingerprints can be obtained from just about any surface. Defense attorneys recognize the limitations of technology, but if fingerprints are not requested, they will try to convince the jury that the investigation was second rate. Inferences are made that if fingerprints had been obtained, their client would be exonerated, his fingerprints would not have been lifted from the evidence.

The point to be made is that the search warrant evidence should be processed with care and professionalism. It is necessary to have at least one person designated as the scribe, the person who records the evidence and marks the evidence containers. In some cases, more than one person must be assigned to this task. It is best if these people are set up at the central work station which has been established. The raid kit should have plenty of evidence containers, marking pens, tags, etc. so that the evidence can be marked as it is recovered. When evidence is found, the affiant should be notified and shown the position of the evidence. The evidence should then be photographed and recovered. Keep the chain of custody to a minimum number of officers. In many cases the defense will not stipulate to the chain of custody, and it will be necessary for each officer who handled the evidence to testify. The officer who recovered the evidence should mark the evidence container with the date and his initials.

In addition to indicating the location in which the evidence was found and who found it—the description of the location should be detailed enough so that there is no question later. Cash evidence should be counted and witnessed before it is taken from the scene. This can be a time-consuming effort at the scene, but it is a must. Counting the cash in front of the suspect is a good idea if the suspect is not belligerent or hostile. Many times suspects will volunteer information about currency which is found. They will often claim that it belongs to them, and if the cash can be tied to the drugs recovered, that statement will be useful. Occasionally suspects, particularly those who have been arrested before, will realize that buy money may be in with the money which has been found or that a dog may hit on the money and consequently will disclaim any knowledge of it. Such disclaimers may be used in later efforts to have the money forfeited.

Once the search is complete a return and inventory must be filled out which represents exactly what items were taken from the scene. A copy of this will have to be left at the place searched or given to the resident or person in control of the premises. What is often standard procedure is to complete the return and inventory at the office so that it can be typed and a copy is then given to the suspect before he is placed in jail. In cases where the person in control is not arrested, the return and inventory should be completed at the scene. It is a good idea to go over the list of items taken so that there is no misunderstanding.

Occasionally, valuable items will be discovered in a search which are not taken. It is advisable to show the suspect the item and tell him or her that it is going to be left where it is. This is a particularly good idea in the case of jewelry and rare coins and other small items. Many complaints of impropriety can be avoided if suspects are made aware of certain things and made to acknowledge that awareness. For example, it would be difficult for a suspect to come back and make a claim that the police stole his watch when it was explained to him that the watch was to be left in the place in which it was found and he witnessed the officer put it back there.

After-Action Reporting

Following a search warrant operation, there should be a routine reporting of the events which took place. This report should include details of forced entry where such was necessary and documentation of any damage done to property as a result. Polaroid pictures are a handy way of recording such damage. Invariably, the owners of the property will want to know who is going to pay to repair the damages, and standard reporting procedures should be in place which document all forced entries.

Any action involving a large number of people or an interagency effort should be reported. Such search warrants may receive media attention, but in any case, the appropriate department commanders should be aware that such an operation did take place. If the investigation is ongoing or for some other reason it is of a sensitive nature, steps should be taken to see that it is reported but that the media are not given access to the details of the reports.

Most after-action reporting of search warrant operations involves the investigation itself. There is too often a tendency for everyone to think that when the entry is made, the excitement has subsided, and the drugs recovered, the rest of the work belongs to the investigator who initiated the case. This is not at all the case. A successful completion of the investigation will be facilitated by a teamwork approach to the after-action phase of the warrant. The teamwork should continue until all the evidence is processed and placed in the property bureau. Three or four people working together to mark and inventory the evidence and complete the arrest processing are much more efficient than one person doing it all alone.

Investigators who have assisted on a search warrant operation have a responsibility to make a statement or report of their actions to the primary investigator. This is imperative where officers recover evidence or witness something significant. Their actions will need to be documented as part of the case preparation. Investigators should make these reports as soon as possible and should exercise the same care in preparing them that they would if the case were their own.

The suspects should be interviewed prior to being placed in jail. Although they will have been advised at the scene of their *Miranda* rights, they should be readvised at headquarters or wherever they are being processed. If they were orally advised at the scene, that should be noted on the written advisement when it is completed. Many times the suspects will not want to talk, but those who do, and do not request that an attorney be present, should be questioned. Specific questions should be asked regarding drugs and currency and other evidence which was recovered. The answers to these questions can be extremely beneficial later.

It should not be assumed that the suspect will not be willing to talk or answer questions. On the other hand, there should be no appearance that the suspect is being coerced into talking. The suspect should not be promised that his case will be dismissed. Only the prosecutors can make those decisions, and even they can only make recommendations. Judges are not bound to abide by any of these arrangements. Information gained from suspects may not immediately result in an opportunity to work up to a higher-level dealer, but it can be solid intelligence for future investigations.

SPECIAL CONSIDERATIONS FOR DRUG LAB RAIDS

Conducting search warrant operations in which the target is a drug manufacturing laboratory of some type requires special expertise and special procedures. A comprehensive plan for these situations should be developed within each jurisdiction. The Drug Enforcement Administration and the California Bureau of Narcotics Enforcement began developing a comprehensive clandestine lab safety program in 1986. Since that time, the plan, developed in accordance with safety regulations set forth by the Occupational Safety and Health Administration, has served as a model for preparedness for the hazards presented by clandestine drug labs. That plan "consists of four basic elements—policies and procedures, equipment and protective clothing, training and medical monitoring."[4]

Investigations focusing on clandestine drug labs will require some special expertise throughout. Many narcotics investigators have little if any experience in investigating these types of cases. Some member or members of each department should be specifically trained in this field to assist or take the lead in these cases. When the investigation has reached the stage that a search warrant operation is imminent, the existence of some plan for dealing with clandestine labs and the related hazards is critical. Lab raids differ from other types of drug raids in several specific areas, all of which have safety implications and all of which should be considered as part of a plan developed beforehand.

Training

Clandestine lab investigations require special training and expertise. One of the main points of such training is the emphasis placed on the

---

4 Randolph D. James, "Hazards of Clandestine Drug Laboratories," *FBI Law Enforcement Bulletin*, April 1989.

need for outside consultation and teamwork. Training should be given to all people who will ultimately be responsible for the safe disposition of a clandestine lab, investigators, chemists, safety coordinators, fire department personnel, and police department tactical personnel. At some point those people who are trained and who have become experts should be called upon to train others within the agency.

Hazards

Clandestine lab investigations have numerous potential hazards in addition to those hazards commonly associated with narcotics investigation. "[T]hese hazards (in order of priority) are: (1) explosions; (2) fires; (3) weapons; and (4) short and long term exposure to chemicals. On a national average, one of five, or twenty percent of all clandestine drug laboratories result in, and/or are discovered through, fires and/or explosions."[5] Gregory and Lazarus went on to cite statistics related to 170 clandestine laboratory search warrants investigated jointly by DEA and the California Bureau of Narcotic Enforcement in northern California. According to those statistics, in 10 percent of those 170 cases, officers were confronted by suspects in possession of fully automatic weapons. In another 10 percent of the cases, agents and officers encountered some type of explosive or chemical booby trap. Finally, in 30 percent of these incidents, some countersurveillance measures were in effect.[6]

Precautions

Chemical

When a raid on a clandestine lab is planned, it is essential that a chemist be consulted in the planning stages. The chemist may be able to assist in accurately assessing the threat level present. The chemist must be present at the scene and take control of the scene immediately after it is secure. The chemist should be responsible for shutting down the lab if it is operational. The chemist will also supervise the collection and processing of evidence.

---

5 Patrick Gregory and Bruce Lazarus, "Safety and Seizure Aspects in Clandestine Drug Laboratories," paper presented at the International Symposium of the Forensic Aspects of Controlled Substances, March 1988, p. 2.

6 Ibid.

Tactical

A lab raid presents a number of additional tactical problems related to the hazards just outlined. As a result, it is necessary to develop tactical plans specifically tailored to these situations.

Special protective clothing must be worn in addition to standard tactical gear. Contingency plans must account for the enhanced threat to the safety of all involved. Hazardous materials specialists and fire department and emergency medical people should be on immediate standby during the execution of the raid.

The immediate goals of the entry plan remain the same as in other raids. Superior manpower and firepower should be deployed with swiftness and surprise so that the suspects can be safely secured. Specialized training relative to clandestine lab investigations and their accompanying hazards will allow for specific tactical preparedness.

Evidence Collection

Search teams also must be provided with protective clothing and should be aware that the chemist will be in charge of processing the search warrant scene. No evidence should be moved without the approval of the chemist. It is advisable to photograph the entire scene immediately after it has been secured. An electronic flash rather than flash bulbs should be used. Positions of light switches should not be changed. The chemist, working closely with the search teams, should see that all finished products and in-process reactions are seized as well as certain precursors. It will be the responsibility of the chemist to determine what items are seized and what quantities. Samples of all chemical found should be taken including those that are contained in marked, sealed containers.

Documentary evidence can be very important if establishing a case for manufacturing controlled substances. All catalogs, recipes, written formulas, and notes should be taken. It may be necessary to obtain a handwriting sample from the suspects and have comparisons made as part of the case preparation.

Disposition of Chemicals

The disposition of chemicals, evidentiary and nonevidentiary items alike, is a critical part of the policies and preparation for these situations. The ramifications of disposing of the chemicals go far beyond the scope of the individual case, and it is necessary to have a plan for safe transportation and disposal which is in compliance with government regulations.

Decontamination

All involved personnel should be decontaminated following the operation and given medical evaluation where the extent of exposure warrants it. Again, long-range safety planning must include comprehensive documentation of exposure and continued monitoring of any side effects which may develop.

CRACK COCAINE: SPECIAL STREET OPERATIONS AND INVESTIGATIVE SITUATIONS

INTRODUCTION

This chapter considers unique problems created by crack cocaine which are experienced in most metropolitan and urban areas across the United States. Crack cocaine has created problems for law enforcement at all levels, but particularly for local police departments and local drug investigators.

This chapter includes a discussion of special operations and investigative techniques that have been developed in response to the crack cocaine problem. Four different investigative techniques and operations will be discussed: extensive use of search warrants to effectively combat street-level crack dealers, street-level undercover buy operations, street sweeps, and street corner reverses.

While the discussion of these techniques is in the context of problems generally related to crack cocaine, the techniques have applicability to a variety of situations. They are commonly used in those other situations, and with the exception of the street sweeps approach and the street reverses, they were in widespread use prior to the emergence of crack cocaine problems. The street sweeps and street reverses are techniques which grew out of a need to address crack cocaine problems specifically.

DEFINITION

Crack cocaine or cocaine base is a highly addictive, smokable drug derived from cocaine hydrochloride. Crack cocaine is easily made from cocaine hydrochloride by mixing the cocaine hydrochloride in powdered form with baking soda and water. The ether with which the cocaine was processed in its initial manufacture and other ingredients used to cut the purity of the cocaine are removed when the cocaine is heated with the baking soda and water. The result is cocaine base or crack, which, after allowed to cool and harden, is in a crystalline form. This is then heated, usually in a glass pipe. The vapors are inhaled and an intense high is achieved.

CRACK COCAINE

Background

The year 1986 is a key date in the development of the crack cocaine problem across the country. Several cities—Miami, Detroit, New York, and Los Angeles, most notably—had experienced severe problems with crack cocaine beginning about 1981. In 1986, however, crack began to spread across the country in epidemic style. A national survey conducted in July 1986 of 30 major cities across the country,[1] revealed 13 cities that reported a severe problem with crack cocaine. Those in that category ranged from New York City where over 1,200 complaints regarding crack dealing were received in a two-week period in the end of May and beginning of June that year, to Oakland, California, where it was reported that 90 percent of the street drug dealers were selling crack cocaine.

---

1 "Major City Survey of Cocaine Crack Abuse," July 17, 1986, U.S. House of Representatives, Select Committee on Narcotics Abuse and Control. Memorandum from Chief of Staff John T. Cusack attached to survey results. (The survey is referred to in this background section on crack cocaine.)

Crack cocaine was already a tremendous problem in major cities such as New York, Los Angeles, and Miami by 1986, and it was becoming a problem in most other major metropolitan areas. During the next year, crack-related investigations continued to rise sharply in most cities, beginning a trend that continued through most of 1989.

In Denver, Colorado, for example, there was one significant location from which "rock" cocaine was distributed prior to the spring of 1986. That location dealt cocaine in rock form, or cocaine base, and it was ingested by smoking it. The cocaine base was not called crack, that term was not yet in use. It was called rock, consistent with West Coast terminology in use at the time. The location had developed into a tremendous source of citizen complaints and was raided on a regular basis. It was a nuisance problem, and each time a search warrant was executed at that location, large numbers of people, 10 to 15, were contacted inside. Invariably, several people were arrested but only small amounts of cocaine base were recovered and often no cases were filed due to the difficulty encountered in establishing possession. With a limited number of narcotics investigators available, this nuisance location was given low priority in the overall enforcement strategy. It was, it turned out, the predecessor of several hundred crack houses to follow by 1988.

During the spring of 1986, the death of Maryland basketball star Len Bias was followed by a news media explosion regarding crack cocaine. In many parts of the country, the term crack was not used prior to its widespread use in the media, both print and electronic at that time. The media attention served to alarm the public as it told of the grave dangers associated with use of crack cocaine and some of the violence attendant to its distribution in major markets across the country. The media anticipated an ensuing crisis. The media reports rightly, as it turned out, foretold of crack houses spreading throughout major cities. The media attention while warning of the dangers of the drug and the situation in general, also seemed to contribute to the popularity of the drug.

Crack became a notoriously evil drug, the distribution and use of which spread equally as rapidly as the warnings of its dangers; several factors worked together to make it the focal point of an American inner-city crisis.

By 1987, nearly every major city in the country was experiencing problems with crack cocaine for which they were not prepared. Crack usage and demand for the product were spreading, and the number of people involved in crack distribution, primarily in inner cities, also increased.

Problems Created by Crack Proliferation

Several characteristics of crack cocaine made it ideally suited for exploitation on the street-level drug market. That is, it is extremely marketable. It can be sold in small quantities for individual consumption, much as marijuana can be sold in individual cigarettes (joints). The possession of a small amount of crack cocaine can be easily concealed from law enforcement officers or discarded and destroyed if that is necessary. Also, like marijuana, it is smoked (in actuality, as the cocaine base is heated a vapor is released and that is inhaled, not smoke in the true sense of the word), which gives it additional mass market appeal. In American culture, smoking is a highly accepted method of ingesting drugs, unlike injection into the bloodstream, which is always associated with hard-core, addictive drug usage.

Crack has the appeal of an intensive high, which coupled with the relatively low cost of individual doses and the fact that it is smoked, makes it preferable to the competition. Finally, crack is easily and safely converted from cocaine hydrochloride (HCl) and is sold at a tremendous profit.

All these factors contributed to the widespread popularity of crack cocaine on the inner-city markets of America in the mid-1980s. With this spread of popularity came problems for drug enforcement officers, unique in many respects.

The way in which the crack cocaine problem manifested itself on the streets across the country can best be characterized as a rage, it did not develop into a problem slowly. It became a problem almost instantly; one day it was not to be found, and what seemed like only the next day, it was being sold on every street corner in certain areas of major cities.

To a great extent, crack was introduced into the illicit street drug market and immediately took on dimensions unequaled by cocaine and heroin in terms of impact on the community. The media attention given crack cocaine, in advance of it becoming a problem in most cities, may have created a public awareness which contributed to adverse public reaction. But much of the adverse public reaction to street crack dealing activity relates to problems inherent in the crack business, not necessarily present in street sales of other drugs.

Many of those problems center on the low price, the highly addictive nature of crack, and the increased profit margin for the dealers. Those three factors taken as a whole moved crack past other drugs in terms of popularity, created a huge demand, heavy foot traffic in sales areas, and in general a very high visibility problem. In addition there were several real and perceived risks to the welfare of the public. People will complain about any drug house in the neighborhood if it is generating a steady stream of traffic, but the traffic and commotion created by crack houses and crack dealers, as crack was first being introduced into a city, far exceeded that generated by other drugs. The low individual dose price of crack cocaine relates to the fact that each dose is cocaine base, almost pure, and very little is required to receive an intense feeling of euphoria. In turn, the high does not last long, and there will usually be a desire initially, and after extended use, a craving to repeat the cycle. A customer may go back to the dealer several times during the course of a day or night, further contributing to complaints about heavy traffic.

Heavy Demand/Heavy Traffic

One of the most serious problems created by a proliferating crack cocaine problem was the heavy traffic and the subsequent complaints and calls for service. In most cases, crack dealing was undertaken in existing street-level drug markets. Crack houses were set up in areas where drugs on the street were not uncommon. In many cases, locations for dealing heroin and cocaine as well as marijuana already existed in the areas in which crack dealing was established. Many police departments experienced a sudden rise in the number of complaints as soon as crack was introduced into the illicit drug market. People who had not complained about traditional drug dealing locations began complaining about the crack dealers. Part of this relates to the fact that traditional dealing was done in a more low-key, low-visibility manner. Dealers were circumspect about who their customers were. They would not sell to somebody they did not know, and they made a point of not attracting attention to themselves. Customers who attracted attention would no longer be served.

Therefore, people frequenting traditional drug sales locations would come and go as unobtrusively as possible. They would go to the door, take care of business, and leave the area. While complaints regarding drug dealers and drug dealing locations have always been a factor in narcotics enforcement, never were complaints generated in the numbers that crack produced and continues to produce in many jurisdictions.

One of the reasons for the tremendous number of people who are part of the problem is that many users and addicts become involved in the dealing process. Never before have so many people taken to drug dealing. In fact, a whole new generation and class of dealers was brought into existence in the areas of cities affected by crack dealing. Many people who were career drug dealers have switched to selling crack; in addition, there is an entire group of new dealers. Traditional lines between dealers and users are erased as many users become dealers. In addition, many people who are not users become dealers motivated by the profit incentives of crack dealing.

Crack users quickly learn that they can do one of three things to make the support of their own habit easier. They can buy a gram or two or even an 1/8 ounce of cocaine HCl and convert it to crack themselves. By so doing, they can sell enough of the crack to cover their initial investment, have plenty for their personal use, and possibly have money left over to buy more cocaine and start the process over again. Another option involves standing around crack sales locations and offering to go to the dealer for customers who come into the area. They then buy a small quantity for which they may be rewarded by the dealer, a commission in a sense, or they will shave off some of the crack destined for the customer and keep it for personal use or resale to another customer. In this manner they can keep themselves supplied at no expense. The third option involves hanging around the crack sales locations and dealing imitation crack (bunk, woo, etc.) and then taking the proceeds and supplying their own habits. Closely related to this third option is simply taking the customers' money and giving them nothing in return.

In addition to the sheer numbers of people involved, there are related difficulties. It is often very difficult to identify the crack dealer at the onset of an investigation when there are so many and they are constantly moving and changing. That coupled with the fact that crack locations attract so much customer traffic creates confusion. Traditional investigative standards have had to be adjusted to cope with the volume of traffic and complaints.

Low-Level Cases

In the initial stages of the crack crisis, most local police departments were not only ill-equipped to handle the extra work load, they had gotten away from working low-level cases. The trend through the early part of the 1980s had been away from low-level street enforcement and toward the middle and upper levels when manpower limitations and overloaded court dockets dictated that some priorities had to be established.

Crack cocaine dealing embodies many of the factors which have been considered grounds for a low enforcement priority: small amounts of drugs involved, low-level street dealers, and dealers whose only criminal records in the area of controlled substance violations consist of use and possession-related cases, not distribution. What the crack cocaine problem does have, however, which makes it a public threat and an enforcement priority is an aura of violence, a rise in attendant crimes against persons and property, and a tremendously low dealer-user ratio. The low dealer-to-user ratio, as mentioned before, is due in part to the potential for profit, the safe and easy conversion of cocaine to crack, and the fact that so many users and addicts become dealers.

But a drug enforcement strategy that targets dealers in an effort to have the most impact for the enforcement dollar requires some adaptation to deal with a huge class of dealers, many of whom commonly possess quantities only slightly above what are generally considered personal use amounts.

Establishing a Teamwork Approach

The spread of crack cocaine dealing not only impacts narcotics investigators but others in law enforcement as well. Patrol districts are deluged with calls for service which are related to crack dealing. Commanders and administrators are pressured into doing something about the drug dealers in their districts. Community relations officers are overwhelmed with complaints about crack houses from concerned citizens and action groups. A crack problem is not only a drug enforcement problem, but a high-priority police problem in general. Because of this, an unprecedented team effort is required to deal with it. Units within the police department must work together, and the police narcotics investigators must work closely with local officers from other jurisdictions and federal law enforcement officers also.

In most jurisdictions which have experienced serious crack problems, drug enforcement priorities have had to be rearranged in order to address the problem. Changing those priorities has required commensurate adjustments on the part of prosecutors, judges, and others in the criminal justice system. Theories emphasizing focus on the upper-level dealers thought to have the most impact on the drug situation in a community had to be revised because of mandates from communities that street crack dealing should be the number one priority of not only the police departments but the courts as well. Attention has been refocused on street-level dealing.

Initial responses to growing crack problems in most cities met with frustration, little success, and the realization that more manpower was needed and new tactics had to be developed. The numbers of complaints and numbers of people involved greatly exceeded the resources available. As the problem continued to grow in scope, there were so many officers committed to working crack investigations spread throughout a given agency that coordination was difficult. Gang units were established, and they generated crack cases. Patrol officers were heavily involved and often generated cases. Part of the frustration and the lack of success experienced in dealing with crack problems initially related to poor teamwork and communication.

The Drug Enforcement Administration has provided local law enforcement a great deal of assistance, manpower, and other resources over the years and has generally played an important role in local drug enforcement efforts. In November 1986, officials from the DEA hosted a conference in Dallas, Texas, to which several local narcotics officers from around the country were invited. DEA was in the process of formulating a strategy, a position with respect to crack cocaine. What came out of that conference was the determination that crack was by its nature a state and local law enforcement problem, not a federal law enforcement problem, a drug problem with which local officers would have to contend.

DEA and other federal agencies have recognized that crack cocaine is potentially a very serious threat in many major cities. However, the evaluation made by DEA in 1986 was correct. Crack was and is still primarily a street-level problem, and as such DEA and other federal law enforcement agencies can provide only limited support.

It is teamwork which has enabled law enforcement to achieve any degree of success in combatting crack cocaine. Local agencies formed regional task forces, many of which were organized and funded by state and federal agencies. Also, federal law enforcement agencies have assisted a great deal in investigating major violators cooperatively with local officers. The U.S. Attorney's office has also provided a great deal of support and has prosecuted many crack cases involving small amounts of drugs based on the rationale that interstate crack trafficking is rightly within the purview of the federal courts given the threat which crack represents to the public welfare. These prosecutions have served warning that crack dealing will be dealt with harshly and have had a deterring effect.

Violence

Violence can be a factor in any criminal enterprise. It has always been a part of drug dealing to varying degrees and will remain so. However, crack dealing brought with it an escalation in the violence associated with drug dealing. The gang involvement in crack dealing accounted for a significant amount of the increased violence as well as the increase in number of weapons encountered.

Another significant factor in the violence associated with crack dealing relates to the competition. The large number of people involved in the drug dealing has led to violent confrontations between dealers in turf battles.

Whatever the causes, weapons were encountered in crack raids in unprecedented numbers as the problem emerged. For example, the Denver Police Department Crack Task Force seized 192 weapons in 246 crack search warrants in 1988. In 1989 the ratio dropped to 175 firearms seized in 350 task force search warrants. The ratio increased slightly in 1990 as 139 weapons were seized in 226 search warrants.

Weapons and violence are very important aspects of crack investigations which must be taken into consideration and which add to the intensity of the work.

Unusual Hours

Not only has crack brought about an increased work load, but it has caused investigators to rearrange their hours on duty. Along with the trend towards complex investigations and prosecutions of upper-level dealers has come a tendency for more narcotics investigators to work during regular daytime hours. Crack can be a 24-hour-a-day problem. In fact, when it first emerged as a problem, most dealers remained active "7 and 24," or "24/7," meaning that dealing was continuous, all day every day.

To be effective, personnel assigned to crack investigations has to be deployed during the hours of peak activity. In addition, the old adage "if he's dealing today, he'll be dealing tomorrow" does not necessarily hold. Consequently, action, if it is to be effective, must often be immediate.

Not only can the hours be unusual, but they are also long. This is of course true of drug investigations in general, but it certainly applies to crack investigations.

Burnout

All the foregoing individual problems—the high number of people involved in selling crack, the heavy work load and unusual working hours, tremendous citizen demands to do something about the problem, the small quantities of drugs involved, the violence, the increased internal pressure caused by so many different people involved in crack investigations and the resultant friction, and the dangerous nature of the work—have created a burnout factor in narcotics investigation units unlike that experienced in the past.

Regardless of how dedicated and hard working a narcotics investigator is, he will get burned out trying to keep pace with a street crack problem, or any other problem for that matter, that is out of control. There is a great deal of pressure inherent in working street-level crack investigations, and there is pressure from the prosecutors to make better cases. Prosecutors want the bigger, better quality cases, and they really can't be expected to get too excited about filing a case involving very small quantities of crack.

There is also considerable pressure from the citizens to keep doing more. People living next door to a crack house want something done about it. They aren't really interested in the fact that 500 crack search warrants have been executed or that 1,000 arrests have been made. They want something done about their problem, and they want it done immediately.

Foremost perhaps as a factor contributing to burnout is the frustration which results from dealing with the same dealers over and over again. The failure of the rest of the system to deal effectively with crack dealers who have been arrested and convicted once or more than once is a big part of the problem. And it is demoralizing to put time and energy into an investigation and see the dealer go right back out and continue dealing, generating more complaints and adding more pressure to the investigator.

It is difficult to keep good people involved in intense work like crack investigations for any considerable length of time without seeing signs of burnout which can have devastating side effects.

When crack dealing takes hold in a community, all these problems will be encountered to varying degrees. The sum is a complex multifaceted threat to public safety which must be addressed with commitment and resolve.

SOLUTIONS TO THE CRACK PROBLEM

In addressing a large-scale problem, traditional investigative methods will be applied. Some nontraditional strategies have also been developed in response to the problems created. Regardless of the course of action taken, an operational doctrine must be developed based on certain principles. While developing this philosophy is an administrative function, it will be based at least in part on input from individual investigators who are the ones in the know and the ones who will be responsible for converting the philosophy into action. The philosophy becomes the backbone and the collective conscience, the strength of which will influence individual and agency survival.

Elements of Operational Doctrine

1. *Enforce the drug laws as strictly as possible.* In essence a zero tolerance goal has to be the optimum, realizing that it will be impossible to eradicate the problem completely but that it is entirely possible to clean up sections of the city one block at a time. If the legislators see fit to make changes in the laws, decriminalization, for example, so be it. In the meantime, file every possible case which can be filed. Operating on this philosophy will require communication with prosecutors and judges. Naturally, it is assumed that the public supports efforts to remove the crack dealers from the streets. Representatives from the prosecutor's office, elected officials, and others should be a part of community meetings and thus made aware of public demands for action.

2. *Determine manpower availability and needs.* It will be necessary in many cases to request that additional officers are assigned on a temporary basis at least.

3. *Assess the problem as a whole and make a threat assessment which prioritizes targets by individual and location.* Those individuals and locations which are having the most impact on the problem should be given priority. Taken into consideration as part of this evaluation is the likelihood that prosecutable cases can be developed.

Inherent in the crack problem are places which generate a great deal of traffic and complaints from citizens but which involve very insignificant amounts of crack and which have very little potential for successful prosecution. Places such as this represent more of a patrol problem than an investigative problem, and uniform patrol officers assigned to work these areas will be as important in eradicating the problems, in many cases more than will the narcotics investigators. If weapons are flourished or fortification is so extensive that disregard for the law is being flaunted, those people and locations should be a priority. Targeting such locations sends a message to the rest of the dealers.

4. *Develop a game plan and contingencies and follow-up plans which enable the reclaiming of neighborhoods which have been lost to crack dealers or are on the verge of being lost.* Coordination with patrol commanders will be essential, as their units will be critical to the success of the various phases of the game plan. The game plan should be calculated to send a clear message to crack dealers.

5. *Put the plan into action.* Have contingency plans prepared and be ready to utilize them frequently. The crack dealers will react to the enforcement action taken as part of the initial plans, and the contingency plans must anticipate and deal with those reactions on their part.

6. *Track all phases of progress but focus primarily on the number of complaints, the crime rates in targeted areas, the number of cases filed, and the progress of those cases in the court system.* By and large, the relative success of a strategy can be measured by evaluating these factors.

7. *Make provisions for reporting to the citizens the kinds of action taken, and the relative success.* Attendance of some representative of the narcotics investigation unit at these meetings is beneficial. Reports to the citizens' groups should be candid. Attending these meetings allows for further input from the citizens.

An operational doctrine such as that just outlined is a must for an effective enforcement program. There must be some goal in mind and some plans for making the goal achievable. A police department cannot back down from any large-scale drug problems and provide some semblance of safety to the citizens in the area at the same time. For the people living in an area overtaken by crack dealing, or any other drug dealing activity for that matter, the concept of drug dealing as a victimless crime has no validity. Entire neighborhoods have been ruined by crack cocaine dealing. The future of an entire generation of young people, primarily from the lower socioeconomic classes, has been jeopardized.

Local police officers, drug investigators in particular, and local police agencies individually have a limited role in the national drug enforcement strategy. Collectively, however, it is the local police departments, the local criminal justice systems which will ultimately decide the success or failure of that strategy. It is common for local police drug investigators to look at the endless supply of drugs coming into the country and feel a sense of frustration. However, the responsibility of local officers is to eradicate drug dealing in their jurisdictions. That goal will never be fully achievable, but it is possible to impact the problem, to clean up certain neighborhoods, and to maintain law and order and control of the streets.

There are a number of techniques, some conventional and some innovative, which can be utilized to attack a large-scale drug problem, specifically for the purposes of this discussion, a crack problem.

Intensified Search Warrant Efforts

Depending on the scope and nature of a given drug problem, the search warrant can be an effective tool in combatting it. In evaluating a problem for prospective avenues of investigation, there are a number of key factors which will affect the decision. If the crack problem consists primarily of street corner sales done open market style, search warrants will obviously not be applicable on a wide scale. In general, warm weather cities face more open market dealing than cities where winter becomes a harsh reality that even crack dealers cannot ignore. The determination to use search warrants as a primary enforcement tool does not preclude the use of other techniques, and in fact search warrants are most effective when used in conjunction with other techniques, such as undercover buy programs and so on. Search warrants based on informant information and controlled buys can be used effectively where undercover operations are for one reason or another not possible or not feasible.

Determining Targets

If a crack problem has at its core a large concentration of indoor crack dealing locations or crack houses, the search warrant, applied on a large scale, can be effective. The relative importance of the crack houses in the overall problem has to be evaluated and determined. If there are, for example, 100 crack houses in operation and only a handful of investigators assigned to the problem, prioritization will be a necessity. If it is possible, determine some objective ranking and hit the targets accordingly. Or if it is possible to determine who the suppliers are, they should be targeted and multiple crack houses may be put out of business if the sources can be prosecuted.

Having members of the prosecutors office involved in the planning and development of strategy is very important when it comes to determining targets. They will be responsible for successfully prosecuting the cases which are developed and for deciding what charges are appropriate. Enforcement action will be a waste of time if the cases are not prosecuted to the fullest extent. If, for example, simple possession of a given amount of crack cocaine has been decriminalized to misdemeanor status, it will be necessary to establish sale or distribution of crack, which is a serious felony, to make the search warrant effort worthwhile. This can be done through undercover buys at the location or established constructively through amount possessed, packaging, and the recovery of other items associated with dealing rather than personal use or simple possession.

In some states the law provides that possession and distribution are both felonies; in fact they may be covered under the same statute. That being the case, the search warrant may have widespread application, as possession of crack will be sufficient basis for prosecution as a felony and whether possession or sale is filed will really not make any difference, although evidence of sale is preferable if and when the case is presented to a jury. Distribution and sale can be established constructively for a more effective prosecution in the absence of undercover buys.

It is important that the prosecutor's office be made aware of the small amounts of drugs which may be involved in crack cases. That is a reality in distribution and possession cases alike many times. There should be no misconceptions on the part of prosecutors. If it is not made clear that small amounts of crack spread among a large number of people characterizes the crack problem, there will be a tendency to resist filing cases based on small recoveries, and it will be impossible to have any impact on the problem. A concerted effort to attack a crack problem, if it is to be successful, has to include filing cases on dealers regardless of amounts involved. This will require that discretion be used in making any plea bargaining arrangements. The impact of an enforcement program can be greatly reduced by concessions in plea bargaining that put the dealer right back out on the street without sufficient deterrent to keep him from continued dealing. He will be the source of more complaints, and indirectly more addiction and attendant crime. Plea bargains should be made in consideration of the likelihood the dealer will continue dealing and in such a way that subsequent cases will be aggravated by the existence of the first case.

A search warrant operation on a crack house can have an impact far beyond just the recovery of a given amount of crack and a couple of case filings. A crack search warrant makes a statement on behalf of legitimate community interests: control of the streets by the drug dealers is an issue which will be hotly contested. To maximize the impact, the target has to be relatively important. Search warrant targets have to be determined on the basis of potential for success of that investigative technique versus other techniques, the relative importance of the violator, and the negative impact that the location is having on the neighborhood. Search warrant operations have a great inherent potential for danger, mishap, and liability and are labor intensive as well. It is, therefore, essential that targets be prioritized. This prioritization is an ongoing process subject to continual revision. What might be a priority tonight might be low on the list tomorrow night.

Timeliness

Crack dealing is an extremely transitory business. Dealers come and go, move locations, change hours, etc., based on several factors. Competition, changes in the weather, fluctuating sources of supply, neighborhood pressure, and the enforcement efforts of the police department all precipitate changes. Any investigative techniques deployed must be used in a timely fashion. This is a critical factor in the use of search warrants, more than in the use of other techniques which are by their nature more flexible.

Widespread use of search warrants against a crack problem is based on the principle that if probable cause exists, a search warrant will be obtained and executed. Executing a large number of search warrants as part of an anticrack campaign requires that the investigators become experts in writing search warrants which will withstand close legal scrutiny later. At the same time, the process has to be streamlined so that what is essentially an unwieldy process by nature is adapted to a fast-moving situation.

There are several steps that can be taken to facilitate the streamlining of the search warrant process so that warrants can be obtained and executed in a timely and effective manner. Following are some of them:

1. A policy should be established that requires that some representative of the prosecutor's office review search warrant affidavits and assist in their preparation when necessary. This will, in theory at least, ensure that warrant affidavits are correctly written. It should facilitate successful prosecution and should at the same time prevent serious and costly mistakes. To be more beneficial, this policy should provide for at least one designated person from the prosecutor's office to perform this function. That representative should be familiar with drug prosecutions and the intricacies of problems encountered which pertain specifically to search warrants. Provisions must be made for this person to be on call. Another facet of this involves a policy which also requires supervisory approval of search warrants prior to presenting them for prosecutorial approval. This is particularly important if the prosecutor is inexperienced, providing the supervisor is competent to make the appropriate recommendations.

2. Investigators should be given special formal training regarding the Fourth Amendment in general and search warrant construction in particular. The best training, however, for becoming proficient in search warrants is actual on-the-job training: writing search warrant affidavits, preparing the cases for prosecution, and testifying in court, specifically in motions hearings. These lessons can be costly if they result in lost cases, but no method of training is more effective. Under the watchful eye of experienced investigators, training will be accomplished, and the job will get done at the same time.

3. There are technological resources which facilitate writing and obtaining search warrants in a timely fashion. Word processing packages are available which not only save time in writing search warrant affidavits, but also make the final product more presentable and professional looking. Systems can also be developed for

facsimilating the warrant to the judge for approval after business hours, which results in time savings and reduced inconvenience to the judge.

4. Special tactical training is required if narcotics investigators are called upon to execute high-risk immediate-entry search warrants. If a tactical unit is available for that purpose, the investigative unit and the tactical unit can develop teamwork for the purpose of achieving mutual goals.

5. Search warrant operations cannot be done on a large scale without the development of a teamwork approach. Every phase of search warrant operations is best accomplished through teamwork, and the need for teamwork is more critical as the number of warrants increases.

Investigative Techniques: Specific Application in the Development of Crack Search Warrants

Controlled Buys

In search warrants used on a large scale to attack crack problems, controlled buys will be the most common means of establishing probable cause. This implies, of course, that informant information and participation will be critical to the success of the effort. Skillful use and careful management of informants will be essential.

Ideally, every time probable cause is developed on a crack house, a search warrant should be written and executed. Of course, this is an ideal and as such will not be completely attainable. However, as the guiding philosophy, it will dictate that informant information be handled quickly and efficiently so that work can be prioritized and warrants executed on as many crack houses as possible.

Controlled buys are frequently made as a means of corroborating informant information in all types of drug cases. Furthermore, they are made for the purpose of gaining additional intelligence sought to guide an investigation. For the purpose of clarification, a controlled buy is a buy made by an informant under controlled circumstances as opposed to an undercover buy which is made by a sworn law enforcement officer.

It should be made clear that controlled buys are not necessarily required in the process of corroborating informant information and establishing probable cause. In fact, if an informant has fresh information, for example, he has been to a given location in the very recent past (within the last few hours), and if he is previously reliable, a controlled buy will not be essential to establishing probable cause. The informant reliability and basis of knowledge will have to be detailed as outlined in Chapter Three. Probable cause will be established by a thorough investigation in addition to and in corroboration of the informant information. The practice of making controlled buys has developed as the ultimate means of informant corroboration, as a means of ensuring warrant correctness, and as a means of fine-tuning the investigation.

The controlled buy is a particularly important technique as crack search warrants are being developed. This due to the fast changing nature of crack dealing which cannot be overemphasized. Based on outside observations, that is, surveillance, a location may appear to be operating. A steady flow of traffic to and from the location would seem to be an indication that dealing is ongoing and that timing is right to execute a search warrant. These observations may not be accurate, however, and controlled buys are an excellent means of verifying intelligence gathered through surveillance and other means.

In crack crisis situations, information will flow swiftly and continuously. There is a great deal of cross-corroboration of information. Informant information will verify, to some extent at least, much of the information received from concerned citizens, and vice versa. Crack informants may know of several locations from which they can purchase crack. While they are active, they will generally provide a steady stream of information, more than enough perhaps to keep one investigator busy. Like all informants, regardless of how reliable they may be they will fluctuate in their degree of dependability. Some of this fluctuation relates to how much crack they themselves may be using. If they become addicted, their dependability will diminish as ultimately also will their reliability and value. While they are willing and able, they can be extremely valuable to an investigator if he can act fast enough.

In crack investigations controlled buys will be made not only in informant-initiated cases, but also in cases which the investigator has initiated through other sources and in which he is using the informant to "cold hit" (make a buy as a first-time buyer unknown to the dealer) to develop the information. In either case, a controlled buy is a sound tactic. It enables the investigator to get some idea of the quality and quantity of crack in the dealer's possession and learn other valuable intelligence which will be necessary in the raid planning and execution.

Controlled buys are also often an important last step in a crack investigation used as a preraid tool to gauge timing. In many crack investigations, the initial controlled buy and the preraid buy may be only hours apart. It is common for crack investigations to proceed with such swiftness that the information is received, a controlled buy is made, other corroborative measures are taken, the search warrant is typed, a preraid controlled buy is made, and the warrant is executed, all within a matter of hours.

When preraid buys are made, the informant should be given specific instructions pertinent to gaining last-minute intelligence. How many people were inside the location, how much crack was visible, were weapons observed, etc. are all important questions which can be answered by a preraid buy. All may have some bearing on whether the raid is conducted as planned or some changes are made. It is not necessary for the informant to be told that he is making a pre-raid buy. In fact it is most often preferable to avoid telling the informant specifically what is planned. Under certain conditions, it may be necessary for the informant to be made aware that a raid will be conducted immediately following the buy. For example, the raid might be planned so the door is hit as the informant leaves, while the door is still open, before it can be locked. In cases of this type, it will be necessary for the informant to be in on the raid planning details to a greater degree than is generally preferred.

One purpose of a controlled buy is to establish the fact that crack, not some imitation substance, is being sold; thus it is almost essential that field test kits be readily available. A presumptive screening is all that is required for the purpose of establishing probable cause, a full test is not necessary.

It is imperative that money lists be made of all controlled buy money. Such currency will often be recovered when the search warrant is executed. If the controlled buy money is found with other currency, it can be important evidence in showing that the other currency is drug proceeds also. This is particularly true in cases where preraid buys are made just prior to the execution of a search warrant. One consideration in identifying the controlled buy money is whether or not the informant will be identified in doing so. If, for example, the dealer has $70.00 in his possession when he is arrested and a $50.00 buy was made just prior to the raid, to identify and separate the buy money tends to identify the informant even without ever giving any specific detail about when or how the buy was made. The dealer may recognize that the currency identified as buy money was that just given to him by the informant. If, on the other hand, the dealer has $1,000.00 in assorted bills when he is arrested, to identify and separate $50.00, for example, will not identify the informant.

Marking the money with a phosphorescent powder which will transfer to the hands of the dealer, while sometimes advisable in undercover buy situations, is not recommended in controlled buy situations if there are no plans to disclose the informant's identity. This technique is very useful in situations in which the dealer is dealing through a slot in a door or through a window or in some other way avoiding face-to-face contact, but its use will require that the person making the buy testify. The powder transferred to the dealer's hands can be detected under a black light, and that coupled with the recovery of the prerecorded buy money can establish a sale case. The undercover officer will have to testify to the facts of the buy, and even though he did not see who handed him the drugs, or to whom he handed the money, powder on the hands may help establish a sale case depending on other factors present when the search warrant is executed. Used in controlled buy situations, the identity of the informant will have to be revealed to get into the details of the buy and the fact that the money was marked with the powder and then given to the dealer by the informant.

When this technique is used, word spreads quickly among the dealers, and they may set up a black light and check money before completing any transactions. Money which has been detected as marked may be kept without an exchange of drugs, or it may be rejected and handed back to the undercover officer.

Having the informant wired during controlled buys improves the control of the buy situation and can give the investigators some direct insight into how the buy went. It does provide for some insurance of the informant's safety also. Having the informant wired is a policy developed by administrators and prosecutors in many jurisdictions. Any recordings made should be kept with the paperwork from the controlled buy, but it is not necessary to transcribe the tapes initially.

Controlled buy paperwork is generally not part of a case filing, that paperwork which ultimately goes to the prosecutors and the court. The paperwork must, however, be kept with the other original paperwork pertaining to an investigation as it may be important later if details of the controlled buys must be revealed for some reason or another. In case of a civil suit, for example, controlled buy paperwork will be very important. Figures 5-1 and 5-2 are sample forms very important to controlled buy documentation. Figure 5-1 is a sample case file cover sheet which was discussed in Chapter One and which can serve as an ongoing log of progress in terms of expenditures and other activities. Controlled buys should be recorded on this sheet as the case progresses. Figure 5-2 is a sample confidential funds expenditure sheet on which must be recorded every expenditure of confidential funds. The controlled buy data on this sheet corresponds to that called for on the file sheet.

Many experienced investigators prefer to keep additional records of controlled buys and other investigative action in their journals. That is a good habit which will enhance case organization.

Controlled buys are cost effective, consistent with information based crack search warrants in general (in terms of confidential expenditures, not manpower expenses). Of course, drug costs will vary from one location to the next depending on the quantities being sold, but it is entirely possible that a good crack search warrant investigation could be assembled for $150.00 to $200.00 and great deal less in many cases. Manpower costs are a different story; crack search warrants are labor intensive and can be expensive in those terms.

Surveillance

Surveillance is a critical investigative tool in the crack search warrant process. Too often, surveillance is viewed as a technique associated with more complex or long-term investigations. Surveillance is as vital to the success of street-level investigations as it is to any other type of case. In crack search warrant investigations, surveillance is generally used to corroborate informant information, to identify the associates and possibly the source of the dealer, and to gain intelligence necessary to prepare raid plans.

In every search warrant, some surveillance will be necessary to corroborate the initial informant information. Many times it will be necessary to take the informant to the location and have him point it out so that there is no mistake. A great deal of valuable intelligence can be learned through surveillance which cannot be developed any other way. In crack search warrant cases, because crack is such a high-visibility problem, surveillance can be especially beneficial in determining amount of traffic, traffic patterns, and something about the emotional climate of the area.

To be effective, surveillance must be undetected, and this is often difficult to accomplish in areas in which a highly visible drug problem

```
                  NARCOTICS INVESTIGATION UNIT

                         FILE SHEET


   FILE NO.:_____    DATE:_____    REPORTED BY:_____

   CASE NUMBER:_____

   SUSPECTS:

   1)  NAME:                       2) NAME:
       ADDRESS:                       ADDRESS:
       DOB:                           DOB:
       PD #:                          PD #:

        (LIST ADDITIONAL SUSPECTS IN NARRATIVE BELOW)

   SEIZURES -    DANGEROUS DRUGS:              TYPE:
                 CURRENCY
                 WEAPONS:
                 DESCRIPTION OF WEAPONS:
                 OTHER SEIZURES:



   EXPENDITURES -
                     EVIDENCE PURCHASED

   1)  DATE:             AMOUNT:         TYPE OF DRUG:
       AMOUNT PAID:                      PROPERTY NUMBER:
   2)  DATE:             AMOUNT:         TYPE OF DRUG:
       AMOUNT PAID:                      PROPERTY NUMBER:
   3)  DATE:             AMOUNT:         TYPE OF DRUG:
       AMOUNT PAID:                      PROPERTY NUMBER:

   INFORMANT PAYMENTS -

   1)  DATE:         VOUCHER NUMBER:         CI NUMBER:
       AMOUNT PAID:     EXPLANATION:

   2)  DATE:         VOUCHER NUMBER:         CI NUMBER:
       AMOUNT PAID:     EXPLANATION:

   3)  DATE:         VOUCHER NUMBER:         CI NUMBER:
       AMOUNT PAID:     EXPLANATION:

   TOTAL ARRESTS:          TOTAL DRUG CASES FILED:
   TOTAL EXPENSES:

   NARRATIVE SUMMARY:

                         FIGURE 5-1
```

exists. An investigator must be sufficiently aware of this possibility to guard against it while not becoming paranoid about being observed or detected. There are situations in which it is just about impossible to get close enough to the location to learn anything useful without being observed. Many crack dealing locations are specifically chosen so that it

NARCOTICS INVESTIGATION UNIT
EXPENDITURE RECORD

DATE:_____

VOUCHER #_____

CHECK #_____

ITEMIZATION		AMOUNT RECEIVED	$_____
EVIDENCE	$_____	RENT/UTILITIES	$_____
INFORMANT	$_____	OFFICE FURNITURE EQUIPMENT	$_____
ELECTRONIC EQUIPMENT	$_____	TRAVEL	$_____
VEHICLE LEASING	$_____	VEHICLE REPAIR AND MAINTENANCE	$_____
COMMUNICATIONS	$_____	MISCELLANEOUS	$_____
		TOTAL EXPENSES	$_____

RETURN RECEIPT NUMBER_____AMT. RETURNED $_____

EVIDENCE

1) DATE:_____AMOUNT PURCHASED_____AMOUNT PAID_____
   PROPERTY NUMBER_____LOCATION/SUSPECT_____
   FILE NUMBER _____COVERING OFFICERS_____

2) DATE:_____AMOUNT PURCHASED_____AMOUNT PAID_____
   PROPERTY NUMBER_____LOCATION/SUSPECT_____
   FILE NUMBER_____COVERING OFFICERS_____

OTHER EXPENSES

_____
_____
_____
_____
_____
_____

INFORMANT PAYMENT RECEIPT

CODE #_____, DID RECEIVE$_____,ON___/___/___

FOR INFORMATION OR SERVICES, (_____)

RE: FILE NUMBER_____.

SIGNATURE OF CI (CODE NAME)_____

PAYING OFFICER_____#_____DATE_____

WITNESS_____#_____DATE_____

SUBMITTING OFFICER_____#_____DATE_____

SUPERVISOR_____#_____DATE_____

COMMANDING OFFICER_____#_____DATE_____

FIGURE 5-2

is difficult for the activity at the immediate location to be observed without detection on the part of the dealers. In other situations where the physical layout does not lend itself to this capability, lookouts are established for this purpose.

Gathering Evidence

There are certain items of evidence which will be essential in successfully prosecuting crack search warrant cases. While most of the evidence will be gathered during the search, there are certain items which must be systematically gathered during the investigation leading up to the warrant. Any complaints of drug dealing at the target location should be documented. Named complainants should be contacted for follow-up information to their complaints. These complainants will not be witnesses in most cases, but the documentation of their complaints may be important, though the information contained is hearsay.

In crack search warrants, establishing possession is often difficult. Crack dealers, like other drug dealers, may go to great lengths to disguise their involvement in dealing activity. An important aspect of this is for the dealer to leave no paper trail which ties him to the location of the dealing. Public utilities will often be contracted using uninvolved people as fronts to arrange the services, or they may be obtained under aliases. This is not always the case, and wherever possible, the investigator should make an effort to obtain subscriber information for phones and utilities. Subscriber information which establishes some tie between the suspects and the location will be very important evidence if the search warrant yields drug evidence and a possession case is filed. Unless the crack is recovered directly on the person of the suspects, proving a possession case will in most cases involve showing some tie between the suspects and the target location. Any paperwork found during the execution of the search warrant which ties the suspects to the location should be taken and careful note made of where it was found.

Recoveries in the form of records pertaining to drug transactions are not too common in street-level crack cases, but occasionally some notes will be recovered, usually on scraps of paper which quite obviously do relate to drug transactions. Numbers recorded with dollar values either followed or preceded by common drug quantity abbreviations such as half, quarter, eighth, and sixteenth should be closely examined. If the dollar figures and the quantities correspond to current market price or if there are other explanatory markings on the notes which can be deciphered as drug values and prices, the notes can be important evidence. The investigator will have to establish his experience and training as the basis for making the determination that the notes recovered are records of drug transactions.

Drug transaction records that are recovered in street-level crack deals will generally show an amount which was paid for a given quantity and possibly a date or day of the week. Those numbers will often be accompanied by another series of numbers which show money generated by sales. For example, "Saturday one-half, $800.00. Sunday (25 + 25 + 25 + 50 + 25 + 25)/175. Monday (25 + 25 + 25 + 25 + 25 + 25 + 125 + 50 + 25)/350." The notes will probably be in vertical columns, may not include any dollar signs, and could be mistaken for a score sheet left over from a card game.

Occasionally a suspect will, after advisement, want to talk and will make a confession about his dealing activity. Usually this is done in conjunction with the desire to work off his case by providing information on other suspects, possibly his source. In these cases, if suspected drug records have been recovered, the suspect should be questioned about the records. An investigator can learn a great deal about such things which will be beneficial in the future and which will contribute to his expertise about drug dealing. Rough notes such as those just explained are a simple and common way that dealers will attempt to keep track of their business. In many cases the notes will have explanations which further help establish that they are indeed records of drug transactions.

Notes such as "J.D. fronted ½, Tuesday" or "D–Dog owes for double-up on Friday" will have some value as evidence if recognized as crack transaction records. "Fronted," "half" or "½," and "double-up" are common terms used in street-level drug dealing. Fronted, of course, means that the one party is given either drugs or money on the promise to deliver the other part of the transaction later. Half can refer to half-grams or half-ounces. In crack dealing, "five-o" or "fifty" is another expression used for what is sold as a $50.00 rock or a "half." "Double-up" is a crack term meaning that double the quantity is being sold for a given price. Essentially two for the price of one is how the term is used. However, double-ups occasionally involve a quality of crack less than pure in which procaine or lidocaine is added to the cocaine before it is turned into crack thereby "fluffing up" the size of the rocks sold without really increasing the actual amount of cocaine base.

In cases where such notes will be used in the subsequent prosecution, a court order for nontestimonial evidence should be secured, and a handwriting sample should be obtained from the suspect. Comparison by experts can then be made between the handwriting on the notes and the sample.

There are several other documents which are commonly recovered and which provide good evidence regarding drug dealing. Many times, personal letters will be recovered in which either the suspect or someone addressing him will refer explicitly to drug dealing and drug use. Occasionally letters will be recovered from concerned loved ones who are pleading with the suspect to mend his ways and quit dealing and using drugs. It is not uncommon to recover notes which children have written which detail the drug involvement of their parents.

The most common line of defense used in crack possession cases involves a steadfast denial of any knowledge of the presence of the crack recovered, denial of any knowledge of crack dealing, and denial of any previous association with the drug. The defense will focus on aspects of the case in which the link between the suspect and the crack recovered are the weakest. This defense is very effective in cases where the recoveries are small and where there are several people inside the target location when the warrant is executed.

Paperwork such as rent receipts, lease or rental agreements, and other documents linking the suspect to the target location should be collected. It will be difficult for the suspect to deny that he lives at the target location when evidence to the contrary is found. Bills from cable television companies, furniture rental companies, and welfare agencies can all be important in showing a relationship between the suspect and the location. This can be true even if the bills are not in the suspect's name, but more investigation may be required to establish the connection. It is quite common for drug traffickers to use the same front person to rent his or her place and set up the telephone and utility service. Finding that person and interviewing him may be necessary in proving that the suspect does have some tie to the location. Occasionally it is possible to show the length of time that the suspect has lived at the target location through old mail and other documents recovered.

Even when there is documentary evidence which links the suspect to the location and to the drugs, the same defense—no knowledge of the presence of any drugs, no knowledge of any drug dealing—is still relied upon frequently as there are few other choices available. When there is no documentary evidence to show some connection between the location and the suspect or directly between the suspect and the drug evidence, an effort must be made to establish this connection through other evidence.

For example, an attempt should be made to tie the suspect to the specific location in which the evidence is recovered. If the evidence is recovered in a closet, other things in the closet which may belong to the suspect should be the subject of the search. Clothes and shoes and hats and other such items which can be shown as being the property of the suspect will help establish that the suspect knew of the presence of the drugs. If the drug evidence is recovered in a jacket pocket, the jacket should be taken as evidence. If the jacket belongs to the suspect, some attempt should be made to show that in some way. For example, maybe the jacket was found draped over a brief case which had several papers and items of identification belonging to the suspect. Careful note of that fact should be made and some of the papers taken, if not the whole brief case, along with the coat and the drug evidence.

The investigators doing the search should be looking for items which tie the whole case together. Finding the right evidence does not usually happen accidentally. When drugs are recovered, the difficulty which may be encountered in showing possession should be anticipated, and there should be a search for some evidence that ties the suspect to the drugs recovered. For example, if a hat is found in the same closet as the drugs, right next to the drugs on a shelf, a photograph of the suspect wearing that hat could be an important piece of evidence.

Photographs can be very valuable in crack search warrants as in other investigations. Photographs which depict the suspect with other known drug dealers should be gathered as evidence. Many times photographs will be found which show the suspect in the target location, often wearing clothing that is also found in the location. To assume that these pictures will have no importance is to underestimate the difficulty of winning a crack possession case in a jury trial.

When evidence is being gathered, overkill should be the objective. No items which have any relationship to the charges being sought should be left behind.

If there is one common error made repeatedly in crack search warrants, it is the failure to process the search warrant scene and handle the evidence with enough care and professionalism. When warrants are done on low-level, street drug dealing locations, there is a tendency to get sloppy in the search, which is a critical phase of a search warrant investigation. To prosecute a possession case successfully in court, the right evidence must be collected, and it must be carefully preserved. When a case goes to trial, it is no longer one of hundreds which have been made; it stands alone as a case in which serious felony charges are pending. It is very important to the defendant, to the judge, and to the jury. Any indication that the investigation was not thorough or professional will be played up to the jury by the defense attorney.

Fingerprints are a good illustration of this point. As any experienced drug investigator is aware, getting fingerprints off drug packaging materials is very difficult and happens rarely. In only a small percentage of cases is it possible, yet in a great many crack possession trials, the defense will make an issue of the failure of the investigators to *attempt* to get fingerprints. If an effort has been made and there has been no success, not getting any prints will seldom be an issue, although the defense may bring it up as a further showing of the defendant's innocence. But if no effort was made to check for fingerprints, that will be played to the jury as slipshod investigative work aimed at convicting an innocent person. The fact that if fingerprints had been obtained, those of the defendant would not have been recovered will be emphasized. Even though there may be only one chance in a hundred that fingerprints will be obtained, it is a good idea to have the critical items of evidence checked. It makes for a more complete, thorough investigation, and when the fingerprints of the suspect are found on packaging materials or scales or whatever, the case is considerably stronger because of it.

Another often overlooked aspect of crack search warrants scene investigations is photographs and diagrams. When crack search warrants are being executed in large numbers to attack a problem of crisis proportions, there is a tendency to cut corners for the sake of expediency. As mentioned previously, at the time the warrant is being done it may just be one of many done that week or that month. When it goes to court, it takes on a different level of importance. It then stands alone, and any investigative shortcomings will reflect on the investigator.

Photographs and diagrams of the search warrant scene are often left out of a crack search warrant investigation. In fact, diagrams and photographs can be very useful in possession cases due to their expressive nature. A photograph of the inside of a crack house can be more illuminating than a 200-word description by an investigator testifying on the stand. A diagram of the inside of the house and the position of the suspects in relationship to the drugs seized will not only refresh the memory of the testifying officer, it will clarify the facts for all who later review them, jurors in particular.

Evidence should be gathered in crack search warrants with care, purpose, and enthusiasm. The goal of any investigation is to win in court, and in crack possession cases, careful gathering of evidence is of paramount importance.

Collateral Investigations

Crack search warrants have one characteristic unique in its frequency of occurrence. That is the number of people wishing to buy crack who come to the door unaware that the police are executing a search warrant. In addition to the fact that several people may be encountered inside the location, thus creating logistical problems and the need for additional officers at the search warrant location, there is the problem of people, sometimes an unending stream, who come to the door wanting to buy crack.

This is an eventuality which must be planned for in crack search warrants. One of two decisions must be made. Police cars and other signs of police presence should be moved away from the target location and the search operation kept very low key, or any further traffic to the location should be discouraged by making the presence of the police obvious. Generally, when the decision is made to keep the operation low key, it is based on the hope that one of the main suspects, not at the location when the warrant was executed, may return to the location while the officers are there.

Doing this is common, but it is usually precluded by a high-profile, dynamic entry. A case in point comes to mind which constitutes an exception to this. A search warrant had been executed in a high drug trafficking area at about 12:30 A.M. on a Saturday. The dealer who was the target of the investigation was a dangerous individual who flourished weapons during his dealings. The house was fortified, and the officers making the entry were compromised by the fortification and a stun grenade was deployed as a diversion. The stun grenade started a fire on a large area rug in the living room. The rug had to be dragged outside and the fire department was called to extinguish the flames. In addition, a water pipe broke at some point, and the small house was flooded with several inches of water. The point is, there was a great deal of commotion surrounding the execution of the warrant. One of the suspects had run out the back door and was apprehended after a short foot chase which was accompanied by a great deal of yelling and screaming. It would seem that there was no way that anyone within three blocks of the area did not know that the place was raided.

The target location was about 100 yards from a street with several bars, gambling shacks, and all night walk-up restaurants. It was a cold night in January so that the foot traffic was lighter than usual. Long after the location had been secured and the commotion had subsided, people began coming to the door. There were a limited number of people inside the location, and it was late in the shift, so it was decided to announce the presence of the police and send them away. This decision had been made in spite of the fact that the main dealer had not been present when the warrant was executed. The rationale was that there had been so much commotion that there was no way he would return.

Just when the operation was about wrapped up, an unknown person was knocking at the door demanding entry. The visibility through the front of the house was minimal looking out and zero looking in. The person on the doorstep could not tell who was inside the house. He demanded entry and was told that the police were there and that he should leave. The person persisted, and finally the door was opened and the person was confronted by two officers who identified themselves as police officers. The officers had been wearing raid jackets and vests but had taken them off and set them aside during the search. In any event, as the suspect was confronted he went for a gun in his right front pocket. He was forcibly overcome by the investigators who disarmed him, removing a .25-caliber semiautomatic from his hand which was inside his pocket. After he was secured, it was discovered that he had a large quantity of crack cocaine on his person in addition to the weapon. A significant amount of cash was also recovered. It was soon learned that this person was the main dealer. He had been at one of the bars on the corner, enjoying Friday night, drinking and impressing the patrons by spending money liberally. He left the bar when it closed with a female whom he had met in the bar and a male companion. These two people stayed in the suspect's car while the suspect came to the door of his crack house to resupply the dealers who were working for him. The male companion who waited in the car was discovered to be armed also. Neither of these people had any idea that a search warrant had been executed at the location, and the dealer showing up with a delivery resulted in an outstanding prosecution rather than just a case against the lower-echelon people.

This example illustrates several points. First, investigators inside a crack house searching should not divest themselves of their vests or raid jackets that identify them as police officers. The occasions when people come to a crack house armed are numerous. Any number of events can take place when they do, and all of them involve risk to the investigators which is much greater if vests and protective clothing are not being worn. The assumption that the presence of the police is obvious should not be made. If it is desired that everyone knows, it should be made so obvious that there can be no mistake. Even when steps are taken to ensure that everyone is aware that a police operation is being conducted, people may show up either to buy drugs or for some other reason.

Another point made by this example is that it is always possible that a suspect of equal or greater importance to those already arrested may come to the location if it is not apparent that a search warrant is being conducted. Some plan should be made for dealing with people who come to the door.

Those who come to the door seeking to buy drugs can become collateral suspects, also subject to criminal case filings. If this is planned, the door should be answered by plainclothes officers who should attempt to get the people at the door to articulate what it is that they want. This message will usually be conveyed in slang terms or in terms referring to a numeric value. For example, the suspects may say that they want a half, or a twenty, or a fifty. That language will most likely be consistent with the information already developed on the location with respect to amounts being sold.

Once the money is exchanged, the suspect can be arrested for attempting to commit a crime, if possession of a controlled substance is a felony and if there are provisions for inchoate offenses or attempts which are applicable to the controlled substance statutes. Generally, these types of offenses are a class or two below the classification of the crime if completed. In other words, they will represent a relatively minor offense.

If these people are to be arrested and charged, it is, of course, essential that the officers are at the location legally for the purpose of executing the search warrant. To be legal, this length of time must be reasonable and the continued presence of the officers must be related to the search operations. To stay in a location after the search has been completed for the purpose of arresting people who come to the door is beyond the scope of the warrant. Courts have generally ruled that "once a search warrant has been fully executed and the fruits of the search secured, the authority under the warrant expires and further government intrusion must cease."[2]

While the search is being conducted, it is not illegal for officers to assume an undercover role in an effort to develop more information about the case. That includes answering the door and dealing with potential crack customers. Even if no effort is made to make a case on these people, they should still be contacted and an effort made to establish the reason for their visit to the location. Many people will show up at the crack house with money in their hands. When questioned, they may not admit that the purpose of their visit was to buy crack, but many of them will. People coming to a known crack house have by their actions aroused sufficient reasonable suspicion that they should be stopped, frisked, and questioned about their actions. Many times these people will be wanted for outstanding warrants.

Notes regarding the number of people who come to the door should be made and later included in the investigative reports. Getting statements from these people and endorsing them as witnesses is also a possibility; however, there is no guarantee that the people will ever show up for court.

Interrogation of the Suspect

Immediately after suspects are arrested, they should be advised of their rights. This should be done verbally and then again in writing on the standard form designed for that purpose. There are generally three positions that a suspect will take. He may refuse under any conditions to talk at all. This refusal may or may not be accompanied by a request for an attorney. Second, he will talk to investigators but will deny any knowledge of contraband or other evidence recovered. Or, third, he will admit knowledge of the drugs and other evidence found. This position is usually accompanied by an expressed desire to work the case off or claims that the drugs belong to someone else. The suspect may or may not disclose to whom the drugs belong, and in any case the suspect will often be lying about that to clear himself.

There are, of course, variations of these three themes, but generally speaking, the suspect assumes one of these postures. If the suspect takes the first position and refuses to talk at all, there is no further interrogation. When there are multiple suspects, the chances that one will be willing to

---

2 *United States v. Gagnon*, 635 F.2d 766, 769 (10th Cir. 1980).

talk are enhanced. Particularly in cases where several people are in a location when it is raided, the chances are greater that one of the people will be willing to talk to the officers, away from the other suspects.

The people inside the location who are customers may identify the dealer. Their statements may be of little value if they are made by people who are unwilling to be witnesses, but occasionally these people may be able to give some clue as to where the drugs may be hidden. Also, they may be able to inform the investigators about what was taking place when the warrant was executed. Those details are sometimes important in finding the evidence and making sure that the right people are the focus of the investigation and are not prematurely released on the misconception that they are merely customers.

The opportunity to talk to people who express a willingness to talk should be seized, particularly when some difficulty is encountered in finding evidence. It is surprising the number of times that suspects will tell investigators where the evidence is hidden.

When suspects are taken into custody and transported to some detention facility, they should be interrogated prior to being incarcerated. The exception is those suspects who have expressed a desire to talk to an attorney and have refused to talk to the investigators. Those suspects should be questioned no further once they have made it known that they wish to speak to an attorney. Those who have not expressed a desire to talk to an attorney should be questioned about the drugs found. These interviews should be recorded in written form at least. It may be desirable to have the suspect give a statement in his own handwriting and elaborate on that through a question and answer session when he is finished. By doing so it is possible to clarify points which the investigator feels are important. Suspects should also be questioned about other evidence found, money, for example. If suspects disclaim any knowledge or possession of money found, that may be important in later efforts to have the money forfeited.

It is not uncommon to recover several hundred or even a thousand dollars in a low-level crack raid. Many thousands of dollars are recovered frequently when the dealers are doing a significant business. Many experienced drug dealers are aware that controlled buys may have been made from them in the process of developing the search warrant. Thus, they may be reluctant to claim any money recovered, fearing that it may be tainted with prerecorded controlled buy funds. Some jurisdictions have developed short-form currency seizure forms which are used in these situations as the basis of later forfeiture actions. Public nuisance and property confiscation statutes include provisions for seizing currency and other assets which are the proceeds of illegal drug dealing activity. These forfeiture actions must be accompanied by an affidavit which details the facts of the investigation and which shows some connection between the money or other assets and the illegal activity. When the suspects disclaim any knowledge of money recovered, it is an important concession, and it will assist in subsequent forfeiture proceedings.

Some jurisdictions faced with serious crack cocaine problems have adapted some short-form currency seizure procedure out of necessity from the standard confiscation procedures. Where several crack search warrants are being conducted per day, the related investigative paperwork will become a tremendous burden. To ease the burden, the short-form seizure approach has been developed. Basically it involves getting the suspect to "sign off" on a carefully worded document which informs him that the currency is to be seized subject to property confiscation laws. The short form then serves as an abbreviated affidavit, taken to court where action is then taken by the judge. By signing the form, the suspect is releasing any claim to the currency, and there is no hearing to contest the seizure. It is signed by the judge, and the currency is thereby ordered forfeited to the designated form.

It is important that interviews with suspects regarding money to be seized be carefully recorded should it later be necessary to refute allegations that the suspects were coerced into releasing their claim to the money. This is one inherent problem in the short-form seizure approach, many suspects may later charge that their money was taken from them by coercion, that they signed the form under duress, and that they did not know what they were signing. If carefully documented, however, an interrogation regarding the money can be critical in refuting those accusations at a later date. The purpose of the short form is to facilitate the seizure of all currency which has been generated by illegal drug dealing. It is not in any way designed to extend the scope of the property confiscation and public nuisance laws or to exploit the small-time dealer unfairly. It is used as an expedient way of seizing small amounts of currency when there is a nexus between the currency and drug trafficking.

Regardless of whether or not the suspect will sign the short-form affidavit, there are certain questions which should be asked of him regarding the money. That assumes, of course, that after advisement, the suspect has expressed a willingness to talk to investigators. Among the questions that should be asked are: How much currency did he have in his possession or in the target location? How was the money earned or derived? Where does the suspect work? All this information can be used in a seizure affidavit if one is subsequently required.

Follow-Up to Crack Search Warrant Investigations

As a way of completing a crack search warrant investigation, there are any number of things which should be checked when the investigative report is being completed and the case is prepared for filing. Unfortunately, there is usually not enough time to check all the things which should be checked and interview all the people who may be witnesses. Particularly in crack cases and other street cases, the value of further investigation has to be weighed against the time it will require and the pressure to move forward with other cases.

When time allows, a more thorough case will result if certain follow-up steps are taken. In the case of rental property, the owner of the property involved should be contacted regarding the person to whom the target location was rented. In cases where the suspect is denying any tie to the target location, a statement from the landlord and a copy of the rental agreement may show that the suspect did indeed rent the property and under what name it was rented. In these cases a photo lineup should be shown to the landlord in the interest of positive suspect identification. Interviewing neighbors may also help establish that the suspect was living at the target location or had some other tie to it.

Many crack cases involve people who are residing in public housing. The housing authority should be contacted for tenant information. Many public housing rental agreements carry with them serious sanctions for drug dealing violations, and notifying the appropriate people of violations allows them to fulfill their responsibilities more effectively to the community.

In areas where a large number of search warrants and street-level cases are being generated, a policy should be developed for notifying the proper health and safety agencies as a matter of routine as well as notifying the owners of private property that their property is being used for drug dealing activity. A policy of this nature will provide for some accountability on the part of persons responsible for the property. In the case of private property, drug dealing activity may eventually be grounds for initiating a public nuisance action of some type and proper notification of the owner will be a necessary step in initiating such action. Many cities have enacted zoning regulations which allow some action to be taken against the owners of nuisance property in addition to and usually prior to any seizure actions.

Many crack cases constitute situations requiring a referral to some social service agency regarding the welfare of children living in the midst of crack dealing and related neglect and abuse. Procedures and guidelines for such referrals are sometimes overlooked by narcotics investigators where the abuse or neglect is not extreme. In fact, so many children are found in these situations that, by necessity, discretion has a great deal to do with which cases are reported. In theory, notification should be made in every case in which children are contacted in a crack house environment. In the process of making such contacts, it is possible that information germane to the investigation will be developed.

Investigators should make an effort to contact probation and parole officers when applicable. These officers are in a position to provide a great deal of information and assistance in an investigation. In addition, they may be able to restrict further the freedom of the suspect aside from the outcome of the current case. Revocation of probation or parole may be in order.

When firearms are encountered in a drug search warrant, additional charges pertaining to the weapons violations may be in order and should be pursued whenever possible. Under the United States Code, the possession of a firearm while involved in the "distribution, manufacture, or importation of any controlled substance" is an offense punishable by a five-year sentence. (See Title 18, Section 924 (c), United States Code.) Agents from the Bureau of Alcohol, Tobacco and Firearms have traditionally provided local officers a great deal of assistance. This has been very much the case in crack cocaine and gang drug trafficking investigations. In addition to the charge mentioned earlier, there are others which may apply depending on the situation. Possession of weapons by a previous offender (convicted felon), falsifying the over-the-counter firearms transaction record (ATF Form 4473), and possession of an illegal weapon are examples of federal and state charges which may apply.

Taking the time to do a thorough and appropriate follow-up investigation can be the difference between a marginal case which gets plea bargained and an exceptional case which results in full prosecution.

Low-Level Undercover Buy Programs

The most common investigative technique used to combat street-level drug dealing in public places is the undercover buy. It is a direct approach whereby sales cases are made against street-level dealers. Generally, this technique is accompanied by immediate arrest of the suspect making it a buy/bust situation. Occasionally, it is preferable to make a series of buys from different suspects or multiple buys from the same suspect, obtain arrest warrants, and then serve them when it is most advantageous to do so.

In many jurisdictions, these operations are conducted with such frequency and so routinely that they may appear to the casual observer to be simple. There are, however, fundamental principles which must be practiced in every case in order to make these operations safe and successful. The following segment of this chapter will discuss the undercover buy as a technique used in street-level drug dealing situations. The planning and execution of these operations will be discussed in a step-by-step manner which, when followed, allows these operations to be conducted easily and efficiently.

Problem Assessment

There are several factors which should be assessed in deciding whether an undercover buy approach is the most appropriate technique for a given situation. Drug dealing done in public, out in the open, usually lends itself to such direct enforcement action. Operational plans will have to be modified to deal with the specific characteristics of each problem. For example, the decision whether or not to arrest the suspect immediately following the buy will be made on certain variables.

If the problem to be addressed involves a number of dealers, dealing in one general area in relatively open view of each other, it may be necessary to delay making arrests until several buys can be made. This is a sound technique if the suspects are sufficiently identified so that they can be arrested later. In some cases, a series of buys will be made over the course of several days, and some positive identification is a prerequisite to utilizing this approach. Employing this approach is calculated on the enhanced impact of making numerous arrests at one time. Much of that advantage will be lost if some of the dealers cannot be identified later.

In many cases where a series of buys will be made, the same dealers will be in a given location nearly every day at approximately the same time, much like legitimate vendors in a downtown mall. When this is the case, identification can be made relatively easily either before or after the buys have been made through routine patrol stops.

If the enforcement action is directed at one particular dealer, it may still be preferable to make more than one buy before arresting him. It may be required that more than one buy is made if it is necessary to have an informant make an introduction of the undercover officer to the suspect. In these cases, the introductory buy will not be filed in the interest of keeping the informant confidential. Subsequent buys can be made, of which the informant has no part, and all those buys can be filed.

Also, the strength of any case will be improved if there are multiple counts. And it may be possible to learn more about the suspect through a series of buys at the same time improving the case. In addition, there is the potential of identifying collaborators and sources and stash locations, all of which, if achieved, will contribute to a more effective, long-lasting solution to the drug dealing problem.

In most cases, however, street-level undercover buys will be planned with the immediate arrest of the suspect to follow the buy. This is the quickest, most direct way of impacting a problem.

Operational Planning Considerations

Determining Operational Objectives

As is the case in any narcotics enforcement action, objectives must be determined before any operation can be planned. This process may be done almost without any conscious effort by experienced investigators, but it must be done and the objectives must be known to those participating in the operation.

The statement of the operational objectives will be simple and straightforward in most street level cases. For example,

> A buy/bust operation will be conducted at 35th and Holly on July 7, 1987 at 2:00 P.M. The target, James Jones, usually deals on the northeast corner of the park near the rec center. Det. Wallis will approach the suspect in an undercover capacity and attempt to purchase a $50 rock of crack cocaine. If the deal is successful, Det. Wallis will drive out of the area and then give the bust sign and the arrest team will move in and Jones will be arrested.

The operational objectives will sometimes be stated in more general terms such as

A series of undercover buys will be attempted in the area of 13th and Pennsylvania in an effort to curtail the open street dealing which is taking place.

Specific objectives will then be developed as plans become more specific. What is critical is that the investigator putting the plan together have some objectives clearly in mind and that plans be formulated to accomplish those objectives.

Determining Manpower Needs

Once the objectives have been determined, it is necessary to figure the manpower which will be necessary to accomplish the objectives. The specific nature of the problem to be addressed will dictate certain manpower needs. For example, the characteristics of each individual problem will necessitate that certain types of people be used in undercover roles. If an informant is going to be required to introduce the undercover officer to the suspect, the undercover officer should be compatible in general appearance and style with the informant. Not all drug investigators possess equal skills in all areas. Some officers are more adept at working undercover than are others by virtue of experience, to some degree. Street-level drug deals can be excellent training grounds for the inexperienced undercover officer. Choosing the appropriate undercover officer will affect the success of the operation; however, the choice is not irrevocable. If one officer is unsuccessful, the plan can be quickly changed, and another officer can make an attempt.

A determination of manpower needs should consider the possible need or desirability of more than one undercover officer. It can be advantageous to have both male and female officers available for undercover work and officers of different racial and ethnic backgrounds as well. Manpower limitations usually restrict the creativity and flexibility with which an operation can be planned.

Once the undercover manpower needs are determined, the number of support people required should be assessed. It is possible in many situations to have officers switch assignments, one time being the undercover officer and the next time being part of the surveillance team. Plans to use an officer undercover in an area will usually preclude using him as part of an arrest team. The number and type of support people needed in a given operation will vary. Support people are generally classified into three groups: surveillance teams, arrest teams, and technical support teams.

Regardless of how routine an operation is, and regardless of the level of the dealer, the need for adequate support people should not be underestimated. Any undercover operation to be done safely and efficiently will require some minimum level of cover: surveillance, and arrest people.

A third and equally important planning consideration is the determination of equipment needs. The equipment actually required for any street-level drug operation is minimal. The use of special equipment should enhance officer safety and improve the quality of the cases when they are presented in court. Equipment such as special surveillance vans, electronic surveillance equipment, and cameras are just some of the types of equipment which can make for a safer and more successful operation.

Elements of Operational Strategy

The success of an operational plan will largely be determined by three things. Does the plan enable prosecutable cases to be made? Is the plan tactically functional, will it actually work on the street? and Will the plan impact the problem to any significant degree?

Legal Effectiveness

To achieve its objectives, a plan must be designed so that legally sound cases are made as a result of the operation. A plan which does not accomplish this is a failure. Drug enforcement strategy in general must have criminal prosecutions as its primary goal. When a problem is being evaluated for possible solutions, the solution chosen should be the one which allows the best chance of a successful prosecution.

Street-level undercover buy operations are based on the premise that the undercover officer will be able to buy directly from the dealer and make a simple sale or distribution case. If the dealer is the type who will not sell to people with whom he is not familiar, this difficulty will have to be overcome. Most street corner crack dealers will sell to unknown people. They are openly advertising their business, in many cases flagging down passing traffic in an effort to solicit customers. In fact, one of the reasons, previously mentioned, that crack dealing in public generates so many citizen complaints is the indiscreet manner in which business is done. If the dealers were more careful about how they did business and with whom they dealt, they would present a much less visible problem and at the same time a more difficult enforcement problem.

The rationale behind making an undercover buy versus just observing the activity and building probable cause to arrest the dealer is that by so doing a more prosecutable case will result. In addition, streetwise crack dealers generally take steps to make it very difficult for police officers to catch them in possession. They may hide the crack away from their person somewhere, in a can under a bush, for example. Or they may hold what they have on them in their mouths and swallow it or spit it out when approached by police officers. This is one major reason that many crack dealers do not wrap their product (pieces or chunks of crack) individually. It is easier to swallow them or otherwise dispose of them if several rocks are wrapped loosely in a small scrap of paper than if they are wrapped in small vials or tiny ziplock baggies.

Legal considerations in street-level sales cases usually revolve around the quantity of crack sold and the quality. Many apparent street-level crack dealers are actually engaged in the sale of an imitation substance which is represented and sold as crack and which creates many of the same problems in terms of disruption of public order. Sale of imitation controlled substances (bunk, woo, etc.) does not carry with it the same penalties as the sale of the real thing in most jurisdictions.

Many jurisdictions have established minimum standards for seizure amounts in order for a case filing to result. This is a necessity due to the fact that a certain amount is required for presumptive screening. Something in the range of .05 grams of crack cocaine would be a minimum amount allowing for a presumptive screening and possibly a full screening at some later point should it be necessary for trial. A street undercover buy operation should be planned so that a sufficient quantity is purchased. It is better to buy a little more, two or three $20.00 rocks if there is any doubt. While prices vary from one part of the country to the next, most street doses sold will constitute a sufficient amount so that prosecution is enabled.

Generally, sale of crack, even small amounts, is a felony. However, prosecutors, defense attorneys, judges, and most jurors do not often regard the sale of a rock of crack cocaine weighing .05 or .10 grams with the same importance that it is given by people living in the neighborhood and narcotics investigators. Because of this, there is a tendency to plea bargain many sale cases involving small amounts of crack. It is essential that the investigator and the prosecutor agree on the importance of this type of case, both working to ensure that it is a neat, thorough case in which every step necessary to making it a success has been taken. An undercover buy case if properly prepared, does have the appeal of being a relatively simple case to prosecute.

Photographs, tape recordings, and videotapes all add to the quality of an undercover buy case. Photographs which depict the suspect involved in several sales prior to and after the undercover buy is made will make the point that the issue is really not just this one sale even though that is all that is charged. The subject of the investigation is a crack dealer whose impact on the community goes far beyond this one undercover transaction. Photographs and videotapes are excellent evidence for presenting the whole picture as well as documenting the specific events from which charges resulted.

Having the undercover officer wear a wire (body microphone) is done in the interest of officer safety and evidentiary considerations. Being able to present an audio recording of the transaction is very beneficial. Unfortunately, the quality of these recordings may often leave something to be desired. In fact they are often of such poor quality that they have little value. A good undercover operation should include provisions for obtaining quality evidence of this type in the interest of a higher-quality case. Doing this will require that people with the necessary skills are available to operate the cameras, video recorders, and other equipment.

A Tactically Functional Strategy

A successful undercover buy operation must be planned so that there is an adequate number of people involved in the operation and that they are properly deployed and properly equipped.

It is often difficult to estimate an accurate number of people required as part of an undercover buy operation. In most cases there is a limited number of people available and the operation is put together within existing limitations. As a general rule, no fewer than *four* officers should be assigned to cover a street-level buy/bust operation which is to be conducted outside or in a public place. Operations which are to be conducted in other locations, a private residence, for example, present some other tactical problems and therefore may require additional people. Types of undercover operations other than street-level buys will be the subject of the next chapter.

A standard operational briefing form should be used for the written plan of the operation, and it may have to be supplemented by diagrams and additional assignment sheets.

The operational plan should contain a clearly worded, brief statement of what is to take place.

> Detective Montoya will attempt to make an undercover buy from Willie C. Smith at the location of 27th and Welton. Det. Montoya will park a block away and will approach Willie C. on foot. Willie C. should be standing on the corner of 27th and Welton in front of the tamale stand. It is likely that Det. Montoya will have to follow Willie C. into the 715 Club at 715 E. 26th Ave. and that the deal will be done just inside the door to the bar. If the buy is successful, Det. Montoya will give the bust sign as he leaves the bar and the arrest team will move in and arrest Willie C. after he has returned to the corner.

This statement of the plan is probably longer than it needs to be. Much of what is written in this plan is normally conveyed verbally during the briefing, whether it is in written form on the briefing sheet or not.

During the briefing, much detail which is left out of the written operational plan will be discussed and the plan will be finalized. The briefing sheet must provide only a fairly specific plan, it need not contain every contingency plan which might be necessary.

It is preferable if the description of the undercover officer and the undercover vehicle are part of the briefing sheet. This is of particular importance when officers from various separate units who may not know each other are involved in an operation. The description of the inform- ant and a brief synopsis of his involvement can also be very important depending on the level of informant participation if any.

The other information needed on the briefing sheet in order to convey the operational plan is standard yet important. A prearranged bust sign, both verbal and visual, should be noted on the sheet. The same applies to the prearranged distress signal.

The space provided for assignments should include a very brief descrip- tion of each officer's role in the plan. For example,

Mahoney	Z-20	Surv., 27th & Cal., notes, camera
Wallis	Z-24	Surv., 2600 Blk. Welton
Demmel	Z-22	Surv., Monitor, Relay Bust Sign
Padilla	Z-26	Surv., 700 Blk. E. 26th
Barker	T-21	Arrest Team, Standby/Nearby
Thompson	T-22	Arrest Team, " "
Shray	T-23	Arrest Team, " "
Montoya	Z-21	Undercover Officer

This operational plan designed for a simple street-level buy/bust with no unusual danger anticipated calls for eight officers. It includes a three-man arrest team consisting of tactical motorcycle uniform officers.

This plan, like most others can be easily adapted to a number of changes which may occur in this scenario or to a number of different scenarios for that matter. For example, assuming that there are a number of street-level dealers operating at that location, 27th and Welton St., this plan could be quickly modified to contend with that scenario. In that case it may not be desirable to arrest Willie C. directly after the buy has been made. There may be other dealers actively involved in selling drugs, and to arrest one suspect may cause the others to become aware of the pressure and to leave.

Therefore, after the undercover officer has made the buy, he could leave the area and assume one of the cover positions, thus allowing one of the other officers to move into the undercover role. As he and the other officer are switching assignments, the transmitter for the kel-kit, which is the actual body microphone, could be transferred as well.

The officer taking the undercover role will have to coordinate with the monitoring officer so that the cassette tape can be switched and an introduction put on the new tape. A new tape should be used for each undercover deal in the interest of simplicity although it is not a fatal flaw to have several consecutive, separate deals on one audiotape. This generally becomes confusing, however, particularly when there are incomplete deals and contacts also on the tape unless the officer monitoring the equipment makes careful notes or a log of times and counter numbers which correspond to each deal. The same is true of videotapes to a lesser degree, it is not nearly as confusing to have several undercover deals on one videotape. It is easier for the person operating the videotape to provide a running commentary and describe what the tape is depicting, whereas this is not possible on an audiotape.

The sample assignment list just given provides for one of the surveillance officers to be responsible for taking notes and using the camera. These two duties are a natural combination as notes are usually made as surveillance photos are taken to record times and subjects for later identification of the pictures. The value of photographs cannot be overstated; however, in nighttime operations surveillance photographs are seldom possible although a night scope fitted with a special video camera can be used. When this equipment is not available, the value of audio recordings increases as there will be no visual documentation of the transactions.

A plan such as that just detailed, include the luxury of uniform officers for use as the arrest team. There are several advantages to a plan that includes uniform officers. In cases where buys are to be made, and the suspects arrested immediately, that can be accomplished by uniform officers with very little notice. In high-crime areas where the presence of uniform police is common, very little attention will be paid to uniform officers contacting a person on the corner. The dealer himself may not immediately associate the fact that he is about to be contacted by the police with the previous sale he just made. He may not realize until some time later that he sold to an undercover officer. If, on the other hand, immediately following a buy, under-cover officers drive to the location and attempt to apprehend the suspect, it is often not as effective. Drug dealers are usually alert for the presence of narcotics investigators, and the dealer may spot the investigators approaching and have time to flee on foot or destroy or dispose of the drugs.

Many times, uniform officers will not be available, and the narcotics investigators will have to move from their surveillance positions and make the arrests. As was mentioned, the presence of plainclothes nar-cotics investigators may serve as a warning sign to the rest of the dealers in the area, and they may temporarily quit dealing.

In planning these types of operations, it is best to consider the most efficient manner in which prisoners can be processed and transported and attempt to implement such procedures. Consideration should also be given to the subsequent case filings which may result. For example, if a large-scale operation is being conducted involving several undercover buys and subsequent arrests, some provisions have to be made for han-dling the prisoners initially and ensuring that all the necessary paperwork pertaining to the arrest and the evidence is completed and put into a packet in some organized fashion.

The following is an example of a typical street-level drug dealing situation, particularly common in areas where crack dealing is rampant. Going through this sample scenario will allow for a comprehensive overview of the principles discussed to this point.

Sample Problem

Development

The problem involves a moderately large public park that has recently been overrun by crack dealing. The park is in a lower-middle-class neighborhood which has a relatively stable family basis. As such, the park has heretofore been used by children for normal activities such as playing ball and hide and seek, using playground equipment, etc. Parents have not had to fear letting their children go to the park by themselves up to this point. Within the past two months, however, the situation has changed dramatically. There are now large numbers of young males most of whom are in their late teens and early twenties who have started to roam the fringes of the park and openly sell crack to people passing by on the streets. The dealing is relatively indiscriminate.

Complaints

Citizen complaints from the mayor's office and through the chief's office are overwhelming. People are also calling the narcotics bureau every day to report the drug dealing and to demand some response. Emergency community meetings have been held to discuss the situation, and pressure is mounting.

Increased Work Load

Members of the narcotics bureau assigned to street-level investigations in that area, investigators and supervisors alike, are being called upon for a solution. In addition, members of the patrol division are deluged with calls for service in the area. Some possession cases are being initiated by street officers, but those arrests and case filings seem to be having no significant impact. When it is possible to keep pressure on the area in the form of uniform officers, activity will slow down; as soon as the patrol officers leave, activity resumes.

PROBLEM ASSESSMENT

The Dealers

In assessing the problem it is determined that the main dealing activity takes place between the hours of 1:00 P.M. and midnight. The dealing is all done out in the open by approximately 10 to 15 people. Some of those people have been fully identified, others have not. The dealers are not always the same people. Efforts to identify the people who are supplying the drugs have been unsuccessful. It appears that some of the dealers work in concert to some degree with other dealers. In addition to the dealers, a fluctuating number of people who are part of the problem as they buy from the dealers and then sell some of what they have bought and use some of it. There are areas in the park where people use the crack they have purchased, but for the most part, people who come to the park to buy leave it as soon as they have been successful.

Quantities Involved

Small street-level quantities of crack are involved. The dealers either keep the crack on their persons or hide it nearby.

Geographics

The park is situated so that close surveillance will be difficult in the daylight hours unless the surveillance teams are concealed in vans. Three blocks north of the park begins a commercial area consisting of warehouses, offices, and manufacturing plants, some of which are now vacant.

PLANNING

Objectives

The objectives of enforcement action are simply to make prosecutable drug-related cases on the violators and to clean up the park and the adjacent area. Based on the nature of the problem, it is decided that some undercover buy operation will be most effective in accomplishing these objectives.

Manpower

It is determined that of the 12 investigators assigned to street-level investigations, 4 will be unavailable to assist in this operation. Eight people are then available. Of those 8, only 2 will be suited for doing any of the undercover work. The impact sought will require an operation larger in scope that 8 people will be able to accomplish. The exact numbers of people required is not immediately known at this time, but rough estimates can be made which will usually be fairly close to what is later required. Members of certain units within the patrol division will be available to assist in the operation as will investigators from narcotics teams and elsewhere.

Equipment Needs

It will be necessary to obtain the use of several additional undercover vehicles, an additional surveillance van, an additional video recorder, and an extra kel-kit (body microphone transmitter and receiving unit) and monitors. The temporary use of additional radios will also have to be arranged.

Documentary Needs

Arrest packets containing all necessary forms for the processing of each arrest should be compiled. Some standard forms can be developed which will enable quick statements from undercover officers immediately following each transaction in which the officer is involved. Some advance planning is required to see that the paperwork flow is smooth and complete. Coordination between surveillance officers and undercover officers will be necessary following each transaction so that notes of times, key words exchanged, recorder counter numbers, etc.

which pertain to the case are accurately recorded. Immediately following each undercover transaction, the undercover officer should make notes on the deal just completed, and the evidence should be marked and turned over to the investigator designated to coordinate paperwork flow. Standard short forms can be made which record the essential details of such transactions. Later reports and case filings can be accomplished much more smoothly if plans are made in advance for correct documentation of the transactions and handling of evidence.

Strategy

It is decided that the strategy will involve a series of undercover buys from all the people who are dealing in the area. After at least two buys have been made from each of the suspects, a roundup will be conducted and all the suspects will be arrested. The operation will be conducted over a four-day period. The buys will be recorded. Each undercover officer will wear a body transmitter, and the transactions will be recorded with a video recorder as well.

IMPLEMENTING THE PLAN

A written plan is developed which specifically details personnel assignments. A briefing for all personnel involved in the operation should be arranged a day or two prior to the operation and should be scheduled for the day the operation is to begin at a central location. Personnel assignments included in the operational plan should be reviewed at the briefing. Equipment should be checked to ascertain that everything needed has been procured and is in working condition.

A command post several blocks to the north in the commercial or industrial area will be established. All people involved in the operation will meet at that location immediately following the general briefing and prior to the start of operations. A final staging will be set, and officers will then report to their assigned positions. In the first three days of the operation, only two officers in uniform will be assigned. They will be responsible for staying in the outer perimeter and responding in case of emergency or in the event that it is necessary to identify suspects. On the final day, several additional uniform people will be assigned to the operation due to the fact that numerous arrests are anticipated. In addition, officers with a prisoner transport vehicle will be assigned then as well.

The supervisor in charge of the operation will work from the command post location. Two members of the narcotics investigation unit will be assigned to the command post to ensure that the paperwork related to each undercover transaction is completed and organized into its own file. The evidence will be obtained from the undercover officer at the command post, and it will be placed in the file also.

The operation is ready to commence when cover officers, probably six in this type of situation, are in their respective surveillance positions and the technical support officers have set up their equipment and have done final checks with the undercover officer. When a van is being used for surveillance on a street-type operation, the van should be driven into the area by a plainclothes officer who will then park the van, get out and lock it, and walk away. People will notice if anybody gets out of the van or not and suspicion will be aroused if a van drives into an area and parks and nobody ever gets out of it.

A final check of the body mike should be conducted and when it appears that all is working, the technical support team will signal the undercover officer to begin. In most cases, at least two officers should be assigned to the surveillance van. To expect one person to operate all of the surveillance equipment which may be involved is unrealistic. Also, officer safety considerations will often dictate the presence of at least two officers in the surveillance van.

Assuming that there are no unusual occurrences such as inclement weather, and assuming that the problem has been correctly assessed and an appropriate plan developed, the operation should show some immediate results. The first undercover officer to go to the location will generally develop some information about the status quo. Once the first successful undercover contact is made, that officer should return to the command post. A plan involving multiple undercover officers and different undercover vehicles will create a minimum amount of lag time. While the undercover officer from the deal just completed and the investigators at the command post arrange the paperwork another deal can be initiated. The undercover officers should make notes pertaining to the transactions immediately. Complete reports can be written later. A cover sheet for use in these operations is helpful. Such a sheet should contain basic information identifying each particular case (see Figure 5-3). Also shown is Figure 5-4, a checklist which can be attached to each suspect's file and will provide a synopsis of what reports are in the file. Both forms are helpful when used in street-level buy/bust and street-level reverse operations.

If any undercover buy is made from a particular suspect unknown to the surveillance team or the undercover officer, he should be identified when convenient but in any case before he can leave the area. Uniform officers assigned to the operation can be deployed for this purpose with instructions to make such identification with a minimum of disruption. They should move in and identify the suspects, and once that is done, they should return to the command post with that information. Officers coordinating the paperwork will then record the information and relay it to the technical support team so that they can put it on their logs.

The operation should proceed in this fashion until buys, preferably at least two, have been made from all the main dealers involved. Multiple buys from the same suspect may result in a case with a stronger plea bargaining position. This can be particularly important where very small amounts are being sold.

Following each day's operations, a debriefing should be held to ensure that information is shared, that all reports are complete, and that corresponding tapes and photographs are in order. The investigators assigned to compile the cases should begin doing so. Arrest warrants should be prepared for the suspects

```
                    UNDERCOVER FACT SHEET

   DATE:_____TIME:_____TRANSACTION NUMBER_____

   UNDERCOVER OFFICER:_____

   LOCATION:_____

   SUSPECT IDENTIFICATION:_____
   _____
             SHOULD INCLUDE DETAILED DESCRIPTION

   VIDEO COUNTER NUMBERS:_____TO_____

   AUDIO COUNTER NUMBERS:_____TO:_____

   CUSTODY OF EVIDENCE GIVEN TO:_____

   BRIEF NOTES:_____

                        FIGURE 5-3
```

```
           STREET UNDERCOVER OPERATIONS REPORT PACKET
                         CHECKLIST

   DATE:_____REPORTED BY:_____

   UNDERCOVER OFFICER:_____

   SUSPECT'S NAME:_____

   EVIDENCE NUMBER:_____CASH RECOVERED: YES___NO___

   SUBSTANCE RECOVERED: YES___NO___NATURE:_____

   ARREST REPORT: YES___NO__OFFENSE REPORT: YES___NO__

   ADVISEMENT: YES___NO___BY_____

   VEHICLE INVOLVED: YES___NO___LIC#:_____

   VEHICLE DISPOSITION:_____

                        FIGURE 5-4
```

involved. The case filings are usually simple in these cases and require a minimum of paperwork. Regardless of how simple the details of the sale may be, making it complete is sometimes difficult when it results as part of a large operation. Accurate statements from the undercover officers are a must. Noninvestigative personnel participating in these operations may not be aware of the importance of the paperwork and must be instructed and trained.

On the final day of the operation another briefing should be held at a central location for the purpose of organizing the roundup of suspects. More uniform officers will be required to accomplish this phase of the operation. Any determination regarding a press conference should be made by the appropriate administrative people, but such media notification should be coordinated with the operational supervisor.

Undercover Buy Options and Variations

The sample problem and the operation planned as a response to that problem are typical. There are a number of options and variations to the manner in which street-level undercover buy operations can be conducted. Specific problems may preclude the use of certain techniques and be ideally suited for others. Manpower limitations will also restrict the use of certain techniques as will equipment availability and the availability of confidential funds. Following are some common variations and options.

Trojan Horse Concept

The Trojan Horse idea involves having cover and arrest teams concealed in the back of the undercover vehicle ready to make their presence known and take immediate custody of the suspect when the verbal bust sign is given by the undercover officer. Obviously, something other than a standard passenger vehicle must be used by the undercover officer. Rental trucks, vans, stake bed trucks, campers, and other recreational vehicles all have some potential for use in this capacity.

This technique in many modified forms has been applied for years by general vice officers as well as narcotics investigators. The plan can be best implemented by having the undercover officer drive into an area of street drug dealing activity and encouraging the suspect to get into the vehicle with him. By doing so, the officer can then drive out of the area and give the bust sign while the vehicle is stopped for some reason. The arrest team can then emerge from the back of the vehicle and arrest the suspect. Taking the suspect out of the area allows for his arrest without other dealers in the target area being immediately aware of it.

Surprise is an important element in the use of this technique. This element will be lost if the technique is used repeatedly in the same area. Drug dealers will learn quickly and will adapt their own methods so that they do not sell to people in large vehicles who may be police officers or not get into those vehicles at any rate.

Renting certain types of vehicles such as moving vans or trucks or recreational vehicles for such operations is a good idea. The vehicles, which will soon be identified as a vehicle being used by the police (burned), can then be turned in when the approach has lost its effectiveness.

Video and Audio Recording

The use of recording equipment, both audio and video, is standard in undercover buy operations at all levels. There have been innovations in the use of such equipment. The Birmingham, Alabama, Police Department, for example, has perfected undercover buy programs which utilize covert audio and video recording devices in the undercover vehicle. The technique was developed due to a shortage of undercover officers. Making one buy and then arresting the suspect immediately, while extremely effective, has negative side effects in that it results in the identification of undercover officers, which greatly limits their future value in that capacity. This is particularly true if the undercover officer, because of manpower limitations, participates in the arrest.

The Birmingham approach entailed widespread use of a technique in which undercover officers would roam through areas of heavy drug dealing and make buys from every dealer they observed. A video camera was hidden in some fashion in the undercover vehicle, inside a gym bag, for example. The officers would attract the dealers to a position in which they would be filmed, close up, by the video camera. The audio part of the transaction was transmitted to covering officers who recorded it and took notes.

Using this approach, several undercover buys were made by one officer. The videotape would later be reviewed by investigators and patrol officers alike, and the suspects would be identified, the cases prepared, and arrest warrants obtained. The technique allowed for 75 percent of the suspects who had been videotaped to be later identified. It was then possible to round up nearly all the suspects, preferably at one time. Making numerous arrests at one time enabled investigators to impact the problem significantly while operating within manpower limitations.

The suspects arrested in an operation of this type may have no idea who the undercover officer was until the officer appears in court nor will they be able to remember any details about the undercover vehicle a month or so after the offense took place. Since a significant number of the cases will be plea bargained, the identity of the undercover officer may not ever be revealed in many cases.

Again, this technique has any number of possibilities for variation and adaptation to specific situations. This is an excellent example of the applied resourcefulness and imagination of narcotics investigators when faced with a difficult problem.

Dealing with Common Problems and Difficulties

Buying from a Middleman

Crack dealing activity on the street commonly involves many people who are free-lance entrepreneurs who know where to purchase crack and who solicit customers for that purpose. These people will seldom have any significant amount on their persons if any at all and represent the lowest possible level of dealer. They are middlemen in the truest sense of the word. While there is nothing wrong with making sales cases against these people, it does not usually have a direct impact on the real source of the crack except inasmuch as the sources may have difficulty recruiting people to replace those who have been arrested.

There is also the risk that the middleman, to whom the money must be fronted, may leave and never return. Traditional narcotics enforcement philosophy prohibiting the fronting of money has had to be revised in order to deal with crack street sales. In some cases, there is no other option than to give the suspect the money and attempt to watch him and see where he goes to get a buy.

It is sometimes possible to overcome these difficulties. Doing so requires identifying the valid targets, who are worthy of directed enforcement action and then attempting to get past the middleman and going directly to the main people. This will involve persistence on the part of the undercover officer who may face verbal hostility from the middlemen whose own crack habits are supported by their activity and who do not wish to be cut out of the action.

If it is necessary to keep the middleman involved, the undercover officer should strive to accompany the middleman to the source. If this is accomplished, cases against both people may result. One risk in this is that the officer will often be going to an unknown destination, covering officers will probably lose visual surveillance, and the undercover officer may be in personal danger if he is not wired or if the transmitter malfunctions. This is the main reason that undercover buys on the street should not be undertaken without a minimum number of covering officers. At least four officers should be part of the cover and arrest team, and the need for more officers may be dictated by sudden changes in the situation. Enough officers should be included in the plan to deal with any eventuality.

The situation can change suddenly from that in which an officer is buying from a man on the street in plain view to one in which the officer is going to an unknown location (tripping) to accomplish the buy. The officer may leave the view of surveillance officers and suddenly be in a situation where he is surrounded by a large group of people. When this occurs, the chances that an undercover officer will be recognized will be greatly increased, and if that happens the officer may be in serious danger.

To be effective, a plan must be flexible and flexibility usually dictates that more officers be involved in the plan.

Buying Imitation Controlled Substances

Another situation frequently associated with serious crack problem areas is the selling of imitation crack. People selling an imitation controlled substance can become a significant part of crack nuisance problems, and at the same time they can be difficult to deal with effectively due to the fact that they may not be selling or possessing any controlled substances.

Anything even closely resembling crack has been represented and sold as crack at one time or another. Pieces of chopped up nuts, parts of aspirin, wax, solidified vitamin B, procaine, and even small pieces of gravel are examples.

The people dealing in imitation crack are usually hard-core users who are trying to generate some cash to support their own habits, or they are just con artists or flim-flam men. Generally, these people will attach themselves to an area in which actual crack dealing is taking place. They will then selectively choose their customers: people with whom they are familiar or people from the immediate area whom they may see again will often be avoided as customers or marks. People new to the area who appear to be just passing through are ideal targets for the bunk dealer in that the dealer will in all probability never be held accountable for his actions by the customer. On the other hand, if they sell bunk to neighborhood people, they may have to answer to them in the future and that can make selling bunk a hazardous proposition.

People selling imitation controlled substances can create difficulty in undercover buy/bust operations. These people require the same level of effort to make cases against with generally a very-low-level prosecution as the result. Some state statutes do not discriminate between the sale of a controlled substance and the sale of an imitation substance represented as the real thing. Where this is the case, people dealing bunk create no special problems. Most jurisdictions, however, have special laws pertaining to the sale of imitation substances. These laws typically classify such offenses in a lower category than sale of an actual controlled substance. Even where sale of imitation controlled substances is a felony, it is the type of case subject to ready disposition in lieu of trial unless the offender has a serious history of similar offenses.

Where problems of this nature are being experienced, the prosecution of these sales cases must be pushed in an effort to deter such activity. Doing this may require having the prosecutor's office develop special guidelines for prosecution of these offenses in target areas. Also, city ordinances can be developed which can provide an alternate means of dealing with these people simply and directly in instances where the facts do not qualify the case for a state prosecution.

The people dealing imitation controlled substances cannot be ignored as they become a significant part of the crack problem. Cases must be filed when the effort to make an undercover buy has been made based on the rationale that the person was actually selling crack. Once the habitual bunk dealers are known, pressure from uniform officers can be somewhat effective in keeping the activity of these people in check. Many of the people who sell imitation controlled substances may frequently be in possession of some legitimate controlled substance for their own consumption. Arresting them for selling the bunk can many times result in a drug possession case as a result of the search incident to arrest.

Evaluation of Effectiveness

Most street-level undercover buy operations do not involve the level of planning as found in the scenario in the sample problem. Isolated instances of crack dealing can be dealt with individually and routinely just as any other street-level drug investigation is approached. On the other hand, large-scale undercover operations in response to serious street crack dealing problems do require significant planning, and all the considerations mentioned will be involved to varying degrees. As noted previously, crack problems of crisis proportions do not just go away; they have to be attacked in the most effective manner suitable.

Following any large-scale operation, the target area should be monitored to determine what, if any, effectiveness the operation had. Generally, the problem will diminish in size and scope for a limited time, and then it will gradually return to its former condition if not given continued attention. Many police departments have had success by using the undercover buy approach to initiate enforcement activity on a large scale in a target area and then following that with intensive patrol efforts and finally with some reverse undercover operations which target the demand side of the problem. Those techniques will be discussed next, as part of a comprehensive drug enforcement approach to street-level crack problems.

Intensified Patrol Efforts

As mentioned earlier in this chapter, dealing with large-scale street drug sales problems involves a considerable team effort on the part of the law enforcement community if there is to be any significant impact on the problem. A major part of this enforcement team is the uniform patrol officers assigned to an area affected by these problems. The role of uniform officers will be discussed in the context of both patrol and special deployment.

Routine Patrol

The role of the patrol officer in drug enforcement is greatly underrated by the average person. A great many cases are developed through the routine work of patrol officers. Not only are a large number of cases filed as a result of this work, but many upscale investigations are also often successful, in part, because of some patrol officer's attentive performance of his duties.

With respect to large-scale problems resulting from street drug dealing, aggressive patrol officers working the area can provide the narcotics investigators with a great deal of assistance. The presence of the uniform officers on a frequent basis keeps the dealers off guard. In addition, the uniform officers will be able to identify problem sources much more readily than will the narcotics investigators, and they can be a valuable source of information for the narcotics investigators who are trying to identify suspects, determine habits, etc. Many good, prosecutable cases will also be made directly by patrol officers who are attentive to drug problems in their areas.

Narcotics investigators must work to cultivate uniform officers as sources of information and assistance. It is the responsibility of the investigators to make the uniform officers who are interested in narcotics enforcement aware of how important they are. This can be achieved by openly sharing information and resources and allowing the patrol officers to remain active in the investigation to whatever extent is possible. Also, the assistance of the uniform officers must be appropriately acknowledged.

In many areas being overtaken by drug activity, saturating the area with directed uniform patrol can be a much more direct and efficient solution to the problem than is the work initiated by narcotics investigators. However, the best solution involves utilizing both resources and making a coordinated effort. In situations which have grown completely out of control, both the effort and the coordination must be intensified in order to have any impact.

Special Deployment

The following situations and techniques depend upon a combined enforcement effort in which patrol officers and investigators are deployed jointly to attack a drug problem. The situations may vary from isolated instances of drug dealing to whole blocks and neighborhoods being taken over by drug dealers. The need for coordination increases as the level of the problem escalates, but the techniques can be applied on a variable scale according to the demands of each situation. The techniques described here are often used in conjunction with other techniques. For example, extensive uniform saturation of an area may be used following undercover buy programs and before the implementation of street reverse operations as a necessary middle stage. Or, if a problem is out of control, some of these patrol tactics will be necessary to stabilize an area before any undercover operations are possible. Likewise, intensified patrol will be necessary to keep an area under control once the problem has been addressed through a combination of investigative techniques.

Surveillance and Arrest

One of the oldest and most successful techniques for handling street dealing activity involves surveillance on the dealing location from a place of concealment, identification of the people who are in possession of the drugs, and the effect of their arrest. A combined effort involving both patrol officers and investigators usually results in a good deal of success using this tactic although the tactic is commonly used by both patrol officers and narcotics investigators. This technique is regularly used independent of other enforcement action, but it is ideally suited for use in conjunction with other techniques as well.

Success hinges on being able to identify the main people and establishing probable cause to arrest those people. It is critical to determine who is dealing and if he is in possession of the drugs or if he has them concealed somewhere nearby.

When those things have been learned, the officers who will be on standby in close proximity will be notified to make the arrests. It is best if the surveillance officers do not have to assist in the arrest. They can maintain their positions for continued surveillance.

This technique is very similar to that in which an undercover buy has been made. The difference is that there is no undercover officer; hence, drug evidence from the buy will not have been obtained, and the success of the action will depend upon apprehending the person before he can dispose of the evidence. The key to the success of this technique is finding a good surveillance post from which the dealing activity can be observed without the dealers detecting the presence of police officers in the area. Many times it requires that at least one of the surveillance officers gets out on foot.

In large-scale problem situations, a combination of uniform patrol officers and investigators should be part of the operation mainly because of the large number of officers and the combination of talents and resources which will be required. When the arrests are made by the investigators, it is preferable if they are in clothing (raid jackets, caps, etc.) which readily identifies them as police officers. Uniform police in marked vehicles can often affect the arrest with less alarm and confusion and in many cases less resistance than can plainclothes narcotics investigators. Also, once the prisoners have been arrested, transportation is a problem, and uniform officers and marked vehicles are again better suited for those functions.

The primary reason for attacking nuisance street drug dealing problems with a joint effort is this: widespread drug dealing activity and the attendant crime and related problems are primarily the problem of the uniform patrol commander in that particular area. It is his responsibility to see that the streets are safe and that crime is controlled. Efforts to control a drug problem in a given area will require the cooperation and assistance of the patrol commander and his officers. It is unrealistic to expect that narcotics officers alone are going to repress a widespread street drug dealing problem satisfactorily. A combined effort is required.

Roadblocks

One technique which has been applied in extreme cases with some success is the roadblock approach. When an area has become an open drug dealing market to such an extent that serious traffic congestions results from street drug deals, it is sometimes necessary to establish roadblocks on the street or streets leading into the area. To be legal there must be a serious state interest at stake, for example, numerous citizen complaints about severe traffic congestion constituting a health and safety threat. If an open drug dealing market is creating serious traffic congestion and hazards to the public in that area, a roadblock can be established to check driver's licenses and vehicle registrations of the vehicles entering the area. The roadblock cannot be established to randomly search cars for contraband or weapons or to detect other violations. To be legal, the technique must be effective in accomplishing what it set out to do and in serving the public interest. Furthermore, the technique must be minimally intrusive to law abiding citizens.

The Washington, D.C., Court of Appeals upheld a roadblock set up by the Washington Metropolitan Police Department in an area of widespread street drug dealing. In addition, the Supreme Court recently upheld highway checkpoints used to detect intoxicated drivers. The factors just set forth were specifically applied in these cases in determining the legality of the roadblocks.[3]

Using this approach would require identifying a serious problem such as traffic congestion which is being created by the people driving in and out of a drug dealing area. When that problem has been identified, using a roadblock approach is legal if it has a clearly stated purpose, for example, to check driver's licenses and vehicle registrations, and if it is effective in diminishing the problem. To be effective, the presence and purpose of the roadblock should be made obvious to people entering the area thus deterring a great many from going forward. The presence of the roadblock will then reduce the traffic congestion, indirectly reducing the traffic to the drug dealing location. The roadblock must be set up according to an organized plan which places strict limits on how the roadblock is carried out. If the roadblock is carried out systematically in accordance with the plan, it is minimally intrusive on the rights of

---

3 *United States v. McFayden,* 865 F.2d 1306 (D.C. Cir. 1989), and *Michigan Department of State Police v. Sitz,* 47 CrL 2155 (1990)). For further information on these issues, refer to *Brown v. Texas,* 443 U.S. 47 (1979), *United States v. Martinez-Fuerte,* 428 U.S. 543 (1976), and *Delaware v. Prouse,* 440 U.S. 648 (1979).

properly licensed drivers. Those who are properly licensed are detained for a very short length of time. Those who are not licensed or have improper vehicle registration will be arrested or receive citations. More importantly, many people will, in all likelihood, be deterred from going into the area.

Roadblocks will most often be used as part of a comprehensive street enforcement program in areas experiencing severe problems. They will be effective if vehicular traffic constitutes a significant part of the problem. If most of the traffic in and out of an area is foot traffic, vehicular traffic congestion will probably not be significant enough to warrant a roadblock.

Street Sweeps

Street drug dealing in the late 1980s grew to such serious proportions in some areas that massive street sweeps were used, generally in conjunction with other techniques, in an effort to control the problem. Crack cocaine and its rapid proliferation caused most of this disruption and chaos. Since that time, street sweeps of varying intensity have been used in many major cities. The street sweep concept is not new. It is based on the theory that saturating an area with police officers reduces crime in those areas. The technique has been used with success in response to other police problems over the years attacking crimes such as burglary, theft, robbery, and common street crimes. When used in those instances, while very effective in reducing the crime rate in a given area, the technique has the undesirable and unavoidable side effect of forcing the criminals to other areas and thus increasing the crime rates in those areas.

Used in instances of widespread drug dealing, the same side effects occur, but to a lesser extent. This is due to the fact that there are two sides of the problem, supply and demand. It is not possible for the dealers to move too far too quickly and still have customers. The buyers rely on word of mouth and the visibility of the dealers to guide them to the sales locations. The highly visible presence of police officers in an area forces the dealers to become much less visible in the affected area whether they move or not. In any case, the technique is effective during the time that the intense pressure is being exerted. Once there is a letup in the high-visibility patrol, the drug dealing will usually resume.

Street sweeps involve directed patrol in a target area to stop people moving in the area, identify the drug dealers and users and others who are part of the problem, and ultimately shut down the activity in the area and reclaim the neighborhood. Implicit in the use of this technique is a recognition that a problem exceeds the capability to deal with it using regular patrol and investigative techniques. As such it is an extraordinary measure requiring a commitment of personnel which exceeds that which is normal. Street sweeps are often used as part of a plan which requires the use of several techniques.

Street sweeps have one major drawback. They are, when used to any significant degree, expensive. Many jurisdictions have found it necessary to use off-duty officers on an overtime basis as part of street sweep operations. The cost is therefore substantial. Street sweeps can be planned on a smaller scale with target areas narrowly defined, thus keeping costs down and still impacting the problem area.

Street sweep operations rely on high visibility and uniform patrol officers are best suited for wide-scale deployment in this manner. It is possible for narcotics investigators to do street sweep operations independently, but they are not as effective. Doing these operations requires that the investigators be dressed in raid jackets and other clothing which identifies them as police officers. Using investigators in this manner may preclude later use of them in undercover roles in the area as well as diverting them from their primary function of initiating quality investigations. Again, these operations used in conjunction with other techniques are most effective, and using combined resources from patrol and investigative units is best.

Inherent in the street sweep approach are some legal problems related to reasonable suspicion to stop and detain people for questioning. Stopping people in a target area requires some reasonable suspicion that the people stopped are involved in illegal activity, i.e., buying or selling drugs. Constitutional rights are not suspended in street sweep operations, although allegations of widespread violations of individual rights are frequently made by defense lawyers and civil liberties groups following such operations.

Conduct of street sweep operations in accordance with predetermined guidelines will ensure that stops are based on reasonable suspicion, which is not difficult to articulate in an area of heavy street drug dealing activity. Those involved in the operation should be briefed on how drug deals are conducted so that they can recognize those who may be in the area for that purpose.

Probable cause to arrest people for buying or selling drugs will commonly exist also. Probable cause, being something greater than reasonable suspicion, will usually require additional surveillance, or additional background information, or both. Many times, probable cause will develop from reasonable suspicion. Discussing these things at a preoperational briefing is a good idea and can minimize problems.

All the patrol techniques discussed in this section are used in conjunction with other techniques to attack large-scale drug dealing problems. Extensive use of search warrants, undercover buy programs, and intensified high-visibility patrol are all used in justifying and setting up the street reverse undercover operations which are to be discussed next.

Reverse Undercover Street Operations

Reverse street operations are those in which the police officers pose as dealers and sell the controlled substance or imitation controlled substance to buyers. The buyers are then immediately arrested and charged with possession. This is another technique which has been developed over the past few years in specific response to the street drug dealing locations which have gotten out of control. This approach addresses the demand side of the problem, and when used following the other techniques, extensive crack search warrants, undercover buys, and intensified high visible patrol, the attack on widespread drug dealing is complete and comprehensive.

Documentation

Prior to using the reverse undercover technique, it is necessary to have a problem fully identified and documented. Accomplishing this requires that the other three techniques have been used to some extent at least. Documentation of a drug problem begins with the numbers and substance of citizen complaints. Those should be corroborated by statistics from other police operations in the affected area. The standard statistics such as numbers of calls for service, numbers of arrests and case filings, recovery statistics, etc. should all be part of the documentation and operational planning prefatory to reverse undercover operations.

Reverse undercover operations done at the street level are not fishing expeditions done randomly. It is necessary to identify a problem and document drug dealing activity, heavy consumer traffic, and increases in attendant crime. Once the problem has been identified, it should be attacked using traditional techniques before implementing reverse undercover operations. Done in this manner, the operations will withstand allegations of entrapment. In addition, as a tactical matter, it is necessary to clear out a great deal of the illegal activity and stabilize the area before reverse operations can be done without a great deal of interference.

Prior Enforcement Action

Once a problem area has been identified, traditional enforcement techniques should be applied in some logical order which leads to the setting up of reverse undercover operations. Reverse undercover operations should be planned when the demand side of the problem is so great that attacking the supply alone cannot thoroughly address it. Traditionally, removing the dealer has removed the problem; buyers go elsewhere. In some crack situations, however, heavy demand can actually perpetuate activity in a given area as the market is so great. In these cases, reverse undercover operations are ideal and absolutely necessary in providing a comprehensive solution to the problem.

Depending on the situation, it may be necessary to apply highly visible patrol tactics to an area as the first step in reclaiming the neighborhood before any undercover operations can be undertaken. It might, for example, be necessary for patrol teams to go through an area and sort out and identify the significant dealers and reduce the level of activity in an area to some manageable level. Once the main dealers have been identified, some undercover buy operations can then be implemented to directly attack the problem.

If a street drug dealing situation is out of control, regaining that control may entail a multiphase plan utilizing all the techniques discussed to this point.

The logical order of events is stabilization of the area through intense visible patrol, undercover buy and search warrant operations in the area to attack both the crack houses and the open market dealers, more intense visible patrol to follow-up and clear the area, and then initiation of reverse undercover operations. It is not feasible to put undercover officers on the street in the role of dealers until the legitimate dealers have been removed. Even when efforts have been made to make cases against and remove all of the dealers, there will be some who remain in the area and who must be dealt with as the reverse operations progress.

An example comes to mind of a problem area which was concentrated on one corner of a densely populated city block. There were three of four crack houses in the area and people dealing on the street corner as well. The preliminary operations included undercover buys and search warrants. It was believed that most of the problems had been removed and reverse undercover operations were initiated. What was not realized was that one of the primary targets who had escaped the search warrant phase of the operation by not being home somehow returned to his girlfriend's apartment during the reverse phase of the operation several hours later and was unaware that the dealer on the corner was part of an undercover police operation. This party emerged from the girlfriend's apartment flourishing a gun and demanding that the officer, whom he thought was a rival dealer, get off his corner. This party was arrested without incident, but it could have been a tragic situation.

To some extent, this type of danger is unavoidable, but caution should be used and preliminary operations should be designed for thoroughness. Cover and arrest teams must be deployed in such a way that they can quickly come to the aid of an undercover officer in distress.

Experience has shown that the success of reverse undercover operations is a good barometer of the seriousness of a given problem. It is possible that the drug dealing activity in an area has been overestimated. If that is the case it will become apparent when reverse undercover operations are used. In moderate traffic areas, where there is not a serious ongoing demand for crack, this will be reflected by low success rates in the reverse operations. When this is the case, it may be a good indication that other measures have been successful in temporarily restoring order to the afflicted area.

Operational Design

Reverse undercover operations at the street level must be designed in such a way that officer safety is ensured, that the defense of entrapment is not an issue and that the suspect is apprehended with a minimum of disruption. If actual controlled substances are being used in the operation, ensuring that the substance is recovered is a vital consideration as well. More on that shortly.

Guaranteeing the safety of the undercover officer necessitates that a significant number of officers be part of these operations. There can be so many variables that it usually requires detailing more officers than are necessary just to cover contingencies.

Successful prosecution of these cases requires that there is good documentation of how the sale went. This means of course that the transactions should be recorded, both video and audio if possible, and that the undercover officer follow strict guidelines. The undercover officer posing as the dealer should not solicit customers nor should he display the controlled substance or imitation substance until the potential customer has initiated a conversation. The point is simply that it must be made clear that the person buying has approached the undercover officer because he thinks he is a drug dealer for the purpose of buying drugs, that he was predisposed to commit a crime, and that he was in the area for that purpose. Videotape, running continuously during an operation, is excellent as it will show both the demeanor and the specific actions of the undercover officer before and during the transaction. The videotape will make it clear that the undercover officer did not solicit the customer, that in fact the opposite occurred—the customer approached the undercover officer and asked if "anything was happening," if he "had anything," if he "had a twenty" or whatever the language was. Common street terms which adequately express the intent of the customer are all that is required.

If the operation is designed to achieve these two purposes, officer safety and a prosecutable case, the only other thing remaining as part of its correct design is that plans are made which enable the suspect to be arrested with a minimum of disruption. Major considerations here revolve around the fact that if an operation is run well, the suspect will be completely surprised when he is approached by police officers and arrested. This being the case, it is essential that the officers be able to approach the suspect quickly, cut off possible escape routes, and make the purpose of their presence immediately known.

Because of this, it is beneficial to have uniform officers available to assist in the arrest. Officers on motorcycles can often accomplish the arrest most efficiently. In any case, the presence of the uniform leaves no doubt in the suspect's mind that he is being arrested; he cannot claim that he ran because he thought he was about to be robbed by several thugs in T-shirts and jeans. Of course, plainclothes officers in raid clothing serve the same purpose. An added advantage of uniform officers being part of the plan is that in the event the suspect drives away before he can be apprehended, uniform officers in a marked vehicle are available to follow the suspect and effect the stop. This is one of the most dangerous aspects of this type of operation, of any type of operation for that matter, namely, the suspect driving away as officers are approaching on foot. The officers are endangered and the success of the operation may be at stake. Therefore, the plan must be designed so that the suspect can be blocked in and arrested without delay and with a minimum of disruption and commotion. Done in this manner, the reverse sales can continue with a minimum of wasted time.

Operational Mechanics

The Undercover Officer

The undercover officer should be dressed in the appropriate attire for the area, and he should be positioned in a manner consistent with the methods of the actual drug dealers who have been operating in the area. If the operation is being videotaped, and it should be whenever possible, how the officer is dressed and where he positions himself may have to be adjusted for better quality filming. White clothing is good at night in low-light conditions particularly where the camera is attached to a night scope. External lighting conditions and natural obstacles will dictate adjustments in clothing and positioning. It is best if the surveillance van is in the area with the equipment set up and ready to go before the undercover officer enters the area. Those officers can then direct the officer into the best position. The undercover officer should be wired, and the wireshould be tested as the officer moves into position.

The undercover officer should not solicit customers or display the product until asked to do so.

As a potential customer approaches the undercover officer, the officer will have to be careful to avoid moving out of the range of the video equipment. The surveillance van should be positioned for some flexibility, anticipating that the undercover officer may have to walk to the curb and talk to some people in vehicles. Once the transaction has been completed, the undercover officer can give details over the wire which will aid the arrest team in isolating the right suspect. For example, if two or three customers approach the undercover officer, the officer should clarify, on the wire, which people are involved in the transaction and should be arrested. "The guy in the red and white shirt with the black cap is the guy I sold to, the other guy isn't with him, he was just standing around."

The surveillance officers can make brief notes pertaining to the times of each deal and some of the identifying characteristics which are distinctive. The undercover officer can then make notes when he is relieved. The money from each sale must be kept separate. It can be passed on to the report writing team through the arrest team or through the close cover officers during the brief break in the action when arrests are being made. That way, the evidence (cash and substance) and the suspect get to the report writing team at the same time. This seems like a minor point, but in heavy traffic areas, the sales may come so quickly and so close together that keeping the details straight can be a problem.

It is preferable to have at least two undercover officers prepared to act as sellers. They can be frequently relieved, and during the times they are not undercover, they can work on the notes and reports from previous transactions. In some cases it is desirable to have two officers working in close proximity to each other, both working simultaneously as sellers. This is not a good idea unless there is adequate electronic and physical surveillance to cover both deals. For one surveillance crew to monitor two separate wires and videotape two deals at once does not work out very well. Spreading the surveillance and cover too thin results in lower-quality work and increases the possibility that costly mistakes will be made and that officers will be injured.

Close Cover

In street crack dealing it is not unusual to have more than one seller on a given corner, or in the event that there is only one seller, there may be several people who just hang around. They may be there hoping that the dealer will be benevolent and give them some crack, or they may try to get into the action in some other way. They may act as bodyguards for the dealer also. This behavior, duplicated in street reverse operations, is ideally suited for providing close cover for the undercover officer. Two or more plainclothes officers can station themselves in close proximity to the undercover officer without arousing any suspicion.

At least two officers should be assigned to the close cover detail. In addition to providing excellent backup for the undercover officer, they will be in a position to assist the arrest teams should they encounter difficulty, and they can detect interference from other people in the neighborhood who may be aware that a police operation is being conducted and who may attempt to warn potential customers. The close cover officers should advise such people that they are interfering with a police operation and that if they continue they will be arrested. In most cases the warning will be heeded, the neighbors will mind their own business, and the officers will have been able to accomplish this with a minimum amount of disruption.

One function that the close cover officers can perform is to watch the suspect as he leaves the undercover officer just prior to being arrested. It is at this time that there is the most risk that the evidence will be swallowed, discarded, or destroyed. Cover officers can observe the suspect without any awareness on the suspect's part that he is being watched. In addition, the cover officers can be useful in discreetly meeting with the undercover officer and taking cash pertaining to a transaction and passing it along to the report writing team. Depending on the level of activity, it may be a good idea to rotate the close cover personnel.

Arrest Teams

Arrest teams should be stationed as close to the site of the operation as can be accomplished without jeopardizing its success. As mentioned previously, uniform officers in marked vehicles are often better suited for arrest duties than are plainclothes officers in unmarked vehicles. There are situations in which the use of plainclothes officers for arrest teams is preferable.

Arrest teams should be instructed to move in and arrest the suspect as quickly as possible. If the suspect is in a vehicle, enough arrest teams should be deployed to block the suspect's vehicle from leaving effectively. Three two-man teams should be assigned to the operation to perform as arrest teams. This number should allow for operations to continue while previous prisoners are being transported to the operational command post where they will be processed. One team performing that function will leave two teams available and the operation can proceed without unnecessary delay.

Arrest teams should be prepared in advance for the distinct possibility that the suspects will attempt to dispose of the evidence. The approach to the suspect has to be either very swift, ensuring that the suspect is taken completely by surprise before he can react, or nonchalant, giving the suspect the false impression that the officers are not going to stop him and that he has no reason for alarm or for disposing of the evidence.

It may be necessary to deploy arrest teams in such a manner that they can approach either on foot or in a vehicle, depending on the situation. If the suspect is on foot, or on a bicycle, approaching him on foot may be better than driving a marked unit or undercover vehicle into the area. In these cases, where the suspect is not in a vehicle, plainclothes officers are often better suited for arrest duties than are uniform officers. Plainclothes officers may be able to effect the arrest drawing a minimum amount of attention to the operation.

If the suspect is in a vehicle, make the arrest teams responsible for the disposition of the vehicle. Part of the impact of these reverse operations involves seizing the vehicle where that can be done within the context of existing public nuisance and property confiscation laws. In any case, whether the vehicle is ultimately seized or not, have it towed or otherwise moved from the scene. It is not suggested that towing of the vehicle be a punitive measure. Rather, it is recommended that to facilitate a smooth-running operation, the vehicle be moved from the operational site; towed to the storage facility or the command post. Many of the vehicles will not be worth seizing, many will have large liens against them precluding their seizure, and in some other cases the circumstances may not warrant seizing the vehicle.

Report Writing Teams

In any street enforcement operation, provisions for handling the paperwork are an essential part of the planning. Failure to provide for systematic handling of arrest paperwork and evidence will result in chaos. At least one team of investigators should be assigned to the command post for this purpose.

When arrests are made, the suspect, the cash which he used to purchase the substance from the undercover officer, and the substance should be brought to the command post. Case packets should be made beforehand which have every form needed in them. Included in such paperwork should be arrest paperwork, evidence containers, and inventory forms. The officers on the report writing team must see that all the necessary paperwork for a case filing is in each packet before the suspects are transported to the detention facility. Each packet should have a checklist on the front of the file folder to ensure that nothing has been overlooked. Refer to Figure 5-3 and Figure 5-4.

In addition, forms can be developed which serve as quick investigative reports which supplant lengthy narrative reports. See Figure 5-5.

Forms such as this can be made and used in the interest of simplicity and case organization. These things are particularly important when numerous arrests are made in a short period of time. Any number of other written reports can be made which will also facilitate organization and later reporting of the operation. The supervisor at the command post should make a master name list including suspects' names, corresponding property numbers, etc. Also, a master vehicle list should be compiled including current disposition of the vehicle and anticipated long range disposition. Included on this list should be license number,

```
                  NARCOTICS INVESTIGATION UNIT
               SHORT FORM SUPPLEMENTARY REPORT
      This report is being made on (date)_____ by Detective
      _____Serial #_____.  It concerns an
      incident at _____, on (date)_____
      at (time) _____.
      CRIMINAL VIOLATION:_____
      REVISED STATUTE NUMBER:_____
      Filing investigator:_____Serial #_____
      This investigative report is made concerning an arrest
      which was made on (date)_____.  The violation took
      place at _____in (City)_____
      (State)_____.
      Detective _____was the officer who was
      acting in an undercover capacity.
      Detective _____was standing at the location
      of_____when approached by
      _____who expressed an interest
      in buying crack cocaine from the undercover officer in the
      following manner:
      _____
      _____
      _____

      Detective_____completed the exchange by
      giving the suspect_____, a previously
      weighed and packaged quantity of crack cocaine in exchange
      for $_____.__ in U. S. currency.

      The suspect_____, was arrested at:
      _____ by the arrest
      team of _____Serial #_____
      and _____Serial #_____
      Date and time of arrest:_____
      Evidence:_____
      Property number:_____.
      This case was presented to _____
      deputy district attorney, on _____.
      Filing: yes___no___Reason for refusal_____
                        FIGURE 5-5
```

brief vehicle description, whether the vehicle was towed, and whether or not the vehicle should be held for seizure or released to the owner.

These details may seem unnecessary to those who have not experienced the demands of after-action reporting and accountability. However, the list of people arrested and the vehicle dispositions will be very important when the operation is completed.

Prisoner Disposition

Prior to undertaking an operation of this type where numerous arrests are anticipated, it is a must that the commanding officers of the detention facility be notified. They can make the necessary arrangements to have additional people working, additional transport vehicles, etc. In general, the cooperation of these people can make for a much smoother operation.

In any case, some provisions must be made to deal with the large number of arrests which may result. At least two officers should be assigned to the transportation detail. The prisoner transportation vehicle, in which prisoners are loaded after processing, can be parked at the command post. When the vehicle is full, those aboard should be taken to the detention facility. More than one transportation vehicle may be required depending on the size of the operation; one can then be used for holding and one transportation.

Surveillance Team

The officers responsible for electronic surveillance and recording of the operation will control the operation to a large extent. The surveillance officers will be in a position to know when a potential customer is approaching and when the deal is consummated. Because they will be watching the transaction and monitoring the audio as well, the surveillance officers should give the verbal bust sign to the arrest teams.

In addition to controlling the tempo of the operation, the surveillance officers should make a log sheet reflecting the undercover activity and corresponding tape counter numbers, both audio and video. In between transactions, these officers can communicate with the report writing officers and others at the command post so that the surveillance logs can be updated with suspect information.

Substance Sold

Street reverse operation can best be accomplished using actual controlled substances. The suspects can then be charged with possession of a controlled substance when the transaction has been completed. There are many jurisdictions in which the prosecutors and police administrators are opposed to distributing actual controlled substances. The objections are based on the risk that the suspect may avoid apprehension and thus the drugs have been lost and put on the street and that, if the substance is not recovered, the police department assumes some liability for any negative effects resulting from its use.

Also, many prosecutors and administrators have difficulty with the underlying philosophy of reverse operations. That is, some argue, the police department should not be in the business of distributing drugs. However, in some severe cases it becomes necessary to address the demand side of the crack problem by attacking it through reverse operations.

Once it has been determined that reverse operations must be a part of the comprehensive solution, the only decision is whether or not actual controlled substances should be distributed. Dealing an imitation substance will result in charges of attempted possession or something along those lines, whereas when actual crack is distributed, possession of a controlled substance can be charged. There is less risk involved in dealing the imitation substance; if it is not recovered, the case is not significantly damaged, and there is no risk accompanying its possible loss. Conversely, if the problem is so serious in scope and nature that it warrants reverse operations, it is probably worth the additional risk involved in the carefully controlled distribution of actual drugs to achieve a better case.

Regardless of whether actual controlled substances or imitations are sold, certain precautions must be taken in the interest of making the operation safer and easier. These are particularly important when actual crack is being used as several key points may become issues in a subsequent trial. The substances should be packaged in plastic. Either small ziplock baggies or miniature vials should be used. Even if this is not how crack is being sold in the area, it should be sold this way during the reverse operation. Crack packaged in such a way is more difficult to swallow, dispose of, and conceal. It is also easier to account for and keep track of packaged crack than loose pieces.

The packages should be similar in total weight. The package sold must be carefully handled upon recovery and placed into the property bureau. The evidence should be tested, just as in other possession cases, even if a test has been done beforehand to determine the level of purity, weight, etc. A statement from the laboratory chemist who prepared the crack for the operation should be obtained as he may be an important witness in the trial.

SUMMARY

The enforcement techniques described have general application to all situations where drug dealing has grown out of control and is threatening the community. They have been applied specifically and with much success to crack problems. There are any number of variations which may be necessary depending on the precise nature of the problems.

A combination of the techniques discussed will ensure that the problem is attacked comprehensively and with the most effectiveness. The techniques which have been described have been developed, modified, and improved upon by narcotics investigators throughout the country. Through training sessions and conferences, problems are shared, and solutions to the problems worked out collectively. A tremendous resource, often overlooked, are the narcotics commanders and investigators whose collective experience has developed and perfected these techniques. Most of these people will readily give advice and share technical improvements upon request.

6

UNDERCOVER OPERATIONS

INTRODUCTION

This chapter deals with undercover operations. Four situations will be discussed: (1) the buy/bust, in which the deal is consummated and following the exchange the suspect is arrested; (2) the buy(flash)/bust, in which the money is flashed and the arrest takes place after the drugs have been seen by the undercover officer; (3) the straight undercover buy, made as part of an ongoing investigation to compound the offense, strengthen undercover relationships, and learn more about sources, and so on; and (4) reverse undercover operations.

Prior to discussing these situations, the three elements critical to the success of any undercover operation are discussed: undercover work, its philosophy, and the undercover officer; planning undercover operations; and surveillance techniques.

The chapter concludes with a general discussion of several of the inviolate precepts and maxims of undercover operations and the situational variables which cause these to be controverted from time to time. There are very few rules which are not broken sooner or later, and while this is necessarily true, there is usually a very high risk attendant to doing so which must be understood.

UNDERCOVER WORK

Philosophy

The theory of undercover investigations is very old, apparently going back to biblical times and no doubt before that. The idea is soundly based on the premise that to gain one's confidence is the only true way of learning of his thoughts and activities. Implicit in the word "undercover" is the concept of secrecy. To function under cover, the true intentions and purpose have to be secret.

In law enforcement, undercover operations are undertaken with the purpose of enabling successful prosecutions of individuals and organizations which would not otherwise be possible. In narcotics enforcement, undercover operations are an integral part of strategy and techniques. Much of the work of a narcotics investigator is done undercover, although probably not within the commonly accepted glamorous cinema and media definitions. Surveillance is no doubt the most commonly utilized undercover technique. It is generally not thought of as such, however. Likewise, the widespread use of informants is undercover police work in a vicarious sense.

Narcotics cases made by undercover police officers are preferable to other cases because a distribution case is often made as opposed to, or in addition to, a possession case and the undercover officer can provide direct testimony regarding the elements of the crime.

Administrative Commitment

There should be a policy in place governing undercover operations in general and providing for procedural regulation of all phases of undercover work. The policy must include a statement of purpose defining when undercover operations should be used. Guidelines for the conduct of undercover operations and provisions for regular reporting and approval of continuing investigations should be included.

This is recommended, though not to be overly restrictive of the discretionary powers of the investigators and supervisors. On the contrary, a clear policy will protect the investigators and supervisors and provide them direction and, more importantly, support in their efforts.

Lacking a clear policy regarding the conduct of undercover operations which provides for administrative accountability, the people at the operational level may be left solely accountable for negative side effects and consequences which may result from good-faith efforts. There is a great deal of risk inherently present in undercover operations. There is risk of personal injury, risk of individual and department liability, and the potential for misconduct. Greater still is the potential that there will be allegations of misconduct which have no basis in fact. To manage all aspects of undercover work effectively, a clearly stated policy must be in place.

There must also be a fiscal commitment by the police administration to undercover operations. Undercover work is expensive, requiring special equipment and specially trained personnel; undercover operations are, by their nature, labor intensive, and to expect that they can be successfully undertaken otherwise is unrealistic. Management must believe in undercover operations. That belief should be manifested in a clearly written policy and should be backed up with the necessary commitment of personnel and equipment.

Selection of Personnel

The personnel selected for undercover assignments will ultimately determine the quality and success of a unit responsible for these types of operations. While this is appropriately an administrative function, the investigators and supervisors will invariably have a great deal of input in these choices. The judgment of those already in place in these assignments will carry a lot of weight. In this way, the collective personality of a unit is perpetuated. The people in place will naturally choose to surround themselves with people whom they like and with whom they get along.

An undercover unit is like any other team in that a number of different skills will be necessary for success. Not everyone in the unit will be an undercover "star." A variety of skills will be required, and people will be asked to do more than one thing well. Selection of an undercover officer must take this into account. The officers selected should be versatile, possessing a number of talents.

It is important that the officers selected for undercover assignments have a work record of reliability and stability. They should also possess initiative to a higher degree than normal. Reliability, stability, and initiative are arguably the most valuable qualities that a prospective undercover officer should possess. The assignment will call for a person who will exercise initiative in making cases where someone less motivated might accomplish nothing. Yet initiative must be tempered by sound judgment. This is a critical balance which will be enhanced through experience if the person has the potential to develop.

There are other aspects of personality and experience which should be considered. While intelligence is important, street savvy is more important. In addition, the officer should be able to communicate well, in writing and verbally: survival undercover and in court can be closely related to how well an undercover officer can communicate. Being bilingual is a distinct advantage for any narcotics investigator. Knowledge of Spanish, if not fluency, is an advantage in a significant number of narcotics cases, particularly in the West and Southwest. Everything else being equal, an officer who speaks Spanish fluently is preferable to one who does not.

Physical fitness is also a requirement for potential undercover officers. There is a great deal of stress inherent in this type of work, and an officer who is physically fit will be better prepared to handle the stress and other demands as well.

Training

There are a number of components necessary in training new undercover officers. Of course, classroom training sessions focusing on undercover work are valuable and should be a part of a new undercover officer's training where possible.

However, the only way that one develops into an undercover officer is through actual experience, on-the-job training. Many departments have extended temporary assignments to vice enforcement units which provide excellent training for future undercover assignments. In fact, general vice work provides an officer with the chance to adapt to working in plainclothes and to gain experience in vehicle surveillances, undercover work of several different types, and case preparation. Officers who have spent considerable time on surveillance of street prostitution deals develop very sharp skills and can follow practically anybody.

Some formal departmental orientation is a must and should focus on the most basic issues. While on-the-job training is the best method of learning how to work undercover and undercover operations, there are several important issues which should be systematically discussed and imparted to the newly assigned officer. Too often, it is assumed that the officer will learn everything which he needs to know through trial and error and informal training. Invariably, certain things go unsaid which later become important. When an officer is assigned to an undercover assignment, he should be advised of the department's informant policy and made aware of much of what is in Chapter Two of this book. Handling informants will be critical to his success. The new officer should be briefed on procedures pertaining to the confidential fund. Finally, the standard operating procedures which provide general guidelines for all undercover operations should be thoroughly discussed. Such procedures usually place limitations on the way an operation is conducted, which will often be stretched by experienced officers, though not always rightly so. The following is a list of ultimatums which are a part of the theory of undercover work and which should be passed on to newly assigned officers. In the final portion of this chapter, some of these maxims will be discussed in the context of when it is necessary to be flexible and ignore them.

1. Always control the location of the deal.
2. Don't be predictable.
3. Never let the money walk.
4. Remove the undercover officer from the arrest scene when possible.
5. Don't give the informant the flash roll.
6. Don't ever flash the money twice in the same location.
7. Don't get over anxious and force a deal.
8. Sense danger.
9. Always have a minimum of four cover officers for an undercover operation.
10. Never give up your gun.

Adapting to the Undercover Role

It is not easy for an officer who has spent considerable time in uniform to adapt to an undercover assignment. Many officers have the feeling that everybody recognizes them just as if they were still going around in uniform. It is a state of mind which must be altered. In truth, in most cities of any size, the officer in plainclothes will not be recognized by most of the people. Those whom he knows well will recognize him, and certain criminal types with which he has dealt will recognize him as well. Otherwise, people for the most part are not going to pay any attention.

The undercover officer must apply the power of "as if." That is, he must act as if he were not a police officer, as if he were actually a person trying to buy drugs or pick up a prostitute or make a wager. When he is in the process of making an undercover deal, whether it is a drug deal or a prostitution deal or just an undercover surveillance in a public place, he must carry himself as if he were not a police officer. Making this adjustment is easier for some officers than others. Some people cannot get over the feeling that everyone knows they are police officers, that they are "burned."

Many times these feelings are intensified by nervousness and fear, forming a negative cycle; they are fearful and nervous because they feel they have been burned, and the feelings of being identified are worsened by the fear and nervousness.

It is best not to force someone into an undercover position; rather, let them adjust their feelings and mind-set gradually and observe a few of the experts at work. Once they have observed several undercover operations they will feel more comfortable trying it themselves.

Again, low-level street drug buys or undercover vice work provide excellent training. An officer who has had the opportunity to gain that experience has a distinct advantage. Making a prostitution deal can require as much quick thinking and ad-libbing as any drug deal will ever require. In essence, the officer learns to develop a line by responding to repeated queries as to whether or not he is a policeman. He also learns how to carry himself and how to look at people to avoid arousing their suspicion. Role-playing exercises can accomplish the same thing, but not with the same realism with which they are learned in actual undercover roles.

As an officer adapts to undercover work he learns what works for him and what does not. One popular way of facilitating the transition from normal police work to undercover work is to grow a beard. This seems to provide a symbolic contradiction to being a policeman in the male ego sufficient enough to overcome much of the self-consciousness about being widely recognized. It is not necessary. Often an officer grows a beard because he is finally free to do so, and it is a matter of preference; sometimes it does help the officer make the transition.

Undercover officers learn to develop a "cover" for their occupations, their family life, and their backgrounds. In most cases, the cover, when it is necessary, should be something which closely resembles the truth. For example, if an officer was an electrician before he became a policeman, that would be a likely cover for him to assume and probably preferable to saying he is a barber if he knows nothing about being a barber. Likewise, if an officer is married and has children, there is no reason that he should change that to make his cover story. Drug dealers have children who go to school and have minor problems and successes just like everyone else. Keeping that as part of the cover will give the officer something to talk about which comes naturally.

The undercover name used should be something simple and easily remembered. The same first name will probably work. Officers often use their middle names or their father's first names or some other name they are not likely to forget. There is no necessity to make any part of the cover too complex. The more fabrications involved, the more difficult it will be to remain consistent.

Undercover driver's licenses and identification are nice to have and may be necessary in some cases. If the undercover role is going to be long term, or one of deep cover, it may be necessary to establish a complete identity. For most drug transactions all that is required is an undercover name. It is not usually necessary to back that up to any significant degree, but it is best to be prepared and having an under-cover identification available is a good idea.

Inherent Dangers

The most obvious danger of undercover work is that the officer will be recognized and that the suspect will take aggressive action against the officer. This is not usually the case in drug investigations. Normally, if the dealer recognizes the officer, he will refuse to sell to him and that is the end of it. He may or may not let the officer know that he has identified him, leaving room for speculation. The informant may be endangered in these situations more than the undercover officer, and his future dealings with the person may have some interesting results.

The most insidious danger in an undercover operation is that the suspect will identify with the officer and, once recognition has been made, will continue dealing with him in an effort to set him up to be injured or killed. This possibility makes it very important that the undercover officer be alert for any subtle changes in behavior on the part of the suspect. The undercover officer should not become paranoid—

that is counterproductive—but there should be a healthy state of awareness at all times.

Another serious threat to the safety of the undercover officer, most often associated with first time dealings with a suspect where significant quantities of drugs and money are involved, is the danger of robbery. Developing a general background and an accurate criminal history profile of the suspect is the most effective way to prevent this from happening. Unfortunately, the advantage of knowing the true identity of the suspects is not always present and an unknown opponent is difficult to assess. In general terms, the less that is known about a suspect, the greater the risk that a robbery or rip-off will occur. This danger is equally as inherent in reverse operations as in undercover drug buys. While operational planning and execution can reduce the risks, they cannot be removed entirely.

In addition to the risks immediately attached to undercover work, there are additional dangers which can build and which may have a cumulative effect on the officers. The most obvious of these relates to stress which may have a variety of symptoms. Another very serious danger is complacency. Officers who have performed in undercover roles for a long period of time may become careless, and the safety of all involved may be jeopardized.

PLANNING

There are basically four types of plans or phases of planning which are part of undercover operations. There is a general plan or standard operating procedure for all undercover operations. This plan should be subject to continual revision to meet the changing needs. In addition, there are the specific undercover plan, the specific surveillance plan, and the arrest plan.

General Operational Plan

Any unit that initiates and participates in undercover operations as part of its regular duties must have a general operational plan in place. The plan can be in writing in the form of official procedures and regulations, or it can be policy written at the unit level. In any case, there are several critical facets of any undercover operation for which some general plan must be in place. The following is a list of the elements to be addressed in a general plan:

1. Suspect identification—minimum standards
2. Preoperational investigation
3. Confidential fund procedures
4. Flash fund availability
5. Communications
6. Surveillance and electronics equipment
7. Standards for minimum cover
8. Raid clothing
9. Special weapons availability
10. Moving to the next level up

Issues revolving around these subjects present themselves repeatedly. To address them in the form of a general plan or standard operating procedure saves dealing with them and resolving them time and time again. The general plan can also be used as the foundation from which all undercover operations are developed. Also, the inexperienced officer will have a systematic way of learning the basics.

Suspect identification is critical, and an effort should be made to identify possible suspects completely in an undercover operation before any action is taken. As a general rule, money will not be invested in a case until the suspect is identified. What constitutes identification will vary.

In cases where money is being flushed (drugs bought, money is spent, arrest deferred until some later time), the case agent and the supervisor will have to determine if the suspect is identified sufficiently enough to justify expenditures. The relative amount to be flushed will have to be weighed in light of case objectives and case potential. There may be only partial identification, in terms of legal name, etc., but there might be a relatively complete identification as a matter of fact. The suspect's address, place of employment, vehicles, etc. may all be known. The general plan should stress identification but should not be so restrictive as to preclude discretion in each case.

In cases where money is to be flashed only or where the buy is consummated and then arrest is immediately made, identification is not as important from an investigative standpoint as from a tactical perspective. Knowing the suspect is extremely important in evaluating the suspect's potential for violence (rip-off), his propensities toward carrying weapons, etc. The more criminal history that can be developed, the better. The general operational plan should stress the need for thorough suspect identification through whatever means are available.

In addition to suspect identification there should be guidelines for other preoperational investigation. The emphasis of all preoperational investigative work is to gain an advantage in planning and executing an operation. Surveillance may be necessary for several days prior to an operation, or it may not. It may be necessary to get utility subscriber information or photographs and records from the department of motor vehicles. The general undercover operations plan need only emphasize the importance of background information to planning.

An established fund for confidential expenditures and appropriate guidelines for disbursement and accounting of funds are essential to an undercover unit. Confidential funds must be readily available if there is to be any chance of successful undercover operations. Confidential funds procedures should have built-in accounting checks and strict reporting of expenditures as a basic part of the structure. The availability of and accountability for such funds must be a planning consideration. Undercover operations require it.

Likewise, buy/bust situations may call for the temporary use of flash money. There should be a separate flash fund established from which there should be no expenditures. The funds should contain a significant amount of currency for showing during a drug deal.

Concern for the cash used in a drug transaction can be a serious source of stress and worry. This is particularly true when large amounts of currency are involved. The fear that the money will be lost will often dictate the manner in which the deal is transacted. There will always be some risk that the money will be lost. This risk should be guarded against through procedures which provide guidelines for how the money is handled. Each situation will be different, and some will involve more risk than others. There can be guidelines only; hard and fast rules as such will be overly restrictive.

Communications will be an important part of undercover operations as it is in any tactical operation. Pagers, voice private radios, and cellular telephones are commonly available today and relatively inexpensively.

They should all be used in the interest of a safer, more successful operation.

The general operational plan should include provisions for the use and maintenance of electronics and surveillance equipment. A certain amount of this type of equipment will be required and used on a regular basis as part of undercover operations. There must be some plan to check and maintain the equipment if it is expected to last. There is so much sophisticated surveillance equipment on the market that the only limitation, and a very real limitation at that, is available funding. What is more important than the type of or quantity of equipment is the condition of the equipment. There is nothing more frustrating than equipment failure. When that happens, a very important tactical and investigative edge is lost. While equipment failure cannot be totally prevented, proper maintenance of the equipment and training in its use must be ongoing.

A general operational plan must make provisions for the general conditions in which undercover operations can be conducted. It must therefore proscribe doing an operation if certain minimum standards are not met. Those minimum standards apply generally to the number of people required for an operation. This is closely related to the individual characteristics of each operation, the personality and history of the suspect, and other factors. Yet there must be some guidelines requiring that some minimum number of people are available for cover.

This is a very critical area of concern. The vast majority of undercover operations are done successfully with ease and without incident. This can lead to an unwarranted sense of well-being on the part of those regularly involved in undercover work. As a result, there will be a tendency to relax the minimum standards regarding the number of people required. This becomes particularly true of the undercover officer himself, who upon recognizing that few people are available for cover, will want to go ahead with the operation anyway.

In situations where an officer is buying from a suspect as part of an ongoing investigation, there will obviously be fewer people required to cover the operation than if the suspect is to be arrested. However, it is a serious mistake to become complacent and allow the undercover officer to make the buy if there are not enough people to cover the contingency that something will go wrong and the suspect will have to be immediately arrested.

It is advisable that every undercover operation is done in such a way that the suspect can be successfully arrested, even when that is not part of the plan. This means that a minimum of four or six officers be assigned to cover each operation. The general operational plan should stress the need for flexibility in any operation.

Minimum standards for cover are often relaxed when an officer is going to be working in a bar, just showing his face, and getting known without any plans to make any buys or otherwise interact with any specific targets. Invariably if these operations are planned with only one cover officer or perhaps two, something goes wrong. Somebody ends up identifying the officer and they have a confrontation, somebody makes them an offer they can't refuse and they end up in a position of jeopardizing the future of the investigation by not going along with the offer, or any number of other things. In spite of the fact that there is a valid reason for officers to work undercover in bars as part of a specific investigation, to do it without sufficient cover to deal with possible surveillance and arrest contingencies is inadvisable. If an investigation is important enough to warrant an officer going undercover in a bar, it also warrants adequate cover.

The subject of working undercover in a liquor establishment brings up another issue which should be addressed in the general undercover operations plan. That is, there must be some set policy regarding drinking while undercover. Again, this should not be overly restrictive, but it must emphasize the need for clear thinking over and above the need to fit in. Depending on the type of establishment, it might not be necessary to drink at all, whereas there are other places where a nondrinker will be automatically suspect.

If each operation is planned to deal with all contingencies, it is necessary that the general operational plan consider the need for special raid gear and possibly special weapons. Plainclothes officers should have raid gear, raid jackets, and caps, and protective vests available to them at all times. They should carry them in the trunks of their undercover vehicles and should be wearing them when arrest of a suspect is a possibility and certainly in buy/bust situations. An example comes to mind. Two narcotics investigators were on the street checking some addresses and doing other routine duties. Some robbery investigators and uniform officers called for an unmarked vehicle to watch an address while they prepared to execute a warrant at that address. The warrant related to a robbery investigation which had occurred the previous night in which the suspects shot at a police officer and got away.

The two narcotics officers were in one vehicle and only the officer assigned to that vehicle had his raid gear with him. He decided that it would be a good idea to put it on even though they didn't figure as part of the raid plans. During the surveillance the suspects left the house and got into a vehicle. The suspects were apparently aware that they were being followed. When they stopped at a stop sign, the driver of the suspect vehicle leaned out of the vehicle and started shooting at the officers. The driver of the undercover vehicle was shot twice, once in the arm and once in the chest by the suspect, who was armed with a .45-caliber semiautomatic pistol. Fortunately, the narcotics officer who was driving had put on his vest, which saved his life. The vest stopped the shot to the chest and the injury to the arm was minor. He also put on his raid jacket which clearly identified him as a police officer to allay any false claims later that the suspects thought they were being assaulted and shot the officer in self-defense. Both suspects were subsequently killed in the exchange of gunfire.

The increase in recent years of drug-related violence has mandated that narcotics investigators be provided with protective vests and other raid clothing. This was not commonly the case only a few years ago, and raids and arrests were often made without the benefit of such equipment. These same concerns, increased drug-related violence, have also necessitated the availability of special weapons. Special weapons such as shotguns and submachine guns can be very useful in certain tactical situations. There is a commensurate amount of training necessary if these weapons are to be part of undercover operations, and only those officers with training and current qualification should be allowed to use them.

The final consideration of a general operational plan for undercover work involves the issue of immediately turning an operation upward to the next level. It is very common for an undercover operation to present the opportunity to go to the next level. The target of the operation may immediately give up his source, but it will require immediate action before word spreads of the arrest of the initial target. These situations will require that fast action be taken, and there should be some plan in place to facilitate that action. In other words, the discretion of the officers making the decision should be guided by policy regarding what consideration can be given the suspect. For example, the suspect will often agree to cooperate if he isn't required to go to jail. As a general rule, getting to the higher source is consistent with the objectives of a case, but no promises of case disposition should be made to the suspect, and he should also be required to go to jail and make bond. It may be possible to have the suspect set up his source and get that accomplished before going to jail. Of course, in addition to the two factors just mentioned, no promises and mandatory detention, there are any number of questions to be answered based on the peculiarities of each deal. Foremost among them is: Can the suspect who is turning be trusted? Is he really turning his source, or is he turning someone below him?

Specific Undercover Plan

Each undercover operation will require a plan unique in many respects. The general issues just discussed will influence the operation to varying degrees. In addition there will be any number of specific considerations. The specific details should be worked out in light of the following.

Setting Time and Location

The officers should set the time and location for a deal as much as possible. While this is not always feasible, the suspect should not be allowed to set up the deal entirely as he sees fit. What happens in most cases is compromise. The suspect will give in on some of his demands, and the officers will have to be flexible in certain areas also.

If the dictates of the suspect go entirely against safety considerations and tactical and investigative preferences, the decision must be made whether or not to proceed with the deal. The location and time of the deal should be chosen to maximize cover and officer safety.

The best locations are those in public places, shopping center parking lots, for example, where the undercover officer will be clearly visible to surveillance and where surveillance can be largely inconspicuous. Public locations, away from the suspect's home, are also preferable to the suspect in most cases. This is particularly true in deals involving large quantities of money and drugs. Again, choice of location and time will be influenced by the individual characteristics of each operation.

Locations which isolate the undercover officer should be avoided. It is best for surveillance to maintain both visual and audio surveillance. If the officer is forced to leave the view of the surveillance team, only the audio surveillance remains and that increases the risk. The main consideration in choosing time and location of undercover operations is to reduce the risk, thus enhancing the potential for success.

Informant Involvement

The degree of informant involvement in each undercover operation will vary. To what extent the informant is involved will dictate how an operation is conducted. Informants will have a tendency to control the manner in which the operation will be conducted. This should be avoided. All conversations between the informant and the suspect which are part of arranging the deal should be monitored. It is also preferable if they are recorded.

If the informant is to testify, then his participation in an undercover operation does not have to be limited for the purpose of confidentiality. It should still be limited as much as possible, however. The less participation the informant has in a case, the better. This is true from both the investigative and tactical perspectives. Regardless of how reliable an informant may be, he is not a sworn officer. He is not trained, his reactions will be unpredictable to varying degrees, and his testimony will not carry the weight of that of a sworn officer.

This is not to say that there are not advantages to informant participation. The informant can often, by virtue of his familiarity with the suspect and the suspect's trust in him, ensure the success of an operation and reduce the risks to the undercover officer.

Conduct of the Operation

The undercover plan should describe the way the operation is to be conducted from the standpoint of the undercover officer. To make the right decisions in an operation, the covering officers must understand and try to view the operation from that perspective. The purpose of the undercover operation, the amounts of money and drugs involved, the bust signs, the distress signs, the vehicles involved, and any other pertinent details should be made known at the beginning of an operation. The operational briefing sheet can be used to outline all the details. The specifics and contingencies can be discussed during the operational briefing.

It is very important that the purpose of the operation is clear. A buy/bust differs significantly from a buy/walk situation. The possibility that the objective of the operation will change based upon certain factors should also be made clear. In other words, the contingency plan and the factors which will activate those plans should be made clear from the standpoint of the undercover officer. The undercover officer will be the key to any changes in the plan, and the covering officers must view and understand the operation from that position. Experience is important in this regard. Officers who have worked together extensively will come to communicate nonverbally. They will understand each others' ways of thinking and can therefore correctly "read" an operation and anticipate danger.

Surveillance Plan

Each undercover operation will require a surveillance plan based on the operational objectives. A good surveillance plan will be critical to the success of the operation. There is no substitute for experience when it comes to surveillance. Likewise, there is no way that a good surveillance can be accomplished without adequate personnel. The following two factors are part of every surveillance plan.

Purpose

Every surveillance will have a specific purpose, usually related to continual observation of a certain suspect or location. With respect to surveillance on a suspect, merely watching the suspect will not be enough. Operational decisions may hinge on the actions of the suspect, and the role of the surveillance officers is not a passive one. They must learn from the surveillance in order to contribute.

The purpose of the surveillance has to be clear so that it does not get sidetracked. Decisions should not be made on speculative observations alone. Too often, the purpose of a surveillance is complicated by officers giving an undue amount of attention to ancillary observations which may have nothing to do with the deal in progress. There has to be a surveillance leader whose responsibility it will be to bring discipline to that part of the operation keeping it focused on its purpose.

Communication

The key to surveillance, particularly moving surveillance, is effective communication. In a moving surveillance, communication is required to avoid losing the suspect. The surveillance leader should be designated before the operation, and he should determine the guidelines for communication. It is usually best if only the person with the "eye" (position of direct observation) at the time talk on the radio in addition to the surveillance leader.

During the actual transaction, there should be a predesignated team of officers responsible for monitoring the transaction on the kel-kit (body microphone and receiver commonly referred to as "the wire"). Usually it is best if this team has the closest visual observation position as well. This team should also make notes as the deal progresses for later conversion into a surveillance report. One of the primary purposes of the close observation team will be the relaying of the bust sign. Both a verbal and visual bust sign should be used in the event that one or the other is missed.

The surveillance leader must ensure that clear communication is facilitated. Each surveillance officer or team will have to react based on the communication which they receive if there is any chance that they are to act appropriately and be in the right position at the right time. In the case of a buy/bust, the surveillance will be complete when the transaction has been observed and the bust sign is relayed; the responsibility then shifts to the arrest teams.

Arrest Plan

Again, each undercover operation will require a specific arrest plan. Some plan for arresting the suspect should be made even in buy/walk situations, if only as a contingency. Every time an undercover operation is conducted, there should be some plan for taking the suspect into custody safely and swiftly.

UC Role in Arrest

The undercover officer should have no planned participation in the arrest of the suspect when the deal is consummated. In fact, if possible, the undercover officer should physically remove himself, if only a few feet, from the arrest scene before the arrest takes place. Removing the undercover officer from the arrest scene will result in reduced danger to him. Depending on circumstances, leaving him immediately next to the suspect may endanger him. He may conceivably become a hostage, or he may be the object of a direct assault by the suspect. There is also the possibility that the undercover officer may be in a cross-fire position during the arrest.

In any case, the undercover officer should not be relied upon to assist in the arrest except as part of a worst case scenario contingency plan. The undercover officer should either remove himself from the area or observantly and preparedly watch the arrest of the suspect. Making it appear that the undercover officer is being arrested can create enough diversion that the suspect actually believes it temporarily, and in doing so, the safety of the undercover officer can be enhanced.

The very beginning of the arrest phase of an undercover operation is the point during which the undercover officer is most vulnerable. Even if the suspect is not the slightest bit suspicious during the transaction, there will be a point at which he realizes that he is about to be arrested. If that awareness comes too soon prior to arrest, he has the opportunity to counter it by fleeing, by attacking the undercover officer, or by taking a hostage. For these reasons, it is best if the undercover officer has put some distance between himself and the suspect. If the suspect is taken completely off-guard and is surprised by the arrest team, his opportunity to react successfully is minimized.

Tactics

Undercover operations are such that they demand tactical knowledge, discipline, and execution to a greater degree than does a standard arrest situation. Training is essential to achieving this. The arrest phase of an undercover operation is filled with tension and stress. In situations of that nature, officers' reactions will be a combination of instincts and training. It is a good idea for investigative teams to train for these operations, much as they do for search warrant operations.

A surprisingly high number of tactical mistakes are commonly made in arrest situations concluding an undercover operation. Many of these result from the lack of a specific plan which governs the actions of individuals, some are the result of lack of training, and some result from lack of discipline.

Improper handling of weapons is foremost among the common mistakes. Too often weapons are brandished about without regard to basic weapons safety and fundamental tactical weapons techniques. For instance, many times the first officers at the arrest scene will shove their weapons through an open car window or otherwise put it in close proximity to the suspect where he would, if so inclined, have an opportunity to grab on to it. Likewise, officers often expose themselves to cross-fire situations unnecessarily. Most of these mistakes are not costly, but they could be, and they can be easily remedied through training.

Advanced weapons training which simulates actual situations, and in which it is possible for officers to train as a team, are very beneficial.

Theory

The prevailing theory governing these arrest situations is based on taking the suspect by surprise with an adequate amount of force so that he is immediately contained and arrested without incident, without injury, and without loss of evidence. Any plan which accomplishes this is a successful one.

TYPES OF OPERATIONS

Buy/Bust

The buy/bust operation technically is any operation in which the drug deal is actually consummated, with drugs and money exchanged, and the suspect is then arrested. It is to be distinguished from operations in which the money is only flashed, though there are only subtle distinctions between the two.

Buy/bust operations, the kind just described, will probably take place only when small amounts of drugs and cash are involved. Where large amounts of cash and drugs are at stake, the risk that the suspect may leave with either before he can be arrested probably will preclude this type of operation and what will transpire will be the flash/bust situation.

The distinct advantage to the buy/bust operation is that the undercover officer will be removed from the arrest scene; thus he is put in a position of significantly less danger. Once he has completed the transaction, he can walk or drive away from the scene, and the arrest team can move into action. This type of operation has the disadvantage, however, that the suspect may get away, which will result in a loss of money but should not adversely affect the case otherwise. An arrest warrant can be prepared and the suspect arrested later.

To use this type of operation to full advantage, the element of surprise should be maintained until the very end. That is, once the undercover officer has left the area, the suspect should be observed and arrested with as little excitement as possible. For example, the deal may be done by having the undercover officer pull up next to the suspect's vehicle in a parking lot. When the deal is finished, the undercover officer drives away and gives the bust sign. The suspect vehicle can be followed and stopped by a patrol officer arousing little suspicion and the suspect can be in custody before he realizes what has transpired.

Of course, there is the possibility that the suspect will flee when the stop is attempted, whether the suspect is on foot or in a vehicle. It is not advisable to let the suspect get too far away. Doing so only increases the risk that surveillance will lose him or that the suspect will burn surveillance and take countermeasures. On the other hand, if there is good surveillance and good communication, the arrest can be timed to maximize the advantage of the arrest team and keep the suspect at a disadvantage.

Buy(Flash)/Bust

This is probably the most often used type of undercover operation in drug enforcement. The technique involves ordering a significant quantity of drugs, and when the suspect shows that he has the drugs and has verbally agreed to complete the transaction with the undercover officer, the suspect is arrested.

There are several features of this type of operation which make it more dangerous than others. First, there is commonly a great deal of money being shown to the suspect. That being the case there is a distinct possibility that the suspect will attempt to rob the undercover officer. Accompanying this danger is of course the undetermined lengths to which the suspect is willing to go to accomplish the rip-off. He may be willing to shoot the officer as soon as he sees the money. The best way to guard against this is through thorough identification of the suspect and careful planning with respect to time and place of the operation.

Another danger inherent in these types of operations is that there will be countersurveillance. This danger can be dealt with if the surveillance is identified and recognized as such. If countersurveillance is good, and is not detected, it can result in suspect awareness of police presence. The deal will then probably not go at all. What is dangerous, of course, is that the suspects have a tactical advantage when they have countersurveillance and it is not identified. This can lead to a number of negative consequences in addition to the deal being foiled: they have the opportunity to identify undercover vehicles and undercover officers, and to study police tactics for future application.

There are a few widely accepted rules of conduct for these types of operations. These rules are based solidly on the philosophy that the police officers should always maintain the tactical advantage, manpower superiority, and firepower superiority.

1. Whenever possible, isolate the suspects and get them on neutral ground to do the transaction.

2. Do not allow the suspects to isolate the undercover officer. The best way to avoid this is by staying on neutral ground. The undercover officer should dictate time and place to the suspects.

3. Flash the money in an open location, isolating the suspects from each other if possible. Do not flash the money twice in the same location.

4. Minimize the vulnerability of the undercover officer during the bust.

5. The undercover officer should always be armed.

One of the worst mistakes that can be made is to try and force a deal, violating some of these basic rules in the process. There are three distinct potential consequences for these operations. The suspect will be able to put the deal together, and if the undercover operation is carefully set up, the suspect will be caught and the drugs recovered. The suspect will not be able to put the deal together, either the suspect or the informant or both has exaggerated the suspect's potential. The third possibility is bad: The deal will go wrong for any of a variety of reasons. Usually this indicates that either surveillance was burned or the deal was a planned rip-off from the beginning.

This third possibility can be potentially very dangerous if there has been poor planning or if the deal is pushed beyond the rules and the scope of the plan. Drug deals are like anything else, if they are meant to happen they usually will go according to plan. The undercover officer and other officers involved in the planning should follow their instincts and "gut feelings" but not to the point that they take unnecessary chances and give away the tactical advantage.

Buy/Walk

Generally these types of buys are made as part of an ongoing investigation where the plan is to make distribution cases while working up the ladder to the source or at least working up to a larger quantity. This type of undercover operation is the simplest in that no arrest is planned, although as mentioned, that eventuality should not be totally discounted.

Conducting this type of operation will require that the suspect has been sufficiently identified. It does not usually make sense to flush on an unidentified person although there may be times when that happens and the suspect is used as an unwitting for the purpose of identifying and getting to his source. The critical decisions in these types of buys center on the conduct of surveillance and whether the money will be fronted to the suspect.

Assuming that the suspect has been identified, there should also be some background information on the manner in which he conducts business. The possibility that the suspect will either desire to or have to go someplace to pick up the drugs should be planned for, and there should be surveillance established to follow him. It is a distinct advantage to know the suspect sufficiently to be able to anticipate where he will go.

The decision whether to front the money or not will again be based on suspect evaluation. If he has the reputation of being a flim-flam man as much as a drug dealer, he probably should not be trusted with the money if any significant amount is involved. Many times, even with substantial dealers, it will be necessary to give them the money and allow them to get the drugs and deliver them. This is now more the case than before as many dealers have changed their methods of operation in response to police techniques. The number of surveillance people should be adequate to follow the suspect and also stay with the undercover officer during the transaction.

As a rule, these types of cases become easier to a point as the undercover officer gains the confidence of the dealer. Yet that confidence will probably never be complete. When the time has come to raise the level and order up a large quantity for a buy/bust (or flash/bust), the deal should be somewhat easier because of previous transactions and a more complete knowledge of the suspect's habits.

From a practical investigative standpoint, it is not wise to make too many buys from the same suspect unless the case is progressing to other levels. From an administrative perspective, cases involving multiple undercover buys from the same suspect should be the subject of regular reports and should also be monitored closely.

Reverse Operations

Reverse undercover operations are those in which the officer acts as the seller rather than the buyer. As such, there is a greater potential for claims of entrapment and a defense based on those claims. To avoid entrapment and any defense based on that claim, there should be some guidelines for the conduct of these operations. Essentially the issues are the same as those discussed in the context of street-level reverses.

The suspect should be identified if possible, and there must be a showing, at some point, that the suspect is predisposed to purchase controlled substances. This can be established through a combination of factors. If the suspect has a record for controlled substances, that will be very important in showing predisposition. Any informant information regarding the activities of the suspect should be corroborated if possible. During the actual transaction, the undercover officer should allow the suspect to make a clear statement regarding purpose. The suspect should state what he is looking for and what price he is willing to pay for it. During conversation of this type the suspect may make other statements which show his predisposition to commit the crime.

Reverse undercover operations are very similar to standard buy(flash)/ bust operations. In them there is the significant attendant risk of being ripped off. Thus, the same general principles for conduct of the operations apply. The risk in these operations is that the drugs will somehow be lost and put on to the street, which creates a liability factor. Handling the evidence which is used in these reverse situations is a matter of some concern requiring special care to assure that the same amount which is checked out is checked back in at the conclusion of the operation.

A related, controversial aspect of these operations involves giving the suspect a "taste" or a sample of the drugs of which he is negotiating the purchase. Most prosecutors and police administrators are against this in principle where cocaine, heroin, and methamphetamine are concerned, although not so adamantly against it where marijuana is the substance involved. Allowing the undercover officer to give the suspect a small sample conforms to the way in which business is conducted between drug dealers, and as such may improve the chances that the deal will ultimately be successful and that the suspect will deliver the currency necessary to consummate the transaction. At the same time, it will usually not be necessary to give the sample if that creates prosecutorial problems. If the substance used has the appearance of good-quality stuff, that will quite possibly convince the suspect to go ahead with the deal.

If a sample is to be dispensed, it should be prepared beforehand and carefully weighed. If it is later recovered from the suspect, it should of course be weighed again. Whether a sample is given or not, the handling and disposition of the evidence used in the operation must be a matter of careful documentation.

GENERAL RULES

This section of the chapter will take one more look at some of the time-honored general rules which govern undercover operations. They are good rules and should be followed in the interest of safety and a successful investigation. There are, however, times when it is necessary to bend, if not break, them. They have all been discussed to this point but they are worthy of a little review.

Control the Location

This is not always as easy as it seems. Experienced drug dealers may be well aware of common police methods, and in an effort to avoid a transaction with an undercover officer, they may set a location for the meeting to which the police would never agree. While it may not be possible to get the suspect to agree to the preferred location, it may be possible to set some control on his location. The bottom line is, if the location is such that the suspect is given a tactical advantage and the undercover officer's safety is being gambled, don't go through with it, no drug deal is worth it. It is possible that through continued negotiations, perhaps one or two small buys, the confidence of the suspect can be gained and he can thus be manipulated.

Do Not Let the Money Walk

This rule has, out of necessity, become more flexible in the past few years due to changes in the drug dealing business. There may have been an increase in the number of people who are brokering the drug deals, and therefore the situation requires letting the money go with the broker. Money is commonly fronted on ounce to quarter-kilo quantity buys when the suspect is identified and there is some reason to believe that he will make good. The key to this decision is whether the suspect is a good risk, and this must be determined subjectively. It would be foolish to give several thousand dollars to everyone who promised to return with the product. On the other hand, operating through a middleman, fronting him the money, is a valid method of getting to the source of supply. If there is any doubt, resolve it in favor of not fronting the money. Many times if the undercover officer is insistent, the broker will introduce him to the source or at least take him along.

Do Not Give the Informant the Flash Roll

In cases where the informant is participating to the extent that he must testify it is conceivable that he would be given the flash roll. For example, if the only way the suspect will do the transaction is if the informant, with whom he is familiar and has dealt in the past, is present. Informants should not be trusted with large amounts of currency. To do so is to tempt fate. However, there are exceptions to the rule and when it is necessary and sufficient control over the informant's actions can be exercised it does not amount to anything more than the average risk involved in the undercover business. The risk cannot be completely removed from this business, and to wait to do a deal when there is *no* risk will translate to not ever doing anything.

Do Not Flash Money Twice at the Same Location

This is another sound rule. There is seldom justification for flashing the money twice at the same location. Once the money has been shown, it is up to the dealer to complete the deal. Showing the money twice usually indicates that robbery is a distinct possibility, the suspect is having trouble putting the deal together, or that the money was flashed to the wrong person. If it is necessary to show the money again, show it under different circumstances at a different location. Change the scenario enough so that a robbery attempt will be foiled or detected or preferably both. It might be advisable to use a different undercover car, or have an additional undercover officer act as the money man. Not taking the money on the second flash is another way of learning the motives of the suspects.

Do Not Force the Deal

With experience comes the ability to determine when to push a deal and when to back away from it. A solid teamwork approach involving input from other experienced officers as a collective decision-making process is good for making this decision. It can be a mistake to get overly anxious and push a deal beyond the limitations of reason and safety. On the other hand, sometimes tremendous police work results from pushing a deal just a little bit.

Do Not Become Predictable

Undercover operations, while adhering to certain basic guidelines, should not be laid out exactly the same way every time. Of course, this does not usually happen as there is a good deal of suspect input in some of the particulars. There is a tendency to fall into patterns, doing the transaction in the same location all the time, for example, that should be avoided. The risk in predictability is that the edge gained through surprise will be lost. Once the element of surprise is lost it can easily be shifted to the suspect's advantage and the possibility of a setup exists.

Remove the Undercover Officer from the Arrest Scene

This is by no means a rule, but it is a good goal to have, when at all practical. Too often, it is impossible to get the undercover officer away from the arrest action. Still, the arrest is much safer when the undercover officer is physically removed from the suspect.

7

ENHANCED INVESTIGATIONS

INTRODUCTION

This chapter focuses on complex investigations and the use of advanced investigative techniques. A great many complex investigations involve no special techniques; rather, they are initiated and developed by intensive application of standard investigative techniques. Many investigations, however, reach a point where the only way in which the full scope of the criminal activity or conspiracy can be uncovered is through some form of electronic eavesdropping. Most often this takes the form of intercepting wire communications.

In this chapter, there is no need to review the standard techniques of narcotics investigation which have been the subject of the first six chapters of this book. Instead, the thrust of the chapter is on developing a case to a wiretap, getting the order for the wire intercept, and successfully managing the investigation so that the objectives are achieved. Case development through the use of pen register and trap and trace information will be discussed in some detail. The entire process of assembling a wiretap case will be examined so that even those who have had no such experience will, after reading this chapter, have a good idea of how difficult and labor intensive these types of investigations can be while at the same time gaining a realization that under the right circumstances, they can achieve success not possible through other means.

There are several basic considerations which are critical in any so-called complex investigation which become more important in investigations which culminate in a wiretap. By definition, a complex investigation for the purposes of this discussion is any investigation aimed at an individual, group of individuals, or organization requiring a long-term commitment of resources and the use of a combination of investigative techniques to bring it to a successful conclusion. The term "complex investigation" implies something above a street-level target and while that is normally the case, it is not necessarily so. It may be necessary to target a street-level organization in a lengthy multifaceted investigation, though very seldom would such activity justify a wiretap or would such an extreme measure be necessary.

To be successful, any complex investigation requires an accurate target evaluation. Common sense, as well as limitations on resources and manpower, dictates that when a target for a complex investigation is selected, that target should be one having a significant negative impact on the community. There are a number of other considerations which become important in deciding whether or not a wiretap is the right course of action, and those will be discussed shortly.

Providing that an accurate target evaluation has been made, what will ultimately determine the success of any long-term investigation will be the manner in which the case is organized. Implicit in the following discussion is this: a good target and a well-organized investigation are essential to a successful wiretap case. Regardless of how well the actual wiretap is conducted, if the target evaluation is wrong, or if the case is not carefully organized, the success of the wiretap will be limited by these two shortcomings.

USE OF PEN REGISTERS

A pen register is an instrument designed to record the numbers dialed from a given telephone line by decoding the dialed impulses. It will provide a hard copy of that information complete with date and time of call, whether the call was incoming or outgoing, and if it was an outgoing call, the number dialed will be recorded. It registers only the numbers dialed from instruments on the affected line. It will not register the numbers from which calls received on that line are made. It does not "intercept" communications within the definition of Chapter 119 of the United States Code, as it does not disclose the contents of conversations and its use is not therefore governed by the provisions of Chapter 119, Title 18.

Legal Requirements

A court order is required to have a pen register installed on a given telephone line. The request for the order must be supported by an affidavit which outlines the facts of the investigation and the need for the installation of the pen register. Essentially, a pen register is a means of obtaining information and written records pertaining to the use of the telephone. Conversations are not intercepted. The affidavit must therefore show that there is probable cause to believe that the information sought through the use of the pen register is necessary to the investigation and that it can be obtained through the pen register.

For example, if information is received that a certain person is dealing drugs and that he uses his telephone in some way to facilitate that activity, the use of a pen register may identify the numbers at which customers and possibly suppliers are contacted. Once those numbers have been identified and subscriber information obtained, the goals of the investigation may be furthered. It may then be possible to develop information on the source or other co-conspirators through surveillance, informant information, and other techniques and ultimately prosecute those individuals.

Many states require that a standard search warrant affidavit be written and a search warrant is then issued, ordering the installation of the pen register and the seizing of the pen register information. The search warrant, in those cases, serves as the order for the pen register. The following is an example of the standard wording of a pen register order, regarding the information which is sought.

> The affiant, Sergeant Paul Mahoney, has filed an affidavit in conformity with the provisions of the Colorado revised Statutes and the Colorado Rules of Criminal Procedure for the following described property:
>> Electrical impulses that can and do designate telephone numbers which are being dialed or pulsed by the user or users of the telephone numbers designated as area code (303) 640-1376, believed to be situated at the place or thing known as the telephone cables of the U.S. West Communications junction boxes located at or near 1331 Cherokee Street, Denver, Colorado; and specifically the telephone cables which are attached to the telephone number described as area code (303) 640-1376. That authorization is hereby

given for use of a pen register on the telephone communication facility associated with the telephone number (303) 640-1376 which service is listed to John Smith, 1331 Cherokee Street, Denver, Colorado. That this order authorizes the use of a pen register as aforesaid for a period to commence November 1, 1992 and to continue any time day or night until the objective herein is achieved or until terminated by this court, but in no event shall this authorization extend longer than thirty (30) days from commencement date. That U.S. West Communications and its agents and employees are hereby ordered to furnish all information, facilities, and technical assistance necessary to accomplish the installation of the aforesaid pen register. It is further ordered that the authorization given is intended to apply not only to the target telephone number listed above but to any changed telephone number subsequently assigned to the same cable par and binding post utilized by the target telephone within the authorized period. That U.S. West Communications and its agents and employees are hereby ordered to provide all subscriber information on any and all published and nonpublished telephone numbers obtained by the aforementioned pen register. It is further ordered that any numbers contained in the speed calling feature connected with (303) 640-1376 be furnished including all subscriber information listing to those numbers. To ensure the effectiveness of this pen register, U.S. West Communications is ordered not to disclose the existence of said pen register to the subscriber or any other person unless by order of this court.

Purpose

The pen register is an investigative tool which can potentially reveal a great deal in the way of intelligence information. Its effectiveness will be related to the extent to which the target telephone number is used in the standard course of drug transactions. If the suspect never makes any contacts related to his drug dealings over the telephone, the value of the information learned through the pen register will be minimal. The names of people learned may be associates, nothing more. On the other hand, if the suspect makes regular contact with suppliers and drug customers, the pen register will generate some very good *raw* intelligence regarding the numbers being called from the target phone and the subscribers of those numbers. That information will very possibly lead to the identification of associates, co-conspirators, and potential grand jury witnesses. It is incumbent upon the investigators to develop it, however.

The pen register will indicate the extent to which the telephone is being used in general. It will give the investigator the whole picture with regard to number of calls, incoming versus outgoing, if the phone is call forwarded, the times when the phone is most active, and so on.

The purpose of the pen register may vary slightly from one case to the next. In a prostitution case involving an escort service, for example, the pen register will probably reveal numbers and subscriber information for the people working for the service as well as the customers. Distinguishing between the two will require some analysis and investigation. It must be emphasized that the pen register will be of little value unless considerable time is spent working on the information which is obtained.

Limitations

The pen register is a sound investigative tool and should be considered for use in any investigation in which the subjects are using the phone in the conduct of their business. In the past, the use of the pen register was often restricted to cases with wiretap potential. It is now being used more frequently not only as a prelude to a wiretap but as an intelligence gathering measure in other cases as well. By its nature, the fact that the content of conversations is unknown, there are limitations on its value. If the subscriber information for the numbers being called are recognizable as known drug dealers, that they are talking about drug transactions during these calls is still just supposition. If they are talking about drugs, how guarded and encoded are the conversations?

It is also possible that many of the subscriber names will not be recognized. The phones could be listed to aliases, or the service may have been obtained by another person. If the information from the pen register is properly and systematically managed, it will be valuable as intelligence in spite of its limitations, and it may serve as the basis for some very important decision making should the investigation proceed to the stage where a wiretap is being considered.

Managing Pen Register Information

Raw Data

The information generated by using a pen register in an investigation is raw data. It is in a form that will render it meaningless unless it is properly managed. There are several different models of pen registers being manufactured by various companies. Some have technical advantages over others, but the basic form of the information generated is the same. Figure 7-1 is a sample pen register printout.

Examined in small quantities it is fairly easy to read the information and to understand what activity took place on the target phone number,

```
                    SAMPLE PEN REGISTER PRINTOUT

        OUTGOING CALL              #1        LINE 1:    (303) 640-1376
        01/01/92   10:51:42     Off-hook
                                   Dialed: 4610805
        01/01/92   10:54:06     On-hook
        INCOMING CALL              #2        LINE 1:    (303) 640-1376
        01/01/92   11:13:02     Ringing
                                    Rings:   7
        01/01/92   11:13:37     Answered
        01/01/92   11:14:08     On-hook
        OUTGOING CALL              #3        LINE 1:    (303) 640-1376
        01/01/92   11:30:09     Off-hook
                                   Dialed: 4610806
        01/01/92   11:33:09     Off-hook


                        ALTERNATE PRINTOUT
        CALL: #4
        DATE:  JAN 01/92
        TIME OF CALL:  11:45:00
        640-5741
        TIME ON HOOK:  11:45:35
        DURATION:  00:00:35




                         FIGURE 7-1
```

in the sample case that number is (303) 640-1376. The information generated by the pen register reveals that call #1 was an outgoing call and that the number dialed was 461-0805, the call lasted 2 minutes and 26 seconds. Call #2 was a short incoming call, and call #3 was another outgoing call lasting 3 minutes. Call #4, printed in the style of another model pen register, was an outgoing call lasting 35 seconds. In this printout, the duration of the call is stated which is useful at times.

Assume for the sake of example that the drug dealer lives with a woman and two children and that an average of 60 calls per day are made from or received at that number. Over a 30-day period, approximately 1,800 calls will be registered and that information printed out. It may be difficult, especially early in the investigation, to determine which calls are being made by the subject as opposed to those being made by the other people living there. Without constant diligent attention, that amount of information will soon become unmanageable. Furthermore, without subscriber information, the information is without any value whatever.

Before the advance of the personal computer age, pen register information had to be handled manually. The tape printout from each day had to be read and from that was extracted the number of outgoing calls, the phone numbers which were called, and the number of incoming calls answered, and those incoming calls which were unanswered. A list of numbers for which subscriber information was needed was then written and submitted to the phone company. The phone numbers were recorded numerically in a book and then cross-referenced alphabetically when the subscriber information was returned. In short, a tremendous amount of paperwork was involved in putting the pen register data into some useful form.

Subscriber Information

One of the most important aspects of using a pen register involves getting subscriber information from the telephone company. In the sample order above, the telephone company is ordered to provide that information to the investigators. That information, when received, must be matched with the pen register data.

Many departments have developed computer software or adapted software products commercially available so that the information from the pen register is downloaded directly to a computer which then sorts it and prints it in usable fashion. When the subscriber information becomes available, most programs have the capability of printing master subscriber lists for each pen register. In addition, the programs should print a chronological daily activity sheet for the number as well as frequency printouts for certain numbers and other information that becomes very helpful in an investigation.

In general, the security departments of most telephone companies will be cooperative in an investigation as long as there is a court order in effect. Such an order mandating their cooperation and the release of subscriber information and billing and service information covers their interests and reduces their liabilities. When a pen register is in use on an active telephone, the investigators will need a great deal of assistance from the service provider in getting subscriber information without which the pen register will be of absolutely no benefit.

Organizing and Analyzing the Information

The pen register information should be organized so that it can be analyzed on an ongoing basis to facilitate the future planning of the investigation. Basically, the information has to be organized so that the investigators can determine who is being called, how often they are being called, and when they are being called. In addition to a subscriber list derived from the pen register, the program should print out a daily activity sheet which shows all the activity on the number in chronological order, and it should also have the capability of producing a call frequency report for any given number.

Figure 7-2 is a sample printout for a day's activity on a pen register. Looking at this report a great deal of important information can be analyzed. For example, assume that one of the calls in this sequence is a prelude to an undercover transaction for a sizable amount of cocaine. The subsequent calls can be analyzed to determine what, if any, calls the suspect made to arrange the transaction. If the incoming call at 4:00 P.M. is the beginning of the transaction, the undercover call during which the suspect told the undercover officer that his shipment had not arrived yet and that they would have to wait until the next day to do the deal, the next few calls could be very important to the investigation. In this case, at 4:02 P.M., the suspect called 698-6000 for which no subscriber information has yet been obtained. He then called a pager number 230-0985 twice and then called 455-5556, the number of a known, upper-level supplier. At 4:30 P.M., the suspect called the undercover phone, 777-9898, and informed the undercover officer that they could go ahead and do the deal, that he had lined up something very good.

A meeting is arranged and the undercover officer goes to the suspect's house at 7:00 P.M. At 7:05 P.M., the suspect, in the presence of the

```
                            SAMPLE

                DAILY ACTIVITY PEN REGISTER PRINTOUT

        Page #_____

        Date Printed_____         Case Number_____

        TARGET #_____         COURT ORDER #_____

  CALL #    PHONE NUMBER CALLED    DATE    OFF HOOK    ON HOOK   TYPE
```

CALL #	PHONE NUMBER CALLED	DATE	OFF HOOK	ON HOOK	TYPE
1	9340800	08/10/91	15:08:10	15:08:40	OUT
2	4610805	08/10/91	15:20:20	15:20:59	OUT
3		08/10/91	15:25:10	15:27:10	IN
4	9352000	08/10/91	15:45:51	15:47:00	OUT
5		08/10/91	16:00:00	16:02:00	IN
6	6986000	08/10/91	16:02:15	16:04:00	OUT
7	2300985007	08/10/91	16:04:19	16:04:39	OUT
8	2300985007	08/10/91	16:05:00	16:05:35	OUT
9		08/10/91	16:10:00	16:12:00	IN
10	4555556	08/10/91	16:17:00	16:18:00	OUT
11	7779898	08/10/91	16:30:00	16:32:00	OUT
12	4555556	08/10/91	12:35:00	16:37:00	OUT
13	6986000	08/10/91	16:50:00	16:50:30	OUT
14	2300985007	08/10/91	16:51:00	16:51:30	OUT
15		08/10/91	16:57:00	16:59:00	IN
16	6986000	08/10/91	19:05:00	19:05:45	OUT
17	4555556	08/10/91	19:35:00	19:36:30	OUT

FIGURE 7-2

undercover officer, makes a call to 698-6000, talks to a party, and arranges the delivery of the drugs in 15 minutes. The deal takes place at 7:30 P.M.; the suspect returns home and immediately calls 455-5556, the number of the known supplier.

In analyzing the pen register data in Figure 7-2, the one category of information which would normally be included but is not here is duration of the call. That, of course, can be figured out but most programs are designed to print that information so, at a glance, it can be determined what the relative lengths of the calls are. Inferences can be drawn from the durations of the calls. For example, calls of 20 seconds were probably not completed for one of a variety of reasons or a pager was called.

Again referring to Figure 7-2 and keeping in mind that an undercover call was made at 4:00 P.M., other conclusions can be drawn from the information which could be very important in the future of the investigation. One important fact is that after calling 698-6000 and talking for almost 2 minutes, the suspect called 2300985007. What this is obviously is a pager call in which the suspect entered 007 at the appropriate time. This indicates that whoever he is calling will recognize that number and return the call. That pager number is called twice and then 455-5556 is called.

It turns out that the pager number and 455-5556 are both subscribed to by a known drug supplier. What may have happened is that upon receiving the page, the supplier called the suspect (incoming call at 4:10 P.M.) and requested that the suspect call him back in a few minutes. The suspect called 455-5556 again at 4:17 P.M.

Continuing with the sample call analysis, the suspect called the undercover phone number, 777-9898, immediately after contacting the known supplier. And immediately after talking with the undercover officer, he recontacted the supplier. The unknown factor in this example is how the person at 698-6000 fits into the scheme of things. The suspect called him immediately after talking to the undercover officer the first time and immediately prior to calling the known supplier on his pager and at home.

When the actual transaction took place, the suspect called 698-6000 in the presence of the undercover officer and a previously unidentified person delivered the cocaine to the undercover officer and the suspect near the suspect's house. Later, the subscriber information was obtained, and it led back to the location to which the source was followed after the undercover transaction. The suspect was tentatively identified, but the connection between the known drug trafficker, the suspect, and the source of this transaction cannot be established through analysis of the pen register information alone.

However, looking at Figure 7-3, some additional pieces of the puzzle are put together. A pattern is evident in which the suspect calls 455-5556 and 698-6000 on August 3, August 4, and August 10. The calls are made within minutes of each other. In this case, where the suspect is a broker for large deals of a quarter-kilo or better, what may be happening is that either these sources are related or they are just separate sources and the suspect calls both until he can put the deal together.

Whatever the case may be, more investigation will be necessary to develop the case fully before a decision can be made whether or not a wiretap is the proper course of action.

Use of Trap and Trace to Supplement Pen Register Data

The pen register will give only the phone number which is called from the target line. Therefore, the subscriber information as a point of departure for identifying co-conspirators will be limited to those calls. It is possible, however, for the telephone service provider to use a trap and trace device which will record the information regarding the incoming calls. The trap and trace will identify those numbers and the dates and times of the calls. With the use of that device, the intelligence to be learned through analysis of phone communications will be complete.

In most cases, the trap and trace will not identify numbers which were called outside of the area code in which the target phone is located. Another disadvantage is that the trap and trace is in the control of the utility company and retrieval of the information may not be as timely as otherwise might be the case. It might also require extra work to integrate the trap and trace information with the pen register data. In spite of these disadvantages, this information is valuable, and the trap and trace should be used whenever a wiretap is a distinct possibility in the interest of thoroughness and a complete preliminary investigation.

The order for the trap and trace is usually obtained at the same time the pen register order is signed, as part of the same order or set of orders and supported by the same affidavit.

```
                         SAMPLE

            PEN REGISTER CALL FREQUENCY PRINTOUT

     Page#_____

     Date Printed_____Case Number_____

     TARGET #_____Court Order #_____

PHONE NUMBER CALLED    SUBSCRIBER     DATE     OFF HOOK    ON HOOK

   (303) 4555556   JOHN PAUL JONES   08/03/91  10:10:23  10:10:59

   (303) 4555556   JOHN PAUL JONES   08/03/91  14:25:10  14:27:25

   (303) 4555556   JOHN PAUL JONES   08/04/91  18:19:00  18:21:00

   (303) 4555556   JOHN PAUL JONES   08/10/91  16:17:00  16:18:30

   (303) 4555556   JOHN PAUL JONES   08/10/91  16:35:00  16:37:30

   (303) 4555556   JOHN PAUL JONES   08/10/91  19:35:00  19:36:30

   COMPARE ABOVE PRINTOUT TO SEPARATE FILE PRINTOUT BELOW

   (303) 6986000   STEVE SMITH       08/03/91  10:08:25  10:09:45

   (303) 6986000   STEVE SMITH       08/04/91  18:21:30  18:23:45

   (303) 6986000   STEVE SMITH       08/10/91  16:02:15  16:04:00

   (303) 6986000   STEVE SMITH       08/10/91  16:50:00  16:50:30

   (303) 6986000   STEVE SMITH       08/10/91  19:05:00  19:05:45

This is an illustration of two sample records of numbers
which are being called from the target line.  With such
printouts as these it is possible to look more closely at
call patterns and determine what calls may be related.
In these samples, it is apparent that the numbers were
called from the target line, in close time proximity on
three separate dates.

                      FIGURE 7-3
```

Developing Pen Register Information

As already emphasized, the pen register information must be developed through investigation to have full value. Subscriber information which is learned must then be checked against criminal histories, driver's licenses, motor vehicle listings, utility company listings, etc. Once this step has been completed, surveillance may be necessary to identify fully the people who might be using the phones at the various locations being called. It is quite possible that the calls to a certain location are being call forwarded to an undetermined location. Determining that may require either a search warrant for records on that phone number or an administrative subpoena for that information. In most cases, however, a great deal can be learned through a combination of background checks and surveillance. The key to this type of investigation is identification.

Drawing Conclusions

Only after the information developed through the pen register has been worked on and more people involved in the conspiracy identified through background checks and surveillance is it possible to evaluate the case accurately. Any determinations made regarding the future of the investigation will hinge upon the accuracy of the assessment of the case after the pen register has been working a while. If the subject of the investigation is using the telephone to arrange his drug deals, the identity of his immediate source, or at least the telephone number he is using, is no doubt going to be revealed by the pen register. The difficulty may reside in identifying the players and their respective roles.

Looking at pen register information for a given date, it is not easy to distinguish criminal calls from social calls, and it may be impossible even to speculate without some, possibly a great deal of, investigation. There are those cases when the pen register quickly reveals numbers of well-documented drug traffickers. When that is the case, it is relatively easy to plan the course of the investigation. It is the cases where none of the subscribers' names are immediately recognizable and where no criminal history is available that drawing conclusions from the pen register is difficult.

If the first 30 days of pen register information are inconclusive, extending the pen register order is normally a simple option. Such an extension assumes that the information being generated is showing some promise, and that is of some value. To extend the order just for the sake of extension is not a good idea. Many times there just is not time to work the information adequately, and in those cases an extension will only compound the problem. If, on the other hand, the pen register is providing good information and the potential for a wiretap case is apparent, the pen register should be continued.

At some point the pen register will be disconnected and the investigators should be prepared to make a final report on the productivity of the pen register. Such information as total number of calls, incoming calls versus outgoing, average number of calls per day, etc. should all be compiled. The investigators must also ensure that the valuable intelligence which has been learned is collated and filed. The intelligence value of a pen register can be potentially tremendous whether the investigation continues or not.

TITLE III INVESTIGATIONS

The Omnibus Crime Control and Safe Streets Act of 1968 included extensive regulation of electronic surveillance. Title III of that act provides the basis for Title 18, Chapter 119, Section 2510 through 2521 of the United States Code, regulating electronic surveillance, hence the common reference to a wiretap as a Title III. In addition to Title III of the act of 1968, the Electronic Communications Privacy Act of 1986 went into effect in January 1987, and it further defined, expanded, and brought up to date Title III. It also provides minimum standards for the state statutes regulating the conduct of wiretaps and electronic surveillance.

Another requirement under the Title III provisions pertaining to electronic surveillance and wiretaps is an annual wiretap report from the Administrative Office of the United States Courts. That report is entitled the *Report on Applications for Orders Authorizing or Approving the Interception of Wire, Oral or Electronic Communications (1990)*. According to the reports for 1988 and 1989 well over half of the wiretaps and other electronic surveillances authorized in those two years involved narcotics investigations (62 percent in 1989, 59 percent in 1988). Gambling and racketeering were the next most frequently named offenses for which electronic surveillance was authorized.

Wiretaps are by far the most common form of electronic surveillance, accounting for about 80 percent of all authorizations in 1989. Oral intercepts and the intercept of electronic communications accounted about equally for the other 20 percent of the orders in both 1988 and 1989. Of the wiretaps and oral intercepts, single-family dwellings accounted for approximately 40 percent of the locations of the facilities authorized for interception in both years.

What are perhaps the most important statistics reflect the increase in the number of court approvals and the cost. In 1988 there were 293 federally authorized electronic surveillances, while in 1989 that figure rose to 310. The number of state wiretaps also rose slightly from 1988 to 1989. The average cost reported in the annual reports for federally authorized electronic surveillances was about $49,000 in 1988. That average cost rose to approximately $81,000 in 1989 federal cases. The average cost for such an investigation at the state level was $32,000 in 1989. In spite of the rising cost of these investigations, they are increasingly more prevalent due to a very successful prosecution and conviction rate. Federal arrests in electronic surveillance cases rose 49 percent in 1989, from 881 in 1988 to 1,312 in 1989. The convictions resulting from those arrests increased 53 percent from one year to the next.[1]

Legal Definitions

This chapter is not intended to be an exhaustive examination of the legal aspects of wiretapping and electronic surveillance. As any experienced investigator is aware, every investigation of this type will be conducted in close concert with the prosecuting attorneys, in the case of federal investigations, the assistant U.S. attorneys. They will be responsible for planning the legal strategy and interpreting legal questions. The investigators must have a relatively thorough understanding of what the law states to make the proper decisions in the investigation, however. The following definitions are pertinent to the understanding of the legal requirements and limitations with respect to electronic surveillances. Some of the definitions are part of many included in Title 18, Chapter 119, Section 2510, of the United States Code. Other terms and concepts defined are discussed elsewhere in Sections 2510 through 2521, Chapter 119, of the United States Code.

Wire Communications

As defined in Section 2510, wire communications "means any aural transfer made in whole or in part through the use of facilities for the transmission of communications by the aid of wire, cable, or other like connection between the point of origin and the point of reception

---

1 *Report on Applications for Orders Authorizing or Approving the Interception of Wire, Oral or Electronic Communications,* Administrative Office of the United States Courts, 1988 and 1989.

(including the use of such connection in a switching station) furnished or operated by any person engaged in providing or operating such facilities for the transmission of interstate or foreign communications for communications affecting interstate or foreign commerce and such term includes any electronic storage of such communication, but such term does not include the radio portion of a cordless telephone handset and the base unit."

As a practical matter, wire communication means telephone communications, including of course, those conducted on cellular telephones. Wire communications cannot be intercepted without a court order authorizing such an intercept. An exception is when one of the parties to the conversation consents to the intercept or where an officer is a party to the conversation. If an undercover officer is calling a drug dealer, for example, that conversation may be intercepted and recorded and the contents later used. The conversation can also be intercepted if, for example, an informant is making the call and he consents to the intercept of the conversation.

Oral Communications

By definition, oral communications "means any oral communication uttered by a person exhibiting an expectation that such communication is not subject to interception under circumstances justifying such expectation, but such term does not include any electronic communication." Essentially, any conversation conducted in private circumstances cannot be intercepted without a court order. Quite obviously, conversations conducted in the privacy of one's home would carry with them an expectation of privacy. To put a transmitter in the house and intercept and record the conversations would require a court order.

In the case of a drug dealer conducting his business inside his home but not necessarily on the telephone, an order for an intercept of "oral communications" may be the appropriate course of action, possibly in addition to an order for the intercept of wire communications.

Electronic Communications

Section 2510 of Chapter 119, Title 18, of the United States Code provides a lengthy definition of electronic communications in paragraph 12. In part, it defines "electronic communications" as "any transfer of signs, signals, writing, images, sounds, data, or intelligence of any nature transmitted in whole or in part by a wire, radio, electromagnetic, photoelectric or photooptical system that affects interstate commerce . . . " It goes on to *exclude* the radio portion of a cordless telephone, that which is transmitted between the handset and the base unit, any wire or oral communication, any communication made through a tone only paging device, and any communication from a tracking device.

In narcotics trafficking, "electronic communications" devices, or digital pagers, are commonly used by suppliers and customers as a means of communicating. There are two contexts in which drug investigators frequently have occasion to intercept these electronic communications. The first occurs in the course of an investigation when a "clone" pager is desired to identify the numbers and codes and, through them, the people with whom the dealer is in contact. A clone pager cannot be issued without a court order under the provisions of Title 18, Section 2511.

A clone pager will reveal information very similar to that learned through a pen register which are excluded from the provisions of the wiretap statute. It will only tell the investigators what numbers are being called. However, inasmuch as codes are also transmitted through these digital pagers, they are looked at not as "registers" of numbers called, but as "electronic communications" devices.

By statute, then, an affidavit supporting the application for a court order must be written just as in the case of the intercept of wire and oral communications. Under the current procedure of the U.S. Attorney General's Office, however, it is not necessary that the applications for the intercept of electronic communications be given the same approval as those for wire and oral intercepts. These applications are approved locally by the U.S. attorney's office. The approval process will be discussed in more detail shortly.

The other context in which narcotics investigators will have occasion to intercept the "electronic communications" of a digital pager is during the course of an investigation, when a search warrant is executed or when a suspect is arrested and his pager is taken as an item having evidentiary value. In such situations, the investigators will encounter a dilemma with respect to the ongoing retrieval of information transmitted on the pager while it is in their possession. This is a relatively new area which will no doubt be subject to continued legal scrutiny and development.

Unauthorized interception of "electronic communications" violates the wiretap statutes. However, if an officer comes across a pager in the course of an investigation, he may be authorized to seize the pager itself and then retrieve the stored messages. When an investigation is known to involve a pager and a search warrant is being prepared, the affiant should include the pager as a subject of the search. Information, from the informant or developed otherwise, supporting the probable cause to believe that the pager is being used in relationship to the drug dealing activity should be included in the affidavit. The pager should then be seized when it is found. Retrieving the information stored on the pager does not violate the wiretap statutes as doing so is very similar to scrutinizing other records which have been seized. Probable cause has been established showing the nexus between the pager and the criminal activity, and retrieving the stored information is reasonable. Likewise, "seizing" new information received on the pager is a continuation of the search which has been authorized. If it is not immediately retrieved, it will presumably be lost as will its potential evidentiary value.

If a pager is encountered and there has been no mention of it in the search warrant affidavit, an additional warrant may be required to retrieve the information stored on the pager. In the affidavit in support of the additional warrant, it will be necessary to establish probable cause that the pager is related to the illegal activity and that the information stored in it may contain evidence pertaining to that activity.

When a person is arrested for a drug dealing offense, for example, and a pager is seized incident to arrest, retrieving the information stored on the pager is possible as an exception to the warrant requirement. If, however, the person is arrested for an unrelated offense, the information on the pager should not be retrieved without a warrant. That is, if a drug dealer is arrested for traffic charges, probable cause to retrieve his messages will not exist based on the search incident to arrest guidelines alone. A search warrant should be obtained.

Once a pager has been legally seized, obtaining the information which is transmitted on it in the form of electronic communications will constitute a search and seizure. Therefore if information is to be obtained from a seized pager on an ongoing basis, a warrant should be obtained authorizing the seizure of that information. Very seldom, if ever, will there be any justification for continued retrieval of this information under an exception to the search warrant requirement.

It is with the court-ordered intercept of these three types of communications that the remainder of this chapter deals. As noted in the statistics earlier, most court-ordered electronic surveillance (80 percent) involves a wiretap, the intercept of wire communications. However, the intercept of oral communications is not uncommon, and the need for the intercept of electronic communications is on the rise with the increasing popularity and use of digital pagers among drug traffickers. Because wiretaps are the most common type of electronic surveillance, most of the discussion in this chapter will be in that context, although issues specifically pertinent to the other types of electronic surveillance will also be discussed.

Preliminary Issues

There are several factors which must be weighed in determining whether or not a case should proceed to a Title III. Some of the more important of these will be discussed at this point.

Target

The target group or individual must be worthy of the effort and expense involved in a Title III investigation. There will always be a certain number of unknown factors making it impossible to predict exactly how much a group is dealing and what the negative impact on the community of that group is. By the time that a Title III is being seriously contemplated the unknowns should be greatly reduced. By evaluating informant information, analyzing pen register data, performing complete background investigations, and doing whatever undercover work is possible and as much surveillance as possible, a clear picture of the target should be forming.

Determining whether or not a Title III is the right approach in a given investigation depends primarily on the amount of drugs being distributed, if the subject uses the phone, and if so, what phone is being used. The second part of the equation must take into account whether or not there is any other investigative means through which the full conspiracy could be uncovered short of a Title III; it should be calculated that such an approach will achieve goals not possible through other types of investigations. Most often this justification rests on the theory that the "source of supply" can be identified and prosecuted.

Legal Feasibility

If the target meets the criteria and qualifies for a possible Title III investigation, the next question to be resolved is whether or not the legal requirements can be fulfilled. Specifically, is there probable cause to believe that the target telephone is being used? If so, can a need for interception be articulated?

It is best to consult with the prosecutors early in an investigation as it begins to develop. Doing so enables them to make a significant contribution to the case as it progresses and to make a more accurate assessment of its potential for a Title III.

Logistical Feasibility

There is no sense considering a Title III if getting it accomplished is not within the unit's potential. If expertise in these types of investigations is lacking within a particular unit or department, the investigators or supervisor should seek outside advice regarding the logistics involved.

There are several undesirable side effects which are a reality of Title III investigations. Because they are so consuming in terms of time and resources, other investigations which may be viewed as important by administrators, prosecutors, and citizens may have to take a back seat. Also, the principal investigators in the case will be effectively lost to the unit for months. Long after the investigation has been terminated, these people may still be preparing for and going to court and consequently they will not be generating new cases. There may also be a little burnout following a lengthy Title III investigation and a resultant temporary drop in productivity. This is natural and healthy to some degree as the investigators will need some time for a mental recovery. The makeup of the unit could be such that these side effects would be devastating, particularly if they are not anticipated.

Quality of the Preliminary Investigation

One other factor which should be considered in determining the potential of a case for a Title III concerns the quality of the preliminary investigation. It is imperative that the preliminary investigation be thorough, complete, and well documented. If these requirements have been satisfied, the investigation will be well organized, and that will manifest itself primarily in the quality of the suspect identification book (crook book) and the surveillance and investigative reports.

The crook book should be compiled as the investigation progresses and should contain all the information regarding each possible suspect and photographs when available. Each time a person with a possible role in the organization is identified he should be added to the crook book. The crook book should be organized alphabetically and a lead sheet filled out for each suspect explaining the role of the suspect in the investigation. (See Figure 1-7, reprinted here as Figure 7-4, for reference.) It is the substance of the lead sheet which is important rather than the form. It is important that the information be accurate and complete.

```
                    INVESTIGATIVE LEAD SHEET

   Case Initiated By:_____Date:_____

   Suspect's Name: _____DOB:_____
   AKA:_____Nickname:_____

   Race:_____Sex:_____Height:_____Weight:_____Eyes:_____

   Hair Color:_____Other Identifying Traits:_____

   Suspect's Address:_____

   Utility Company Information:

   Public Service:_____

   Telephone Company:_____
```

```
                INVESTIGATIVE PLAN AND NOTES
   _____
   _____
   _____
   _____
```

```
                    VEHICLE INFORMATION

   1) _____
        License number    Make      Model      Year    Color

   2) _____
        License number    Make      Model      Year    Color

   Listing #1_____

   Listing #2_____
```

```
   P                             |  Suspect Identification
   H                             |
   O                             |  Police Dept. #_____
   T                             |
   O                             |  Drivers License #_____
   G                             |
   R                             |  NADDIS Check  [ ]  [ ]
   A                             |
   P                             |                yes   no
   H                             |
```

FIGURE 7-4

What may be most preferable in terms of a lead sheet is a form which is generated by a computerized data base. The form may not be the most attractive, as many computer-generated forms are not, but having the information in a computer file, which can later be integrated with phone subscriber lists, etc. will be of tremendous value.

At some point in the investigation, the crook books will have to be copied and distributed to other investigators participating in the case. With this in mind, the information regarding each subject should be as detailed and self-explanatory as possible.

The surveillance and investigative reports are equally as important as the crook book. When an investigation spans several months' time, it is important that each surveillance be carefully documented. Likewise, the progress of the investigation should be documented by investigative reports. The lead investigators should organize their case file so that every important aspect of the case is a matter of record. The following is a sample of how a case might be organized.

1. *Case crook book:* alphabetical file of all possible subjects in a case. Updated immediately as new subjects are identified.

2. *Case file*

    A. *Investigative reports.* Complete copies of all investigative reports made throughout the course of an investigation must be part of the case file. For example, if public service information is obtained on a certain date, that information should be part of an investigative report and included in the case file in some logical (chronological is good) order. Likewise, informant debriefings and any other significant information which sheds light on the case should the subject of an investigative report.

    B. *Surveillance reports.* A surveillance report should be made each and every time a surveillance is conducted. What is learned should be noted on the report, and the report should include an indexing section at the bottom wherein vehicles, suspects, and addresses can be listed for indexing purposes. A critical flaw in many investigations revolves around the failure of investigators to document surveillance. Accurate, complete surveillance reports are a must when the time comes to prepare an affidavit; surveillance notes made on the back of a matchbook cover or a napkin will have long since disappeared it they are not translated into an official report.

C. *Buy reports.* Complete records of each buy, whether an undercover buy or a controlled buy, should be retained. The report packet for each buy should include the surveillance report for each buy, a buy report if the buy was made by an undercover officer, and a statement if it was made by an informant, property invoices, and lab results. Also copies of the money used for the buy should be retained with the buy packet. It is also a good idea to keep copies of the expenditure records pertaining to the buys with the rest of the paperwork.

D. *Informant documentation.* When an informant is participating on a long-term basis in a complex investigation with Title III potential, documentation of informant activities and payments should be kept in the case file. This is a good idea even though in conformity with department policy it may be required that they are kept elsewhere too. It is important that the relationship between the informant and the investigators be documented in a major case, particularly if the informant has agreed or may be required to testify.

E. *Photographs.* Surveillance photographs should be maintained as part of the case file as the investigation is being developed. Photographs of suspects should be kept with the crook book information. If a case becomes a Title III investigation, surveillance photos of suspects, residences, and businesses, and suspect vehicles will be very important in the process of educating the investigators assigned to assist in some part of the case.

F. *Case chronology.* A case chronology or case progress report should be maintained as a means of charting the course of the investigation. The report can be a continuing outline, in chronological order, of the development of the case or it can be in the form of periodic narrative reports which detail the developing nature of the case.

G. *Index.* A master index of suspects, suspects locations, and suspect vehicles is extremely handy. Programs such as Lotus 1–2–3 are ideally suited for such indexes, and the ability to sort by various criteria is built into them. Some word processing programs also have resident indexing capabilities. The index will require continual updating; incomplete lists and indexes are a source of frustration.

If the case files are neat and well organized, evaluating the investigation for further action will be more easily and accurately accomplished. More importantly, preparation of the Title III affidavit will be greatly facilitated.

Affidavit Preparation

Any investigator who anticipates writing a wiretap affidavit should consult Title 18, Sections 2510 through 2519. If not Sections 2520 and 2521, which are less critical to the investigator at this stage of the process. An annotated book of the code is best inasmuch as it includes case law development with respect to the important aspects of the statutes.

There are requirements in the statute which mandate the way the affidavit should be written and the information that it should contain. An investigator preparing to write a Title III affidavit should also read the affidavits of the other officers which have been successful in the past. While a great deal of the language and style of the affidavit is boiler plate, there is room for individual style and organization to a point.

This section of the chapter deals with the content and organization of an affidavit in a general sense pertaining specifically to wiretap affidavits rather than affidavits for the intercept of electronic or oral communications.

The investigator who has not written and submitted a wiretap affidavit in the past should be prepared for some nuances related to these affidavits which do not usually accompany other written work and investigations. To begin with, the affidavit, particularly if submitted in the federal system will be the subject of close scrutiny by many people. If the investigation is being done with a federal agency, the FBI, for example, supervisors and members of the legal department of that agency will review the affidavit. Through each draft, changes will be recommended. By and large, the changes recommended will be constructive although some changes are suggested seemingly just for the sake of change or for stylistic reasons rather than having any factual or legal basis.

What can seem like an endless review and revision process does serve to make for a good final product. The investigator should be prepared to make many revisions and should not take the criticism of the affidavit personally.

In many jurisdictions, some abbreviations are commonly used in search warrant affidavits and seizure affidavits, even though these are certainly legal documents. Some abbreviations such as St. for street and Det. for detective are allowed. In a federal wiretap affidavit, the use of abbreviations is not acceptable.

The affidavit should be written in a clear, straightforward style. It should be thorough and concise, and much of the revision should involve bringing the important details of the investigation into sharp focus and eliminating the extraneous information. What is far more important than style is substance; style is important only to the extent that it can facilitate the expression of the content.

Affidavit Organization

The affidavit must be organized in such a way that the reader is taken through the investigation from its incipient stages to the status quo. To accomplish this, arranging the facts in chronological order is generally the most effective, although it may be necessary to organize the facts in some other logical order in combination with a chronology of events. The following are several general categories of information which must be present in the affidavit in some form. The titles of the sections may be varied, and some sections can be combined, but the arrangement of the content of the affidavit should generally conform to that which is presented here.

It is preferable, in the interest of clear reference, in a lengthy affidavit, that the paragraphs be numbered consecutively throughout the affidavit.

Introduction and Identification of the Affiant

Title III affidavits, like those supporting the request for a search warrant and other affidavits, should begin with an introduction of the affiant. The introduction should be more detailed than is normally the case in a search warrant affidavit however. It should begin with a paragraph of general introductory information followed immediately by a paragraph in which the purpose of the affidavit is stated. The purpose should be stated succinctly and should include the fact that the affidavit is in support of an application seeking authorization to intercept wire communications. The telephone number and then the address at which the phone is located should be stated. Subscriber information should follow and then a statement regarding the identification of persons known whose communications are to be intercepted. The naming of interceptees is a critical aspect of the affidavit, and it will be discussed shortly, following this section.

This section of the affidavit should continue through several more paragraphs and should detail the experience and training of the affiant which would in effect qualify him to conduct such an investigation and to draw inferences from facts based upon that expertise. If the affiant has written previous Title III affidavits, that information is very important as such experience gives him a higher degree of credibility.

The purpose of detailing the training and experience of the affiant is that the facts of the investigation will later be intercepted to some degree in light of the qualifications of the affiant. The observations of an expert differ from those of an inexperienced investigator. An experienced investigator who has written hundreds of search warrant affidavits and who has participated in several hundred drug investigations is probably an expert in certain aspects of the field of illegal drug trafficking, if not the field in general. That experience, taken together with formal training and informal discussions with other officers and informant and citizen debriefings, forms the basis of a good deal of knowledge which distinguishes that person from other police officers. That the affidavit and the investigation upon which it is based are that of an expert should be made clear from the very beginning. Many of the decisions made in a complex drug investigation are based to some extent on inferences drawn from the facts at hand. The conclusions reached by an "expert," a person with extensive experience and training, will carry more weight and have a higher expectation of accuracy than those of a novice or a casual observer.

Statement of Objectives

This section of the affidavit should state the purpose of the wiretap in a few concise paragraphs and should include the names of the persons involved in the alleged drug trafficking conspiracy, the specific violations which are occurring, and what the use of a wiretap on the desired phones is expected to produce in terms of evidence.

Named Interceptees

The persons whose communications are desired to be intercepted will have previously been named in the second or third paragraph of the affidavit. As mentioned in the discussion of the introduction, the naming of interceptees is an important part of the affidavit and is not something which is done arbitrarily or on the basis of speculation. To name a person as an interceptee, there must be probable cause to believe that he has committed or is about to commit one of the specified offenses. In addition to that, probable cause must exist to believe that communications pertinent to those offenses will be obtained through the interception and that the premises where interception will be made are being used in furtherance of the specific offenses.[2]

The fact that a person is a known associate of the target does not constitute probable cause to believe that he has been or is about to be involved in the conspiracy.[3] There must be some other facts learned through the investigation which lead to probable cause. For example, a pen register information showing that the target is calling a known drug trafficker shows only that they may be associates. For that matter, they may not even be associates; their wives may be friends or their children may go to school together. Just the fact that the number is being called is not enough to establish involvement in the criminal activity.

If, however, the known drug trafficker is observed meeting with the target before a drug transaction, that, coupled with the suspect's record and other facts learned through the investigation, will help to establish the probable cause necessary to name him as an interceptee. Through investigation it may be possible to show that the person is the source or is participating in some other way in the criminal activity.

If probable cause to name a person as an interceptee does not exist at the time that the affidavit is being prepared, the information pertaining to that person, including the fact that he is being called, should be listed in the section detailing the facts of the investigation. While it may not establish probable cause to name the person as an interceptee, it should be included in the interest of supporting the probable cause to believe that the target is involved in the specified criminal activity. Should probable cause to name that person or other person not originally

---

2 *United States v. Armocida,* 515 F.2d 29 (Pennsylvania 1975).

3 *United States v. Johnson,* 539 F.2d 181 (D.C. 1976).

named as interceptees be developed during the intercept, the order can be expanded to include them as named interceptees. Such expansion would normally be included in the daily report to the prosecutor who makes regular reports to the judge.

List of Violations

This section of the affidavit should also include a list of the violations which are believed to be occurring. This can usually be accomplished in one paragraph that starts out with the names of the interceptees and continues through an enumeration of offenses being committed. For example,

> John Smith, John Jones, John Johnson, and others yet to be identified are committing acts in violation of Title 21, United States Code, Section 841(a)(1), Distribution of Controlled Substances (cocaine); Title 21, United States Code, Section 846, Conspiracy; Title 21, United States Code, Section 843(b), Unlawful Use of a Communication Facility; . . .

All violations which are believed to be being committed should be listed in this paragraph, although when new violations are uncovered, the order can be expanded to include them just as in the case of new interceptees. Some sections of the code, less specific than those mentioned in the sample, should be researched for applicability. Offenses such as continuing criminal enterprise; importation and conspiracy to illegally import; interstate and foreign travel in aid of racketeering enterprise; and racketeer influenced and corrupt organizations may very well apply.

What the Wire Communications Will Reveal

The remaining part of this section, Statement of Objectives, should be devoted to detailing what will be learned through the intercept of wire communications. This again can often be accomplished with one paragraph and five or six subparagraphs. The following is an example:

> There is probable cause to believe that this telephone, number (303) 333-3333, has been used, is being used, and will continue to be used specifically by John Smith, John Jones, John Johnson (sometimes referred to hereafter as the Smith/Jones/Johnson group), and other co-conspirators yet to be identified in carrying out the offenses listed in paragraph (appropriate paragraph number) above. Further, the wire communications of the above-named people and other yet-to-be-identified co-conspirators using telephone number (303) 333-3333 pertaining to those offenses will concern:

1. The dates, times, places, and manner in which controlled substances (cocaine) are delivered to or by the Smith/Jones/Johnson group.

2. The amount of currency which is paid for or received by the Smith/Jones/Johnson group and the dates, times, places, and manner in which these transactions are conducted.

3. The nature and extent of the controlled substances importation, transportation, and distribution system of the Smith/Jones/Johnson group.

4. The identity of currently unidentified co-conspirators in the Smith/Jones/Johnson group and their respective roles and participation in the above listed offenses.

5. The identity of the sources of supply of controlled substances (cocaine) for the Smith/Jones/Johnson group and the yet-to-be-determined origin of the supply.

6. The manner in which the illegal proceeds from these offenses are dispersed and utilized and the locations where these proceeds may be concealed.

Identification of Communications Facilities Subject to Interception

This section is necessary to describe the premises where the telephone is located. The legal address, a physical description, and whatever subscriber information for the telephone which has been acquired should be included in this section.

Identification of Individuals Whose Communications Will Be Subject to Interception

This section of the affidavit contains a detailed description of each named interceptee. The description should include all vital statistics. Name, aliases, date of birth, FBI number, social security number, police department numbers, Naddis number, address, telephone numbers, and a complete physical description should all be part of this section. It is preferable if this information is in a block format for each named interceptee, and each block can be given a subparagraph designation as part of the initial paragraph containing the introductory statement of the section. The introductory statement must simply state that "The following individuals are suspects in this investigation about whom probable cause has been developed and which probable cause is detailed in this affidavit. Based on that probable cause, it is believed that the following people have used, are using, and will continue to use the telephone number (303) 333-3333 in furtherance of the offenses listed in paragraph 12 above."

Confidential Sources

Somewhere in the affidavit there should be a section which introduces the reader to confidential sources and describes their respective involvement in the development of the investigation. It is preferable to put this section before the Facts and Circumstances section.

Each informant who has provided information in the case, and to whom subsequent reference will be made, should be given a designation for future reference, such as CS (confidential source) One, CS Two, etc. The information which the informant has provided and his participation in the investigation should be detailed inasmuch as it is necessary to the development of probable cause. Beyond that, the informant information included should be that which most effectively demonstrates his credibility and basis of knowledge. Information pertaining to the importance of keeping the informant(s) confidential should also be included in the close of this section. Invariably, the most important reason for not revealing the identity of an informant has to do with his physical safety. If there is specific information regarding a history of violence or showing a propensity toward violence on the part of one or more of the people involved in the conspiracy, that information should be included.

Facts and Circumstances

Once all the preliminary and introductory portions of the affidavit are complete, the affidavit should then proceed to the meat—those facts which establish probable cause; probable cause to believe that the persons named are or will be committing offenses, that evidence of those violations will be obtained through the wire intercept, and that the premises where the interception will be made are being used in connection with the offenses.[4]

These three settings in which the existence of probable cause must be demonstrated are repeated again here to emphasize their importance. This section of the affidavit is the most critical, and only that information which reflects on the issue of probable cause should be included. In the interest of keeping the affidavit to a reasonable length, there should not be any unnecessary detail. Unnecessary details about an undercover buy, for example, which add nothing to the probable cause and do not shed light on the facts of the case should be omitted.

The investigation should be chronicled in some logical manner. It is

4 *United States v. Armocida,* 515 F.2d 29 (Pennsylvania 1975).

very likely that the case was initiated through informant information, and if that is the case, then this section of the affidavit can flow naturally from the previous section in which the informant was introduced. In that section in which the confidential sources were listed, some of the information which they provided and which was corroborated will have been described. It may be necessary to have a great deal more information which has been provided by the informant in the beginning of this section as a way of informing the reader how the investigation began. Also, it will no doubt be necessary to include some of the facts regarding the informant's active participation in the investigation, that is, controlled buys, undercover introductions, etc.

The following are some critical areas which should be addressed as probable cause is being established.

1. *Target information:* All information which has been learned about the target or targets should, of course, be included. Criminal history, work background, and other biographical information which helps form a picture of the target in relation to his criminal activity is important and should be covered. Unnecessary detail is not desired.

2. *Drugs on the table:* If the investigation to its current state has resulted in the purchase or seizure of drugs, including controlled buys, the details should be discussed. If buys have been made, some details regarding how the purchases were arranged and transacted can be very important. The results of the analysis should also be included. What is not necessary is too much detail regarding every last fine point of the transaction. Only those facts which show who was involved and how and when the transaction was completed are necessary.

3. *Use of the telephone:* All information which indicates that the target is using the telephone to conduct his illegal activities should be included in this section. Under ideal circumstances, an undercover buy can be arranged on the target number with the target at the target location. Even better perhaps would be the target calling his source from the target number in the presence of the undercover officer. What enhances the value of this type of information is that an officer will be able to testify in later hearings, whereas the same information provided by an informant whose identity the prosecution does not wish to reveal becomes hearsay. In any event, any

information directly linking the target and the target telephone number to the illegal activity should be described in detail.

4. *Pen register information:* Pen register information will not only support the conclusion that the target telephone is being used in connection with the offenses enumerated, but from this information inferences can also be drawn about the overall conspiratorial nature of the case. Pen register information can either be integrated into the investigative facts section in chronological order, or it can be brought up in logical order as co-conspirators are discussed.

5. *Co-conspirators:* Information regarding possible co-conspirators, whether they have been named as interceptees or not, should be included in detail. Some of these people who are potentially co-conspirators may have been uncovered through pen register information, through surveillance, or other investigative means. When the facts pertaining to the main target or targets have been detailed, these people, as they relate to the investigation, should be discussed.

6. *Corroborative facts regarding the target(s):* While this entire section is corroborative in nature, there are some subtle facts about the target or targets which may seem unimportant but which can serve to complete the picture. For example, it the target has been the subject of some extensive surveillance and has been observed to drive in a manner designed to detect surveillance, that is a noteworthy fact. Likewise, seemingly insignificant statements which the target may have made to the informant or the undercover officer should be included if they have a bearing on his activities or reflect behavior consistent with drug traffickers. If the target is unwilling to introduce the undercover officer to his source or sources, that is of course important and consistent with the manner in which drug dealers operate.

7. *Freshness:* The information included in the affidavit, regardless of its importance, will be of little value in establishing probable cause if it is stale. The information in a historical context is valuable, but the affidavit has the burden of establishing the continuing nature of the offense. Current information is critical.

When the investigation has been described from its inception to status quo, including all the historical and current information which falls roughly into the general categories just listed, probable cause should be clear. A reasonable person should find probable cause relative to the three settings: that the target has or is about to commit the offenses; that communication pertinent to the offenses will be obtained through the intercept; and that the target location is being used in the furtherance of the offenses.

Need for Interception

Once the probable cause has been sufficiently discussed, it is then necessary to explain, in some detail, why a wire intercept is necessary. It is important in this section to show that the intercept of wire communications will succeed where routine investigative techniques are bound to fail. This section should emphasize that normal investigative techniques have been exhausted where that is the case, although the use of electronic surveillance is not necessarily reserved for use only as a last resort. It is, however, necessary to demonstrate that a wiretap is likely to succeed, whereas the normal or routine investigative measures are either unlikely to achieve the objectives or they are too dangerous to pursue.[5]

Demonstrating the need for interception involves going through each investigative measure which has been tried or which could be tried and explaining why it has failed or would in all likelihood fail or why it has been or would be successful to only a limited degree.

The reluctance of witnesses to testify against drug traffickers for fear of personal reprisal is demonstrative of a traditional investigative measure (the grand jury approach) being minimally effective and thus failing to uncover fully the scope of a conspiracy. Likewise, interviewing people is only going to have limited value if people are reluctant to talk to investigators and later testify. Also, those with valuable information might be reticent due in part to their own involvement in the conspiracy, and if they are deeply involved, they should be defendants, not witnesses.

Essentially, this section of the affidavit should show that the investigation has proceeded as far as it is going to go, that there is much more about the conspiracy to be learned if it is to be fully uncovered and prosecuted, and that the intercept of wire communications will succeed where the other measures have fallen short. There will be unique characteristics of each investigation which are important in making this point

---

5 *United States v. Licavoli,* 456 F.Supp. 960 (Ohio 1978); also see *United States v. Falcone,* 364 F.Supp. 877 (New Jersey 1973), and *People v. Gallina,* 95 A.D.2d 336 (New York 1983).

and those should be included. Such things as the reluctance of the targets to introduce someone to their sources, particularly at the higher levels, and the resultant limitations on an undercover approach; the fact that the targets are very surveillance conscious and wary; and indications which point to concealment of assets, etc.—all may be important in showing the need for interception.

Conclusion

The conclusion consists of a very brief paragraph requesting that, based on the facts contained in the affidavit, there is probable cause and that an order should be issued.

Period of Interception

This section is usually written in standard language, some of which is derived directly from the wording of Title 18, Section 2518. Paragraph 5 of that section states that

> No order entered under this section may authorize or approve the interception of any wire, oral, or electronic communication for any period longer than is necessary to achieve the objective of the authorization, nor in any event longer than thirty days. Such thirty-day period begins on the earlier of the day on which the investigative or law enforcement officer first begins to conduct an interception under the order or ten days after the order is entered.

The wording of this section of the affidavit usually contains a statement to the effect that because of the conspiratorial nature of the offenses involved, it is quite likely that the types of communications sought will be intercepted and yet the objectives of the authorization have will not be fully met by virtue of that fact alone. Due to the possible number of people involved, it should be requested that the intercept be allowed to continue, rather than terminating it when the described types of communications are first obtained.

Technical Assistance

This section of the affidavit also consists of very standard language, and the purpose of it is to request that the provider of communications be ordered to furnish such technical assistance as is necessary to conduct the interception in an unobtrusive manner. It should be made clear that the police department and the sponsoring federal agency will be responsible for expenses necessarily incurred pursuant to the authorization.

In this section also is the request that the order include the use of a pen register. This is a standard request even though the use of a pen register always accompanies a wire intercept and in spite of the fact that the use of a pen register is not covered under Chapter 119. It should be included in the affidavit and subsequent orders so that a separate order for a pen register is not necessary.

This section also includes a request that the telephone service provider be ordered to provide subscriber information in a timely fashion. This request should be worded in such a way that it is clear that there will be some urgent requests for subscriber information, for example, a call to a number for which no subscriber information has yet been obtained arranging a transaction to take place immediately. In a situation such as that, knowing the subscriber information can be a matter of extreme importance. What is being requested is that the telephone company be ordered to provide that information immediately in those circumstances.

Prior Applications

Paragraph 1(e) of Section 2518, Title 18, United States Code, requires "a full and complete statement of the facts concerning all previous applications known to the individual authorizing to intercept ... involving any of the same persons, facilities or places specified in the application, and the action taken by the judge on each application ... " Fulfillment of this requirement involves checking the various indices of the state and federal agencies which would reveal the existence of prior applications or orders. Normally, checking with the respective state attorney general's office, the U.S. attorney's office, and the DEA and the FBI should suffice. As a practical matter, the case agents will know by this stage of the investigation, whether or not any other investigations, particularly any having reached this stage, are currently in progress.

Minimization

The final paragraph of the affidavit is a statement to the effect that all interceptions will be minimized in accordance with Chapter 119, Title 18, namely, that when conversations occur and it has been determined through voice identification, physical surveillance, or other means that none of the named interceptees or their confederates is involved in the conversations, the interception of those communications will be suspended immediately. Likewise, if one of the named interceptees is a party to the conversation but the conversation is not criminal in nature, that type of interception, too, shall be suspended. The monitoring and recording of nonpertinent calls will be minimized. Defining what is pertinent and what is nonpertinent is very subjective and will be discussed in the monitoring section of the part of this chapter dealing with conducting the wiretap.

Preoperational Logistics

There are a number of tasks to be done while the affidavit is being prepared in order to be ready to do the wire when the order is finally approved.

Locating the Listening Post

Arrangements must be made to rent an off-site location at which the listening post will be established. The location should be one which will be physically capable of meeting the demands of a wiretap. It must have adequate utility capacity. When a potential site is being considered, the technical people who will be installing the equipment and otherwise charged with maintaining the technical side of the operation should be consulted regarding the location. There may be characteristics which will make the installation of the phone lines particularly difficult or expensive. The narcotics investigator may not recognize these inherent problems, whereas a good technical man will.

There are other considerations to be made when choosing the location of the LP. A wiretap is physically demanding and stressful on the people involved. A location should be chosen that will be comfortable and which will easily accommodate the number of people who will be working in it.

If a large number of people will be coming and going, the location should be one where that amount of traffic will not attract attention. A commercial location may be better than a residential area for that reason.

Setting Up the LP

Once the location for the listening post has been chosen, the advance work for setting it up should begin. Ordering the necessary phone lines and equipment from the service provider should be done well in advance of the anticipated start-up date. It can often take two weeks to install the necessary lines on which the actual wiretap will be conducted. In addition, it may be necessary to order some of the tape recorders, pen registers, printers, and other equipment which will be needed.

One good system consists of a console containing three cassette recorders for each line being intercepted. Three exact tapes are generated simultaneously. One becomes the work copy, one the transcriber copy, and of course one is designated as the original copy. Each console is controlled by a pen register which, when activated by the target phone, sets off an alarm, and the recorders operate automatically.

Establishing a Surveillance Post

Many of the same considerations mentioned with regard to locating the LP also pertain to establishing a suitable surveillance post. The surveillance post will, at certain times, be the site of considerable traffic, and for that reason it is advantageous if it is located in a place where the movement will be inconspicuous. The surveillance post should be located reasonably close to the area where the most activity is anticipated for the sake of convenience. It should not be situated so close that the surveillance officers will be observed by the target or one of his associates on the way to and from the target location.

In some cases, the surveillance post can be set up in the same location as the listening post. That is a convenient arrangement which facilitates good communication between the monitors and surveillance leaders, but separation of the two also has its advantages. The listening post operation functions more efficiently with the fewest distractions. Having the surveillance post in the same building as the LP tends to encourage too much traffic and too much noise in and around it. Some policy which limits the people entering the LP should be established, particularly if the SP and LP are situated in the same building.

Arranging for Personnel Assignments and Scheduling

One of the most difficult tasks related to a Title III operation involves the scheduling and assignment of personnel. The size of the operations, the fact that temporary personnel assignments are usually required, and the fact that overtime is a factor make this the case.

Not all narcotics investigators are equal, and this is certainly true when it comes to a Title III case. There are some investigators who have the ability and the desire to work on someone else's investigation with the same vigor as if it were their own. Then there are inevitably some who seek the assignment just to get paid overtime or other benefits which might be involved. If the job is to be done right, both the surveillance post and the listening post require people who are interested in the case and skillful in most phases of investigative work. It might be necessary to recruit experienced specialists to monitor the wire, to run the surveillance teams, and to assist at the LP with the review of the logs and other daily functions. The services of a good technical man will have to be arranged, and some people skilled in surveillance photography will be a necessity as well.

Preoperational Briefings

While the orders are being prepared, when it has become apparent that the initiation of the wiretap is imminent, a preoperational briefing or perhaps a series of briefings, should be held.

Monitor Briefing

Depending on the nature of the case and the experience of the people involved, it may be necessary to hold a separate briefing for the monitors. This is extremely helpful if some or all of the people who will be monitoring have never been monitors on a Title III before. A briefing exclusively for the monitors allows an opportunity for the case agents, the technical assistants, and perhaps the prosecutor to explain how the equipment works, what the objectives of the wire are, and what types of conversation are anticipated.

If a briefing of this type is held, the mechanics of monitoring should be discussed in some detail. Doing so may alleviate mistakes when the wire is in progress. Such things as labeling the tapes, writing an accurate synopsis of the call on the log, changing tapes at day's end, and sealing the court copy of the tape are all important, and though they are relatively simple tasks, they can be confusing and doing them wrong will create minor headaches if not major problems later.

General Briefing

Sometime immediately prior to the beginning of the wiretap, a general briefing should be held for all people who will be assigned, regardless of what their function will be. Such a briefing can serve as a forum for special deputations and other procedural matters, and the case can then be discussed in sufficient detail that everyone understands what the mission is. The crook books can be passed out at this briefing also. If the briefing is done a day or two prior to the start of the wire, the officers will have a chance to review their books and become familiar with the main people, vehicles, and locations which are likely to come up repeatedly throughout the investigation.

Minimization Briefing

When the order has been signed, before the intercept is initiated, it is recommended that the prosecutor conduct a minimization briefing. At that time the prosecutor will go over written guidelines pertaining to the conduct of the electronic surveillance. These instructions, if carefully written, will provide direction pertaining to recording the conversations, daily reporting requirements, privileged communications, minimization, preparation of transcripts, and termination of the intercept.

It is important that all case agents and monitors attend this briefing. Although it is probably not necessary that every officer involved in the case be at a briefing of this type, it is preferable if they are. For one thing, a properly conducted briefing of this type by an experienced attorney will be informative and beneficial training, particularly for officers lacking experience on a Title III.

Conducting the Intercept

Monitors

The monitors will be the key people in any Title III. They will be responsible for making several important determinations each time a call is intercepted, for example, Is the call pertinent? Should surveillance be dispatched to cover some meeting discussed in the call? Who are the participants in the call? Can the codes be broken? etc.

The first responsibility of the monitors is to listen to and make some determination as to the content of the call. When codes are being used, particularly early in the intercept, it may be difficult to determine not only who is talking, but what it is that is being discussed. Very seldom will the language be clear and open to the extent that weights and prices are discussed other than in some guarded reference.

The codes being used probably relate somehow to the background of the people involved, although there are some terms which are common, in fact so common that using them as codes has very little effectiveness. Such terms as "whole one" and "big one" and "half" and "small one" are obvious references to drug quantities depending on the context in which they are used. There will be individual code words such as "tires," "rooms for rent," and "work" which may be difficult to decipher. A monitor who is experienced as a street cop and as a narcotics investigator can be invaluable in reading between the lines and evaluating the context of these conversations. Also knowing the case and being able to make a quick determination of who the speakers are will be very important.

Even when codes are used, the participants in the conversation may be careless and break the code themselves. For example, if a person calls the source and states that he needs a tire and wants the same size as before, that could conceivably be a legitimate conversation regarding tires. However, when the source responds that he has no big tires left, that all he has are several small yellow tires and the other party orders five of the little yellow ones, that leaves little room for doubt that it is not tires which are being discussed but drugs. Observing any subsequent meets arranged becomes very important. If a meet takes place and no tires are exchanged, in particular no small yellow tires, what little doubt there may have been is removed: a conversation of the type sought as evidence of the conspiracy has been intercepted.

The monitors will have the responsibility of determining what calls will require a surveillance response. It will be important that they make an interpretation of the meaning of the call and then keep the surveillance people informed about what action on the part of the target is anticipated. Interpretation of the call and making a sound judgment of its content are key. This is true in English-speaking wires, but it is of even greater importance in foreign language intercepts. Sharp monitors will ensure that the initial interpretation as well as the immediate response to the call is accurate.

Aside from the cognitive aspects of monitoring, there is the mechanical side—the upkeep of the logs and the handling of the equipment and the tapes. The following is a list of paperwork and hardware with which the LP should be well stocked as well as some suggestions for using them.

1. *90-minute cassette tapes.* A moderately busy telephone will require approximately two tapes per day considering that the tape is changed at midnight whether it is full or not. Using the 3-cassette system for monitoring, 6 tapes per day or 180 for a 30-day wire would be an accurate estimate. There is no excuse for running out of tapes. The orders will require that all intercepts are recorded, and running out of tapes will not be an excuse for failing to record a portion of

the intercept. Also, if more than one phone is the subject of an intercept, the printing on the labels and logs should be of different colors to prevent confusion. One line would have red logs and red labels, another black, a third line blue, etc.

2. *Log sheets.* Figure 7-5 is a sample wire intercept log. The page numbers of the log sheets should be consecutively numbered throughout the period of intercept, including any extensions. Likewise, the tapes and the calls should be consecutively numbered. The "R" on the far left-hand column is reserved for marking the call as a relevant or pertinent call. If a call is relevant, the column should be marked with an "R." If it is not a relevant call, the column should be left blank. The call number is then inserted in the next column followed by an "I" or an "O," indicating whether the call was incoming or outgoing. Whether or not the call was minimized should be logged, and the time that it was minimized. If a call is minimized, the monitor can periodically go back on and check to see if the substance of the conversation has changed to some relevant subject. The times those periodic checks are made should also be logged. The number called and the subscriber information should be logged. If the call is an incoming call, the information derived from a trap and trace, if one is in effect, can be logged on the administrative copy of the log sheet. More on the copying and distribution of the logs will be presented shortly.

The summary of the conversation should be succinct and accurate. It should be detailed enough so that someone reading the log will have an understanding of the essence of it.

The remaining spaces on the log are for marking what language the call was in, "E" for English, "S" for Spanish, etc.; indicating whether or not surveillance was generated by the call; and the initials of the monitor.

3. *Pens and supplies.* The LP should be furnished with an ample supply of pens and note pads. The pens used on the log should be of the same type black ball point so that the logs all look alike. It is a minor point, but neatness is important. Most monitors will take notes pertaining to the call on a scratch pad and then transfer them to the log sheet when they have time. Note pads and pens are valuable commodities in the LP.

WIRE INTERCEPT LOG

PAGE # _____

COURT ORDER NUMBER _____

INTERCEPT # ____ DATE ____ TAPE # ____ DATE TAPE ON ____ DATE TAPE OFF ____ TIME ON ____ TIME OFF ____

R CALL NO.	I/O	TAPE REVS FROM	TO	TIME CALL BEGAN	END	MINIMIZED Y/N	TIME	NUMBER CALLED	SUBSCRIBER	SUMMARY	LANG	MONITOR

FIGURE 7-5

4. *Case information.* The LP should have a copy of the crook book, the affidavits and the subsequent orders, and an updated subscriber list. Of these, the subscriber list will be the most used. To understand the call fully and make an accurate interpretation, the monitor is going to need to know who is being called. Also, the subscriber information should be noted on the log sheet, and the monitors will need to have a list they can check each time an outgoing call is made. Many computer programs, designed for handling a pen register operation, will generate complete number lists which can be used for reference once the subscriber information has been obtained and updated on the program.

In most cases, the orders will make some provision for obtaining subscriber information. Usually that enables the monitors to call the phone company, even after business hours, and obtain such information when it is a new number for which no subscriber information is available.

5. *Other equipment.* Among the other equipment probably necessary at the LP will be at least one telephone line and a portable radio for communicating with surveillance. The radio should be tested as some frequencies have a tendency to interfere with the operation of the wire when transmitting.

Two or three sets of headphones should be in the LP as should at least one additional tape recorder, identical to those being used on the console as a work machine for the monitors. Tape boxes will also be needed for storing the work and transcriber copies of the tapes. The court copy of the tape should be immediately sealed and put in a lock box. Also among the additional equipment needed is a high-speed tape duplicating machine should it be necessary to make copies of any of the tapes for reviewing purposes.

If the line being intercepted is active, at least two monitors will be necessary to keep up with the activity on the phone and the other duties also. Many times the conversations happen so quickly and in such rapid succession that the monitors will not be clear on the identity of the participants and the content of the calls. The three cassette system is designed so that the work copy can be taken from the machine at any time and reviewed. Another work copy will be inserted in its place and marked with the appropriate call and tape revolution numbers. Therefore, while the transcriber and court copies will be identical, the work copies may differ significantly. It may be necessary to pull the work copy three or four times during the course of one full tape. In that event there will be three or four work copies covering the period of calls which were all recorded on one transcriber and court copy of the tape.

During busy periods, the monitors may momentarily fall behind, and they will have to rely on the pen register for times, numbers called, and duration of the calls many times. The only thing that the pen register won't provide are the counter numbers on the machines. If the monitors lose track of those temporarily, they can pull the work copy and check the counter numbers as they are reviewing the content. When the activity slows down, one of the monitors may be busy for an hour making sure that the sequence of calls, times, revolution numbers, numbers called, and an accurate summary are recorded on the log correctly.

SURVEILLANCE RESPONSIBILITIES

The surveillance people will be responsible for covering the selected meetings and transactions as well as keeping track of the principal targets in the investigation. For the surveillance people to be effective, they must have a good working knowledge of the investigation and stay current with the events which happen.

Each member of the surveillance team should keep a log of his or her observations such as that depicted in Figure 7-6. This is essential since each member of the team may have different assignments during the course of a shift, and even on the same surveillance and the observations of one team member will differ from the observations of another person on the same surveillance in a different location. Over the course of a long wiretap, it will be impossible to keep track of who observed what without accurate surveillance logs.

At the end of each shift, the surveillance leader should collect the log sheets and from those compile a summary report of the day's surveillance activities. The summary report and the logs will then be distributed. The original should be given to the case agent, and a copy should be put in the SP and LP surveillance report book in chronological order. There should also be an administrative copy of the surveillance reports and logs for use as an ongoing reference by the case agents.

```
                 NARCOTICS INVESTIGATION UNIT

                      SURVEILLANCE LOG

    DATE :_____CASE NUMBER:_____

    DAY OF WEEK:_____WEATHER:_____

    OFFICER INITIALS_____=_____SERIAL NO.:_____

    OFFICER INITIALS_____=_____SERIAL NO.:_____

    ON _____,a surveillance was conducted in the area of

    _____pertaining to _____

    The following observations were made:
                                      PAGE___OF___
```

TIME	INITIALS	OBSERVATION

FIGURE 7-6

Photographers

At least one surveillance photographer will be necessary on each shift. In a surveillance in conjunction with a wiretap, you will want an experienced photographer. There will be many opportunities, however, for more than one surveillance officer to take photographs of a meet, giving inexperienced photographers a chance to experiment and get familiar with the equipment.

One surveillance officer should be assigned responsibility for seeing that all the film to be developed is dated and appropriately marked so that the prints can be identified by photographer, subject, and date. When the film is processed and returned from the photo lab, the photos should be initialed and marked by the person who took them.

The photos can then be filed either in chronological order or by subject. The best of these can be displayed on a wall or bulletin board along with copy of the surveillance report for that day. In this manner, all officers involved in the investigation can study the photographs and keep up with the case by familiarizing themselves with people and events which they may not have witnessed.

In addition to displaying surveillance photos, photos of vehicles and properties with seizure potential can also be displayed in a separate location designated for asset photos.

It should be emphasized that several hundred photographs may be accumulated during a thirty-day wire. It is essential that someone be charged with keeping these in order as they are developed. When the case is completed, the case agents and prosecutors will determine which photographs will be used as evidence; probably only a small percentage will be used, but it is likely that copies of all of them may have to be furnished to the defense at some point in compliance with discovery requirements.

Case Agent's Role

The case agent will be required to keep up with the progress of the wire in every aspect to make the decisions which will be demanded of him in bringing the case to a successful conclusion and in preparing the case for prosecution. To accomplish this, at least two or three officers in addition to the case agent and the supervisor should be responsible for staying on top of the case. The following are some of the more critical areas of responsibility.

1. *Review and recap of the LP logs.* The log sheets from the previous day's monitoring activity must be reviewed and recapped each morning. They must be checked for accuracy and content. It is possible that there will be numbering mistakes or other such prob-

lems which are minor as long as they are remedied immediately. By reviewing the logs, the case agent will stay current with the progress of the case and any new developments. When the log has been reviewed and corrected as necessary, the calls can then be categorized. There should be four general categories of calls:

☐ Pertinent (relevant)

☐ Non-pertinent less than two minutes in duration

☐ Non-pertinent greater than two minutes in duration

☐ Incomplete calls, recordings, etc.

When the review of the previous day's activities is complete, the amount of calls in each category should be recorded as well as the number of each type which were minimized. In addition, the call numbers of pertinent calls should be noted, as should any additional subjects or violations for which expansion is desired, and any technical problems which were experienced.

2. *Daily report.* The review of the log sheets of the previous day forms the basis for the daily report to the prosecuting attorney. Figure 7-7 is a sample format for a daily report. This particular form is done on a computer program with the capability of making all of the necessary calculations. With this type of format, the case agent or supervisor can take the figures from the four basic categories, the total number of each, and the number minimized and enter them in the appropriate place in the upper portion of the report. The figures are then transferred below and calculated automatically.

When reviewing the daily reports there are two or three areas of particular interest. The total number of pertinent calls and the percentage, pertinent of complete, are important. Likewise, the number of pertinent calls over 2 minutes in length and the percentage of those which were minimized is important. As the wire progresses, there should be about a 90 percent minimization of nonpertinent calls over 2 minutes in duration. In the early days of the intercept, when the monitors are unfamiliar with the participants and the code words used, a somewhat lower percentage of lengthy (over 2 minutes) nonpertinent calls minimized is acceptable.

The minimization of nonpertinent calls under 2 minutes in length is not as critical. Something less than 2 minutes is not a long

```
                         SAMPLE DAILY REPORT

        DATE:

        TO: (ASSISTANT UNITED STATES ATTORNEY)

        FROM:  TITLE III AFFIANT

        DAILY REPORT CONCERNING COURT ORDER #:_____

        DATE OF INTERCEPTION:_____DAY NUMBER_____

        TARGET TELEPHONE NUMBER:_____


I.  INTERCEPT CLASSIFICATION        NUMBER   NUMBER MINIMIZED

    A.  PERTINENT                      7               0
    B.  NON-PERTINENT < 2 MINUTES     15               4
    C.  NON-PERTINENT > 2 MINUTES      6               6
    D.  INCOMPLETE, RECORDINGS, OTHER 13               0

    TOTAL NUMBER OF ALL INTERCEPTIONS  41             10

II. INTERCEPT ANALYSIS

    A.  INCOMPLETE CALL ANALYSIS

        1.  TOTAL INTERCEPTS                        41
        2.  TOTAL INCOMPLETE, ETC.                  13
        3.  PERCENTAGE INCOMPLETE                31.71 %

    B.  COMPLETE CALL ANALYSIS

        1.  TOTAL NUMBER OF COMPLETE CALLS          28
        2.  PERCENTAGE - COMPLETE CALLS OF ALL CALLS 68.29 %
        3.  TOTAL NUMBER OF PERTINENT CALLS          7
        4.  NUMBER OF PERTINENT CALLS MINIMIZED      0
        5.  PERCENTAGE - PERTINENT OF TOTAL      17.07 %
        6.  PERCENTAGE - PERTINENT OF COMPLETE   25.00 %
        7.  PERCENTAGE OF PERTINENT CALLS MINIMIZED 00.00 %
        8.  TOTAL NON-PERTINENT < 2 MINUTES         15
        9.  PERCENTAGE - NP < 2 MINUTES OF TOTAL 36.59 %
        10. NON-PERTINENT < 2 MINUTES MINIMIZED      4
        11. PERCENTAGE - NP < 2 MINUTES MINIMIZED 26.67 %
        12. TOTAL NON-PERTINENT > 2 MINUTES          6
        13. PERCENTAGE - NP > 2 MINUTES OF TOTAL 14.63 %
        14. NP CALLA > 2 MINUTES MINIMIZED           6
        15. PERCENTAGE-NP CALLS > 2 MIN MINIMIZED 100.00 %

                         FIGURE 7-7
```

conversation, and to listen to the entire conversation to determine content when one or more of the named interceptees is involved in the conversation is not unreasonable. When none of the named interceptees participates in the conversation, minimization will usually be a clear-cut decision resulting in immediate minimization.

Determining whether or not a call is pertinent is the most important part of the daily review of the logs. The monitors will have made an initial determination and marked the log accordingly. However, upon reviewing the log, the case agents should carefully evaluate each call to see that they agree with the initial decision of the monitor.

Any call in which drugs are discussed is, of course, pertinent. Many calls of which money is the subject will be pertinent, as might calls regarding out-of-town or out of country travel. Calls to pagers belonging to suspects in the conspiracy should be classified as pertinent calls rather than incomplete or nonpertinent, clearly so if the pager has been used in the past as a communication device for setting up drug transactions.

The second part of the daily report, not depicted in Figure 7-7 will contain more narrative information than statistical. This part of the daily report should explain

☐ Persons named in court order whose communications were intercepted.

☐ Persons not named in the court order but whose communications are desired for expansion of the order.

☐ Violations other than those named in the court order, but which are desired for expansion of the order.

☐ A list of pertinent intercepts by call number.

☐ An explanation of nonpertinent calls greater than 2 minutes which were not minimized. Some brief explanation such as "caller was on hold almost 2 minutes and was calling one of the named interceptees, therefore call was not minimized," will be sufficient.

The daily report should give the prosecutor some idea of how the intercept is progressing. It will not, however, take the place of frequent verbal briefings. The verbal briefings let the prosecutor know exactly how things are going. The written daily reports and subsequent periodic reports form the basis of the prosecutor's report to the judge.

3. *Periodic reports (weekly or 10-day reports).* The daily report format shown in Figure 7-7 is designed for automatic statistical recap over given periods of time. For example, the judge may desire that the

prosecutor make weekly or 10-day reports to him concerning the progress of the wire. The statistical information from the bottom of Figure 7-7 is easily transferred, in this program and others as well, to a cumulative report. Such a report allows the case agents to see the overall picture. From these statistics, graphs can be made showing the relationship of the different types of calls, minimizations curves, etc.

This information is not captured just for the sake of statistics. Having the information readily available allows for positive changes in the conduct of the wire which may result in a better prosecution and in any case will discourage and disarm later defense attacks in this direction. Eventually this information may be requested, and there will be no excuse for not having it.

4. *Ongoing Affidavit Preparation.* The case agents will also have the responsibility of ensuring that the affidavits which will be necessary at a later stage of the investigation are being prepared as the case progresses. Search warrant affidavits, civil seizure affidavits, and affidavits for expansion or extension of the intercept should be prepared as part of a continuing effort rather than waiting until the time when they are needed and writing them in a crisis mode. The case agent should designate one person to be responsible for each task and the tasks can be completed when they are needed.

5. *Disposition of the tapes.* The case agent will have to see that the court copies of the tapes are properly marked and sealed and placed in the property bureau. When the case has been completed, the case agent must arrange for official sealing of the tapes in the presence of the judge.

6. *Preparation of transcripts.* Transcripts of pertinent calls should be prepared as the case progresses. This particular task, especially in a foreign language intercept, can be overwhelming. There will be a limited number of people capable of transcribing calls spoken in a foreign language and a specialist may have to be hired for this purpose, although the monitors may be able to do some of them. In the case of English calls, the tedious job of transcribing the calls may have to be spread around and some assigned to everybody.

When the transcripts have been prepared, the case agent should review them, have the person who transcribed them review them again against the content of the conversation, and they should then be typed. When they are finished the originals should be maintained as evidence and at least one copy put in a book in numerical order of the calls.

7.   *Pertinent call summary and index.* Preparing a summary of pertinent calls may seem redundant in light of the fact that there is a summary on the log sheet and there will be a complete transcript. A summary of pertinent calls will serve as a guide for the case agents and may contain more editorializing and supposition than is desired on the log sheet. Figure 7-8 is a sample of a pertinent call summary. A book of the summaries can then be assembled and can be arranged in any order determined to be the most helpful to the case agents in analyzing and preparing the case for trial. Figure 7-9 is a computerized index of the pertinent calls which is necessary whether or not a summary is desired. This type of index allows the investigators to sort calls by participants and readily pick out the calls which will be important in the prosecution of each defendant.

8.   *Pertinent call package.* A pertinent call package should be prepared for each conspirator. This can be undertaken at about the midpoint of the wire when there is clear idea of how many conspirators will ultimately be indicted and who they are. These packages should contain a transcript of each pertinent call in which the particular conspirator is a party, a copy of the reports of surveillance which may have been generated by the call, and a copy of the index listing all the pertinent calls in which this conspirator participated. Copies of photographs related to the surveillance can also be included. This information will aid grand jury presentation, and after indictment, when discovery conferences and pretrial meetings occur, the separate package pertaining to each defendant will be readily available.

The case agent may have many other incidental responsibilities in addition to those listed, most of which will relate to the spontaneous containment and correction of small problems. The case agent's immediate supervisor will have the responsibility of seeing that everything gets accomplished and that the case agent is given all the help he needs.

Supervisor's Role

The supervisor will have the primary responsibility for seeing that the logistics of the wiretap remain workable and that everybody is doing

```
                          SAMPLE

                   SUMMARY OF PERTINENT CALL

    CASE NUMBER_____

    TARGET NUMBER_____

    Call Number_____Date_____Time_____

    Tape Number_____revolutions_____to_____

    Participant #1_____(at target phone)

    Participant #2_____

    Incoming_____Outgoing_____NUMBER CALLED_____

    SUBSCRIBER INFORMATION_____

    _____
```

```
                         SYNPOSIS

    The synopsis should be a brief narrative describing
    the content of the call.  An interpretive analysis of
    the call is permissible in this whereas the summary
    in the monitor log should be brief and factual.

    The purpose of the pertinent call summary is to provide
    the case agents with a summary of each pertinent call,
    without having to consult the log, which has all calls,
    or the complete transcript of the call.
```

```
                        FIGURE 7-8
```

his or her share of the work. There is probably nothing in narcotics work like a wiretap in terms of stress, long hours, and burnout. Without careful supervision, the distribution of work may become unbalanced, a few people doing most of the work and suffering most of the headaches, while others, usually those inexperienced in investigations of this type,

```
                          SAMPLE

                    PERTINENT CALL INDEX

                    TARGET PHONE _____
```

DATE	CALL #	PARTICIPANT #1	PARTICIPANT #2	OTHER
052391	3	JONES, JOHN	JOHNSON, PETE	
052391	5	JONES, JOHN	JOHNSON, PETE	
052591	40	JONES, JOHN	JOHNSON, PETE	
052391	7	JONES, JOHN	LNU, JOSIE	
052691	51	JONES, JOHN	LNU, MARIE	
052491	22	JONES, JOHN	WILLIAMS, JOHN	
052391	14	SMITH, MILTON	BLACK, WILLIAM	
052691	60	SMITH, MILTON	BLACK, WILLIAM	
052791	91	SMITH, MILTON	BLACK, WILLIAM	
052391	11	SMITH, MILTON	DANIELS, JACOB	
052791	98	SMITH, MILTON	DANIELS, JACOB	UNKNOWN
052391	17	SMITH, MILTON	LNU, TERRY	
052891	105	SMITH, MILTON	LNU, TERRY	

```
     This index is a list of all pertinent calls from the
     target phone number.  The number one participant is the
     person talking on the target phone.  The number two
     participant is the person calling in or being called.
     in some instances there will be a third party involved
     in the call.

     An index such as this can be sorted by participant's
     name or by date or by a combination of factors.  For
     example, this list is sorted by first participant,
     then by second participant and finally by date of call.
     The participants in each call in which John Jones was
     a party are listed in alphabetical order and the calls
     in which each participated are listed in ascending order
     by date. The same is true for Milton Smith's calls.
```

```
                    FIGURE 7-9
```

become bored and fidgety, thus contributing further to the stress and pressure on the case agents and supervisors.

The supervisors assigned to the wiretap will have to take positive steps to keep all the surveillance and LP people interested in the case in order to keep morale high. One important way of accomplishing this is to keep everybody informed of the progress of the case and involved in the decision making process through informal discussions, etc. Narcotics investigators who are accustomed to working their own investigations independently should be allowed to contribute to the success of a case and to exercise some initiative in the conduct of surveillances and other aspects of the investigation.

In addition to maintaining high morale, the supervisors have the responsibility of planning the course of the investigation based on events, many of which are anticipated, and assigning people to the various tasks based on both current and anticipated needs. This planning process is ongoing in any case, but particularly so in a wiretap where the commitment of resources is so much greater than the average investigation.

Another primary responsibility which will rest with the supervisors will be that of maintaining good interagency cooperation. A cooperative endeavor will require some give and take in order to fulfill the needs of all the agencies which are participating. Conflict is not inevitable, however. A good supervisor will be able to resolve differences of opinion and align the varying objectives so that mutual benefit will result. Doing so will demand that the supervisor play the role of mediator and peacemaker and look for ways of making the situation work rather than giving in to the negative forces.

The supervisor should also stay on top of the expenses which are incurred and make sure the lead representative of each agency participating in the case understands what portion of the expenses will be the responsibility of their agency and that they get the necessary approval to make such financial commitments. The other side of that involves agreements pertaining to the way in which forfeitures will be divided. Very seldom will problems develop if these and other issues are addressed and resolved consensually in advance.

Achieving the Objectives

The ultimate standard by which the success of a wiretap investigation will be measured is whether or not the objectives, those stated formally in the affidavit and stated and hoped for informally otherwise, have been achieved. The objectives are generally the same in all cases, that is, to gather evidence concerning the dates, time, and places of the transactions; the amounts of currency which are exchanged; the nature and extent of the distribution network; the identity of currently unidentified co-conspirators;

the identity of sources of supply; and the manner in which the illegal proceeds are dispersed and utilized.

The wiretap statutes require that when the objectives have been achieved, the wiretap must be terminated. Determining if the objectives of the investigation have been accomplished will be primarily the decision of the case agents and the supervisors. Making the decision will involve more than simply going down a checklist and checking accomplishments against stated objectives, it must be done in light of any number of other real considerations and intangible factors as well. Ideally, the accomplishment of objectives will coincide with other timing considerations, such as the delivery of a load and the identification of the source or sources. Too often, however, there is a tendency to judge the quality of a wiretap case based on seizures and assets rather than the extent to which the conspiracy will have been exposed, the organization disabled and dismantled, and the quality of the conspiracy prosecution which will result.

It is not likely that each and every objective stated in the affidavit will be accomplished to the degree desired. What is likely and what should happen is that the case will reach a point where most of the objectives have been met and a solid case will be the product, providing the initial evaluation of the target was accurate, the case was well organized, and the intercept was planned and conducted thoughtfully and carefully.

The following is sample of how a typical case might progress with commentary afterward regarding the accomplishment of the objectives.

Synopsis of Activity

☐ *Day 1:* Conversation is intercepted regarding tires; two or three suspects are called but the only named interceptee involved is the main one, on whose phone the intercept is being conducted.

☐ *Day 2:* A conversation is intercepted between the main interceptee and a possible suspect. The possible suspect states that he will stop by the house later. Surveillance covers this meeting, and it is the consensus that the meeting was either a delivery of money or a pickup of drugs, maybe both. This suspect is positively identified.

☐ *Day 3:* A conversation between the main interceptee and a person thought to be his source is intercepted. However, the conversation is about tickets and money. The main interceptee tells the source that he has some tickets which he wishes the source to pick up, but later goes on to say that so much money is a temptation, apparently breaking his own code: tickets equals money. Surveillance is established, and the meeting between the two is observed.

☐ *Day 7:* The main interceptee makes several attempts to contact his suspected source, finally doing so late in the afternoon. He tells the source that he has a party who wants a whole tire, that the party is the guy from the other day, and that he only has half the money now, but that he is good for the rest of it. The source tells him to call when he is ready. The main interceptee then calls the possible suspect from day 2, and asks him if he is ready. The guy states that he is, that he wants a whole one, and if it is okay that he only has half the money. The main interceptee tells him it's okay and to come and get him in half an hour. The main interceptee then calls the source and they arrange to meet in about 40 minutes; he tells the source that he is bringing the guy with him, that the guy is okay but that he will make him wait in the car in any case.

Surveillance is established on the possible suspect, the main interceptee, and the location of the source. Surveillance observes the main interceptee being picked up by the buyer, in the same vehicle which he was driving on day 2. They are then followed to the location where the source is located at which point the main interceptee goes into the house and comes back a few minutes later with something under his jacket. He hands it to the buyer who then leaves by himself. The main interceptee goes back in the house, and a short time later he and the source leave in the source's car. The source takes the main interceptee home.

☐ *Day 8:* The main interceptee calls the buyer and asks "How was it?" to which the buyer responds "It is really good stuff."

☐ *Day 10:* The buyer from day 7 calls the main interceptee and says that he has something to drop off and that he will be by in 20 minutes. Surveillance follows the buyer from his house to the main interceptee's house where the buyer enters, stays a minute or two, and then leaves. The main interceptee then calls the source and tells him that he has some tickets for him. The source is observed by surveillance going to the main interceptee's house where he and the main interceptee meet briefly in the front yard. The source then leaves.

☐ *Day 11:* The main interceptee is called by a second suspect, out of town, who states that he will be down in two days to pick up a transmission. He states that he wants a whole one, a good one. He then states that it has to be good because his people are going to test it with a spike and a spoon. The main interceptee says he will have it ready.

☐ *Day 12:* The main interceptee calls the source and tells him he needs another tire, the same size as before. The source says that he will bring it over later. Surveillance is established on the source's house and he is observed going to the main interceptee's house and he and the two people meet again in the front yard. It is difficult for surveillance to see if anything is exchanged, but they can tell without a doubt that the source was not carrying a tire.

☐ *Day 13:* The main interceptee receives a call from the second suspect, who states that he has just arrived in town and asks the main interceptee if he is ready. The main interceptee tells him to come over. Surveillance observes the meeting in the front yard, but the two go inside the house and no exchange is observed. The second suspect emerges from the house a short time later and leaves. He is not carrying a transmission. He is followed by surveillance until he is well out of town, presumably headed home.

☐ *Day 14:* The main interceptee calls the source, tells him that he has some tickets for him, and says that he wants him to get them as soon as possible. The source is observed going to the main interceptee's home and going inside briefly. He is then followed home.

Analysis

Through the first 14 days a great deal has been accomplished. Much about the method used to arrange delivery of drugs and payment has been learned. The code language has been deciphered: "tires" and "transmissions" and possibly other car parts are used to mean drugs, and "tickets" is a code word used for money. The first day, when conversation was intercepted between the target and an unknown regarding tires, it was not recognized as pertinent conversation. In retrospect, however, those calls take on a different significance and shed light on later activities.

The main interceptee has been intercepted on the phone numerous times arranging drug transactions. Two buyers have been identified and the drug transactions in which they were involved has been documented by surveillance. The source has been identified, and conversations in which he arranged for the pickup and delivery of drugs and currency have been intercepted. Good surveillance has documented these transactions and these violations can be charged.

In this scenario, the main interceptee, his source, and two of his customers have been wrapped up and will be indicted and charged. However, what is apparent is that the main interceptee is a broker for the source, and through informant information, it is learned that the source has several other brokers such as the main interceptee in this case and that he gets a delivery of about 5 kilos a week from his source in California. The informant information also indicates that on day 13, the source had 3 kilos in his possession, at the location at which phone calls to him from the target phone as well as surveillance has established that he is staying.

The objectives of this intercept may have been accomplished at this point in time. The main interceptee, his source, and the buyers can all be prosecuted for their part in the conspiracy. Search warrants could be executed at the target location, the source's stash location, based on all the information available, including the fresh informant information, and possibly on the residences belonging to the two buyers. Significant recoveries may well result, but whether they do or not, the case will have been successful.

Another option, probably the one which will be chosen, involves expanding the intercept to include the source's telephone number. Based on the circumstances detailed, there is good probable cause to believe that the source was using his telephone in furtherance of his illegal drug dealing activities. Furthermore, it is logical to assume that he sells to other people, in addition to the initial target, and an intercept of his phone should result in the prosecution of those people. Also, it is likely that the source's source in California may be identified and wrapped up in the overall conspiracy.

While the objectives have been achieved, there is more than adequate justification for staying up on the initial target's phone and expanding to the source's phone. That is, the conspiracy will be more completely uncovered in doing so than it is to this point. There are still approximately two weeks remaining on the original order. Ideally, this confirmation of the source's identity will have been anticipated, and an affidavit for expansion will be well along. This being the case, it is entirely possible that the new order could be signed and the second intercept initiated before the authority of the original order expires.

If the facts have been correctly evaluated to this point, the second intercept will not have to go long before the source contacts the California source and arranges a delivery. It could be anticipated well in advance that when the delivery is made, it will be taken off and both intercepts concluded. Without question, the objectives of the case as a whole and each intercept individually will have been accomplished satisfactorily.

Culmination of the Intercept

Concluding or bringing down the wire can be extremely hectic. In most cases there will be a number of things, such as the roundup of suspects, execution of search warrants, and the seizure of assets, to be accomplished almost simultaneously. This stage of the investigation will require planning and forethought to be successful. Each investigation will require some unique manner of conclusion, some unique order to the way things are done. The following are some areas of concern.

Timing

In wiretap investigations, as in other narcotics cases, timing is everything. A few minutes or hours can make the difference between a large seizure and a successful case and no seizure. Of course in a wiretap, there is the distinct advantage of intercepting the conversations of the suspects and getting inside information which can be of considerable help in deciding the right time for the conclusion of the intercept.

It is, however, a misconception that listening to the conversations of the conspirators will ensure impeccable timing, that it will be easy to recognize the delivery of a load and take it off as a means of concluding the intercept. This is far from the case. The truth is that in most cases, the conversations will be subject to a variety of interpretations and whether or not a load is imminent and whether or not it should be taken off will be the subject of controversy and debate.

What is invaluable in timing the conclusion of the intercept is input and discussion from several experienced people familiar with the development of the case. A variety of experience should be represented in these discussions. Those with a good deal of experience in wiretap cases will have valuable suggestions based on similar cases in the past. Those with a great deal of experience in street narcotics enforcement will have the benefit of a keenly developed sixth sense based on years of timing street drug deals so that maximum results are achieved safely. The prosecutors too should be consulted, and many times they will have suggestions and think of angles which the investigators have not considered.

Arrest of Principal Conspirators

As the wiretap progresses and moves toward its end, there should be some planning regarding how the indictments and arrests will be handled. If it is feared that some or all of the suspects will leave the country when it becomes known that a wiretap has been done, arrangements should be made so that these people are indicted prior to the wrapup of the case.

When a delivery or other climax to the investigation is anticipated, indictments can be obtained, even if only limited indictments which will later be superseded by complete indictments, so that the suspects can be arrested when the timing is right and held for a detention hearing. At the detention hearing, evidence can be given which indicates that the suspect may be a flight risk, but it will probably be necessary to unseal the affidavits and make public the fact that a wiretap was done.

Another option, when there is not a significant risk that the suspects will flee, is to bring down the wire, execute search warrants, and not arrest the conspirators. Leave them to be indicted later.

A combination of the two approaches may be in order. Obtain indictments and be prepared to arrest the ones who are a flight risk and not arrest the others; rather indict them as the postwire investigation continues as part of other grand jury testimony.

Search Warrants

One search warrant affidavit should be prepared on a continuing basis throughout the wiretap. The one affidavit can establish the probable cause for any number of places to be searched.

Deciding what places are to be searched will be influenced by the amount of probable cause in existence and its freshness. It may be difficult to establish fresh probable cause for some of the places even relying on the ongoing nature of the offenses and the existence of records and proceeds to support probable cause which, though once in existence, has grown stale. Locations for which there can be established fresh probable cause should be hit in some timely sequence in conjunction with the conclusion of the intercept.

Seizure of Vehicles and Other Assets

The affidavit for the seizure of vehicles and other assets should be prepared as the investigation proceeds. It will be necessary to assign at least one person to this task. As vehicles are used in a drug transaction, the title research should be done, and the facts qualifying them for seizure under property confiscations or public nuisance laws should be detailed in the affidavit. In addition to the affidavit, a list of the vehicles and other property to be seized at the conclusion of the wire should be maintained. When it is time to bring down the wire, the affidavit and seizure orders can be close to completion, lacking only some finishing details to make them ready to serve.

SUMMARY

Electronic surveillance is the ultimate investigative technique. No other techniques involve such a high degree of intrusion into one's privacy. So that this intrusion is not taken lightly, an investigation of this type carries with it a commensurately high degree of responsibility on the investigative agency and the prosecutors to be right and to conduct the intercept strictly in accordance with the laws.

The intercept of wire and oral communications can enable the prosecution of criminal conspiracies not otherwise possible. But at no small price. Title III investigations are costly in terms of resources and manpower, they are time consuming, and they place high demands on the skill and professionalism of the officers and prosecutors involved.

8

ATTITUDE AND PROFESSIONAL RESPONSIBILITY

INTRODUCTION

The first seven chapters of this book have been devoted to a discussion of those techniques most commonly used in narcotics investigations. Professional narcotics investigators will achieve varying degrees of proficiency in the use of those skills. They are all methods and operations which can be learned through practice, and it is possible that a narcotics investigator will become an expert in most of these areas. Generally speaking, each investigator will be limited only by his or her desire to continue learning and to improve himself or herself. It is not technical skill alone which ultimately distinguishes the truly outstanding professionals in the field from the mediocre; it is a combination of traits embodied in an officer's attitude.

This chapter will focus on some of the nontechnical aspects of narcotics investigation, personal characteristics such as integrity, commitment, responsibility, survival instincts, and burnout. These personality factors compositely form an investigator's attitude, and it is attitude, above all else, which will define personal and professional success.

Narcotics investigators are in a position of public trust and confidence to a greater extent than any other law enforcement officers. They are entrusted with a specific mission, the successful completion of which directly affects the success of all others in law enforcement and public safety in general. Yet it is an area of law enforcement sensitive by its nature. Public support for narcotics law enforcement is by no means unanimous nor is it consistent. There are inherent contradictions in a society which spends millions of tax dollars for drug enforcement, education, and rehabilitation yet implicitly condones personal use as harmless and possession of personal use amounts as a victimless crime.

It is within the context of contradiction and double standards that the professional narcotics investigator must function. If he is to survive, he must have integrity and a sense of personal responsibility. If he is to become a credit to his profession he must have the right attitude.

RESPONSIBILITY

Every law enforcement officer who becomes a narcotics investigator takes on additional professional responsibility to himself or herself, the public, and fellow law enforcement professionals.

In the law enforcement community, narcotics investigators hold a special position. While the assignment is recognized as a difficult one, it is not without benefits. The hours are long, but there is flexibility, unlike most uniform assignments. Working in civilian clothes is also a benefit. Also, many narcotics assignments include paid overtime, take-home undercover cars, pagers, and other fringe benefits.

Within a police organization, narcotics officers are viewed with emotions ranging from respect, envy, and jealousy to disdain and distrust by fellow officers and command officers. It is the responsibility of each individual narcotics officer to do the job in such a manner that not only is he or she respected for the job that he or she does, but there is a positive transfer to the image of all narcotics officers. Earning this respect requires that the individual officer not violate the trust that has been given; it requires that the officer not forget from whence he or she came, that he or she perform his or her job with pride but without arrogance.

Each individual has a responsibility to earn the benefits of the assignment, and this requires dedication and professionalism well beyond the norm.

Narcotics investigators should work aggressively to avoid alienation between patrol officers and themselves. This can best be accomplished by an attitude of openness and willingness to help. Granted, there will be some fellow officers and administrators who will retain a natural bias against narcotics investigators regardless of how hard an individual works to overcome it. Those will be few, however, and they can be ignored. When individual investigators have the right attitude, a good collective image is formed, and the entire law enforcement community benefits.

Being a narcotics officer is a special assignment, a chance to be one of the elite, a chance that only a few are offered. That being the case, each individual narcotics investigator owes himself or herself an all-out effort to be the best that he or she can be. The investigator must also engage in a rigorous ongoing process of honest self-evaluation. The benefits of being a narcotics investigator will often lead a person into a false sense that he or she has those things by some right, that he or she is entitled to those benefits whether or not he or she continues to do the work which earns them. This generally happens to young officers who have forgotten what working the street in uniform was like, working holidays, taking lousy vacations, rotating shifts, etc. When narcotics officers allow themselves to forget that they are brothers and sisters to the uniform officers, that they have a common mission, that they could be uniform officers again tomorrow, they probably need a serious reminder, possibly even a transfer back to uniform.

If each individual narcotics officer continues to evaluate his or her performance and attitude to ensure that he or she is being the best that he or she can be, it will be reflected in both the quality and quantity of work. He or she will work to give back more than he or she receives, to make a contribution consistent with his or her responsibility. This requires dedication. It will mean working grueling hours and making personal sacrifices that not everyone is prepared to make. It will mean taking an enormous pride in one's work, on the street, in written work, and in court. A narcotics officer should be his or her own worst critic, never settling for sloppy surveillance work or poorly written reports replete with spelling errors and faulty grammar.

In addition to his or her responsibility to himself or herself and to his or her fellow officers, each narcotics officer has added responsibility to the community. That portion of the community which supports an all-out antidrug effort deserves only the best effort. Those citizens do not expect failure, incompetence, or corruption. They expect and deserve a high degree of professionalism. It is their perception that only the best, the most dedicated, hard-working officers get to be narcotics officers.

On the other hand, that part of the community which does not support drug enforcement or supports it only half-heartedly will not be surprised by sloppy investigative work, poor judgment, corruption, and a general betrayal of trust.

INTEGRITY

Every police department has rules and procedures governing individual conduct. Most have procedures specifically applicable to handling evidence. The aim of these procedures and regulations is to ensure the highest degree of collective integrity possible within the department.

It is not these rules and procedures alone through which this is accomplished. It is the responsibility of each officer to maintain high individual standards of integrity and honesty, such that newly assigned officers are impressed with that indelibly as the foremost characteristic of the individuals that comprise the unit.

The integrity of a narcotics officer is challenged in primarily four areas: first, the handling of evidence, cash, and drugs; second, the handling of confidential funds; third, the ethical management of informants and matters concerning them; and fourth, his or her testimony in court.

The scandals which are so well publicized—those involving officers who steal money or drugs, those who divert confidential funds to their own use, or those who use an informant illegally—are the product of compromised integrity. Such breakdowns in integrity can be influenced by a number of factors against which the individual officer has to always be on guard.

SURVIVAL

Survival for a narcotics officer is defined in very limited terms. A narcotics officer survives only if he or she continues to be effective in his or her mission: taking drugs off the streets and bringing criminal prosecutions against drug dealers. To be effective, the narcotics officer must be tough and smart, he or she must relentlessly attack the target, but the attack has to be disciplined within the parameters of law and ethics. It is a difficult balance to achieve; however, there are some who ferociously pursue the mission without ever crossing the line. A good many become burned out and are no longer effective; some are never effective; and some give up, compromise their integrity, and become criminals themselves.

Narcotics work can be extremely frustrating. It is difficult to make good cases and to get them all the way through the system. The realization that the accomplishment of each individual narcotics officer or narcotics unit does not begin to impact the problem, does not have any direct effect on the flow of drugs into the country can be a depressing one. The temptations represented by large amounts of cash and drugs are real. The dangers of working undercover and executing search warrants are also real, they can create tension in an individual which builds over time and can become troublesome and cause real changes in personality.

There are no simple formulas for surviving, but certainly one of the keys to survival is self-honesty and that has to be part of a process which can only result from awareness rather than denial. An officer must be honest in evaluating himself or herself and recognize when he or she is succumbing to burnout and job-related stress. The officer must be willing to look at his or her performance with some objectivity and be able to admit that he or she is no longer effective, if that is the case, and move on to something else. Granted, the supervisors have a great deal of responsibility in this area as well, but the ultimate responsibility rests with the individual.

COMMITMENT

A complaint, commonly heard in discussions about the current state of affairs in this country, is that Americans can no longer build a decent automobile, that there is no sense of craftsmanship left among the auto workers, no pride.

Narcotics investigators too are judged by their product. Does the product exhibit pride and craftsmanship? Is there an obvious commitment to excellence? It is the responsibility of each individual to make this commitment in the interest of personal and professional success.

INDEX

385